SKEPTICISM AND POLITICAL THOUGHT IN THE SEVENTEENTH AND EIGHTEENTH CENTURIES

SKEPTICISM AND POLITICAL THOUGHT IN THE SEVENTEENTH AND EIGHTEENTH CENTURIES

Edited by John Christian Laursen and Gianni Paganini

Published by the University of Toronto Press in association with the UCLA Center for Seventeenth- and Eighteenth-Century Studies and the William Andrews Clark Memorial Library

www.utppublishing.com

ISBN 978-1-4426-4921-7

Library and Archives Canada Cataloguing in Publication

Skepticism and political thought in the seventeenth and eighteenth centuries / edited by John Christian Laursen and Gianni Paganini.

(UCLA Clark library series)
Includes bibliographical references and index.
ISBN 978-1-4426-4921-7 (bound)

1. Skepticism – Political aspects – History – 17th century. 2. Skepticism – Political aspects – History – 18th century. 3. Sextus, Empiricus. 4. Skeptics (Greek philosophy). I. Laursen, John Christian, editor II. Paganini, Gianni, 1950–, editor III. Series: UCLA Clark Memorial Library series

B837.S563 2015   149′.73   C2014-907042-X

This book has been published with the help of a grant from the UCLA Center for Seventeenth- and Eighteenth-Century Studies.

University of Toronto Press acknowledges the financial assistance to its publishing program of the Canada Council for the Arts and the Ontario Arts Council, an agency of the Government of Ontario.

Canada Council for the Arts   Conseil des Arts du Canada

University of Toronto Press acknowledges the financial support of the Government of Canada through the Canada Book Fund for its publishing activities.

Contents

SKEPTICISM AND POLITICAL THOUGHT IN THE SEVENTEENTH AND EIGHTEENTH CENTURIES

Introduction

JOHN CHRISTIAN LAURSEN AND GIANNI PAGANINI

This is a book about ideas about knowledge and politics. More precisely, it is about lack of knowledge, or skepticism, and what it can mean for politics. Presumably, if we have wide access to truth and knowledge, it must be pretty easy to figure out what to do in politics. But if we do not have such confidence, what should we do? This is a question that many thinkers have pondered over the centuries. And this is a book about some of the ideas they have developed in order to answer it.

The idea that we should not have much confidence in our knowledge is widely referred to as skepticism. And people have attributed a wide range of political implications to it. On the one hand, it has been said that if one cannot know much, one should not try to do much, but rather remain conservative or quietistic. On the other hand, if the status quo is not supported by truth and knowledge, then perhaps we should feel free to make radical changes, to undermine and subvert everything. The very idea that such opposite implications have been attributed to a concept cries out for a wider and deeper analysis of it.

What Is Skepticism?

We can start with the point that the word "skepticism" means different things to different people. In very general terms, it is an attitude that foregrounds the difficulties in deciding on the truth or falsity of any proposition. Any attempts to bring out more specific features come up against the reality that there is no single accepted meaning of the word, but rather a family of meanings. It is worth observing that if writers claim to detect related concepts such as Platonism, Aristotelianism, Stoicism, or Epicureanism in the writings of historical figures, they are obligated to make some remarks about the historical traditions designated by those terms. But skepticism has long been different: many writers who use the term clearly have little or no appreciation that there is a historical tradition behind it.

This does not mean that skepticism had no history, but rather that skeptical thinkers seldom put much effort into placing themselves into a historical context. If they did, they would have discovered that the history of two traditions of skepticism dates back at least to the age of Hellenistic Greece.[1] One is called Pyrrhonism, and is named after Pyrrho of Elis (ca 365–275 BC), who is supposed to have lived the life of a skeptic. Ancient authors Diogenes Laertius and Sextus Empiricus are our main sources about this tradition. As Sextus put it, the Pyrrhonians found equipollent arguments on both sides of any argument (*isosthenia*), so they suspended judgment (*epoché*), and found themselves in tranquillity (*ataraxia*).[2] This did not mean they stopped enquiring: they were also called *zetetics* or enquirers because of their ongoing investigations. They reported that the outcome of all of their work was *metropatheia*, or moderated passions.[3] Emidio Spinelli's chapter, below, provides a much more in-depth introduction to the Pyrrhonists and the political implications of their ideas.

The other tradition was a development from Plato's Academy, and thus was called Academic skepticism. Arcesilaus and Carneades were skeptical successors to Plato as heads of the Academy. The Roman thinker Cicero is our main source here.[4]

Pyrrhonism was characterized by suspension of judgment and living with appearances, not by flat-out denial of knowledge or truth. Academic skepticism provided rules for living in the absence of truth by evaluating probabilities and looking for good reasons. However, the word spread out to cover much more than the historical traditions. Doubt, suspicion, and any number of other reasons to hesitate to accept truths or knowledge have accreted to the concept.[5]

One way to bring many of these meanings together is that what they have in common is that they oppose dogmatism, or the claim to access to truth and knowledge. It is well known that dogmatisms or claims to truth have any number of political implications.[6] Skepticism and dogmatism are two ends of the spectrum of epistemology, or the theory of knowledge. A couple of the figures in this volume are actually dogmatists, but they provide some of the best analyses of skepticism even as they oppose it.

It should be observed that skepticism is not the same as relativism, which is a dogmatic theory that everything really is relative to everything else. It is not the same as pessimism or other negativisms, which say that things really are bad, declining, or worse. A skeptic would have to suspend judgment about those claims as well.

The early modern thinkers who are evaluated in this volume were inheritors of the traditions of skepticism, and sometimes of the wider use of the term. The work of Richard Popkin since 1950 was an inspiration for a revival of the study of skepticism in this period. He was the pioneer in the synoptic study of early modern skepticism, entitling the first edition of his major work *The History of Scepticism from Erasmus to Descartes*, expanding that to ... *from Erasmus to Spinoza* in the third edition, and to ... *from Savonarola to Bayle* in the last edition.[7] In these books and in dozens of articles he scoured the philosophy of the age for signs of the influence of skepticism, bringing together many otherwise-forgotten figures and bringing out the often-unnoticed skeptical aspects of the work of some well-known figures. He was widely influential for arguing that skeptics could be religious, relying on faith rather than knowledge, a religious position he termed "fideism."

Gianni Paganini's *Skepsis: le débat des modernes sur le scepticisme* [Skepsis: the debate of the moderns about skepticism] is the fullest overview of the tradition of skepticism from Montaigne to Bayle since Popkin.[8] He went more deeply into the philosophy of some of the figures Popkin had reviewed somewhat briefly, and brought into the debate some of the dogmatic philosophers such as Tommaso Campanella and Thomas Hobbes, who taught us a lot about skepticism by using it as well as trying to refute it. This expanded the field from the study of skepticism towards the study of controversies about skepticism. He provided what amounts to a change of paradigm: Popkin understood skepticism as an anti-metaphysical movement allied with natural science that was emancipating itself from metaphysics. For Paganini, skepticism was an important element in the debate about the metaphysics of modernity. In his interpretation, the skeptical epistemology of Montaigne is based on his metaphysical assumptions about cognitive processes. Unnoticed before, Paganini found that Campanella wrote on skepticism as a prelude to a new metaphysics long before Descartes, but it was plagiarized by Marin Mersenne before being published in 1638. And he argued that Hobbes's confrontation with skepticism was decisive for his reform of *prima philosophia*. Paganini also added to Popkin's analysis of the uses of skepticism in religious matters by exploring the anti-theological and anti-religious uses of skepticism by La Mothe Le Vayer and the author of the *Theophrastus redivivus* (1656).[9]

In the last decade numerous collective volumes have surveyed figures in the period.[10] The founding of the International Society for the Study of Skepticism and its journal, the *International Journal for the Study of Skepticism,* have placed the study of early modern skepticism within a much wider and longer study of skepticism throughout history and down to the present.[11] But the focus of most of that work was not on the politics, and that is the purpose of this volume.[12]

Can Skeptics Live Their Skepticism?

One of the classic critiques of skepticism was that a person could not really live in accordance with skepticism, because either 1) they would walk off cliffs because they would not believe they were really there (the *apraxia* [impossible to live] argument), or 2) they would be amoral, because they could have no belief in the truth of morals (the *immorality* argument). So in order to stay alive and be reasonably good people, the skeptics would have to believe in some truths, whether openly or surreptitiously. Let us proceed to see if this is true.

The skeptics patiently answered the charges that they could not live their skepticism by pointing out that in the absence of truth one can live in accordance with appearances. In lieu of knowledge, one can live by habits and customs. Sextus Empiricus provided a list of the rules by which skeptics live: follow the guidance of nature, go along with the compulsion of states like hunger and thirst, conform to laws and customs, and learn an art or trade.[13] Naturally, he had to add the caveat that skeptics do not live like this because it is true or right, but simply as what to do in the absence of dogma.

Cicero adapted the skeptical Academy for Roman purposes by translating Carneades's *pithanon* as *probabilitas,* claiming that skeptics can live in accord with probabilities in the absence of truth. The point of all of this is that a thriving human life can be described in terms that eschew truth and knowledge.[14]

The Politics of Skepticism

What does this mean for politics? Sextus Empiricus does not give us an extended account of the implications of skepticism for politics. Nevertheless, as Emidio Spinelli explains in chapter 1, he did sketch out what a skeptic might do if ordered by a tyrant to carry out some horrible task: either obey or disobey, depending upon "ancestral customs and habits," not on dogma.[15] Spinelli spells out more of what this might mean, but for our purposes in the introduction it is enough to see that it is not obvious that skeptics would behave very differently from non-skeptics, who might obey or disobey depending upon their dogmatic principles and their ability to act consistently with them.

The implications of Academic skepticism for politics start from the famous story of Carneades's mission to Rome in 156–5 BC. On one day he lectured in favour of virtue, and on the next against it, providing equal arguments on both sides that would lead to suspension of judgment. Cato the Younger was so incensed that he moved to grant the Athenians' appeal and get them out of Rome before they could subvert the youth of the republic. His belief, of course, was that republics depend upon dogma.

Augustine of Hippo shared some of Cato's concerns, writing *Contra Academicos* against Academic skepticism in 386 AD. Skepticism remained alive and well in the Middle Ages, represented by figures such as Peter Abelard, John of Salisbury, Nicholas of Autrecourt, and John Buridan, and it could also be found in the Islamic world.[16] Political implications included John of Salisbury's arguments for toleration.[17]

The Renaissance saw a major increase in attention to skepticism, in part because of translations into Latin of Sextus Empiricus.[18] Michel de Montaigne was among the most prominent and influential thinkers to adapt ancient skepticism for his own purposes, and there is an immense literature on his philosophy and politics.[19]

It has been mentioned that most students of skepticism after Popkin are indebted to his work in one way or another. But Popkin had little to say about the implications of the tradition he studied for politics. John Christian Laursen fleshed out the implications for three early modern figures: Montaigne, David Hume, and Immanuel Kant.[20] He found a pervasive, but certainly not dogmatic, skepticism at the foundation of Montaigne's politics. Others had explored Montaigne's political thought and variously argued that it was conservative, liberal, or radical. Laursen concluded that if Montaigne was a conservative, he was a skeptical conservative; if he was a liberal, he was a skeptical liberal; and if he was a radical, he was a skeptical radical. With respect to Hume, Laursen found a political stance that could be described with the slogan that all politics takes place within a history of custom and habit. In the absence of truth, Hume thought, people are forced to rely on politeness, manners, and opinion for their political decisions, and it behooves us to study how they work. Finally, Laursen brought out some of the unexpected aspects of the influence of skepticism on Kant's politics. It is true that Kant was absolutely certain that politics should take the form of a republic, but he also insisted that we can never know if any particular government actually is a republic. In his terminology, we can know the apodictic laws that should apply, but not whether they are instantiated in the world.

This volume takes up the story of the influence of skepticism in political thought from half a century after Montaigne, when François de La Mothe Le Vayer was writing (1630s–60s). In contrast to Montaigne's private skepticism and public acceptance of the prevailing authorities, La Mothe Le Vayer publicly challenged some of the authorities of his day along with the accepted political science of Aristotle and Machiavelli and their followers. Some have thought his attitude was complete rejection of any political knowledge, but in chapter 2 Daniel Brunstetter brings out a kind of paradox. La Mothe Le Vayer can be understood as arguing in favour of a kind of political science that values freedom of thought, tolerance, and enquiry by examination of the pros and cons, which in turn ends in praise for moderate monarchy, which can make all of this possible. That means that he is not fully skeptical about the merits of skepticism in politics. He favours a political system that enables skepticism and uses his skepticism to enable that system.

In chapter 3, on Hobbes, Gianni Paganini brings out the importance of his experiences in France in the 1640s. His philosophical psychology was clearly influenced by Montaigne, Charron, and La Mothe Le Vayer. An emphasis on the role of vanity and vainglory in human behaviour and politics can be understood as a form of skepticism about the high-sounding claims people usually make for their actions. Hobbes's growing naturalism, or the treating of humans as similar to animals, has obvious roots in the skeptics. Hobbes's reliance on empirical observations and introspection seems closely related to the skeptics' phenomenalism, or acceptance of appearances. One limit on the influence of the French skeptics was that Hobbes does not stop at skepticism but thinks he can go beyond it and arrive at truths in politics. But these truths are very peculiar because they are rather the effects of language, of linguistic conventions, than of dogmatic knowledge.[21]

In chapter 4, Jean-Charles Darmon examines the implications of the fact that Cyrano de Bergerac's heroes were Socrates, Democritus, and Pyrrho. The latter is a model of *libertas philosophandi* or freedom to philosophize as one will. Skepticism is not so much a philosophy as an attitude, and for the writer one of its chief merits is that it provokes literary invention. If so much of life is illusion, imposture, and paradox, these causes of skepticism must have political implications as well. Among other such implications are those that come from the essential nature of man as the animal that lies. Not only do we lie, but we want to be lied to. Nothing is permanent: even politics is constantly in flux. Cyrano's writings help us get used to that.

Samuel Sorbière's *Discours sceptiques* were published in 1657 as a refutation of skepticism from its catastrophic results, with an argument for natural law as an alternative. The arguments for natural law may not have much originality, but in chapter 5 Sylvia Giocanti shows that his refutation of the skeptics has the philosophical merit of answering Montaigne in his own terms. Thinking through the idea of a society making most of its decisions on the basis of law and custom, he shows how this could easily lead to barbarity and suffering.[22] Giocanti also shows that in order for Sorbière to make his case the most compelling, he had to downplay Montaigne's reservation of a large private sphere, taking the commitment to customs and laws as something close to a dogma. As with many attempts at a *reductio ad absurdum*, Sorbière's reduction of skepticism requires an exaggeration of the position to the point that it might not have been recognizable by the members of the skeptical tradition. And in that he stands for many of the critics of skepticism, who will not or cannot appreciate its nuances.

In chapter 6, on Bernard Mandeville, Rui Romão, brings out the skepticism inherent in his theories, often by showing the roots of his ideas in Montaigne and other skeptics. A wide range of ideas in common with the skeptics include an anthropological pessimism, distrust of ideals, unorthodox political conservatism, emphasis on the power of the passions, and naturalism. There is more: as a physician, Mandeville exhibits in his own life the long tradition of fruitful interaction between medicine and skepticism. Romão argues that Mandeville belongs right in the centre of a skeptical moral and political tradition. He observes that Mandeville's suggestion that we arrive at the best possible social order by not trying too hard to create it sounds rather like a parallel to Sextus Empiricus's analogy of skepticism to the painter Apelles, who achieved just the effect he wanted by giving up trying and just throwing his brush at the canvas.

In chapter 7 Andrew Sabl looks at the political and historical writings of David Hume, discovering a form of skepticism that does not depend heavily on philosophy.[23] The methods that Hume uses turn the study of history into a calming project, eroding dogmatic assumptions. Hume draws the reader along in fact-checking, examining the arguments of both sides, drawing balances of pros and cons. Good intentions are contrasted with actual results, and the complexity of history undermines easy side-taking. Sabl recommends Hume's practices for the contemporary world, observing that wider use of them would moderate political passions. We shall see if his advice is followed.[24]

In chapter 8 Whitney Mannies begins from the point that our notions about the schools of ancient philosophy and their heritage can be misleading if they lead us to think that one must be either an Epicurean or a skeptic, but not both. Denis Diderot was a skeptic precisely because he was an Epicurean materialist, and found the material world so complex and dynamic that it was almost impossible to grasp and hold. The implications of this view in politics were to favour limited government, reform over revolution, tolerance, and freedom of thought. In literature, Diderot pushed to the limit a naturalistic writing style that foregrounds both the protean nature of our world and the uncertainties of our knowledge, giving every reader the skeptical experience.

In chapter 9, on Rousseau, María José Villaverde brings out one of the most striking characteristics of his philosophy.[25] Rousseau apparently thought he could be thoroughly skeptical about philosophy and theology and yet thoroughly dogmatic about morals and politics. So we have the paradox of a thinker who has done his best to undermine claims of knowledge in one area of life who believes that the truths of another area can be insulated and untouched by the demolition of truths in the first. In this way, Rousseau stands as an early model for later thinkers who thought that skepticism could be given free rein in some areas and refuted or tamed for other purposes.

Adam Smith learned a lot from both Mandeville and Hume. As Pierre Force shows in chapter 10, Smith wanted to blunt the rather amoral implications of at least one reading of Mandeville by bringing out the ways in which self-interest can be genuinely harvested for the common good. Drawing on his friend Hume's discussion of the ways in which sympathy can harness our selfishness, he gives us a cleaner, less selfish-looking beehive: it is actually in our interest to render honest services to each other. Thus, there is skepticism about the foundations of our moral and political systems: there is no higher truth in them than what we perceive as utility. But that is sufficient for what we perceive as a thriving polity.

In chapter 11 Rodrigo Brandão provides us with a fresh take on Voltaire according to which he is not the complacent purveyor of deism that he has often been made out to be, for example, by Jonathan Israel. Rather, his arguments for deism are so weak that one should suspect his sincerity. His understanding of natural science was close enough to skepticism if it is understood as a phenomenology, just a theory about appearances. And in morals and politics Voltaire fights systemization and dogmatics at every level but the most basic, where he is indeed a dogmatist: the common good is a universal morality. Skepticism is a propaedeutic for political action, but one does not suspend judgment where one sees injustice. Like Rousseau, Voltaire wants to have his skepticism and eat it, too.

One of the strangest cases for having your skepticism and dropping it upon impulse was Brissot de Warville. As Sébastien Charles explains in chapter 12, Brissot planned out and sketched one of the most wide-reaching summaries of skepticism with apparent sympathy. Then he threw himself wholeheartedly into radical activism in politics. Charles observes that this may have been a product of the times: when the customs and laws that the tradition of skepticism relied on all fail together in revolutionary times, how should one act? One answer is to take on impulse any goal as a truth, and act on it. One can imagine a politics in which all the parties know that there is no guaranteed truth behind any of them, but in which all play their roles with fervour and commitment.

In chapter 13, on Carl Friedrich Stäudlin, John Christian Laursen looks at a thinker who worried about the negative implications of skepticism when it reached wider audiences, but admired a properly philosophical skepticism. This tension can be found in his treatment of Kant as deeply skeptical and yet at the same time an antidote to the worst kinds of skepticism. As he notes, Stäudlin was not alone among his contemporaries in understanding Kant as a skeptic. In some ways, Stäudlin was an inheritor of a tradition of philosophers at the Prussian Academy who domesticated skepticism. Among other things, they translated Hume in ways that rendered him and other skeptics middle-of-the-road, moderate, and harmless to church and state.[26]

At one end of the spectrum, the conservative Edmund Burke has been interpreted as a skeptic, and in the twentieth century Ludwig Wittgenstein has been called both a skeptic and a political conservative – although this latter judgment is subject to some debate.[27] At the other end of the political spectrum, in the nineteenth century Friedrich Nietzsche brought out some of the radical implications that can be found in the tradition,[28] and in the twentieth century Anatole France thought of himself as a skeptic while at one point being very sympathetic to the Bolsheviks.[29] By this point, our survey of skepticism and politics might lead to suspension of judgment about any necessary implications of the skeptical tradition, and further enquiry into the concrete conclusions drawn by specific skeptics in specific times and places.

The Late Twentieth Century and Contemporary Skepticism in Politics

In the language of late twentieth-century and current political theory skepticism has a very broad and general meaning, again implying various and sometimes opposite political positions. On one hand are those who see some of our prevailing contemporary institutions as skeptical. Michael Oakeshott contrasted the politics of faith and the politics of skepticism in a book of that title.[30] He described the former as a perfectionist theory based upon a doctrine of human nature, and the latter as a simple "reading of human nature." Significantly, he associated Hobbes – usually considered a dogmatic philosopher – with skepticism taken in this particular meaning.[31] He also wrote that the Constitution of the United States is "the most profoundly skeptical constitution of the modern world."[32] In his last book, co-authored with Avrum Strull, Richard Popkin echoed Oakeshott on what he termed "skeptical democracy": "the very structure of modern democratic government – as designed by Locke, Bayle, Hume and Jefferson among others – was the result of a fundamental skepticism about human beings being able to find true and unquestionable answers about how people should live."[33]

On the opposite side, Will Kymlicka has claimed that "liberals do not endorse skepticism."[34] He refers to Rawls, who did not include an entry for skepticism in the index of his *A Theory of Justice* (1971), even though one could object that his ideal of a "neutral state" and the basic condition of the "veil of ignorance" imply a kind of skepticism.[35] Rawls often speaks of uncertainty and of choices made in conditions of uncertainty. The word does appear in the index of *Political Liberalism* (1993), where Rawls argued that his notion of liberalism "does not argue that we should be hesitant and uncertain, much less skeptical, about our own beliefs."[36] He worries that if liberalism is "indifferent or skeptical" it would be "in opposition to numerous comprehensive doctrines, and thus defeat from the outset its aim of achieving an overlapping consensus."[37] But his solution to this conundrum is that "a political conception of justice" suggests that some things can be set aside or removed from the political agenda.[38] Aside from the point that indifference and skepticism are not the same thing, in this and several other places where he claims to reject skepticism he may in fact be relying on it. Another way of describing his liberal separation of church and state is that it is based on the inability to reconcile opposing positions and thus an agreement to disagree on them while agreeing on so-called political matters.

But even if Rawls could not recognize his own place in a skeptical tradition, other thinkers of the end of the last century and the beginning of this one are much more aware of their positions. Tobin Siebers saw much of the literary theory of the latter half of the twentieth century as a product of the politics of skepticism.[39] He recruited all of the major figures such as Derrida, Foucault, and Lacan into the company of skeptics, albeit without any significant connection to other traditions of skepticism. In contrast, Renato Lessa has recently drawn a chain of skeptical connections from Montaigne to Hume to philosopher Nelson Goodman, Primo Levi on the lessons of the Holocaust, and Elaine Scarry on the body in pain.[40] It is possible to read a great deal of contemporary culture as implicated in skepticism and its corresponding politics.

This volume cannot be expected to solve the theoretical problem of the connection of skepticism with any particular political theory or practice for all times and all places, nor to identify particular authors or trends in history that best embody the principles of skepticism – supposing that skepticism could be qualified as a homogeneous system having its own principles. It is surely wiser and more fruitful to examine the ways in which various different skeptical notions, tools, and texts in their contexts shaped the early modern approach to politics and social life. That, we hope, is the contribution of the chapters in this book.

NOTES

1 For a short presentation, see Gianni Paganini, "Skepticism," in *The Classical Tradition*, ed. Anthony Grafton, Glenn W. Most, and Salvatore Settis (Cambridge: Harvard University Press, 2010), 889–92.

2 Sextus Empiricus, *The Skeptic Way: Sextus Empiricus's Outlines of Pyrrhonism*, tr. Benson Mates (Oxford: Oxford University Press, 1996), 89–90.

3 Sextus Empiricus, *The Skeptic Way*, 89, 92–3. On the vocabulary of the skeptics, see Emmanuel Naya, *Le vocabulaire des Sceptiques* (Paris: Ellipses, 2002).

4 For a recent general survey, see Richard Bett, ed., *The Cambridge Companion to Ancient Scepticism* (Cambridge: Cambridge University Press, 2010).

5 For a wider and looser take, see Jennifer Michael Hecht, *Doubt. A History* (New York: HarperOne, 2004).

6 See John Christian Laursen, "Anti-skepticism and Political Thought in the 18th Century: Jean Pierre de Crousaz and the Political Illiberalism of Mitigated Dogmatism," in *La centralità del dubbio. Un progetto di Antonio Rotondò*, ed. C. Hermanin and Luisa Simonutti (Florence: Olschki, 2011), 169–89.

7 See Richard Popkin, *The History of Scepticism from Erasmus to Descartes* (Assen: Van Gorcum, 1960; second edition, New York: Humanities Press, 1964); *The History of Scepticism from Erasmus to Spinoza* (Berkeley: University of California Press, 1979); *The History of Skepticism from Savonarola to Bayle* (Oxford: Oxford University Press, 2003). See Jeremy Popkin, ed., *The Legacies of Richard Popkin* (Dordrecht: Springer, 2008).

8 Gianni Paganini, *Skepsis. Le débat des modernes sur le scepticisme: Montaigne – Le Vayer – Campanella – Hobbes – Descartes – Bayle* (Paris: Vrin, 2008); see also Paganini, "Scepticism," in *Routledge History of Seventeenth Century Philosophy*, ed. Dan Kaufman (London: Routledge, forthcoming).

9 Anonymous, *Theophrastus redivivus*, first critical edition eds. Guido Canziani and Gianni Paganini (Florence: La Nuova Italia, 1981–2), 2 vols.

10 Gianni Paganini, Miguel Benítez, and James Dybitowski, eds., *Scepticisme, Clandestinité et Libre Pensée/Scepticism, Clandestinity, and Free Thought*(Paris: Champion, 2002); Gianni Paganini, ed., *The Return of Scepticism from Hobbes and Descartes to Bayle* (Dordrecht: Kluwer, 2003); José Maia Neto and Richard Popkin, eds., *Skepticism in Renaissance and Post-Renaissance Thought* (Amherst, NY: Humanity Books, 2004); Sébastien Charles, ed., "Le scepticisme à l'âge classique," theme issue of *Philosophiques* 35 (2008): 161–290; José Maia Neto, Gianni Paganini, and John Christian Laursen, eds., *Skepticism in the Modern Age: Building on the Work of Richard Popkin* (Leiden: Brill, 2009); Gianni Paganini and Sébastien Charles, eds., *Scepticisme et Lumières*, special issue of *Libertinage et philosophie* 12 (2010): 139–234 ; Diego Machuca, ed., *Pyrrhonism in Ancient, Modern, and Contemporary Philosophy* (Dordrecht: Springer, 2011); Sébastien Charles and Plinio J. Smith, eds., *Scepticism in the Eighteenth Century: Enlightenment, Lumières, Aufklärung* (Dordrecht: Springer, 2013).

11 International Society for the Study of Skepticism = http://isoss.wordpress.com; *International Journal for the Study of Skepticism* = http://www.brill.com/publications/journals/international-journal-study-skepticism.

12 The only two books directly on the topic are John Christian Laursen, *The Politics of Skepticism in the Ancients, Montaigne, Hume, and Kant* (Leiden: Brill, 1992) and Petr Lom, *The Limits of Doubt: The Moral and Political Implications of Skepticism* (Albany: State University of New York Press, 2001).

13 *The Skeptic Way: Sextus Empiricus's Outlines of Pyrrhonism*, tr. Benson Mates (Oxford: Oxford University Press, 1996), 92.

14 See John Christian Laursen, "Yes, Skeptics Can Live Their Skepticism and Cope with Tyranny as Well as Anyone," in Maia Neto and Popkin, *Skepticism in Renaissance and Post-Renaissance Thought*, 201–23.

15 Sextus Empiricus, *Against the Ethicists* (Oxford: Oxford University Press, 1997), 27.

16 Dominik Perler, *Zweifel und Gewissheit. Skeptische Debatten im Mittelalter* (Frankfurt: Klostermann, 2006); Paul Heck, "Skepticism in Islamic Philosophy," in *Skepticism: From Antiquity to the Present*, ed. Diego Machuca and Baron Reed (London: Bloomsbury, forthcoming).

17 Cary Nederman, "Toleration, Skepticism, and the 'Clash of Ideas,'" in *Beyond the Persecuting Society: Religious Toleration Before the Enlightenment*, ed. John Christian Laursen and Cary Nederman (Philadelphia: University of Pennsylvania Press, 1998), 53–70.

18 Gianni Paganini and José Maia Neto, eds., *Renaissance Scepticisms* (Dordrecht: Kluwer, 2009).

19 See, recently, the chapters dedicated to Montaigne in Maia Neto, Paganini, and Laursen, *Skepticism in the Modern Age.*

20 Laursen, *The Politics of Skepticism*, passim.

21 For the general attitude of Hobbes, positive and at the same time reactive, toward the skeptics, see Paganini, "Hobbes among Ancient and Modern Sceptics: Phenomena and Bodies," in Paganini, *The Return of Skepticism*, 3–35, and Paganini, *Skepsis*, 171–227.For the topic of language in the ancient context, see Lorenzo Corti, *Scepticisme et langage* (Paris: Vrin, 2009).

22 For a much more positive attitude toward skepticism in some of Sorbière's work, see Lorenzo Bianchi, "Absolutism and Despotism in Samuel Sorbière: Notes on Skepticism in Politics," in Maia Neto, Paganini, and Laursen, *Skepticism in the Modern Age*, 193–210.

23 See also Dario Castiglione, "The Practical Value of Hume's Mitigated Skepticism," in *The Skeptical Tradition around 1800: Skepticism in Philosophy, Science, and Society*, ed. Johan Van der Zande and Richard Popkin (Dordrecht: Kluwer, 1998), 221–34; J.C. Laursen, "David Hume on Custom and Habit and Living with Skepticism," *Daimon: Revista Internacional de Filosofía* 52 (2011): 87–99.

24 For the skeptical implications of Hume's attitude, see now Gianni Paganini, "Theism, Atheism, and Scepticism. Bayle's Background to Hume's *Dialogues,*" in *Gestalten des Deismus in Europa*, ed. Winfried Schröder (Wiesbaden: Harrassowitz, 2013), 203–43.

25 Compare Sergei Zanin, "L'entremise du scepticisme. Jean-Jacques Rousseau et la composition du *Discours sur les sciences et les arts,*" in *Scepticisme et modernité*, ed. M.A. Bernier and S. Charles (Saint-Étienne: Publications de l'Université de Saint-Étienne, 2005), 155, 66.

26 John Christian Laursen, "Tame Skeptics at the Prussian Academy," *Libertinage et philosophie* 12 (2010): 221–30.

27 Iain Hampsher-Monk, "Burke and the Religious Sources of Skeptical Conservatism," in Van der Zande and Popkin, *The Skeptical Tradition around*

1800, 235–60; Vicente Sanfélix, "Was Wittgenstein a liberal?" in *Ethical Liberalism in Contemporary Societies*, ed. K. Wojciechowski and J. Joerden (Bern: Lang, 2009), 117–36.

28 Tamsin Shaw, *Nietzsche's Political Skepticism* (Princeton, NJ: Princeton University Press, 2007), betrays no knowledge of the skeptical tradition, while Jessica N. Berry, *Nietzsche and the Ancient Skeptical Tradition* (Oxford: Oxford University Press, 2011), situates Nietzsche in it.

29 Carter Jefferson, *Anatole France: The Politics of Skepticism* (New Brunswick, NJ: Rutgers University Press, 1965).

30 Michael Oakeshott, *The Politics of Faith and the Politics of Scepticism* (New Haven, CT: Yale University Press, 1996). Note that there is almost no recognition of the ancient skeptical tradition in Oakeshott's work: see John Christian Laursen, "Oakeshott's Skepticism and the Skeptical Traditions," *European Journal of Political Theory* 4 (2005): 37–55.

31 Oakeshott, *The Politics of Faith*, 75–6.

32 Oakeshott, *The Politics of Faith*, 80.

33 Richard Popkin and Avrum Stroll, *Skeptical Philosophy for Everyone* (Amherst: Prometheus, 2001), 280.

34 Will Kymlicka, *Contemporary Political Philosophy* (Oxford: Clarendon Press, 1990), 201. Kymlicka argues that skepticism does not support self-determination; he also mistakes skepticism for a kind of relativism.

35 John Rawls, *A Theory of Justice* (Cambridge: Belknap Press, 1971).

36 John Rawls, *Political Liberalism* (New York: Columbia University Press, 1993), 63.

37 Rawls, *Political Liberalism*, 150.

38 Rawls, *Political Liberalism*, 151.

39 Tobin Siebers, *Cold War Criticism and the Politics of Skepticism* (Oxford: Oxford University Press, 1993).

40 Renato Lessa, "The Ways of Scepticism (Then and Now)," *Iris: European Journal of Philosophy and Public Debate* 1 (2009): 513–27.

chapter one

Neither Philosophy nor Politics? The Ancient Pyrrhonian Approach to Everyday Life

EMIDIO SPINELLI

1. In Search of the Political

If we sought to provide a textual foundation for a historical enquiry into the stance adopted by ancient skepticism, especially in its Pyrrhonian version, with regard to politics, we would no doubt find ourselves in a tight spot. First of all, we would run up against an objective lack of works or textual fragments *explicitly* devoted to the topic. Most importantly, however, we would have to deal with a range of opinions, or rather genuine prejudices, that have been expressed over and over from antiquity down to the present day, and according to which a skeptical approach would *ipso facto* serve as a basis and cause for the worst and lowest of all political behaviour available to human beings.

This final and irrevocable verdict would appear to bring together a number of authors who are very distant from one another in chronological terms, as well as in terms of their philosophical merit. Thus for instance in Aristocles (1st century AD?) we read:

> one should consider also the following things: what sort of *citizen*, or *judge*, or *counsellor*, or *friend*, or simply human being would such a man make? Or on what atrocity would the man not venture who thought that nothing was really honourable or shameful, or just or unjust? For one could not even say that such men are *afraid of the laws and their penalties*; for how could they, who are free from emotions and troubles, as they say?[1]

No warmer would be a voice far closer to us and more widely heeded, at different latitudes and in unquestionably highly refined milieus. At the end of an extremely polemical article criticizing the alleged "equilibrium" of the skeptical stance on politics, while clearly endorsing the idea of a profound engagement "about what is right and what is wrong," Martha Nussbaum writes:

> we see how profoundly *selfish*, indeed *solipsistic* the sceptic program is, seen as a program for philosophy in a needy and troubled world containing urgent human problems toward whose solution philosophy in the Rawlsian spirit may possibly make a major contribution. If philosophy is only capable of making the individual practitioner feel calm, *then Socrates's enemies would be right*: philosophy is a dangerous form of self-indulgence, *subversive of democracy*, and its teachers are corruptors of the young. *Fortunately, philosophy is capable of much more than that.*[2]

In the light of these unequivocal and almost outraged remarks, why should we continue our enquiry? Why should we search for traces of a political attitude in philosophers – ancient skeptics, especially the ones connected to the current of Pyrrhonism – who are structurally incapable of distinguishing between good and evil, between just and unjust, and of establishing any fixed points, any positive and universal *values* on which to anchor their dealings with and among others?

I believe that surrendering to this alleged non sequitur, which has been forcibly or even disdainfully imposed, would be a sign of historical as well as theoretical weakness. On the contrary, it seems far more appropriate to me as a matter of philosophical research, as well as far more correct as a way of assigning "equal opportunities" to all (including the poor Pyrrhonists of antiquity), to follow a different path. The (perhaps ambitious) aim of this paper, then, will be to once again carefully examine those passages of Sextus Empiricus's corpus – the most valuable source for reconstructing ancient Pyrrhonism (if for no other reason but because it is the most extensive one) – from which it seems possible to draw rather weighty and relevant information regarding the skeptical approach to political issues.

2. The Last "Mode" and the Laws ...

As already noted, while Sextus's writing covers all the parts into which dogmatic philosophy was traditionally divided (logic, physics, and ethics) and even extends to the examination of the *technai* that later entered into the canon of the so-called liberal arts (grammar, rhetoric, geometry, arithmetic, astrology, and music),[3] nowhere in his works do we find any *independent* and *self-standing* chapter devoted to the *politike techne* or *episteme.* Indeed, "political science" (*politike episteme*) *stricto sensu* is only discussed in a couple of parallel passages where Sextus attacks and sets out to demolish Plato's definition of human beings as "broad-nailed two-footed featherless animals capable of political knowledge."[4] This is a "mimetic" quote, so to speak, borrowed from the technical vocabulary of the Platonic Academy; Sextus not only does not agree with it, but even ridicules it by resorting to both genuinely Pyrrhonian arguments and similar criticism possibly of Epicurean origin.[5]

The lack of any circumstantial treatment of the attributes and features of what Aristotle had termed "the most controlling science, the one that, more than any other, is the ruling science,"[6] does not however imply a complete uninterest in political topics and issues on Sextus's part. The presence of these issues is no doubt more difficult to detect within the wider framework of Sextus's attacks on his dogmatic opponents and of the rare yet valuable instances in which he personally presents the genuine (and in his view coherent) Pyrrhonian approach. Still, we do find some texts and contexts that betray a need to address problems that are either explicitly or implicitly political in character.

A privileged starting point for grasping Sextus's stance is represented by his treatment of the tenth and last mode,[7] which by widely and parasitically drawing upon more ancient dogmatic material,[8] "especially bears on ethics, [and] is the one depending on persuasions and customs and laws and beliefs in myth and dogmatic suppositions" (*PH* I 145). While it is true that Sextus here consciously narrows down the field of action of this trope, it seems equally undeniable to me that when he speaks of *ethics,* this is to be broadly understood as "the study of value in general and not exclusively of *moral* value."[9] It is therefore legitimate to extend Sextus's arguments to support his genuinely skeptical conclusions concerning political issues as well. Besides, it would be difficult not to note the explicit mention made of laws or *nomoi* among the factors listed right from the start. Indeed, this suggests that there is *also* a political streak in what Sextus is arguing. Sextus strives to (and arguably delights in) illustrating the widest possible range of differences in terms of habits, customs, prejudices, and assumptions and legal practices among the various places and peoples under consideration, recording conflicting *logoi* of equal weight related to these elements as a whole. Yet, these conclusions should be regarded not as a form of descriptive moral or political relativism, but rather as a specifically and genuinely skeptical view: for *diaphonia* (dispute or dissonance) leads one not to believe that all the various stances are *true* in a relative sense, but rather to suspend judgment on all moral value. Indeed, in the final section of the argument we read:

> We could have taken many other examples for each of these oppositions, but in a brief account this will suffice. Thus, since so much anomaly has been shown on objects by this mode too,[10] we shall not be able to say what each existing object is like in its nature, but only how it appears relative to a given persuasion or law or custom and so on. Because of this mode too, therefore, it is necessary for us to suspend judgement on the nature of external existing objects. (*PH* I 163)[11]

The gamut of examples mentioned by Sextus may be subsumed within the interweaving of five factors (for a total of no less than fifteen intersections). These factors inevitably engender conflicting representations and are enough to lead us, from a Pyrrhonian perspective, to a healthy *epoché* (suspension of judgment) (see also *infra*, 21) concerning the real nature of the objects or behaviours taken into consideration (including political ones). Without going into the details of Sextus's heated anti-dogmatic argument, I believe it is especially worth focusing on the third of these factors.

This factor consists of the contradictions related to the proliferation of different and conflicting laws. Law is defined as "a written contract among citizens, transgressors of which are punished" (*PH* I 146). In his detailed account, Sextus shows that he is familiar not only with specific judicial laws adopted by different peoples both of Greek (e.g., the inhabitants of Rhodes: *PH* I 149) and of non-Greek origin (e.g., "the Tauri in Scythia": *PH* I 149), but also (and perhaps especially) with those adopted by the Romans.[12] Several mentions are made (*PH* I 146, 152, 159) of the legal ban on adultery, which officially entered the Roman law with the *lex Iulia* (1st cent. BC). Mentions are further made of other Roman laws about renouncing one's paternal inheritance (*PH* I 149), homosexual intercourse (*PH* I 152, 159), intercourse with one's own mother (*PH* I 152, 159), marrying one's own sister (*PH* I 152, 159), beating a free man from a good family (*PH* I 156), and committing murder (*PH* I 156).

Leaving the issue of the trustworthiness of Sextus's account aside, what must be stressed is the fact that the law in his view does not play any special role or possess an absolute and untouchable status, and cannot be spared the clash of opinions that characterizes all other forms of behaviour or human choices. In other words, even one of the cornerstones of political thought, the idea of *nomoi* (whether regarded as *phainomena* [things which appear] or *noumena* [things which are thought], as *pragmata* [facts] or *logoi* [accounts]) would appear to be subject to the genuine philosophical skill and ability of the skeptic, if it applies "in matters of opinions," according to the definition, or rather programmatic premise, clearly stated at the beginning of the *Outlines of Pyrrhonism*: "Scepticism is an ability to set out oppositions among things which appear and are thought of in any way at all, an ability by which, because of the equipollence in the opposed objects and accounts, we come first to suspension of judgment and afterwards to tranquillity."[13]

3. A Wider Strategy at Work ...

In illustrating the purpose and limits of laws in the context of skeptical criticism in accordance with the tenth mode, Sextus almost seems to adopt the vantage point of an external observer satisfied with displaying a strong *diaphonia* [dispute] and thus attaining the kind of *epoché* that will grant him *ataraxia* [absence of trouble or tranquillity].[14] The strategy he adopts when seeking to level a more sweeping polemical attack against dogmatic ethics *tout court*, by contrast, appears far more complex and articulated. Here Sextus cannot limit himself to shattering the moral constructions of his opponents, but must also defend himself against the well-known, recurring, and often ill-founded dogmatic (and especially Stoic) accusation of inactivity or *apraxia*. He must therefore operate on two fronts: he must counter any attempt to anchor behaviour to absolute norms, but at the same time must also provide a coherent alternative for shared living that may be implemented through his action plan (also – it is reasonable to suppose – in the political field). The picture, then, grows clearer: rejecting the dogmatic perspective founded on objective and absolute values does not mean being doomed to inaction, to an unacceptable plant-like condition.[15] For there is also room to move in another direction, which enables one to steer clear of the presumptuousness of philosophical discourse by anchoring oneself to points of view supported by empirical and "non-philosophical" (albeit not necessarily anti-philosophical) forms of acceptance of what Sextus in several sections of his writing describes as "common life," or *koinos bios*.

Sextus, in other words, seeks to identify the outcome of his interaction with the world with an external as well as internal disposition (*diathesis*) capable of ensuring a genuine kind of skeptical "happiness," marked by the simultaneous presence of "tranquillity" (*ataraxia*) and "moderation of feeling" (*metriopatheia*).[16] When Sextus provides a criterion for his own action in the form of what is apparent, or rather the representation of *to phainomenon*, his claims come to reflect the underlying logic of his philosophical approach.[17] Sextus does not formulate any strong dogmatic assertions (i.e., he does not slip into what is referred to as *diabebaiousthai* [to positively affirm]) in his technical jargon, as if he wished to and could establish with absolute certainty the confines of good and evil, and give the final word "about what is right and what is wrong" (as Nussbaum would like to do), or about the strict *rules of engagement* in ethics as well as politics. The linguistic form he lends his moral conclusions is not intended to disclose any absolute plan for human action, but simply to turn every "is" into "appears,"[18] and thus to provide an account of a complex autobiographical event. In this respect, Sextus's suggestion of an ethical and political scenario that could actually be achieved even (or perhaps especially or indeed exclusively) by Pyrrhonists shows itself for what it really is and is intended to be: a "confession" of one's own inner affections that is made public and hence probably *also* charged with persuasive (yet never veridically cogent) power. After registering the progressive and reciprocal checkmating of all the various dogmatic doctrines, the Pyrrhonist does not seek to give the final word on the alleged existence of objective values in the ethical and political field. Rather, he simply regulates his own conduct on what currently or on each occasion *appears* to be good or bad, according to a clearly articulated mechanism of (polemically) active removal of the obstacles set by dogmatic opinions and at the same time of passive reception/impression/transmission of unavoidable phenomena connected to the condition of our everyday existence.

This broader strategy would appear to be at work both in the second section of the third book of the *Outlines of Pyrrhonism* (*PH* III 168 ff.) and in the complex account of *Against the Ethicists* (*M* XI). Without examining all the various phases of Sextus's polemic in detail, the core of his objections may perhaps be summed up by quoting Julia Annas's words: dogmatic definitions "cannot give the essence or nature of good. A definition that did would put an end to controversy: but controversy has manifestly not ceased, so these definitions must have failed to make the essence of good clear."[19]

Everyday life unfolds outside of philosophers' circles and their disputes, which take place on the level of mere opinion (*en tois doxastois* [in matters of opinion], as Sextus often likes to say). In other words, there exists a further level on which affections of another kind impinge upon us. These are all those situations in which we are forced to experience necessary events ("matters forced upon us"[20]) that escape our will to intervene and are in any case determined by factors that fall outside of our control. In this case, the behaviour of individual agents can neither appeal to absolute moral principles, nor be regulated by mere personal will. As the Pyrrhonist limits himself to controlling his own reactions within the framework of his "moderation of feeling" (*metriopatheia*), the action he describes and accepts must be seen to stem from the acceptance of a series of conditions already at hand that are connected to one's physical constitution, education, and belonging to a specific social and political milieu.

What guides us in this context cannot be the abstract force of philosophical arguments. Rather, we regulate our life on the basis of what everyday experience has offered in the past and continues to offer today. As we shall see soon, this is what Sextus means when, against the charge of *apraxia* [inactivity] or *anenergesia*, he claims that the Pyrrhonist can act[21] "according to the non-philosophical observance" (*kata ten aphilosophon teresin*: *M* XI 165) or – "without holding beliefs" (*adoxastos*) – "according to the observance of everyday life" (*kata ten biotiken teresin*: *PH* I 23).[22] This latter field is not open to abstract speculation, since it has to do with "matters forced upon us" and thus imposes a series of inevitable points of reference, on a natural level (given that as human beings we cannot avoid perceiving, thinking, and experiencing emotions and affections) as much as on a cultural, social, or political level. After all, we are not living on Mars but in the *here and now* – in both a geographical and historical sense – and are constantly conditioned by our education, by the rules or laws of the community to which we belong, and by the technical know-how which all around us seeks to use experience for the service of our needs.[23]

The horizon within which it seems inevitable to place this Pyrrhonian ethical option is that of an everyday life articulated into manifold ways of living, freed from the rule of any dogmatic practical reason. Operating in the background is an original *Gegenbenheit* in which each one of us finds himself to have been "thrown" and which cannot therefore be ignored.[24] Is this too poor a scenario? Worse still, does it pave the way for unacceptable forms of quietism or conservatism in ethics, but also – and especially – in politics? In other words, by foregoing any strong rational and theoretical apparatus in moral reflection, does the Pyrrhonist ultimately doom himself (and us as well, if we choose to follow his example) to paralysis, boredom, and the loss of emotional involvement? Or rather – and worse still – is he taking a dangerous and unworthy course destined to turn him into a vile creature who is utterly passive in the face of strong forms of authoritarianism,[25] or a slave to ruling norms of conduct, including the unspeakable ones that will be at work in a completely unjust, racist, and cruel society,[26] a society governed by a tyrant, to mention an extreme example, a genuine case study for political reflection *tout court*?

4. And What If a Tyrant ...?

Before broaching the question of what the relations between a Pyrrhonist and a tyrant might be like, it is worth stressing once again that the former is someone who lives, act, and reacts – at least according to Sextus's writing in defence of a coherent skeptical praxis. The Pyrrhonist is capable of addressing the many needs he faces in his ordinary existence – including, as we shall soon see, an extreme situation such as pressure exercised by a tyrant. Whether the Pyrrhonist acts as a hero or proves himself to be a coward, his reaction depends on what kind of man he is, or rather what kind of man he has become through the varied and complex experience of being in touch with the *world of life*. This moral and empirical itinerary followed by the Pyrrhonist, which is connected to specific situations and historically conditioned, nonetheless allows his journey to be a peaceful one. He can live in accordance with the *world's course,* free from the dogmatic pretension of assigning absolute value to norms of conduct that are simply an integral part of our *koinos bios* [common life] and that stem from a constant engagement with the reality of praxis. His actions, however, are not arbitrary, but are rather regulated by the four *fundamental categories* mentioned by Sextus in a famous passage of his *Outlines of Pyrrhonism* (*PH* I 23–4 – with one of these categories, the third, clearly possessing traits that may also be regarded as political *lato sensu*):

1. nature's guidance, the specific fate which human beings must be subject to as creatures equipped with sensibility and reason;
2. the need intrinsic to elementary affections or primary needs, such as hunger and thirst, and the mechanical reactions they engender;
3. the tradition connected to ruling laws and customs, which asserts itself as the acceptance of the norms of conduct of one's community – so much so that even the sceptic, for instance, regards religious piety as something good and impiety as something bad;[27]
4. the teaching of the arts, understood as the passive learning of specific rules, which is to say of the know-how promoted by given *technai.*

The final and staunchest appeal made to this moral attitude, which definitely stands in contrast to strong, dogmatic ethics, rejects the alleged value that many – philosophers as well as private persons ("idiots"/ *idiotai* in the etymological sense: see *PH* I 30) – assign to the theory. Instead, Sextus pursues a different horizon: that of a clearly qualified *teresis*, which is to say a specific form of "observance" and empirical generalization, albeit one set within well-defined boundaries. This is an explanatory model Sextus is extremely fond of.[28] He not only uses it to argue in favour of epistemological schemes related to certain conceptual turning points typical of ancient medical empiricism, but also applies it to the ethical sphere. This enables him to provide guidelines for human conduct in agreement with that "common life" (*koinos bios*) which it seems so difficult to escape from and whose "norms" – created over a long period of time, and possibly with much toil, through the development and consolidation of our historical condition – it seems really impossible to ignore.

However, if our Pyrrhonist chooses to accept this frame of reference, were it only for a moment, he would once again be pressed by the dogmatists: "and what if a tyrant ...?"

In one lengthy passage (*M* XI 162–7[29]), Sextus starts by recapitulating the dogmatic charges that the skeptic would be doomed to total inactivity and complete inconsistency. In order to clearly expose this inconsistency, Sextus's opponents resort to the example of a tyrant.[30] If a tyrant wished to compel the skeptic to perform vile and unspeakable actions (such as killing one's own father[31]), what would the skeptic do? The answer would appear to boil down to a clear-cut alternative: either he will disobey the tyrant and choose to take his own life, or he will yield to his request, thus perpetrating parricide. In both cases, the dogmatists reason, the skeptic's behaviour will be dictated by a choice (and corresponding refusal) based on a higher criterion for distinguishing between what is truly good and what is truly bad. The skeptic, then, while in principle rejecting all normative ethics, will *de facto* act like the dogmatists, which is to say like those who "have apprehended with confidence [*meta peismatos*] that there is something to be avoided and to be chosen."[32] Sextus's reply is reported in a passage worth quoting in full (*M* XI 165–6):

> (165) Indeed, in stating these things they do not realise that the sceptic does not live according to philosophical reason (for with respect to this he is inactive), but that through non-philosophical 'observance' he can choose certain things and shun others. (166) And when forced by a tyrant to commit any of the prohibited things, he will perchance choose one thing and

shun another on the basis of a preconception [*prolepsis*] connected to his ancestral laws and customs; and he will more easily endure hardship compared to the dogmatist, since unlike the latter he opines nothing in addition to these things.

To adequately understand the conceptual premises and arguments of these few, dense lines, it is necessary first of all to once again emphasize how Sextus is certainly aware of the fact that it is impossible to remain completely inactive.[33] His battle, therefore, is not one for quietism or mere resignation, since the skeptical solution will only cause this outcome among those who, by really straining Sextus's texts, will treat the dogmatic moral approach as the *only* possible guide to ethical phenomena.[34] Indeed, if we firmly cling to the dogmatic prejudice according to which each choice or rejection stems from philosophical reasoning or *logos* – which is theoretically strong, since it is anchored to an indisputable definition of true and false, just and unjust, decent and indecent, i.e., of good and bad – anyone who, like the Pyrrhonist, lacks any such unwavering certainty is bound to strike us as being inappropriate or eccentric, or even scatterbrained. If the "militant" intervention of rationality is to be accepted, given that "the reasonable belief is *precisely* and *by definition* that whose *acceptance* – to the very best of our available knowledge and belief – affords the best *promise* for realizing our goals,"[35] we then ought to regulate all our behaviour, as Sextus himself suggests, "according to the philosophical theory" (*kata ton philosophon logon*). Only in such a way will we be authorized to speak of a coherent and especially justifiable praxis, to the point of proposing an articulate but dogmatically rigid "art of life" (*techne peri ton bion*).[36] Only in such a way will we be able to determine and display those underlying beliefs that lie at the basis of the acceptance of given values, as much as of the rejection of or, if necessary, all out war against other, alternative ethical models.[37]

On the whole, these dogmatic assumptions – be they ancient or modern – would appear to leave very little room for the poor skeptic and the alleged liveability of his life, which from a dogmatic perspective is clearly marked by repeated rational shortfalls and incomprehensible irrational acts of surrender. Despite such enduring and radical objections, however, Sextus believes he can overcome this impasse by assigning skeptical moral action an autonomous and legitimate field of action.

Sextus sets out almost provocatively – and probably conscious of his own originality – by rejecting the very moral rules established once and for all by dogmatists of all ages and latitudes. Far from dooming him to paralysis or inactivity, this gesture represents the first step in the formulation of a more profound alternative suggestion. The skeptic believes that she can act consistently in the face of the countless tight spots and decisions of moral life without turning into a kind of vegetable. She does not rely upon the cogency of any philosophical *logos* [reason][38] or on any rigid normative rationality, but rather formulates choices and rejections "according to the non-philosophical observance" (*kata ten aphilosophon teresin*).[39] By thus deploying an ethical sensitivity that, as the term *teresis* clearly suggests, operates in close contact with a form of repeated and consolidated experience, the skeptic is able to act not only with respect to the lesser events of everyday life, but even in the extreme scenario of coercion at the hands of a tyrant. Should the latter wish to compel the skeptic to face an alternative between two extreme forms of behaviour, as in the case of the order to kill one's father, the skeptic will not lack decisional resources. Her moral life may in no way be envisaged simply as a blank slate or empty page lacking any guidelines. As Sextus more accurately and technically explains, the skeptic will lend her behaviour this or that direction case by case,[40] according to an inner preconception (*prolepsis*) that is logically and chronologically prior to all moral action. The real difference compared to the ethical doctrines upheld by the dogmatists lies precisely in the meaning that must be assigned to this *prolepsis*. It is not established *a priori* on the basis of prejudiced theoretical choices, nor is it a vague intuition.[41] Rather, it proves to be the outcome of an empirical engagement with the customs and habits of the traditional norms and laws of our country.[42] What conditions the operative choices and everyday behaviour of the skeptic, therefore, is an articulate and complex system of pre-existing points of reference, a network of possible decision elements integrated within his own broader and all-round natural and intellectual background.[43] This consists in the range of rules of conduct that the skeptic has assimilated through her education or which govern the society she lives in, or indeed in a set of principles or points of reference that in her eyes prove more functional to her present attainment of intellectual tranquillity and a moderate control over her own unavoidable "passions"/*pathe*.[44]

Many people have felt, feel, and probably will feel offended by the passiveness (or perhaps "conformism")[45] the above approach seems to entail. But is this really the case? To get back to our extreme situation, there is nothing to prevent our Pyrrhonist from resisting and rebelling against the tyrant, if from the cradle with her mother's milk she has imbibed a strong-rooted anti-tyrannical inclination;[46] and conversely, there is nothing to prevent the skeptic from having been predisposed towards an absolute form of personality worship. In both cases, it may legitimately be suggested perhaps that the skeptic's behaviour will at least be free of the kind of fanaticism, intolerance, and overzealouseness typical of those headstrong dogmatists who over the centuries – in the name of good, or rather of the Good – have sacrificed their lives on the altar of glory, but who – again, always in the name of good, or rather of the Good – have also proven capable of committing the kind of atrocities that no passive and detached Pyrrhonist could ever even imagine, *pace* Aristocles or the more "democratic" Nussbaum.[47]

It would be possible to invoke here further "factual counter-examples" or articulate "intellectual experiments."[48] We might ask ourselves, for instance, what kind of son would be most desirable for a father in the face of a threat from a tyrant: a skeptic or dogmatist with an heroic temperament who is ready to sacrifice himself, and hence turn his parent's life into endless mourning? Or instead a skeptic or dogmatist "somewhat" inclined to surrender, a coward perhaps, yet one who is alive, who continues to breathe the very life his parent freely bestowed upon him out of sheer biological disinterest and which therefore represents the highest of all values, to be safeguarded at all cost? Or again: would the most desirable son be a skeptic who has been educated to resist tyranny, or rather a dogmatist attached to a strict theodicy, for instance, that might (perhaps passively) drive him to view the murder of his own father simply as a stage in the accomplishment of the grand, unfathomable plan drawn by a providence that is nonetheless good? And again: would the most desirable son be a skeptic who has been educated to the worship of the political hierarchy to such an extent that he will do away with his father without any remorse, or rather a dogmatist who is a faithful adherent to Epicurean teaching and hence is completely detached, since he is used to thinking that death – one's own or anyone else's – amounts to nothing at all?

This play of questions could be endlessly extended. The time has come, however, to end this analysis of a Pyrrhonian option that appears to enable one to do without philosophy as well as politics, understood in strong, dogmatic, and absolutist terms. For while the Pyrrhonist neither possesses nor seeks to possess any ethical beliefs of absolute validity, he can still construct a coherent and justifiable moral world for himself. This scenario, which is clearly also applicable on the political level, appears to be historically related to the public and private development of the age in which the skeptic finds himself living. Finally, it would almost appear to gradually turn into a kind of ethical habit, perhaps not a very solid habit (since not rooted in an inflexible dogma), nor a particularly attractive one (especially for those flying the flag of absolute values and universal principles), yet one that functions pragmatically *here and now*.

NOTES

1 Aristocles F. 4 (my italics; *Aristocles of Messene. Testimonia and Fragments* [Oxford: Oxford University Press, 2001], 27; see also the commentary at 129–31).

2 M. Nussbaum, "Equilibrium: Scepticism and Immersion in Political Deliberation," in *Ancient Scepticism and the Sceptical Tradition*, ed. J. Sihvola (Helsinki: Hakapaino Oy, 2000), 194 (my italics).

3 On Sextus's attack on these *technai*, see E. Spinelli, "Pyrrhonism and the Specialized Sciences," in *The Cambridge Companion to Ancient Pyrrhonism*, ed. R. Bett (Cambridge: Cambridge University Press, 2010), 249–64.

4 *PH* II 28 (tr. J. Annas and J. Barnes, eds., *Sextus Empiricus: Outlines of Scepticism*, Cambridge: Cambridge University Press, 2000, 74); see also *PH* II 211 and *M* VII 281–2. For another attack on "outrageous" dogmatic political theories (more precisely Stoic ones, maybe highly influenced by Cynicism), see *PH* III 245–9 and *M* XI 190–6 (on this last passage, see E. Spinelli, ed., *Sesto Empirico. Contro gli etici* [Naples: Bibliopolis, 1995], 355–61; and R. Bett, ed., *Sextus Empiricus. Against the Ethicists (Adversus Mathematicos XI)* [Oxford: Clarendon Press, 1997], 205–10).

5 On this specific question, see E. Spinelli, *Questioni scettiche. Letture introduttive al pirronismo antico* (Rome: Lithos, 2005), 68–75.

6 See Arist., *EN* I 1, 1094a26–7 (tr. T. Irwin, ed., *Aristotle. Nicomachean Ethics* [Indianapolis/Cambridge: Hackett, 1985], 2).

7 See *PH* I 145–63(tr. Annas and Barnes, eds., *Sextus Empiricus: Outlines of Scepticism*, 37). Subsequent references are to this edition and are cited parenthetically in the text. See also III 198–234.

8 This ranges from occasional literary quotations (e.g., from Homer: *Il.* XXII 201, *PH* I 150; *Od.* XXII 423, *PH* I 157; *Il.* XVI 459, *PH* I 162) to more or less actual laws (see therefore *supra*, 20–1).

9 J. Annas and J. Barnes, *The Modes of Scepticism. Ancient Texts and Modern Interpretations* (Cambridge: Cambridge University Press, 1985), 157; see also D. Machuca, "Moderate Ethical Realism in Sextus' Against the Ethicists?" in *New Essays on Ancient Pyrrhonism*, ed. Machuca (Leiden: Brill, 2011), 144.

10 For "the anomaly in things" as the primary, puzzling, and troubling starting point of the Pyrrhonian enquiry, see *PH* I 12.

11 See also *PH* III 235.

12 For the important role played in the very poor biographical data about Sextus by this insistence on Roman customs and laws, see at least D.K. House, "The Life of Sextus Empiricus," *Classical Quarterly* 74 (N.S. 30): 1980, 227–38; and E. Spinelli, *s.v.* "Sextus Empiricus," in *DPHA*, vol. VI, ed. R. Goulet (forthcoming). For Sextus's relationship with "die römische Sittlichkeit," see also M. Gabriel, *Antike und moderne Skepsis zur Einführung* (Hamburg: Junius, 2008), 79–81.

13 *PH* I 8 (tr. Annas and Barnes, eds., *Sextus Empiricus: Outlines of Scepticism*, 4); see also *PH* I 31–3 and more generally L. Corti, *Scepticisme et langage* (Paris: Vrin 2009), 16–18, as well as B. Morison, "The Logical Structure of the Sceptic's Opposition," *Oxford Studies in Ancient Philosophy* XL (2011), 265–95; and E. Spinelli, "Sextus Empiricus et l'ombre longue d'Aristote," *Philosophie Antique* 12 (2012): 275–7. For the ethical "application" of this Pyrrhonian *dynamis*, see *M* XI 111.

14 See also F. Grgić, "Scepticism and Everyday Life," in Machuca, *New Essays on Ancient Pyrrhonism*, 75.

15 For the Platonic and Aristotelian roots of this polemical metaphor, see respectively Plat. *Theaet.* 171d and Arist. *Metaph.* IV 4, 1006a14–5 and 1008b10–9; see also G. Striker, "Sceptical Strategies," in *Doubt and Dogmatism. Studies in Hellenistic Epistemology*, ed. M. Schofield, M. Burnyeat, and J. Barnes (Oxford: Oxford University Press, 1980), 63n25; and F. Decleva Caizzi, ed., *Pirrone. Testimonianze* (Naples: Bibliopolis, 1981), 266.

16 The key passage is undoubtedly *PH* I 25–30. On skeptical *eudaimonia* and/or happiness, see also the recent R. Bett, "Can an ancient Greek sceptic be *eudaimôn* (or happy)? And what difference does the answer make to us?" *Journal of Ancient Philosophy* 6/1 (2012), online: http://www.journals.usp.br/filosofiaantiga/index.

17 See esp. *PH* I 21–2.

18 See *M* XI 18–19 and Spinelli, ed., *Sesto Empirico. Contro gli etici*, 164–6; for a different explanation, see Bett, *Sextus Empiricus. Against the Ethicists (Adversus Mathematicos XI)*, 58–60, whose conclusions are however critically examined by Machuca, "Moderate Ethical Realism in Sextus' Against the Ethicists?" 163–71.

19 J. Annas, "Doing Without Objective Values: Ancient and Modern Strategies," in *Ethics*, ed. S. Everson (Cambridge: Cambridge University Press, 1998), 198.

20 See *PH* I 25 and 29–30, but especially *M* XI 141–4.

21 Or perhaps and better: he can "be active." For the very subtle distinction between *to act* ("in the robust sense of the dogmatist's theory of human

action") and *to be active* (in the sense that Sextus's sceptic "goes *through the motions* of an ordinary life"), see K.M. Vogt, "Scepticism and Action," in Bett, *The Cambridge Companion to Ancient Pyrrhonism,* 171–2.

22 See also *PH* I 231, 237; II 102, 246, 254, 258; III 235; M VIII 158. The translation of the formula *kata ten biotiken teresin* might not be a very flowing or charming rendition (if we wish to stress the real meaning of *biotikos,* for instance, should we rather opt for a periphrasis like "in accordance with the needs of life," as proposed by M. Burnyeat, "The Sceptic in His Place and Time," in *The Original Sceptics: A Controversy,* ed. M. Burnyeat and M. Frede [Indianapolis/Cambridge: Hackett, 1997], 105n17?). At any rate, that translation wrongly seems to introduce the notion of "ordinary" into the description of one's dependence on "common/everyday life." For an apparently (although not always usefully) interchangeable use of "ordinary"/"everyday," see Grgić, "Scepticism and Everyday Life."

23 See *infra,* § 4. On the "quite ingenious" notion of "forced assent" and the related proposal of a kind of "undogmatic assent" (both intended as anti-Stoic attitudes), see Vogt, "Scepticism and Action," 174–5. For the hypothesis that this special attitude towards everyday life might even transform the Pyrrhonist into a "deep reformer," see Grgić, "Scepticism and Everyday Life," 74–7.

24 See esp. M. Hossenfelder, ed., *Sextus Empiricus. Grundriss der pyrrhonischen Skepsis* (Frankfurt am Main: Suhrkamp, 1968), 83; on the possible "côté sartrien" of Sextus's position, see also S. Marchand, "Sextus Empiricus et les effets politiques de la suspension du jugement," 20–1 (forthcoming; pagination quoted from the typewritten version kindly sent to me by the author).

25 This is one of the negative political implications stressed by Nussbaum, "Equilibrium: Scepticism and Immersion in Political Deliberation," 192–3; Gabriel, *Antike und moderne Skepsis zur Einführung,* 86–92, attacks instead "die zentrale Inkonsistenz des Quietismus" in Sextus and his version of Pyrrhonism.

26 Such a strong 'bill of indictment' is invented *disserendi causa* by H. Thorsrud, "Is the Examined Life Worth Living? A Pyrrhonian Alternative," *Apeiron* 36/3 (2003): 248, who also tries, however, to offer at least two possible replies, more or less genuinely in the vein of ancient skepticism.

27 I cannot here enter into the details of Sextus's attitude towards religion, although this is a question which might *also* have political implications and consequences. I shall only provide some recent bibliographical references: J. Annas, "Ancient Scepticism and Ancient Religion," in *Episteme, etc.: Essays in Honour of Jonathan Barnes,* ed. B. Morison and K. Ierodiakonou (Oxford: Oxford University Press, 2011), 74–88; H. Thorsrud, "Sextus Empiricus

on Skeptical Piety," in Machuca, *New Essays on Ancient Pyrrhonism*, 91–111; R. Bett, "Against the Physicists on Gods (*M* IX.13–194" (forthcoming in the Proceedings of the 2007 Symposium Hellenisticum); Marchand, "Sextus Empiricus et les effets politiques de la suspension du jugement"; E. Spinelli, "'Le dieu est la cause la plus active': Sextus Empiricus contre la théologie dogmatique" (forthcoming).

28 On the positive role played by the notion (and praxis) of *teresis* in Sextus's more general approach to knowledge and ethics, see E. Spinelli, "Sextus Empiricus, l'expérience sceptique et l'horizon de l'éthique," *Cahiers philosophiques* 115 (2008): 29–45.

29 On the parallel anti-skeptical objection reported by DL IX 107–8, see now Corti, *Scepticisme et langage*, 44–55.

30 Among several possible references, besides the "logical" schemes in Corti, *Scepticisme et langage*, 32–9, see esp. Spinelli, ed., *Sesto Empirico. Contro gli etici*, 326–37; and Bett *Sextus Empiricus. Against the Ethicists (Adversus Mathematicos XI)*, 172–81. The best treatment of Sextus's response to the extreme situation created by the tyrant's order remains J.C. Laursen, "Yes, Skeptics Can Live Their Skepticism, and Cope with Tyranny as Well as Anyone," in *Skepticism in Renaissance and Post-Renaissance Philosophy*, ed. R. Popkin and J. Maia Neto (Amherst, MA: Humanity Press, 2004), 201–34: his very subtle and deep analysis also offers reasonable counter-arguments against some hard (yet not always well grounded) polemical attacks put forward against the Pyrrhonian solution by Annas, "Doing Without Objective Values: Ancient and Modern Strategies," esp. 209–13; and M. Nussbaum, *The Therapy of Desire* (Princeton, NJ: Princeton University Press, 1994), esp. 313–15, as well as Nussbaum, "Equilibrium: Scepticism and Immersion in Political Deliberation." See also J.C. Laursen, "Skepticism, Unconvincing Anti-skepticism, and Politics," in *Scepticisme et modernité*, ed. M.A. Bernier and S. Charles (Saint-Etienne, France: Publications de l'Université de Saint-Etienne, 2005), 167–88; and Id., "Escepticismo y política," *Revista de Estudios Políticos* 144 (2009): 123–42.

31 This is the paradigmatic example explicitly quoted in DL IX 108.

32 Tr. Bett, *Sextus Empiricus. Against the Ethicists (Adversus Mathematicos XI)*, 27. On the strong/technical (i.e., Stoic) meaning of the verb "apprehend"/*katalambano* used in this passage, see 176, while on Sextus's opposition to any dogmatic assertion made "with firm conviction (*meta bebaiou peismatos*)" – in this case in the field of natural science or *physiologia* – see *PH* I 18.

33 See again *PH* I 23 and also *M* VII 30.

34 For some clever reflections about this topic, see Hossenfelder, ed., *Sextus Empiricus. Grundriss der pyrrhonischen Skepsis*, esp. 66 ff.

35 N. Rescher, *Scepticism* (Oxford: Basil Blackwell, 1980), 223 (my italics).

36 On Sextus's attack on this ethical *techne*, see *PH* III 239–79 and *M* XI 168–256.

37 Nor should we forget the dangerous prospect of a strong conflict among radically different absolute values or – to use an expression more *à la page* – the actual risk of a "clash of civilizations" (this expression refers to the title of S.P. Huntington, *The Clash of Civilizations and the Remaking of World Order* [New York: Simon & Schuster, 1996]; see also S.G. Azzarà, "La crisi della globalizzazione e il conflitto delle civiltà. Una lettura critica di Huntington," in *Die Philosophie und die Idee einer Weltgesellschaft*, ed. D. Losurdo and S.G. Azzarà (Pisa: Millepiani Editore, 2009), 827–59.

38 On Sextus's attitude towards the *logos* and more generally his "way of speaking," see also S. Marchand, "Sextus Empiricus' Style of Writing," in Machuca, *New Essays on Ancient Pyrrhonism*, 113–41. One should also remember that "the use of sceptical language in politics might imply a certain civilizing effect. Rather than claiming truths and knowledge, skeptical political actors would have to argue in terms of appearances and use vocabulary like 'perhaps' and 'maybe'. If, on the one hand, this precludes the dogmatic defense of much-loved political positions, it also precludes dogmatic offense on behalf of other less savory positions" (Laursen, "Skepticism, Unconvincing Anti-skepticism, and Politics," 170).

39 Bett, *Sextus Empiricus. Against the Ethicists (Adversus Mathematicos XI)*, 26, prefers to translate: "in accordance with non-philosophical practice" (see also Grgić, "Scepticism and Everyday Life," 73). Mates's suggestion ("regimen": B. Mates, ed., *The Skeptic Way: Sextus Empiricus's* Outlines of Pyrrhonism [Oxford: Oxford University Press, 1996], 92) is surely fascinating, not least for its evident medical flavour; see also *supra*, n. 22.

40 Namely "au cas par cas," as proposed by Marchand, "Sextus Empiricus et les effets politiques de la suspension du jugement," 13 and 19, who also reports Estienne's translation ("*si res ita ferat*"). I believe that if we wish to opt for an alternative version, we should choose not "perhaps" (Bett, *Sextus Empiricus. Against the Ethicists (Adversus Mathematicos XI)*, 27) or "peut-être" (Corti, *Scepticisme et langage*, 31n2), but rather "as it happens (to me)" (*tychon*: see therefore LSJ, s.v. *tygchano*, A.2, speaking "of events, and things generally"). This is the same nuance of meaning Sextus seems to give to the expression *hoion tychikos* ("as if by chance," R.G. Bury, tr., *Sextus Empiricus*, vol. I: *Outlines of Pyrrhonism* [Cambridge & London: Loeb Classical Library, 1933], 21; "wie zufällig," Hossenfelder, *Sextus Empiricus. Grundriss der pyrrhonischen Skepsis*, 100; "as it were fortuitously," Annas and Barnes, eds., *Sextus Empiricus: Outlines of Scepticism*, 11; "fortuitement," P. Pellegrin, ed., *Sextus Empiricus. Esquisses pyrrhoniens* [Paris: Éditions du Seuil, 1997], 71) at *PH* I 29, where

he describes the "mechanism" by which tranquillity follows from the suspension of judgment. In addition, the presence of *tychon* (if one accepts the *lectio* of the manuscripts as legitimate and correct: see also Bett, *Sextus Empiricus. Against the Ethicists (Adversus Mathematicos XI)*, 172) suggests that "the sceptic will do whatever results from the various psychological forces within him, and there is no way to predict what this will be" (ivi, 179). For the sake of completeness one should also mention Blomquist's suggested correction (*stoichon* instead of *tychon*: J. Blomquist, "Textkritisches zu Sextus Empiricus," *Eranos* 66 (1968): 99–100), now accepted by Corti 2009, 31n2.

41 *Pace* Annas, "Doing Without Objective Values: Ancient and Modern Strategies," 209–11.

42 Especially because "nous commençons par faire avant de penser, et nos sentiments moraux et politiques proviennent d'abord de ce sol-là" (Marchand, "Sextus Empiricus et les effets politiques de la suspension du jugement," 9). See also *PH* I 17; II 246; *M* IX 49, as well as again DL IX 108, where – maybe under Timon's influence? See DL IX 105 – the role of "habit" and "laws" (*synetheia* and *nomoi*) is explicitly underlined; see finally *M* VIII 368.

43 See Hossenfelder, *Sextus Empiricus. Grundriss der pyrrhonischen Skepsis*, 72; and Bett, *Sextus Empiricus. Against the Ethicists (Adversus Mathematicos XI)*, 178–9. It might be interesting to draw a comparison between Sextus's attitude towards political and/or legal "Pyrrhonian pre-conceptions" and Epicurus's emphasis on the role of *prolepsis* (that can also change according to different times and places; for his notion of what is just/*to dikaion*: see at least his *Principal Doctrines* 37 and 38).

44 For a similar approach, see Thorsrud, "Is the Examined Life Worth Living? A Pyrrhonian Alternative," 246–7; see also Bett, "Can an ancient Greek sceptic be *eudaimôn* (or happy)? And what difference does the answer make to us?" 9. What is important, anyway, is that the Pyrrhonist avoids any "set of additional beliefs," any kind of *prosdoxazein*, as rightly suggested by Grgić, "Scepticism and Everyday Life," 89; see already Spinelli, ed., *Sesto Empirico. Contro gli etici*, 330.

45 See however Marchand, "Sextus Empiricus et les effets politiques de la suspension du jugement," 10 and 13.

46 See also Machuca, "Moderate Ethical Realism in Sextus' Against the Ethicists?" 173n45.

47 On some crucial features of the moral attitude of ancient Pyrrhonian skepticism (passivity, detachment, mildness), see B. Morrison, "The Ancient Sceptic's Way of Life," *Metaphilosophy* 21 (1990); esp. 213 ff. There are even some scholars, such as A. Botwinick, *Scepticism and Political Participation*

(Philadelphia: Temple University Press, 1991), 60, who maintain – although possibly only for rhetorical purposes – that precisely because he is not epistemically involved (but only emotionally and psychologically), the skeptic can better guarantee an egalitarian and open-minded behaviour, useful even for a wider form of political participation and social engagement.

48 See also Spinelli, *Questioni scettiche. Letture introduttive al pirronismo antico*, 143–5.

In this chapter I have not examined the political attitude of ancient academic skepticism (if indeed there was any at all), but rather concentrate my attention on the Pyrrhonian side, as attested and represented by the works of Sextus Empiricus (fl. c. 180–210 AD). I warmly thank Stéphane Marchand and Francesco Verde for their helpful comments on a previous version of this chapter, which is part of the research project PRIN-MIUR 2009 "Le filosofie post-ellenistiche da Antioco a Plotino."

chapter two

La Mothe Le Vayer and Political Skepticism

DANIEL R. BRUNSTETTER

Introduction

François de La Mothe Le Vayer (1588–1672) was part of a group of scholars living in seventeenth-century France and known as *les libertins érudits.* They have been portrayed as opponents of superstition and fanaticism who doubted everything in order to challenge the authority of tradition and to satisfy their own intellectual pleasure.[1] La Mothe Le Vayer's literary achievements, what Richard Popkin describes as "pedantic imitations of Montaigne," earned him considerable renown in France.[2] He was elected to the Académie Française, was the protégé of Cardinal Richelieu, and was a teacher of Louis XIV. Influenced by the works of Sextus Empiricus and Montaigne, and consumer of a vast array of travel writings that exposed him the variety of the world, he was at the very heart of the *crise pyrrhonienne,* an intellectual movement centred on skepticism that overtook France by attacking the authority of almost every purveyor of knowledge, from Aristotle to Galileo.

At first glance, La Mothe Le Vayer presents a monolithic version of complete skepticism. He appears to scrupulously doubt all authoritative claims, marshals copious evidence as to the diversity of moral behaviours and political possibilities in the world, openly discredits the vanity of the purported sciences, hails the philosophical hedonism of Epicurus, and is seduced by the allure of stoic retreat. In his *Petit traité sceptique sur cette façon de parler, n'avoir pas le sens commun* (1647), La Mothe Le Vayer's explicit thesis demonstrates that one's senses are unreliable and that one therefore cannot have any certain knowledge. In his *Discours pour montrer que les doutes de la philosophie sceptique sont de grande usage dans les sciences* (1669), he illustrates how Pyrrhonian skepticism eliminates any serious concerns for scientific research because the process of doubt reveals that the logic of all sciences is unreliable. His *Hexaméron rustique* (1670) paints the portrait of a sensual non-believer who discredits commonly held notions of morality and undermines the moral basis of revealed religion. Yet, while many paint him as a total skeptic, it is important to recognize that La Mothe Le Vayer is a thinker of several types of skepticism, each with its own degree of doubt: scientific, moral, religious, skepticism for *divertissement*, and political skepticism.[3]

In this essay, I examine La Mothe Le Vayer's political skepticism. In his *Discours pour montrer les doutes de la philosophie sceptique sont de grand usage dans les sciences* one finds a brand of skepticism aimed at challenging the possibility of, and interest in, popular forms of scientific research. La Mothe Le Vayer's skepticism raises doubt about the possibility of true knowledge by calling into question the adequacy and reliability of evidence, the methods used, the observations undertaken, and the assumptions that buttress any claim to true knowledge. But does his method of skepticism leave the quest for knowledge about the moral and political world without any theoretical claims? Just as the categories of skeptic and believer are not mutually exclusive insofar as the former raises perennial doubts, but can still be part of the latter by choosing to accept some religious beliefs even if there is no certain knowledge or irrefutable evidence of the existence of God, so too can a skeptic of political science be a political scientist, of sorts.

In contrast to the view, advanced by Popkin, that La Mothe Le Vayer's writings lack theoretical structure, employing instead merely an illustrative writing schema, I suggest that the thesis-antithesis methodology he used in the "Dialogue traictant de la politique sceptiquement," a chapter in his first published work – the *Dialogues faits à l'imitation des anciens* (1630) – dissimulates La Mothe Le Vayer's own contribution to political science.[4] To philosophize like the ancients – the theme of the book implied in the title – as La Mothe Le Vayer explains in the "Lettre de l'auteur," leads him to practise the "ancient eloquence full of the liberty to speak as one thinks" (12). In terms of political enquiry, this results in a form of political skepticism that neither suspends total judgment about others nor passively acquiesces to the customs under which he lives. His reflections remove political science from the throne of superiority its practitioners claimed it had attained across the centuries of interpretation and reinterpretation by washing away, as it were, the false certitudes of Aristotle, the dreams of the utopians such as Campanella and More, and the political expediency of Machiavelli. La Mothe Le Vayer judges in a negative light the cruelty of recent regimes (including sixteenth-century Spain [Aristotle] and France [Machiavelli]), while praising the monarchy under which he lives. His skepticism shares similarities with his contemporary, René Descartes, namely, in the importance he gives to bringing into questions the means by which we know what we claim to know, and thus undermining philosophically entrenched dogmatic presuppositions. His concerns about the status of religious truth, God's existence, and the nature of the soul helped to set the stage for Descartes's preoccupations in the *Meditationes de prima philosophia*.[5] However, whereas Descartes employed doubt as the first step towards a method of knowledge, La Mothe Le Vayer's conclusions in the "Dialogue traictant de la politique sceptiquement" remain more exploratory in nature: the claims that survive his skeptical cleansing are the skeleton of a political philosophy that is partially dissimulated in the multiple layers of the dialogue, the scope of which we will explore in this essay.

Politics and Skepticism

It is clearly possible to be skeptical and political at the same time, because acting in a political manner does not require certainty. But political science is different from politics; politics, to employ Laursen's definition, "refers to a wide variety of attitudes, positions, strategies, and actions concerning government, international relations, and the public realm," while the vocation of political science purports to demonstrate some level of certainty about the causes and effects of human and state behaviour.[6] If done well, the vocation of political science will help humanity to overcome false beliefs and live well. However, skeptics doubt this is possible; or rather, as in the case of La Mothe Le Vayer, reject the idea that those who claim to have done so are correct in their assessment of the human condition.

The roots of political science date to the ancients. Aristotle famously wrote in the *Nicomachean Ethics* that political science was the architectonic science "which uses the rest of the sciences, and since, again, it legislates as to what we are to do and what we are to abstain from, the end of this science must include those of the others, so that its end must be the good for man."[7] For Aristotle, enquiry into politics was the key to deriving universal codes of moral conduct in order to construct political regimes that promote virtue. This vision of political science – as the "first, most noble and most advantageous of all [sciences]" – is the view La Mothe Le Vayer sets out to dethrone in his dialogue on politics (394).

Aristotle's authority on political matters was such that deep into the sixteenth century, he was considered by some, including the Portuguese thinker Diogo Lopes Rebelo and many of the Spanish scholastics, to relate the truths of Nature. His knowledge about virtue and politics was thus seen as a valuable guide to future kings who sought to rule well.[8] That said, his political and moral authority was the target of many modern political philosophers. For example, Machiavelli rejected the interpretations of political science made by the ancients, but saw value in a version of political science that illustrated the effectual truth. Such a science of politics, which he purports to provide, would deliver useful knowledge to would-be princes, albeit very different from the views expressed by Aristotle, about how to rule.

Both of these claims to political knowledge concerned La Mothe Le Vayer because when the science of politics according to Aristotle or Machiavelli was implemented, this historically resulted in great cruelty. In the modern world, La Mothe Le Vayer was well aware of the troublesome Spanish monarchy's cruel conquest of the New World fuelled by scholastic Aristotelianism. Certain Spanish theologians, such as Juan Gínes de Sepúlveda, turned to Aristotle to provide the Spanish Crown with a source of philosophical authority to justify conquering the native populations.[9] As an avid reader of Montaigne, La Mothe Le Vayer would have been aware of this link between authority and conquest, and thus gleaned from Montaigne's musings cause for critical skepticism.[10] Closer to home, the recent history of France's period of religious civil war, deformed by Machiavellianism, gave La Mothe Le Vayer more reason to doubt the utility of political knowledge. Once again through the lens of Montaigne, who warns those who would find value in Machiavelli's teachings that emphasize the uses of cruelty and dissimulation – "those who preach to princes such an attentive distrust, under the guise of preaching them security, preach them their ruin and shame"), – La Mothe Le Vayer bore witness to the dangerous link between political knowledge and violence. Like Montaigne, who viewed with distaste the coupling of Machiavellianism and French politics – "this new-fangled virtue of hypocrisy and dissimulation, which is so highly honored at present, I mortally hate it" – La Mothe Le Vayer's skepticism questions the purported benefits of such political knowledge.[11]

These examples provided good reason to be skeptical of political enquiry as being good for mankind. Although he does not directly name Aristotle or Machiavelli as his targets, his reflections on the Spanish monarchy and on his native France, as we shall see below, implicitly identify them as two philosophers in the crosshairs of his skeptical dethronement of political science.[12] In this, La Mothe Le Vayer was following in the footsteps of Montaigne, although his skepticism had a different purpose.[13]

Skepticism, by promoting doubt, can serve as a mechanism that removes what is perceived to be false dogma in order to replace it with true knowledge. Descartes and Hobbes are good examples. The risk, however, is that the "true knowledge" replacing "dogma" serves the political whims of the ruler at the expense of others, who suffer great cruelty when this knowledge is applied to the political realm. On the other hand, skepticism could lead to total suspension of judgment, and therefore the rejection of certainty. Montaigne's skepticism, for example, practised during the period of religious civil wars, led him to suspend judgment on customs of others while accepting the customs of his own country and seeking refuge in his "arrière boutique."[14]

La Mothe Le Vayer's political skepticism, however, was different insofar as he did not build, like Hobbes, a theory of politics once he was through repudiating the political science of others. And unlike Montaigne, he did not retreat into the private sphere and passively accept the mores of his own country. Rather, he left certain foundations of a theory of politics standing – namely, the intellectual freedoms allowed by his king – and publically affirmed his support of these political characteristics in order to pursue a career as a public intellectual skeptic.

This reading of La Mothe Le Vayer parallels Popkin's stance that his skepticism was necessarily incomplete. Challenging the pervasive opinion that La Mothe Le Vayer sought to make religious belief seem ridiculous and absurd to the rational person, Popkin argues that La Mothe Le Vayer marks the continuation of a form of skepticism found in Montaigne. This form of skepticism was not an anti-religious movement destined to undermine Christianity. Rather, he suggests that La Mothe Le Vayer's project was ultimately compatible with Christianity. "I think it is perfectly possible," he writes,

> that the continual emphasis on Christian skepticism in his writings was intended as a sincere view, at least as sincere as that of Montaigne and Charron. In this I know I stand alone except for the eighteenth century editor of La Mothe Le Vayer's *Dialogues*, L.M. Kahle. But it seems perfectly possible that the point of the so-called *libertinage érudite* was not to destroy Christianity but to serve as a buttress for a certain type of liberal Catholicism as opposed to either superstitious belief or fanatical Protestantism.[15]

The same could be true for political skepticism. Rather than seeking to destroy the vocation of political science, it is also plausible that La Mothe Le Vayer could be a skeptical political scientist, that is to say, one who doubts the Aristotles and Machiavellis of the world because their conceptions of politics, if put into practice, would lead to political behaviour resulting in nefarious outcomes, but also one who enquires into the politics of human affairs in order to offer "a few light suspicions according to the reach of our humanity" (451). This view is compatible with the claim that La Mothe Le Vayer's skepticism is geared towards liberating human beings from the grip of dogma by means of a mode of amusement that, like Montaigne's *Essais,* delivers him from the bitterness of life. However, my interpretation also suggests that La Mothe Le Vayer's amusing skepticism served to teach his readers important lessons about politics.[16]

La Mothe Le Vayer's Political Skepticism

La Mothe Le Vayer expresses his skepticism about political science in a dialogue entitled "Dialogue traictant de la politique sceptiquement." The literary device of dialogue allows La Mothe de Vayer to juxtapose two opposing ideas, and take the reader through a series of mental exercises that lead him or her to reject the commonly held view in favour of what, at first, appears to be a more unorthodox view. In the case of political science, he hopes to persuade the reader that the popular view that "the study of the government of the state, which we ordinarily call politics, is one of the most worthy forms of contemplation" is problematic (387). Rather than helping to improve the lot of humanity, the study of politics, he claims, has been plagued by utopian visions – he alludes to the likes of Plato, Thomas More, Tomasso de Campanella, and Francis Bacon, whose political explorations amount to "chimeras" (390), ignore the vicissitudes of fortune, and occupy and trouble philosophical minds with "vain things" (391). He cites numerous examples of the diversity of the world in order to suggest that studying politics does not lead to universals. In addition, he shows that its study does not produce good rulers, implicitly denouncing Aristotle and Machiavelli through his criticism of sixteenth-century Spain and France. Thus, rather than providing knowledge of politics that is useful for the good of humanity, political science facilitates dogmatic claims that lead to fanaticism and cruelty. I will contend this is a surface reading of La Mothe Le Vayer.

One could read in La Mothe Le Vayer's skepticism a purely destructive act that wipes away all possibilities of knowledge. As Popkin argues, "unlike his contemporaries Bacon and Descartes, the value of the method of doubt lies in clearing away the science as well as all scientific interest. What remains is the suspension of judgment on all matters, and the divine Revelation."[17] According to this reading, nothing would remain from La Mothe Le Vayer's doubting of the sciences, including political science: no knowledge about the human condition, no assumptions that could serve as the basis of judgment, no foundation for political enquiry; nothing but some vague sense of God. If this were true, then the only conclusion to draw would be that the vocation of political science is, indeed, not a worthy endeavour. But this conclusion does not seem to fit the textual evidence. An alternative reading is that La Mothe Le Vayer's rejection of past attempts to impose a universal political science yields a version of political science of its own.

The key to such a reading of La Mothe Le Vayer lies in the methodology he uses. While he clearly takes some pleasure – *divertissement* – in his intellectual forays into the diverse political modes and orders of the world, there is more to his political skepticism. In keeping with the skeptical methodology that undergirds La Mothe Le Vayer's dialogue on politics, each claim can be countered by its opposite, with the latter disproving the former. The beginning passages set up the thesis-antithesis dynamic that structures the skeptical dialogue on politics, as it moves from the view that political science is a worthy endeavour to the counterclaim that it is not.

The dialogue begins with one of the interlocutors, Telemon, defending the utility of political science based on three claims. First, because it is the architectonic science, it is useful for aiding peoples across the globe to live happily: "By its utility, which extends to so many peoples which it teaches to govern themselves and live happily, [it] should perhaps be called the first, most noble, and most advantageous of all [sciences]" (394). Second, it is unfair to expect its axioms to be mathematical in order to be useful; rather, its maxims, gathered carefully over time, can generally be useful if founded on "reason and good discourse" (395). Third, disregarding the study of politics causes one to neglect the love of one's own country. Here, the assumption seems to be that political science leads to the conclusion that one's own laws are the best laws. Note that this is precisely what La Mothe Le Vayer comes to implicitly conclude at the end of the dialogue by rejecting previous interpretations of political science and praising the regime under which he lives, a point to which I return below.

There is good reason to reject each of these claims, even if La Mothe Le Vayer does not really reject the last one. The main reason to reject them, communicated through the voice of the other interlocutor Orontes, is that the societies purported to be the most civilized, that is, the ones that claim to have perfected and implemented the study of politics, "caused the wars, tyrannies, plagues, famines, and generally almost all of the evils that we suffer ... One thing we cannot doubt is that they threw the shackles onto the feet of that beautiful natural liberty whose loss cannot be compensated for" (397). Linking purported knowledge of universal truths to cataclysmic historical events, La Mothe Le Vayer rejects the scientific authority of political science as a vocation that could instruct princes how to rule well. But then he goes further:

> In what you describe as the first and most noble of sciences, having its fundamental reasons and certain principles, I would easily admit to you that there is no other science that is so full of pomp and circumstance as she, vaunting that it dominates over all the others. She speaks only in reasons and maxims of state, and possesses all the great charges, and is adored by all that is inferior to her. But all that false luster, and that fastidious monster, can only fool an ignorant people, and becomes ridiculous in the eyes of those who look at things in their essence. (397)

Political science appears to be nothing more than dogma embellished with cute maxims ("false luster") that trick the masses to follow their king, while hiding something terrible (a "fastidious monster") underneath. On the surface, this supports La Mothe Le Vayer's deeply skeptical argument outlined in the *Discours*, namely, that we cannot really know anything for certain. However, La Mothe Le Vayer, who sees things for what they are, is not duped. This suggests that there is another layer to the dialogue beyond the simple thesis-antithesis dichotomy.

La Mothe Le Vayer alerts his readers to the reality that history provides "antitheses without limit" to each authoritative claim (407). The rejection of political science is no exception. If the rejection of political science must be juxtaposed with its antithesis, then what is this antithesis? The answer, logically, is the rejection of the rejection of political science. If taken literally, this would be implicit in the very act of La Mothe Le Vayer's writing the dialogue on political skepticism itself. But what does this act yield politically and philosophically?

The act of writing has two purposes. On the one hand, it is a public act of skepticism. Taking a page from Montaigne, La Mothe Le Vayer exclaims, speaking of the skeptical approach: "O inestimable antidote against the presumption of knowledge of the pedants."[18] Montaigne's skepticism encouraged the individual to withdraw to one's "arrière boutique" – a private act – to seek one's own path to happiness amidst the trials and tribulations of the human condition. Departing from Montaigne, La Mothe Le Vayer makes skepticism a public vocation that forces the process of doubt into the public sphere. His fascination with the diversity of the world, books, and history, coupled with the political nature of his writings that challenged taboos and dominant mores, even if undertaken for his (and other's) intellectual amusement, deals unavoidably with the human condition and politics. As Salazar observes with regard to La Mothe Le Vayer's subsequent work, his skepticism has at least one exception, found in the admiration of a society "regulated by *philia* and the skeptical application of knowledge. In effect, a society of free thinkers, that is to say, citizens."[19] This exception is not arbitrary; it marks the keystone of his own science of politics – the benefit of a political system that enables what he values above all, the freedom to be a skeptic. I will have more to say on the political and philosophical implications of this predilection in the final section of this essay.

A second purpose of writing is to undertake an act of meta-philosophical enquiry – an enquiry about enquiries – that contributes to the vocation of political science. Stated differently, behind the thesis-antithesis veil lies La Mothe Le Vayer's own participation in the vocation of political science. By employing a skeptical methodology in seventeenth-century France to discredit previous attempts at political science, La Mothe Le Vayer participates in a conversation about politics spanning the ages. What is more, he pronounces judgment on the most famous question that plagued the minds of great thinkers from Plato to Aristotle, Aquinas, Machiavelli, Hobbes – and later Rousseau, Kant, Rawls, and so on: What is the best regime? His contribution is a necessary dose of skepticism to render the study of politics useful in two ways. First, his critical look at philosophers of the past helped him to judge negatively the manifestations of their philosophies in the contemporary world. And second, the act of practising skepticism through writing led him to judge positively the regime under which he lived and offer theoretical claims about what a good regime is and how it can come to ruin.

Repudiating Certain Regimes

La Mothe Le Vayer turns to a classic skeptical tool to criticize, on the surface, the potential of political science to provide knowledge about the best regime by cataloging the diversity of the world. He thus illustrates that those who claim to have such knowledge are misled because so many versions of alternative ways of life exist. His examples include the Incas, the Aztecs, the Persians, the Tartars, the Turks, the Arabs, the Chinese, the Greeks, the Romans, and the Spanish, among others. Paying particular attention to this trope, Popkin argues that La Mothe Le Vayer sought nothing more than to "develop evidence about variations in ethical and religious behavior" in the world without seeking to make political claims.[20] However, insofar as La Mothe Le Vayer passes judgment on some of these, there is more to the process. The Spanish are his favourite target. "Who would not take the Spanish today," he asks rhetorically, "for the best statists and the most refined political analysts that live?" (410).

The choice of the Spanish is important. Conquerors of the New World, rulers of an expansive empire at the apex of European power steeped in religious, scholastic, and thus Aristotelian dogma, perpetrators of great crimes of cruelty against the Indians at the hands of the Machiavellian conquistadors, the Spanish "best regime" was paid for in blood and vice. Seeking to provide an antithesis to the view that the Spanish represent the apex of political philosophy, La Mothe Le Vayer exclaims: "According to my nature, which is no stranger to paradoxes, I think I can reasonably support [the claim that] there does not appear a nation under the heavens that is less born to rule others than [the Spanish], and who did not more prudently maneuver amidst the great advantages of the times and fortune that were presented to her to arrive at the status of universal monarchy" (410). This is an attack on Aristotelianism, which buttressed and informed the Spanish kings' ruling practices. Echoing Montaigne, La Mothe Le Vayer forcefully repudiates the view that the Spanish rise to power was due to good political science. Rather, he cites "good fortune" – the religious schisms in England and France, the weakness of Italy, and the indifference of Germany – as the catalyst for Spain's dominance.

More poignantly still, he critically reflects on Spanish cruelty in subduing the New World: "But whoever will gaze upon from the other side [the conquistadors'] evil behavior, and the irreparable errors of [the Spanish] government, how much evil she employed to extract the gold from Peru ... [and] the manner by which she attracted the hatred of the rest of the human species ... by way of insatiable avarice and cruelties of the most inhumane nature" will recognize that Spain is not, despite its position of power, a model to be admired by anyone seeking knowledge of the science of politics (411). He concludes that Spain's success was not due to prudence and good mores – which he equates broadly with erroneous attempts at political science (grouping Machiavelli and Aristotle together as equally mistaken), but rather to "the ordinary outcome of the revolution of states" (412).

Praising Certain Regimes

There is more to La Mothe Le Vayer's musings than negative criticism. Following his attack on Spain, he opines that each prince assumes he has arrived at some universal principals, despite diverse predilections: "There is not a Legislator who has not thought he has found the finest level of Politics, despite the fact that each has his own particular laws, and that [one prince's laws] often permit what is categorically prohibited by [the other prince's laws]" (415). This would suggest there is no basis to ascertain whether certain laws are good in general. However, La Mothe Le Vayer himself does offer praise of certain laws, which he garners not from purported authorities of political science, but from experience. In the passage that follows, he praises the King of France as "the greatest king who has ever handled the scepter" for permitting the skeptical musings of philosophers like himself (416). He then undertakes a lengthy critique of royalty – which yields key clues provided to the reader to decipher La Mothe Le Vayer's own political science that I explore below – before once again openly praising the current monarch of France for allowing him to think and express his thoughts openly:

> You see, Telemon, with what frankness I am disposed to treat ... such a fickle subject. The goodwill of our great monarch, and the happiness of his government having permitted me to say what I would have had to suppress under a prince with less heroic virtue. It is necessary to have the rule of an Augustus, or a Trajan, or a Louis the Just to dare express oneself [like I have]. (433–4)

If La Mothe Le Vayer is sincere in his praise, then he is essentially making a statement about what a good regime is, namely, one that promotes a certain level of tolerance. But are we to take La Mothe Le Vayer seriously in his praise of the king? Could this be one of those empty statements of flattery that often accompany works of philosophy?

Scholars are divided on how sincerely to read La Mothe Le Vayer's writings. One school holds that La Mothe Le Vayer's views must be read through the lens of dissimulation – i.e., he could not say openly what he thought, but had to hide his true views between the lines.[21] Building on Leo Strauss's claims in *Persecution and the Art of Writing*, this school of thought suggests that we need to be cautious about taking his words at face value. While certainly true of sixteenth-century France, when authors such as Montaigne had to be careful to avoid upsetting the ruling figures and the censors, and for the early seventeenth century as well, was it the case for those writing during the time of La Mothe Le Vayer? On the one hand, he originally published his dialogue on politics under a pseudonym. However, there was little doubt throughout his career about his public reputation as a skeptic, which suggests that he did not have to hide it. His candour even led him to being embroiled in controversy surrounding the possibility of revolt against the monarchy. Thus, as Popkin argues, owing to the climate of tolerance under the reign of Louis the Just, La Mothe Le Vayer was ultimately not worried about expressing his true opinions.[22] This did not mean he did not dissimulate certain views, such as his own political claims, within a treatise on political skepticism for the intellectual amusement of himself and others. Indeed, dissimulation that could be uncovered by careful readers creates the intellectual paradoxes of which he was so fond (410). I am thus inclined to agree with Popkin's assessment that La Mothe Le Vayer's praise of Louis the Just, while perhaps embellished in the form of flattery, was sincere.

One could interject here that La Mother Le Vayer is simply using a typical trope employed by skeptics, that of bearing the yoke of the regime under which they live, while suspending judgment about others. La Mothe Le Vayer admits as much: "We do not obey the laws or the prince because they are good and just, but simply because they are law and he is the prince" (433). However, as we saw above, La Mothe Le Vayer does not entirely suspend his judgment about other regimes, and he does more than passively accept the regime under which he lives. By praising the French monarchy under which he lives, La Mothe Le Vayer effectively suspends his skepticism to lay the foundation of a political theory based on toleration of a wide and vigorous intellectual life. His praise of Louis the Just is thus more than mere flattery, and reflects a trait also found in Augustus and Trajan, whom he also praises. Each of these rulers ushered in an era of peace after a time of tumult and governed without brutality and with tolerance.

Such praise was not an isolated moment in La Mothe Le Vayer's early thought. In the chapter of the *Dialogues* entitled "Dialogue sur le subjet de la divinité," to counter those who employed the cruel methods of the dogmatic Inquisition to keep the public order, La Mothe Le Vayer praises the maxims of Tertullian and supported the pre-Christian claims that the

"the Romans were in this sense the most just … being content to make the inhabitants of the empire observe their laws without being violent to anyone in terms of religion" (337). He also favourably cited the laws of Jovien and Valens, who permitted the liberty of belief, authorizing and equally approving all existing religions.[23] The upshot is that La Mothe Le Vayer consistently praised certain political characteristics – namely, religious freedom, liberty of expression, and toleration more generally. As with Hume, for whom freethinking was more important to his underlying philosophy than most scholars recognize, La Mothe Le Vayer understood that his ability to be a freethinker was essential to his identity as a public, and at times radical, skeptic.[24] This tolerance then enabled a deep skepticism of dogma that allowed intellectuals to raise questions about commonly held beliefs regarding human nature, natural law, the viability of mores and customs, the universality of religion, the place of cruelty in politics, and the stature of the monarchy.

Political Implications: La Mothe Le Vayer's Political Science

La Mothe Le Vayer offers us more than just the standard skeptical suspension of judgment on all matters. While suspending judgment on politics abroad by appreciating the diversity of political possibilities in the world at large, he was willing to apply criticism or praise closer to home, within the common heritage of Europe. Thus, despite proffering, on the surface, a scathing critique of political science, La Mothe Le Vayer's skeptical turn shadows his participation in the vocation of political science.

The impact of a climate of skepticism on intellectual advances should not be underestimated. One need only compare an active climate of skepticism to historical instances when such doubt was not permitted (i.e., the Spanish Inquisition or any modern authoritarian regime). The legitimacy of doubt facilitates alternative forms of scientific enquiry, including political enquiry, by rendering public the most critical opinion, which in turn disarms dogma and opens the intellectual pathway towards a shift away from accepted "truth." In addition, this skepticism provides an intellectual tool that opened the path for a comparative analysis of beliefs, rites, social organization, mores, and political systems across cultures and time.[25] Finally, it contributed to a culture of enquiry and doubt that had a broader effect on the evolution of political ideas in France through the Enlightenment.[26] Even if his own political enquiry does not take the form of the treatises of a Bodin or Montesquieu, La Mothe Le Vayer's career did produce claims about the human condition and has had a lasting influence on the intellectual landscape of France. To the extent his skepticism left in its wake of doubt certain assumptions that could help his readership during his lifetime and his intellectual heirs to think about the relationship between politics and the human condition, he provides a philosophical foundation that survives his skeptical scythe and that others could build on (or be forced to reject).

That said, in the spirit of a skeptic, La Mothe Le Vayer recognized the limitations of his own theoretical gaze. The first limitation, building from the age-old maxim that good regimes eventually decline, is that tolerant regimes are never everlasting. Rather, they are always subject to the vicissitudes of fortune: "That supposed science of states ... does not have any principles that are so certain that ... the slightest accident of fortune, the slightest diversity of time cannot easily shake them" (440–1). The recognition that fortune may intervene to countermand the maxims of the science of states should not, however, discount the possibility of useful knowledge. Machiavelli, who was hardly a skeptic, also recognized the role of fortune in political affairs. However, he believed that by reading history and following the examples of great men one could find political maxims that could enhance the probability one could dominate over fortune. Notwithstanding the fact that the goal of Machiavelli's science of politics was vastly different from La Mother le Vayer's, the French philosopher agreed that some level of knowledge about politics was possible. Thus, in the concluding passage of the dialogue, before the interlocutors head off to a feast, the reader is presented with the following position: "Let us be happy with what others make into a profession of having such certain sciences, to be witnesses, if we are constrained to do so, to possess a few light suspicions according to the reach of our humanity" (451). This position marks a middle ground between the thesis found at the beginning of the dialogue articulated by Telemon, the view that political science is useful, and the antithesis articulated by Orontes that the science of politics is incendiary, and therefore worthy of repudiation. This middle ground – which parallels La Mothe Le Vayer's own view of politics delineated above – implies that nature provides human beings the inner instinct and tools to search for the truth of things, even if it may be impossible to arrive at certainty. La Mothe Le Vayer's political skepticism thus translates into a tamer political science – a skeptic's political science – by replacing claims of certainty with "light suspicions" about the political, which are nevertheless philosophically important.

La Mothe Le Vayer's skeptical political science reveals what a good regime looks like, but it does not enumerate how to get there or how to preserve it. However, he hints at how good regimes unravel. Returning to the example of Spain – though this could apply to any regime – he writes: "Like a wispy and particular interest, an unpremeditated moment, made in haste or with hesitance, makes or unmakes the most important actions of a ruler" (412). Fortune can lead to the downfall of princes, whether they are good or bad rulers. Taking a page from Montaigne, he observes that whatever principles princes follow, "one often arrives at the same end by different paths, and that the causes which appear contrary can produce the same effect" (416). But once again departing from Montaigne, La Mothe Le Vayer elucidates the negative circumstances that lead to a regime's ruin.[27]

In a long passage that follows his repudiation of Spain and between the two passages where he praises the French monarchy as cited above, La Mothe Le Vayer undertakes a philosophical enquiry into royalty: "I want presently to focus on the royalty, to examine the [related] maxims in my own way. Such a task I will undertake willingly given that, having such a good and just prince, we can speak freely about this subject, and without fear of any sinister reaction" (416). In this section of the dialogue, he first lists a series of theses/antitheses of examples to challenge the view that monarchs are superior to regular men. Then he remarks: "It seems that God operates much more distinctly on the hearts of Kings ... than those of the rest of mankind. From this, many consider [kings] to be much more obligated [to follow] a more correct morality, and be more conscientious than others." This caveat points to an exception to the thesis/antithesis methodology, as if revealing a moment when La Mothe Le Vayer is dialoguing directly with kings or would-be princes: "Thus we observe an infinity of princes whose vices and unlawfulness led them to perish miserably." Significantly, this statement does not have an antithesis, which suggests that La Mothe Le Vayer sees a causal relationship between princely vice and political ruin. The warning continues as he returns to the thesis-antithesis methodology to show how dissimulation, that Machiavellian virtue which some esteem as essential to ruling, renders a prince "suspect" in the eyes of the people, and "undermines his interests." Finally, he provides an antithesis to the French predilection for hereditary monarchy by showing how many countries thrive with monarchs chosen through election (420–2).

The implications of this reflection on monarchy are twofold: first, a further rejection of Machiavelli insofar as a king who rules through vice will come to lose his throne. The second is that royal succession is no guarantee that the good, tolerant regime of one king will be passed on through the bloodline. This conclusion reveals a substantive problem with La Mothe Le Vayer's endorsement of a tolerant absolutist regime, one that he clearly recognized and perhaps feared would come to pass. While good for intellectual enquiry, a tolerant absolutist regime provides no guarantees of political permanence. Absent political checks, such a regime can turn intolerant very quickly because there is nothing to stop the king from imposing his whims on the people. Indeed, this fear did come to pass in the case of the very regime La Mothe Le Vayer praised. The death of Louis the Just in 1643, only three years after the publication of the *Dialogues*, saw the rise to the throne of Louis XIV, whose reign eventually veered towards intolerance. La Mothe Le Vayer proved unable to imagine a political solution to instil greater permanence, though he did recognize the problem and combatted it through a shift towards more radical skepticism as his career unfolded.

The culture of doubt La Mothe Le Vayer helped to sustain did, however, sow the seeds for future reflection that deepened enquiries about the sanctity of divine monarchy, and led later philosophers to look for ways to institutionalize tolerance. A century later, Montesquieu, writing with the experience of La Mothe Le Vayer's era and in particular the intolerance during the reign of Louis XIV in mind, ultimately came to conclude that the good regime requires some sort of institutionalized legal checks.[28]

Concluding Remarks

La Mothe Le Vayer can be read as a political scientist who was a skeptic. To the extent that he uses a certain skeptical methodology to make political claims about political philosophers of the past and the human condition, he is participating in the very vocation of political science that, on the surface, he ridicules. It is thus important to parse out two levels of his critique of political science: on one level is his criticism of previous attempts at political science that do not yield beneficial rules about the science of the state – Aristotle and Machiavelli are among his favourite targets. This political skepticism is a destructive skepticism that undermines claims to political knowledge made by authoritative philosophers, but also dissimulates his targeting of certain political practices, namely, cruelty, princely vice, religious dogma, and intolerance. On another level, there are the assumptions that remain once the purported certainties of others are washed away and his ironic praise of Louis the Just is unmasked, namely, the importance of tolerance and the intellectual climate of skepticism permitted by it. This is La Mothe Le Vayer's foundational political science, a paradox he dissimulated within the perpetual thesis-antithesis cycle of his dialogue on politics.

There are two final notes to contemplate when putting La Mothe Le Vayer's early foray into skepticism via a dialogue on political enquiry into context. Speaking of La Mothe Le Vayer's *oeuvres*, my analysis of his political skepticism suggests that he employed different types of skepticism across his career, at least one of which was incomplete because it betrayed political claims of theoretical substance. This illustrates the need to parse out the levels of skepticism he employed in his other works, and the relationship of his ideas to the political stability and upheavals of his lifetime. Speaking of the broader process of political enquiry across time, which La Mothe Le Vayer wittingly dissimulated his participation in, his skepticisms – including his political skepticism – firmly established a culture of critical thought regarding certain political traditions. Thus, although the *crise pyrrhonienne* of the seventeenth century may have temporarily appeared to undermine humanity's quest for scientific and religious knowledge, this skeptical culture, which brought into question some aspects of politics while praising others, paved the way for future philosophers to reconstruct, in their own manner, the science of politics. His original works went through multiple editions until well into the eighteenth century, while the essence of his ideas was published in abridged form for popular consumption, in addition to an interpretive biography of his life.[29] Tracing the reception of his skepticisms across the changing philosophical landscape in France can yet yield further insight into his legacy as a skeptic and a political scientist.

NOTES

1 See René Pintard, *Le libertinage érudit dans la première moité du XVII* siècle (Paris, 1943) and Françoise Charles-Daubert, *Les Libertins érudits en France au XVIIe siècle* (Paris: Presses Universitaires de France, 1998).

2 Richard H. Popkin, *The History of Scepticism: From Savonarola to Bayle* (Oxford: Oxford University Press, 2003), 83.

3 On the strategies of expression utilized by La Mothe Le Vayer, see the chapter dedicated to him in Jean-Pierre Cavaillé, *Dis/simulations: Jules-César Vanini, François La Mothe Le Vayer, Gabriel Naudé, Louis Machon et*

Torquato Accetto: réligion, morale et politique aux XVII siècle (Paris: Honoré Champion, 2002).

4 Popkin, *History of Scepticism,* 84. I use the version of La Mothe Le Vayer's "Dialogue traictant de la politique sceptiquement" found in François de La Mothe Le Vayer, *Dialogues faits à l'imitation des anciens* (Tours: Librarie Arthème Fayard, 1988). All translations are my own and appear in the text.

5 Roger Ariew, John Cottingham, and Tom Sorell, eds., *Descartes' Meditations: Background Source Materials* (Cambridge: Cambridge University Press, 1998), xvii.

6 John Christian Laursen, *The Politics of Skepticism in the Ancients, Montaigne, Hume and Kant* (Leiden: E.J. Brill 1992), 4–5.

7 Aristotle, *The Nicomachean Ethics,* translated by David Ross (Oxford: Oxford University Press, 1998), 2.

8 Daniel R. Brunstetter, *Tensions of Modernity: Las Casas and His Legacy in the French Enlightenment* (New York: Routledge, 2012), 24–5, 45–9.

9 Daniel Brunstetter, "Old World Philosophy in a New World: From Natural Slave to Natural Man," in *Old Worlds, New Worlds. European Cultural Encounters, c.1000 – c.1750,* ed. L. Bailey, L. Digglemann, and K.M. Phillips (Turnhout, Belgium: Brepols Publishers, 2009), 101–20.

10 See the passages in Montaigne's essays "Of Cannibals" and "Of Coaches" where the author of the *Essais* specifically challenges the link between philosophical authority and the conquest of the New World; Michel de Montaigne, *The Complete Works of Montaigne,* translated by Donald Frame (Stanford, CA: Stanford University Press, 1958), 150, 693.

11 Montaigne, *Complete Works,* 491.

12 For historical background on the targets of skepticism, see chapters 2 and 3 of Richard Tuck, *Philosophy and Government: 1572–1651* (Cambridge: Cambridge University Press, 1993). On France and Machiavellianism, see Edmond M. Beame, "The Use and Abuse of Machiavelli: The Sixteenth-Century French Adaptation," *Journal of the History of Ideas* 43, no. 1 (1982), 33–54.

13 For direct criticism of Aristotle, see Montaigne, *Complete Works* pages 403, 429; for explicit criticism of Machiavelli, see page 497.

14 Montaigne, *Complete Works,* 177.

15 Popkin, *History of Scepticism,* 87.

16 Sylvia Giocanti, "La Mothe Le Vayer: Modes de diversion sceptique," in *Libertinage et philosophie au XVIIe siècle,* 2, 1997, 33–48.

17 Popkin, *History of Scepticism,* 84.

18 La Mothe Le Vayer, *Petite traité sceptique sur cette façon de de parler,* in La Mothe Le Vayer, *Oeuvres,* vol. 9, 280.

19 Philippe-Joseph Salazar, *La Divine Sceptique: Ethique et rhétorique au 17eme siècle; autour de La Mothe Le Vayer* (Tübingen: Gunter Narr Verlag, 2000), 78; my translation.

20 Popkin, *History of Scepticism*, 82.

21 See Peter Zagorin, *Ways of Living: Dissimulation, Persecution, and Conformity in Early Modern Europe* (Cambridge, MA: Harvard University Press, 1990).

22 Popkin, *History of Scepticism*, 88–90.

23 For a discussion, see Gianni Paganini, *Skepsis: Le Débat Moderne Sur Le Scepticisme* (Paris: Vrin, 2008), 80.

24 Paul Russell, *The Riddle of Hume's Treatise: Skepticism, Naturalism, and Irreligion* (Oxford: Oxford University Press, 2008).

25 Paganini, *Skepsis*, 77.

26 Skeptical culture in general was influential in contributing to the shift from support of divine monarchical legitimacy to the long period of political criticism leading up to the French Revolution. See Jacob Soll, who focuses on translators, editors, and commentators in sixteenth- and seventeenth-century France; *Publishing The Prince: History, Reading, and the Birth of Political Criticism* (Ann Arbor: University of Michigan Press, 2008).

27 This assumes that the common interpretation of Montaigne as a pure skeptic is accurate. One could also argue that dissimulated in his skepticism are the foundations of a political science born out of the violence of the religious wars – namely, a rejection of the politics of cruelty and the need to establish a political system based on tolerance. If Montaigne was also dissimulating political preferences of his own, and La Mothe Le Vayer interpreted Montaigne this way, it could be just as accurate to say he was following in Montaigne's dissimulationist footsteps. On Montaigne, compare Alan Levine, *Sensual Philosophy* (London: Lexington Books, 2001) and Laursen, *Politics of Skepticism* (chs. 4 and 5).

28 See, for example, the last five books of *De l'esprit des lois*, which can be read as demonstrating the need for autonomous judicial bodies to protect the liberties of the nation and the inviolability of the law by thwarting the natural despotic tendencies of absolute monarchy.

29 See La Mothe Le Vayer, *Oeuvres de François de La Mothe Le Vayer*, 14 vols. (Dresden: M. Groell, 1756–9; Charles-Antoine-Joseph Leclerc de Montlinot, *L'Esprit de La Mothe Le Vayer* (S. l., 1763) and Pons-Augustin Alletz, *La Vie de la Motte Le Vayer, Consellier d'État, et Précepteur de Monsieur, Frère Unique du Roi Louis XIV* (Paris: Chez la Veuve Duchesne, 1783).

chapter three

Hobbes and the French Skeptics

GIANNI PAGANINI

1. Hobbes and the Challenge of French Skepticism

The relations between Hobbes and skepticism are still in dispute. On the level of theory, some recent studies have established historical connections regarding specific aspects of Hobbes's thought, from the theory of knowledge to the principles of first philosophy. On the grounds of moral and political philosophy it seems that the guidelines of criticism can be basically reduced to two:

a) There is scarce or no relation at all between Hobbes and skepticism. For Hobbes, the great divide does not run between dogmatists and skeptics in the Pyrrhonian meaning of these terms, but beween "*mathematici*" (in the Greek extended meaning: those who know and then can really teach the others) and the "dogmatists." The former, according to Hobbes, proceed according to the method of sciences, by clear definitions and rigorous deduction; the latter, especially those who speak about passions, morals, and politics, are not able to "teach" but only to "persuade": taking "for principles those opinions which are already vulgarly received," they proceed "without any evident demonstration." It is clear that this distinction is tantamount to the opposition between science, or true knowledge, and rhetoric, which is for Hobbes no real knowledge but only a practical effort to gain assent ("with passion [they] press to have their opinions pass everywhere for truth"). Paradoxically, the field of the dogmatists is the realm of "doubt and controversy" that "they have very much multiplied."[1] Faced with this strong opposition, it seems that skepticism would not be an alternative worth taking into account. In the French milieu that Hobbes participated in during his Parisian exile, one that was fully acquainted with the topics of Pyrrhonism, Marin Mersenne took up this peculiar meaning of dogmatism, praising Hobbes for "setting up the dogmatic philosophy on very solid grounds" and urging his friend Samuel Sorbière (with leanings towards skepticism) to abandon "Your epokhē [suspension of judgment] and skeptical trifles."[2] Even today some historians seem to be trying to "purify" Hobbes's character by removing from him almost any trace of his contacts with the skeptical tradition. For example, Quentin Skinner acknowledged in the past the importance of the Hobbes-Montaigne relationship especially in the field of moral and anthropological considerations;[3] more recently, however, the same author has stressed more and more Hobbes's non-involvement in the Pyrrhonian tradition,[4] reducing its relevance to the minimum trace of the skeptical background to the rhetorical "paradiastolē" (rhetorical redescription, by which one can disparage virtue and excuse vice).[5] If French political thought, which was nourished by skepticism, had any influence on Hobbes, it would have been only for the category of "interest," coming from the theories of the "raison d'état," not exactly a skeptical notion.[6]

b) The second alternative sees Hobbes as a post-skeptical thinker, one who has elaborated his own response to Pyrrhonism, having it in mind as a challenge to some of his own philosophical conceptions. There are many variations of this formula, which range from Popkin to Tuck, and myself. Popkin and Tuck agree that Hobbes took the challenge of skepticism seriously enough to lead political discourse to a new ground: "a political theory of truth" for Popkin who mostly treated religious and political issues;[7] a philosophy of the intellect that "limits or binds itself," renouncing its own independence, for Tuck who considered the epistemological topics.[8] I have explored Hobbes's theory of phenomena, which relies upon the Pyrrhonian theme of the "mixtures" between the subject, the object, and the middle, as it was redeveloped by Montaigne and his disciples in France.[9]

There are elements of truth in both interpretations, but I would like to outline a third scenario, whose historical and theoretical elements are as follows:

Hobbes did not confine himself to rejecting (as in claim a) or to overcoming (as in claim b) skepticism, but really learned from it and tried to answer its challenge. There are many aspects of the seventeenth-century skeptical *koinē*, and especially of the modern one, which are also at the basis of Hobbes's thought: we shall explore here mostly anthropological, psychological, and moral elements that figure in his description of human conduct. These aspects represent an essential part of the descriptive background against which Hobbes's moral and political theory is built. Hobbes made acquaintance with authors such as Montaigne and Charron already in England or during his trips to the Continent, but a new incorporation of skeptical elements most likely happened to an even greater extent at a particular stage of Hobbes's life and work, when, during the decade of his exile in France (1641–51), he was fully immersed in the context of "Continental skepticism"[10] (two of his most prominent interlocutors, Mersenne and Descartes, extensively argued with skeptics). Therefore, it is especially in *Leviathan* that one can see the impact of these trends and also his reactions to them, even though some skeptical topics were already present, to a lesser extent, in some of its previous works. The reason why this skeptical background has been scarcely considered or even overlooked by the interpreters depends on the main focus being put on ancient pure Pyrrhonism whose political side is very scant and goes no further than the topic of the relativity of ethnic and normative constitutions.[11]

A very different outlook could be obtained if one considers not the ancient but the modern skeptics.[12] Moving from the controversial plane of contrasting phenomena to the more positive study of actual human conduct, modern skeptics did not confine themselves to develop Sextus Empiricus's tenth trope, by collecting the disparities between peoples, temperaments, traditions, and societies, but finally they came to identify some constants of human behaviour. They came up with especially two: on the one hand, the irresistible tendency to self-preservation, and on the other hand an equally strong tendency to glory and vainglory. They were especially interested in finding out the real motives of human action behind the alleged normative paradigms offered by the morals and the politics of the dogmatists. From this point of view the modern skeptical approach to the substantive doctrines of good is significantly different from the ancient one. Whereas the ancient Pyrrhonists tried to show that there were irremediable conflicts about norms, that any dogmatic theory is not only unsustainable but also unnecessary and even harmful for the achievement of happiness,[13] the modern Pyrrhonists focused not only on the uncertainty of any ethics, but also on the contrast between the duties preached by morals and politics on the one hand and on the other the actual springs and modalities of real human behaviour.

There is in the modern skeptics a realistic vein in the description of human behaviour that goes much beyond the famous description of the fourfold rule of common life that is set forth in Sextus Empiricus. Furthermore, the relatively brief remarks about the "normal rules of life" according to natural and cultural appearances (respectively, guidance of nature and constraint of passion on the one hand, tradition of laws and custom, and instruction in the arts, on the other hand)[14] are developed by the modern skeptics into a refined and complex psychological analysis of which we have no comparable example in the ancients.

Moral psychology is perhaps the least developed branch of ancient skepticism. One might wonder whether the realistic anthropology of the authors such as Montaigne, Charron, La Mothe Le Vayer, and others depends on or is consistent with their general skeptical approach, especially with certain aspects of their skeptical epistemology. This question would open the way to quite different considerations that would be mainly related to the existence of a normative or essentialist definition of what skepticism in morals and politics should be: a very interesting and controversial issue that much exceeds the boundaries of this chapter and would require a separate treatment. We stick here to a rather empirical and historical definition, assuming that the modern skeptics are represented by the authors who considered themselves to be so, and that their themes are, as they actually are, tightly intertwined, so that the issue of consistency between the various realms of their speculation is superseded, for our aims here, by the recognition of their coexistence into a general mood that can be rightly considered to be wholly skeptical.[15]

2. Self-preservation and Pride: The Skeptical Background

Regarding the many points that highlight the skeptical influence (in this broad and modern meaning) on Hobbes we can distinguish between a *pars destruens* [destructive part] and a *pars construens* [constructive part]. The former is better known and can easily be summarized by some major points. Certainly some outstanding features of Hobbes's moral theory derive from these skeptical debates: criticism of the ancient doctrines of the highest good ("*agathon aplos,*" or "simply good"), the inability to determine a hierarchy of moral values in terms of sheer ethical discussion, the endless disagreements that divide not only schools but also individuals, because everyone thinks that what he likes is good.[16] All these topics are already clear in the text of *Elements of Law* yet they are at the same time commonplaces that were largely brought up by the seventeenth-century skeptical crisis when doubt was applied to every kind of dogmatic knowledge, including ethics and politics. Montaigne had already denounced "such a bitter and violent struggle among philosophers concerning the highest good," remembering Varro's calculation according to which at least 288 conflicting sects had arisen on that particular topic[17]. Once in France, Hobbes hardened in this opinion, as already expressed in the *Elements,* by reading Montaigne as well as the pages of the libertine skeptic La Mothe Le Vayer, with whom he had friendly relations. In his dialogue *De l'ignorance louable* La Mothe described in even greater detail the variety of philosophical doctrines about the "souverain bien."[18]

The *pars construens* is quite famous as far as it concerns Hobbes: his approach to the human tendencies to self-preservation and to glory (and most of all vainglory) is well known and can be found in every treatment of Hobbesian philosophy. By contrast, the points that Hobbes picked up from reading the French skeptics are much less known and therefore worth commenting upon.

Regarding the first human trend, self-preservation, Montaigne had already indicated a close correlation between "Fruition de la vie" and "crainte de la perdre."[19] In John Florio's translation, which became a classic in sixteenth- and seventeenth-century England, the full quotation sounds like similar expressions used by Hobbes: "we embrace and claspe this good [life] so much the harder, and with more affection, as we perceive it to be less sure, and feare it should be taken from us."[20] For Florio as for Hobbes, this is an impulse that affects all living beings and comes directly from nature: "Nature hath imprinted in beasts the care of Themselves and of Their Preservation."[21] One could object that this very topic was so widespread in classical and early modern culture that Hobbes did not necessarily find it in the skeptical texts. This is correct. What is typical and exclusive, however, of both the skeptical trends and Hobbes's thought is the connection of this basic impulse to the more complex topics of glory and vainglory. As is well known, Leo Strauss had the great merit of pointing out the relevance of this connection, even though he completely neglected the French context in which Hobbes was embedded during his decade on the Continent and from which he drew this specific relation.

Strauss indicated at the basis of Hobbes's political philosophy a sharp antithesis: on the one hand vanity, meant as the root of natural appetite, a kind of vanity basically unfair, and on the other hand, the fear of violent death, meant as the passion that leads us to think and to reckon, so a fundamentally important passion.[22] At the same time, Strauss claimed the moral character, not a mechanistic one, of the distinction between the right of self-esteem and its deviation in pride and in vainglory; furthermore, he showed that a progressive decline of aristocratic ethics focusing on the concept and practice of honour took place in the passage from *Elements* to *Leviathan.* Strauss's references to Hobbes's sources basically went in two directions: for the *Elements,* the theory of the passions contained in Aristotle's *Rhetoric* (albeit an Aristotle with some vague qualification: "seen from a humanistic point of view").[23] On the other hand, especially for *Leviathan,* he looked at Descartes's *Passions de l'âme.* We shall soon see that these two references are insufficient to understand the bulk of Hobbes's position, and that it should be sought among the seventeenth-century French skeptics.

First of all: on the theme of vanity, the famous Aristotle-Hobbes synopsis drawn by Strauss, which puts side by side Aristotle's *Rhetoric,* and Hobbes's *Elements, Leviathan,* and *De homine,* leaves a blank space because Strauss is unable to find in Aristotle something that could be compared to the Hobbesian treatment of this passion.[24] Strauss also seems to forget that criticism of the aristocratic ethic (emblematically represented for him by *Il Cortegiano,* the book of Baldassare Castiglione)[25] was one of the basic aspects of the skeptical crisis that developed into a more general dismantling of any kind of pride; hence skepticism went so far as to become the fiercest opponent of any sort of human vanity, including anthropocentric prejudices. Leaving aside the sociological issue of chivalrous ethics, which was replaced at that time by the new figure of the *bourgeois-gentilhomme* (a theme well explored by George Huppert),[26] we shall concentrate here on the relationship between anthropocentrism and vanity, and then on the connection of skepticism with criticism of vainglory. As a matter of fact, it is among the French skeptics that passions such as "présomption " (Montaigne), "vanité" (Charron), and "philautia [love of oneself]" (La Mothe Le Vayer) were described as deeply affecting the human condition. For Montaigne, presumption is "notre maladie naturelle et originelle,"[27] for Charron vanity is "la plus propre essentielle qualité et de l'humaine nature."[28] La Mothe Le Vayer's "philautia"[29] is not the simple and right attachment to oneself, but means a systematic distortion of one's judgments in favour of a supposed sense of superiority, which was widely exemplified by the "dogmatists" of his time. Therefore, in order to read authors denouncing vainglory, one does not need to wait for the moralists of the second half of the seventeenth century like Pascal, Nicole, and Bayle, who actually were influenced by Hobbes through Sorbière (this latter introduced into his French translation of

De cive the very phrase "amour propre," so widely used by the French moralists). Furthermore, these moralists were highly conditioned by the Augustinian heritage that prompted them to reframe passions such as vanity and glory into the opposition between self-love and love of God, up to the point that in order to save the former from the blame falling on the selfish passion, Malebranche had to distinguish between positive "self-love" from negative "*amour propre.*" On the contrary, the previous generations of Montaigne, Charron, and Le Vayer were not so haunted by the idea of sin accompanying almost any kind of self-love; as a matter of fact, they stuck to a more neutral approach when describing human passions and left aside depreciative evaluations. This phenomenological approach is very akin to the one adopted by Hobbes. As for Hobbes passions are natural ("the desire and other passions of man are in themselves no sin"),[30] so for the French moralists of the early seventeenth century passions may be "diseases" to treat, even serious inconveniences for the social life, but they are not necessarily "sins" to expiate. Rather than being a vice or a guilt, presumption or vainglory is primarily an obstacle that prevents men from perceiving proper relationships with others: so it has a social – or better an antisocial – connotation, much more than any other moral or religious evaluation.

Let us go back to the grandfather of French skepticism, Montaigne. For him it is so important to correct the fault of presumption that he developed a strong idea of equality among men, and even among all living beings, up to the point of basing this idea on true metaphysical foundations. For him, criticizing presumption primarily means to dismantle anthropocentrism. His famous tirade in the *Apologie* declares that all men and animals as well share a kind of "equality" and commonality within the natural order of the world, where neither dominant positions nor particular privileges are allowed to anyone. It is in this connection that Montaigne considers the social impact of presumption: being a self-deceiving attitude, presumption is much more a matter of imagination than of reality. Presumption is a true narcissistic construction that feeds on "opinion," "fantasies," and "imagination," altering the perception of what is "real" and what is "false." Therefore, vanity is a typically human passion, since animals lack it; however, this peculiar and specific endowment does not represent an advantage for humankind. Regarding this kind of presumption, Montaigne writes ironically that: "c'est un avantage qui luy [à l'homme] est bien cher vendu et duquel il a bien peu à se glorifier, car de là naist la source principale des maux qui le pressent: peché, maladie, irresolution, trouble, desespoir."[31]

The condemnation of anthropocentricism is not only a metaphysical topic regarding the ranking of humanity in the ladder of nature; it becomes for Montaigne also an occasion to attack the much harsher domination that some men exercise over other men. The presumption of inequality that some people assume over other men is even worse and harder than that over the animals. The result is that "men who serve do so at a lower price and for a less interesting and less favourable treatment than the one given to birds, horses, and dogs."[32]

It is also notable that, although the *Essais* do not establish a direct connection between vanity and presumption, on the one hand, and aggression and oppression on the other, as Hobbes does in his *Elements,* the consequences of this focus on the passions of vanity and presumption are nearly the same in both authors. Weighing the damages brought about by this sort of vainglory, both Montaigne and Hobbes reach the same conclusion: the compelling need for a strong and unquestionable authority in order to stop the attacks of the vainglorious against the moderate. This is directly expressed by Hobbes in political terms, whereas Montaigne has a more general discourse, including political regulations in a wider web of constraints; he recommends turning off the presumption indeed "by giving the human spirit the most rigid barriers that we can," which explicitly means both laws and religions, either with mortal or immortal rewards and punishments.[33]

Furthermore, when reading these famous pages of the *Apologie de Raimond Sebond,* one has to bear in mind that in the ancient sources as well as in the early modern thinkers the comparison between men and animals always had a clear political significance, as seen in Aristotle's famous discussion of the behaviour of *animalia politica.* It is not by chance that these peculiar topics, that of political animals and that other, more general, comparison of animals to man, are both taken up again by Montaigne and Hobbes, albeit with different intentions: the former mostly to compare the advantages and disadvantages of human and animal societies, the other rather to emphasize the necessary artificiality of men's politics.[34]

In Charron, a close disciple of Montaigne, the social and political background of passions such as "vanity" and "presumption" turns out to be even more evident. In the economy of the whole treatise *De la sagesse* these kinds of affections are not included in the detailed list of the passions (such as love, ambition, avarice, hate, envy, anger, fear, sadness, compassion, cruelty, etc.) that represent in turn part of the "first consideration of man, that is natural because of all its integral parts."[35] "Vanity," "weakness," "inconstancy," "meanness," "presumption" are isolated in a special section that is supposed to provide the reader with a "general depiction of man," and vanity is so prominent that it is emphatically placed right at the beginning, whereas presumption concludes the whole picture.[36] Vanity, which is "the most essential and typical quality of human nature," reveals itself in comparisons to others: it makes us "live only in relation to others."[37] Furthermore, vanity joins with presumption, and they widely overlap. Their definitions are formally different but very close as to content: "s'estimer trop et n'estimer pas assez autruy" can be rightly said of both of them.[38]

3. Vanity and Equality: Hobbes and Montaigne

To sum up the main results of our analysis thus far, we realize that both the diagnosis and the treatment of human presumption have many aspects in common in both the French skeptical texts and Hobbes. Vainglory, or vanity, or presumption is among the worst and the most typical affections of humans; what is more, vanity and equality oppose each other up to the point that every attempt to restore the truth of the human condition passes through recognition of equality and unmasking of presumption. One might object that these maxims spring from common knowledge of human psychology, according to the Socratic precept that both Charron and Hobbes place straight at the start of their masterworks: "Nosce te ipsum, Read thy self" (Hobbes);[39] "s'estudier et apprendre à se connoistre" [study yourself and learn to know it] (Charron).[40] It might be common wisdom too, but one still has to explain why this illustrious recommendation to self-knowledge does not play any role in the traditions emphasized by Strauss as relevant for Hobbes (Aristotelian and Cartesian ethics), whereas it is peculiar of the early modern skeptical psychology. In addition, the passion of vanity and its unmasking are so crucial both for Hobbes and the skeptics, although they are lacking (Aristotle) or marginal (Descartes) in the ancient and modern mainstreams.

One should not underestimate vanity also in the field of politics. Only when people give up vainglory that makes them assume too much of their power, citizens become able to recognize each other as equal; only then are they amenable to making a contract. So vainglory is the first and main obstacle to agreeing upon social covenant. All this is nicely summarized in a couple of paragraphs in the *Elements:* "Men by nature equal. By vain glory indisposed to allow Themselves to equality with others."[41]

What impulse might Hobbes have drawn from reading French skeptical texts? And what kind of response could they have provoked, since for a great author such as the English philosopher the category of influence should be replaced by that of resilience, which includes both reception and reaction? In order to answer these questions, a closer examination of the concept of equality, both in Hobbes and in the French skeptical *milieu*, is needed.

Hobbes's theory about equality is extremely realistic; for him, equality basically consists in the like and mutual vulnerability to aggression by others and consequently to the danger of violent death.[42] Only afterwards and in the second place equality can also be considered a structural property of the right that nature has given to all. Very seldom are the French skeptics so harsh. For example, the brief definition of La Boétie, the great friend beloved by Montaigne, is halfway between realism and idealism, because it is founded not only on equality of strength but also on a sense of universal fraternity: "La nature nous a tous faits de même force, et, comme il semble, à la même moule, à fin de nous entreconnaître tous pour compagnons et ou plutôt pour frères" [Nature has given us the same strength, and it seems, in the same mould, in order that we recognize that we are all companions and even more, brothers].[43] Montaigne's own definition is already more deflationary, dropping brotherhood and focusing mainly on equality of means available to all men. Thus in John Florio's translation: "For men to be all of one kind, and except the most or least, they are furnished with like meanes to judge and instruments to conceive."[44]

In other passages of the *Essais* the representation of equality is even more concrete, relating to one of the examples most cherished by Hobbes himself: the example of the American tribes. Looking at Brazilians in the essay *Des cannibals,* Montaigne describes these so-called barbarians, noticing that among them natural law was still in force ("les naturelles loix leur commandent encore"); they enjoyed perfect peace and freedom; neither covenants nor authorities were set up in their small societies ("nul nom de magistrat, ny de superiorité politique; nul usage de service, de richesse ou de pauvreté; nuls contrats" [no name of magistrate, nor of political superiority, no services for others, no wealth or poverty, no contracts]).[45] Among the Brazilians, "the laws that nature gave us" are still in force. Many features of the state of nature as described by Hobbes in the *Elements, De cive,* and *Leviathan* are very similar, as is well known.

Even the structure of their arguments is comparable. Both Hobbes and Montaigne start from man's natural equality as opposed to vainglory (Hobbes) and presumption (Montaigne). Both focus on the rights that all men share by nature and that should prevent them from falling into any inequality, either of wealth or power. There is however a notable contrast. While Hobbes stresses how much we have won (peace) by abandoning the equality and the complete freedom of the state of nature, Montaigne underlines by contrast what we have lost when entering society. It is a loss for which – so says a true skeptic, disciple of Montaigne, and contemporary of Hobbes – there is no compensation: "Une chose ne peut-on nier, que ce ne soient elles [ces belles Polices] qui en mille façons ont jetté les fers aux pieds à cette belle liberté naturelle, dont la perte ne peut recevoir de compensation" [One thing cannot be denied, that it was them (these good laws) that have tied chains around the feet of that beautiful natural liberty, the loss of which cannot be compensated].[46] Even if they know very well the primitive condition of the Brazilians, Montaigne and his followers still consider that the state of nature, as well as the Brazilians' simple life, are better than "the Golden Age,"[47] whereas the same condition is described by Hobbes as "solitary, poore, nasty, brutish, and short."[48] There is also another big difference: it seems that aggression and the danger of violent death haunt Hobbes much more than Montaigne or the modern skeptics. It is noteworthy that according to the latter, man's vulnerability in the natural state would come more often from fighting with animals than from clashing with other men, in contrast to Hobbes's analysis of the natural condition.

Having reached this point, we can summarize the complex intertwining of Hobbes's thought and his nearly certain readings in skepticism. Skeptical authors had fully understood the web of relationships and oppositions that took place in the natural state between freedom and equality, on the one side, and vainglory and presumption, on the other side. From a moral point of view, skeptical analyses were very close to Hobbes's. On the contrary, skeptics were not much shocked by the potential or current aggressiveness that features in the state of nature, and all the more so since they often considered politics as more or less concealed violence. All these convergences and divergences, however, are already easily recognizable in the text of *Elements of Law*, written in England before Hobbes fled to France. It is true that Montaigne and Charron had been translated into English and published several times in England (Charron's *Of Wisdom* had many editions in London: 1612, 1630, 1651, etc.). This means that Hobbes did not need to wait until his arrival in France in 1641 for an acquaintance with the Continental skeptical tradition, and we should also take into account his many trips to the Continent as a chaperon of the Newcastles. For example, during his stay in Venice, Hobbes got in close touch with Fulgenzio Micanzio, secretary of Paolo Sarpi, and we know by the *Pensieri* of this latter that the great Venetian was fond of skeptical books such as the *Essais* and *De la sagesse*.[49] Since the beginning of this chapter, however, we have anticipated that the full immersion in the Parisian *milieu* imparted a new impulse to Hobbes's skeptical connections and that one can see clear signs of this wider acquaintance with the authors and the topics of French Pyrrhonism by reading the work entirely conceived and written in France, *Leviathan*. In order to demonstrate this hypothesis we must focus on the novelties that mark *Leviathan* in comparison to the previous works (especially *Elements*) and show that they can likely be explained by Hobbes's reactions to the French skeptical ambiance.

4. *Leviathan*, the New Handbook of Politics and Early Modern Skepticism

The first hint regards the structure itself of *Leviathan*, which connects psychology and politics, thus giving a completely new table of contents to the typical early modern handbook of government. This point has already been suggested by Anna Maria Battista,[50] yet – as we shall soon see – it needs further clarification and some corrections, especially with regard to the connection between psychology and epistemology of politics, both in Hobbes and the skeptical authors of seventeenth-century France. In reality, Anna Maria Battista overlooked the conventional aspect that is prominent in Hobbes's epistemology, and that represents his own response to the general crisis of knowledge featuring in the skeptical trends of that time.

In short: the new book of politics as it developed out of Hobbes's previous works (especially *Elements* and *De cive)* is neither a manual recommending skills of action in the tradition of Machiavelli's *Prince* or Lipsius's *Politicorum libri*, nor a treatise about the virtues of the ruler, as in the mainstream of medieval and Renaissance "mirrors of the prince." The proper knowledge that the new handbook wants to provide the reader with is science ("civil science"), neither "prudence" nor morals, which means that its foundations are neither normative ethics nor strategy of government, but basically knowledge of man that is afforded by psychology. This new structure is already evident in the *Elements*, where political matters, which start in chapter XIV (the natural condition of men and natural right), are preceded and prepared for by a wide range of chapters that – with the only exception of chapter XI, dedicated to knowledge of God and spirit – deal with matters of psychology (human faculties, sense, imagination, reason, pleasures, passions, difference of wit, deliberation and will, language, etc.).[51]

This psychological agenda is addressed again in *Leviathan*, yet in this latter work it is largely renewed and built with new materials, most probably in order to cope with new data, new requirements, new issues that were especially at the heart of French Pyrrhonism. Even though there is no explicit allusion by Hobbes to these skeptical texts, it is highly unlikely that he did not have them in mind when dealing with topics largely debated in his Parisian context. There are four main areas where *Leviathan* makes substantial innovations in comparison to *Elements* and that reveal at the same time probable influences coming from the skeptical *milieu*. (There are of course other major innovations in *Leviathan* that cannot be related to the skeptical context, such as the theory of authority, or many of the theological matters in the second half.)[52] Since these cross-references typically and exclusively point to skeptical influences, one can hardly believe that, fully embedded in the French context, Hobbes did not get these innovations from there, either as an influence or as a response. We must add that in Hobbes's case any influence always implies a double process of reception and reaction, as we have already said. These four areas are 1) sharp naturalization of man, so as to establish a bridge between animal and human psychology; 2) strong emphasis on the method of introspection and its consequences for the architecture of the system; 3) widening of the causal explication of the passions. The fourth area is a matter rather of reaction than of influence: 4) the bifurcation of passions and language, hence the artificiality of the "science of just and unjust."

1) The first area is in the very middle of Hobbes's psychological and anthropological project as it evolved since his first book. *Leviathan* begins with a book "Of Man" that is the necessary prologue to the properly political book "Of Commonwealth." The "man" Hobbes speaks about is a part of nature, as in Montaigne's or Charron's writings, and in *Leviathan* man's naturalization is pushed to an extent that has no equal in Hobbes's earlier works. There are also obvious continuities: in actual matter, Hobbes sticks to the mechanistic explanation of the main psychological operations (sensation, imagination, memory, and thought) that are already present in *Elements;* in *Leviathan*, however, he develops a new kind of comparative approach, constantly putting side by side human and animal psychology. This way of dealing with human faculties in connection with the animal ones is new in Hobbes's

philosophical career, but it was very common in the works of Montaigne, Charron, and later French skeptics such as La Mothe Le Vayer. Probably relying on their description, Hobbes for the first time states explicitly in *Leviathan* that man's psychological faculties are not basically different from those of animals, even though the former bring about more important results than the latter. It seems clear in *Leviathan* that men are not distinguished from animals because of a different metaphysical stock, which is excluded by the thesis of the integral materiality of the soul and by reduction of all psychological operations to the effects of matter and movement. The real divide between men and animals consists in two features that seem to be functional rather than natural: the first is curiosity, which is still a "passion," yet a specific one that is proper only to man, and the second turns out to be the use of an artificial and conventional technique such as language. Reason itself is for Hobbes no longer the hallmark of a spiritual and immortal soul; it is instead the combined effect of curiosity and industry driving men to seek not only the causes, but also and foremost the possible effects of the causes, whereas animals are confined more sluggishly to seek just the causes of the effects they are immediately interested in. Even the practical and moral side of human condition is strongly naturalized by Hobbes during his French period. After describing the process of deliberation as a complex web of desires, expectations, and forecasts, Hobbes denies that men are provided with something like the Aristotelian *dianoetike orexis* (rational appetite). Therefore, he argues provocatively the thesis that animals also "deliberate" and do it nearly the same way as men. While not ignoring the negative effects coming from the passions in social life, Hobbes sticks to the thesis of the full naturalness of emotional life. Thence, the great divide between men and animals is not to be found in some metaphysical and mysterious substance, the supposed immaterial soul, but in the different functioning of the same basic psychological operations, which in the case of men are driven by a specific curiosity and developed by linguistic techniques, whereas animals meet the immediate appeal of the desired effects. In man, reason is much more a matter of psychological construction, where curiosity, industry, and words are the main factors, than a matter of natural, let alone metaphysical, endowment.[53] Even though the expression is not present yet, a kind of "natural history" of reason is already implicit in *Leviathan*, and this reconstruction is based on a close comparison to the animals, unlike the previous works. It is clear that a strong impulse towards this naturalization, through the comparison between man and animal, derived from the skeptical Continental authors, even though Hobbes came to an original position that represents a step beyond the skeptical crisis: as we pointed out elsewhere, a new kind of scientific humanism was developed in this dialogue with skeptical humanism, without being reducible to it.[54]

Besides drawing ideas for the naturalization of man, *Leviathan* took over two other typical aspects of the skeptical tradition, at first on the side of method.

2) Much more than in the previous works, Hobbes sets out in *Leviathan* the value for the political science of empirical observation and introspection. This is very akin to the phenomenological approach of Pyrrhonism; yet, what is new and typically modern (referring to Montaigne and Charron) turns out to be an in-depth analysis of the psychological contents of common experience. Especially referring to the study of the passions and the human mind, Hobbes makes this point in the introduction to the book: "this kind of doctrine admitteth no other demonstration."[55] This simple admission breaks with the ideal deductive order that should drive from the simpler to the more complex, from the general to the particular, that is, from the body to the man up to the citizen, according to the original chain of systematic order Hobbes had conceived for developing his own philosophy. The outburst of political matters that chronologically invert the systematic order (*De cive* and *Leviathan* were published before *De corpore* and *De homine*) is not only the result of Hobbes's strong concern about the troubled English situation; it is also the effect of an epistemological crisis concerning the scientific pattern proceeding by definitions and deductions, which obliges him to have recourse to empirical observation in order to provide the data that cannot be drawn by analysis from the basic definitions. This new opening to the practice of observation and introspection is clearly indebted, from the standpoint both of method and contents, to the wide psychological explorations made by the French skeptics.

Leviathan restarts exactly from the point where moral skepticism had led Hobbes to declare in *Elements* the crisis of the *summum bonum* and to accept individual subjective preferences as the criterion of the good (a weak "criterion," in the same way that Sextus spoke about a "criterion of skepticism," very different from the dogmatic one):[56] good is always *bonum sibi*. However, in *Leviathan* Hobbes goes a step further since he suggests distinguishing between the objects of the passions, which are always mutable and different from one person to another, and the passions in themselves, which are on the contrary quite uniform and constant enough to support certain knowledge, even though not "demonstrative" knowledge. Human passions can be studied and even be defined, as in Hobbes's *Leviathan,* independently from the shifting nature of their objects. Thus, both the "civil scientist" and the sovereign can study "the similitude of *passions,* which are the same in all men," without any need of assuming what is impossible to ascertain, "the similitude of the objects of the passions," given the definition of the good as *bonum sibi,* which implies a radical individualization of the objects of the appetites.[57]

We have already stressed the Socratic origin and the modern skeptical reintroduction of introspection. The existence of common passions can be found by introspection, according to the famous motto "Nosce te ipsum, Read thy self," which is recommended by Hobbes in the introduction to *Leviathan.* What is interesting now is that Hobbes, by taking over the famous motto, shifts it from the field of morals to the political one; the message is not addressed as before to the philosopher or straight to the individual man, but directly to the sovereign. Moreover, the recommendation takes on a cognitive value, because the sovereign is warned to "read in himself not this or that particular man, but mankind"; only in this way will he be able to decipher "the characters of man's heart," going beyond the lies and dissimulation that conceal the truth.[58] Once again, Hobbes's position can be understood as a move replying to similar moves made by the representatives of modern skepticism. When mentioning the Socratic motto, Hobbes most probably had to recollect the general program developed by Montaigne in the *Essais,* when the French author declared to seek in himself, in his own individuality accurately described, not the mere accidents of a single man but the universality of the human form.[59] The main difference consists in the fact that, thanks to his own "civil science," Hobbes is able to give introspection a stronger epistemological status as well as a political impact, which is completely lacking in Montaigne's approach, mainly focused on general knowledge of humanity.

Most probably, the missing link between the purely skeptical category of introspection as developed by Montaigne and the political use of the same by Hobbes must be found in Charron's *Sagesse.* There, a new kind of philosophical anthropology is outlined with some similarity in structure and method to *Leviathan's* section, "Of Man." In *De la sagesse* political topics are already preceded and founded by a descriptive anthropology that is based on self-knowledge ("De la connoissance de soy et de l'humaine condition" [Of knowledge of oneself and of the human condition])[60] and where (as we have already seen) the catalogue and description of passions occupies a conspicuous part. From this point of view, Hobbes's insight of grounding politics on psychology was not totally new, being anticipated by skeptical thought, especially in the more systematic form it had taken in Charron. Yet, once again, alongside this structural analogy, there are also notable differences that cannot be overlooked. The most striking one can be described as follows. Charron establishes a direct connection between the study of the passions and theory of the virtues, including moral and political virtues (justice, prudence, strength, temperance). In the architecture of *De la sagesse* book I (on anthropology, psychology, theory of passions, etc.) lie the foundations on which book II is built, containing the general rules of wisdom, some of which already regard political issues.[61] From these general grounds derive "the specific counsels of wisdom," in the fourfold partition of the virtues. Therefore *De la sagesse* claims to be but a straight line going from psychology to politics, despite all the originality belonging to the Charronian theory of wisdom. Hobbes, as we are going to see a little later, introduces between psychology and politics the dimension of rights, obligations, and contract, which involve a break in Charron's more straightforward scheme. Yet, before seeing this relevant shift, let me underline another major change in *Leviathan* that depended, in my opinion, on Hobbes's exposure to the skeptical topics.

3) The transition from the *Elements* to *Leviathan* is also marked by the recognition of a wider variety of causes and forms in the genesis of passions. Previously, in the *Elements*, Hobbes had reduced the variety of appetites to the prevalence of a single object of desire: power. Therefore, the whole treatment of passions had been preceded by a discussion of power and honour, since – writes Hobbes in *Elements* – all passions "consist in conception of the future, that is to say, in conception to power past, and the act to come"; as a "conception of future," every desire is above all "conception of power able to produce something."[62] A monocausal explanation of passions is outlined that focuses on *power*, despite the recognition of the variety of "goods." In the next work, *De cive*, Hobbes's psychology of the conflict gets more complex: men fight not only for power, or goods they cannot share, or for rights they cannot renounce, but especially because of "certamen

ingeniorum" [the combate of Wits], the result of which is mainly the feeling of self-complacency ("possit magnifice sentire de sé ipso").[63] As in the previous analysis of Montaigne and Charron, men's vanity becomes here a sort of self-contained passion rather than an intellectual mistake in assessing the comparison of the respective powers. Furthermore, Hobbes highlights the force of "libido laedendi": much more a potential psychological drift than an actual will to aggression. Not surprisingly, this "libido" is more easily satisfied in a pose of contempt of others than in a real fight against them.[64]

In *Leviathan* this change from the primacy of power to self-consideration gets more and more evident, and impinges on the structure of the work. Now the chapter on power (chapter X) comes long after the one on the passions (chapter VI) and, what is more, has little relevance to their explanation; in *Leviathan* there is one only passage saying that the idea of power produces a passion, specifically, the passion of glorying. Two general features affect the world of passions in *Leviathan*: passions become less competitive and their variety multiplies. Even the nature of happiness turns out to be less agonistic, consisting in the more neutral success of any undertaking, whereas in the previous works it consisted in surpassing competitors.

Also behind these many changes, one might easily recognize the influence of the skeptical authors who had studied in depth the world of human passions. The shift from the hierarchical and monocausal theory of the *Elements*, focused on the primacy of power, to the more descriptive one of *Leviathan* has many parallels in the empirical and phenomenological approach adopted by Montaigne and Charron.

5. Hobbes's Response to the Challenge of Political Skepticism

Besides the first three areas of cross-reference that outline major influences from the skeptics on Hobbes, the fourth area rather features Hobbes's reaction to political skepticism. This is the "dogmatic" side of Hobbesian philosophy, the peculiar response of "civil science" to the doubts of its contemporaries.

4) Consistently with their conceptions, the skeptics assumed that, being based on psychology, politics could not go beyond the level of "prudence,"[65] while for Hobbes politics must be a science. This assumption

opens the crucial epistemological issue. How can this step towards science be justified if the study "Of Man" does not go further than the study of "the similitude of passions," as Hobbes himself, along with Montaigne's disciples, admits?

If one has a look at the chart (see p. 74) that accompanies chapter IX ("On the Classification of the Sciences")[66] of *Leviathan*, a major change can be seen, regarding the place and foremost the "generation" of politics, in comparison to the skeptical authors we have analysed. For these latter, and for Charron first of all, the transition from psychology to politics is consistent and could be portrayed by a kind of straight line: there is a sort of linear progression from the former to the latter, politics simply being the deployment of human psychology with its faculties, appetites, and passions.

This immediateness is still featured in the chart that accompanies the *Elements of Law*.[67] This chart is bipartite, according to the partition of the text itself. The second part ("Concerning men as a body politic") parallels the first one ("Concerning men as persons natural"): there is no mirroring of one to another, but it is implicit that the political person is a consequence or a qualification of the natural person. The transition from "Man" to "Commonwealth" is more complex in *Leviathan* and requires a peculiar path that is different from the one starting from the passions, that is, from the basic psychology of man. Given the broad definition of science as "knowledge of the Consequence of one Affirmation to another" (science always is "Conditionall" and not "Absolute"), in the chart the "Consequences from the *passions* of men" pave the way to "Ethics," yet not to the "Science of Just and Unjust." After all, Hobbes admits that moral duties could be drawn from knowledge of human psychology, and foremost from the human passions; however, he does not think, at least in *Leviathan*, that any "science," especially any "science of just and unjust," can be derived from there.

There is a sharp bifurcation before this "science" comes up, and the watershed runs between passions and language. As a matter of fact, the science of right depends on "consequences from *speech*," i.e., on the use of language "in *contracting*," and not from the consequences "from the passions of men." It is still true that passions and ethics belong to the "qualities of *men in particular*" and that without any knowledge of them any human construction, including covenant and commonwealth, would be condemned to arbitrariness or meaning-

SCIENCE, that is, Knowledge of Consequences; which is called also PHILOSOPHY.
Consequences from the Accidents of Bodies Naturall; which is called NATURALL PHILOSOPHY.
Consequences from the Accidents common to all Bodies Naturall; which are Quantity, and Motion.
Consequences from Quantity, and Motion indeterminate; which being the Principles, or first foundation of Philosophy, is called Philosophia Prima.
PHILOSOPHIA PRIMA.
Consequences from Motion, and, Quantity determined.
Consequences from Quantity, and Motion determined
By Figure,.......
By Number......
Mathematiques,
GEOMETRY.
ARITHMETIQUE.
Consequences from the Motion, and Quantity of Bodies in speciall.
Consequences from the Motion, and Quantity of the great parts of the World, as the Earth and Starres,
Cosmography,
ASTRONOMY.
GEOGRAPHY.
Consequences from the Motion of Speciall kinds, and Figures of Body,
Mechaniques, Doctrine of Weight,
Science of ENGINEERS.
ARCHITECTURE.
NAVIGATION.
PHYSIQUES, or Consequences from Qualities.
Consequences from the Qualities of Bodyes Transient, such as sometimes appear, sometimes vanish, ...
METEOROLOGY.
Consequences from the Qualities of Bodies Permanent.
Consequences from the Qualities of the Starres.
Consequences from the Light of the Starres. Out of this, and the Motion of the Sunne, is made the Science of..
SCIOGRAPHY.
Consequences from the Influence of the Starres,..................................
ASTROLOGY.
Consequences of the Qualities from Liquid Bodies that fill the space between the Starres; such as are the Ayre, or substance aetheriall.
Consequences from the Qualities of Bodies Terrestriall.
Consequences from the parts of the Earth, that are without Sense,
Consequences from the Qualities of Minerals, as Stones, Metalls, &c.
Consequences from the Qualities of Vegetables.
Consequences from the Qualities of Animals.
Consequences from the Qualities of Animals in generall
Consequences from Vision,.........
OPTIQUES.
Consequences from Sounds,........
MUSIQUE.
Consequences from the rest of the Senses.
Consequences from the Qualities of Men in Speciall
Consequences from the Passions of Men,..............................
ETHIQUES.
Consequences from Speech,
In Magnifying, Vilifying, &c.
POETRY.
In Perswading,..
RHETHORIQUE.
In Reasoning, ..
LOGIQUE.
In Contracting,..
The Science of JUST and UNJUST.
Consequences from the Accidents of Politique Bodies; which is called POLITIQUES, and CIVILL PHILOSOPHY.
1. Of Consequences from the Institution of COMMON-WEALTHS, to the Rights, and Duties of the Body Politique, or Soveraign.
2. Of Consequences from the same, to the Duty, and Right of the Subjects.

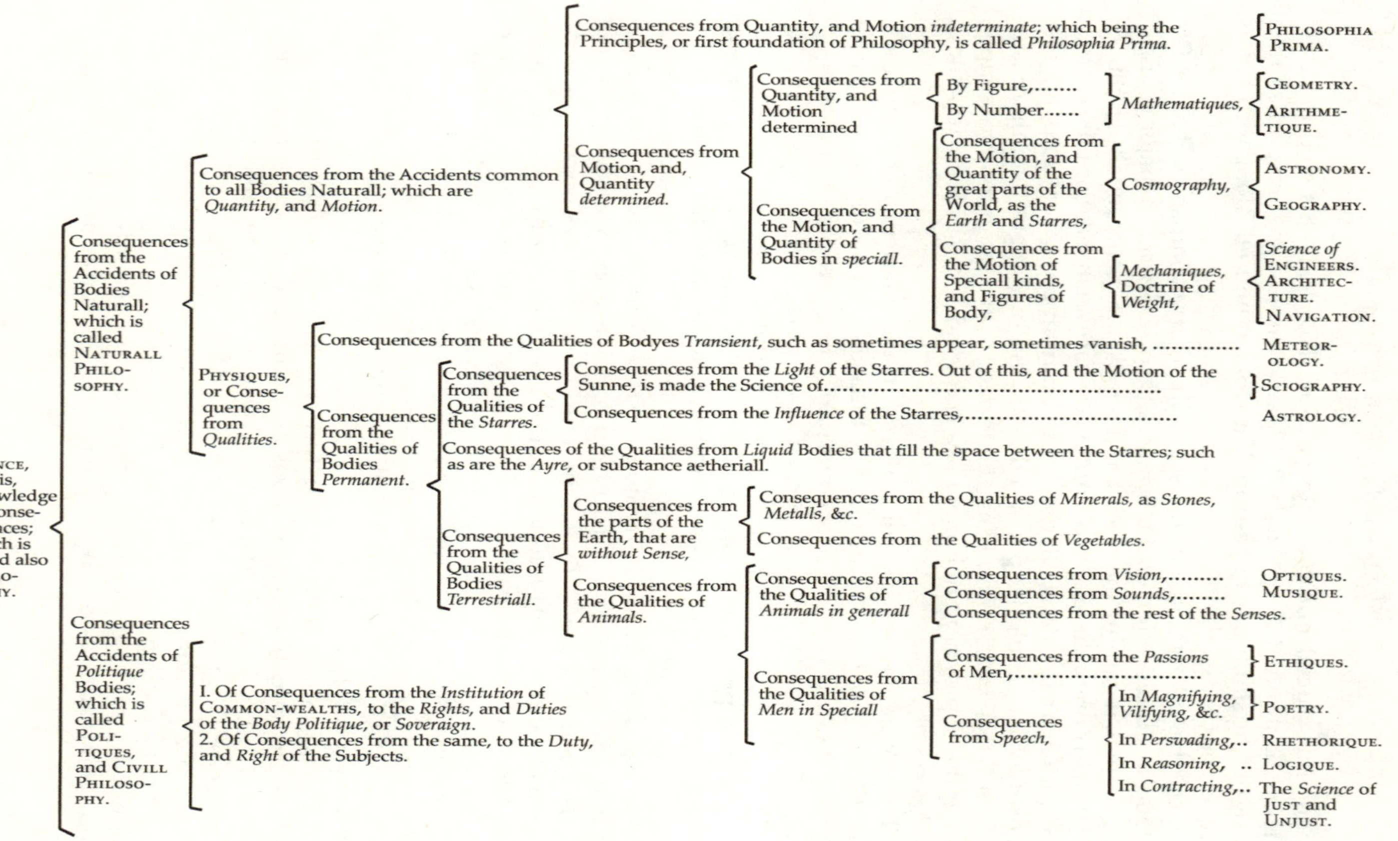

Chart 1

lessness. Literally, the words of the political contract would be devoid of meaning because they would have no reference (in Hobbes's theory of knowledge a concept is a way of conceiving a body, so that there is no meaning without reference). Thus, the study of passions and ethics is absolutely necessary for the foundation of politics; however, it is not sufficient for the development of a "science of just and unjust" as such. Language ("Consequences from Speech") is the requirement for this kind of science. This discourse is valid for the establishing of politics, not for politics once already established: in this latter meaning (as "Politiques and Civil Philosophy") politics depends not so much on language as on the "Consequences of the accidents of the *Politique* bodies," and therefore it is placed in another place of the chart, on the left side, independently from the "science of just and unjust." Hobbes thus sharply distinguishes between the science of creating the bases of the commonwealth through definitions of the just and unjust, on one hand, and on the other hand the science able to draw all the consequences from the accidents of the political bodies already built up.

Going back to the first meaning of the civil science, we can see in the same chart the importance of this very bifurcation between consequences from the passions (psychology and ethics) and consequences from speech (contracts and science of the just). This bifurcation between the two different branches is a result of a major divide separating Hobbes from the French skeptics. Hobbes could not find the notions of right and wrong, conceived as the "Consequences from *speech* in *contracting*," in authors who rejected as unrealistic and impossible the idea of grounding politics on an original contract as a conscious and voluntary stipulation. Montaigne, Charron, and the French skeptics subscribed to the very opposite formula of the "fondements mystiques" [mysterious foundations][68] of any political authority. Of course, that formula was full of irony because by mystical or mysterious foundations they did not mean the "divine" origin of authority; rather they meant that the origin of political power should be "mysterious" and necessarily kept hidden because it is always plunged in violence and cheating. The skeptical authors were so distrustful towards politics that they did not see any possibility of establishing society and power on mutual agreement. Thence the decisive importance they gave to religious and political impostures as well as to *coups d'état* in order to establish the political machinery: a reasoned consensus would have been the last thing they thought necessary for establishing the state. Seventeenth-century skeptical authors lacked the very notion of covenant. By contrast, the whole framework of Hobbes's political philosophy is built on the idea of a mutual agreement between the citizens about the authorization of the sovereign.

Despite this move, which is the main feature of Hobbes's philosophy in comparison to his skeptical interlocutors, Montaigne's and Charron's lesson was not simply crossed out. With this idea of the contract as a "consequence from speech," Hobbes managed to maintain his own idea of science as a "conditional" construction and at the same time to overcome political skepticism without giving up the modern approach to the passions that had developed into making psychology the necessary premise of politics. We are here at the heart of the main epistemological issue of Hobbes's philosophy: how to articulate his strong conventionalism that relies on the power of linguistic stipulations, on the one hand, and on the other the indispensable function of hypotheses that are supposed to be based on experience, wherefrom he draws his generalizations.[69] To simplify a matter much more entangled: without linguistic conventions, politics would stop at the level of "prudence," like the skeptics,[70] and would not reach the level of "science"; yet, without hypotheses coming from experience and definitions relying on its data, "consequences from speech" would be devoid of any real meaning. As we have shown in this study, the intertwining of the two levels was not only the result of the internal development of Hobbes's thought, but – at least in the field of politics – also the effect of his encountering the challenge of skepticism.

NOTES

1 *The Elements of Law Natural and Politic*, ed. Ferdinand Tönnies. Second edition, ed. M.M. Goldsmith (London: 1969; first ed.1889) I, XIII, 3–4, pp. 65–7. Nearly the same topic is taken up again in the dedicatory epistle of *De cive*: *De cive*: *The Latin Version* ... ed. Howard Warrender (Oxford: Clarendon Press, 1983), 74.

2 Letter from Mersenne to Sorbière, 25 April 1646, in *De cive*, ed. Warrender, 86.

3 Quentin Skinner, "Thomas Hobbes: rhetoric and the construction of morality," *Proceedings of the British Academy* 76 (1990), 1-61: on Montaigne, 27–8, 44–9.

4 See Skinner's most assertive statement in "Reason and Rhetoric in the Philosophy of Hobbes," in Quentin Skinner and Yves Charles Zarka, *Hobbes. The Amsterdam Debate*, ed. Hans Blom (Hildesheim: Olms, 2001), 21–2: "I see no evidence that Hobbes was even faintly interested in Pyrrhonism, let alone relativism. He is not I think responding to an epistemological crisis

at all. [...] Nor was he at all interested in the technical claims put forward by self avowed skeptics, whether pyrrhonian or academic. What I try to show is that that points us in the wrong direction. What Hobbes is really preoccupied by is the neo-classical art of rhetoric and its view about what it is to conduct an argument."

5 Cf. Quentin Skinner, *Reason and Rhetoric in the Philosophy of Hobbes* (Cambridge: Cambridge University Press, 1996), 128, 340, which stresses the skeptical background of the oratorical theme of "paradiastole."

6 Skinner, *Reason and Rhetoric*, 428–30, with references to Rohan, Silhon, Béthune, and La Mothe Le Vayer.

7 See the important articles by Richard H. Popkin reprinted in *The Third Force in Seventeenth-Century Thought* (Leiden: Brill, 1992): "Hobbes and Scepticism I," 9–26; "Hobbes and Scepticism II," 27–49, esp. 49.

8 For Hobbes as a "post-skeptical thinker," see Richard Tuck, "Hobbes and Descartes," in *Perspectives on Thomas Hobbes*, ed. G.A.J. Rogers and Alan Ryan (Oxford: Clarendon Press, 1988), 11–41; and Tuck, "Optics and Sceptics: the philosophical foundations of Hobbes's political thought," in *Conscience and Casuistry in Early Modern Philosophy*, ed. Edmund Leites (Cambridge: Cambridge University Press, 1988), 235–63. For the passage quoted, see Tuck, *Philosophy and Government 1572–1651* (Cambridge: Cambridge University Press, 1993), 307. According to Tuck, Hobbes's post-skeptical move consists of replacing a "natural agreement" (mostly in political matters) by an "artificial agreement." Modern commentators and some of Hobbes's contemporaries were puzzled by this "self-destructive character of judgement."

9 For my interpretation of Hobbes's place in relation to the history of early modern skepticism, and for further bibliography on this topic, see Gianni Paganini, "Hobbes among Ancient and Modern Sceptics: Phenomena and Bodies," in *The Return of Scepticism: from Hobbes and Descartes to Bayle*, ed. Paganini (Dordrecht: Kluwer, 2003), 3–35; Paganini, "Hobbes and the Continental Tradition of Skepticism," in *Skepticism in Renaissance and Post-Renaissance Thought. New Interpretations*, ed. Richard H. Popkin and José R. Maia Neto (Amherst, NY: Humanity Books, 2004), 65–105; Paganini, "Hobbes's Critique of the Doctrine of Essences and its Sources," in *Cambridge Critical Companion to Hobbes's Leviathan*, ed. Patricia Springborg (Cambridge: Cambridge University Press, 2007), 337–57.

10 For Hobbes's acquaintances in Paris, see Quentin Skinner, "Hobbes and His Disciples in France and England," *Comparative Studies in Society and History* 8 (1966): 153–67 (reprinted in Skinner, *Visions of Politics*, vol. III, *Hobbes and Civil Science* [Cambridge: Cambridge University Press, 2002], 308–23);

Noel Malcolm, *Aspects of Thomas Hobbes* (Oxford: Clarendon Press, 2002), esp. 459–69. On Hobbes's relations with Gassendi, see Paganini, "Hobbes, Gassendi e la psicologia del meccanicismo," in *Hobbes oggi*, ed. Guido Canziani and Andrea Napoli (Milan: Franco Angeli Editore, 1990), 351–446; Paganini, "Le néant et le vide. Les parcours croisés de Gassendi et Hobbes," in *Gassendi et la modernité*, ed. Sylvia Taussig (Turnhout: Brepols, 2008), 177–214; Paganini, "Hobbes, Gassendi und die Hypothese der Weltvenichtung," in *Konstellationsforschung*, ed. Martin Mulsow and Marcelo Stamm (Frankfurt: Suhrkamp, 2005), 258–339. On the connenctions with the libertine circles in Paris, cf. Paganini, "Hobbes et les libertins," in *Philosophes, libertins et free-thinkers*, ed. Lorenzo Bianchi, Nicole Gengoux, Gianni Paganini (Paris: Honoré Champion, forthcoming).

11 For more details see the chapter by Emidio Spinelli in this volume, which shows that the skeptical notions of *biotike teresis* (observance of everyday life) and *koinos bios* (common life) lie in the background of any skeptical political considerations, even though they are not immediately political in themselves. For further bibliography on the political side of skepticism and the accusations of *apraxia* addressed to it, see Spinelli, the same chapter.

12 More generally, on the features of modern skepticism, see: Gianni Paganini, *Skepsis. Le débat des modernes sur le scepticisme. Montaigne-Le Vayer–Campanella–Hobbes–Descartes–Bayle* (Paris: Vrin, 2008).

13 For a general overview of ancient skeptical criticism of morals, see Emidio Spinelli, ed., *Sesto Empirico. Contro gli etici* (Napoli: Bibliopolis, 1995), intro. and commentary; Richard Bett, ed., *Sextus Empiricus. Against the Ethicists (Adversus Mathematicos XI)* (Oxford: Clarendon Press, 1997), intro. and commentary.

14 Sextus Empiricus, *Pyrrhoniae Hypotyposes* I, 21–4.

15 On this broad topic see John Christian Laursen, *The Politics of Skepticism in the Ancients, Montaigne, Hume, and Kant* (Leiden: Brill, 1992).

16 See *Elements*, I, VII, 1–3, pp. 28–9. There is also another specific criticism put forward by Hobbes, according to which it is impossible to imagine in men "an utmost end," since "while we live, we have desires, and desire presupposeth a farther end" (6, p. 30).

17 Montaigne, *Essais*, II, xii, Pierre Villey, ed. (Paris: PUF, 1999), 577.

18 François La Mothe Le Vayer, *Dialogues faits à l'imitation des anciens*, ed. by A. Pessel (Paris: Fayard, 1988), 266–302. It is highly unlikely, however, that Hobbes knew, when still in England, this work which had a confidential diffusion in France at the beginning of the 30s and was not translated into English.

19 Montaigne, *Essais*, ed. P. Villey (Paris: PUF, 1999), II, xv, 817.

20 The translation by John Florio (1603) was quite famous in England. See the ed. by George Saintsbury (London: D. Nutt, 1893), vol. II, 341.
21 *Essais* III, xii, 1055; Florio's trans. vol. III, 317.
22 Leo Strauss, *The Political Philosophy of Thomas Hobbes: Its Basis and Its Genesis* (Chicago: University of Chicago Press, 1952 [orig.1932]), 18–20.
23 Strauss, *The Political Philosophy*, 35.
24 Strauss, *The Political Philosophy*, 38–43.
25 Cf. Strauss, *The Political Philosophy*, 45–59.
26 George Huppert, *Les bourgeois gentilshommes* (Chicago: University of Chicago Press, 1977).
27 Montaigne *Essais*, II, xii, 452.
28 Pierre Charron, *De la sagesse*, 229. We quote from the second edition: Pierre Charron, *De la sagesse* (Paris, 1604), reproduced in the modern edition, ed. by Barbara De Negroni (Paris: Fayard 1986), with the main variants taken from the first edition (Bordeaux, 1601).
29 La Mothe Le Vayer, *Dialogues*, 364–9 ("De l'opiniâtreté").
30 Hobbes, *Leviathan*, edited with an introduction by C.B. Macpherson, (Harmondsworth: Penguin Books, 1985), XIII 62/187 (the first number refers to the Head edition pagination, the second to this modern ed.).
31 Montaigne, *Essais*, II, xii, 460.
32 *Essais* II, xii, 461: "Les hommes qui nous servent, le font à meilleur marché, et pour un traitement moins curieux et moins favorable que celuy que nous faisons aux oyseaux, aux chevaux et aux chiens."
33 *Essais*, II, xii, 559: "Nostre esprit est un util vagabond, dangereux et temeraire: il est malaisé d'y joindre l'ordre et la mesure. [...] C'est miracle s'il s'en rencontre un rassis et sociable. On a raison de donner à l'esprit humain les barrieres les plus contraintes qu'on peut. En l'estude, comme au reste, il luy faut compter et reigler ses marches, il luy faut tailler par art les limites de sa chasse. On le bride et garrote de religions, de loix, de coustumes, de sciences, de preceptes, de peines et recompenses mortelles et immortelles ; encores voit-on que, par sa volubilité et dissolution, il eschappe à toutes ces liaisons." The context of Montaigne's phrase is not immediately a political one; yet his warnings take place in the course of a general reflection about the danger that liberty turns into license ("licence d'opinions et de meurs," "licence effrenée"). Against this danger Montaigne presses for a tight regulation ("tutelle"), either by custom ("le train accoustumé") or constraint (ibid.).
34 On this topic of *animalia politica* in Hobbes and his ancient (Aristotle, Epicurus) and modern sources (Gassendi), see my article: Paganini, "Political animals in seventeenth century philosophy: some rival paradigms,"

in *Ethical Perspectives on Animals in the Renaissance and Early Modern Period*, ed. Cecilia Muratori (Florence: SISMEL – Edizioni del Galluzzo, 2013), 285–98.
35 Charron, *De la sagesse*, 51 ff.
36 Charron, *De la sagesse* , 227–80.
37 Charron, *De la sagesse*, 231.
38 Ibidem, 271.
39 *Leviathan*, introduction. 2/82. Hobbes traces a peculiar interpretation of this motto: see below, p. 70.
40 Charron, *De la Sagesse*, 44.
41 *Elements*, I, xiv, 1; 2–3, 70.
42 *Elements*, I, xiv, 70–4.
43 Etienne de La Boétie, *De la Servitude volontaire ou Contr'un*, ed. Malcolm Smith (Geneva: Droz, 1987), 41.
44 Montaigne, *Essais*, I, xiv, 51: "les hommes sont tous d'une espece, et sauf le plus et le moins, se trouvent garnis de pareils outils et instrumens pour concevoir et juger." Florio's trans. vol. I, 273 (in this translation Essay xiv is displaced, becoming xl).
45 *Essais* I, xxxi, 205–6. Montaigne highly praises this natural simplicity ("une nayfveté si pure et simple"), even though recognizing that these so-called savages have their own culture, made of priestcraft and prophecy, divination, war etc. (208–9). Montaigne is not so disingenuous (or primitivist) as to forget that among them reason is still at the zero degree, which does not mean that they are worse than us. They can be even better than us: "Nous les pouvons donq bien appeller barbares, eu egard aux regles de la raison, mais non pas eu esgard à nous, qui les surpassons en toute sorte de barbarie" [We can thus call them barbarians by the rules of reason, but not in comparison to ourselves, who have surpassed them by all sorts of barbarisms] (210).
46 La Mothe Le Vayer, *Dialogues* ("De la politique"), 397.
47 Montaigne, *Essais*, xxxi, 206: "il me semble que ce que nous voyons par expérience en ces nations là, surpasse non seulement toutes le peintures dequoy la poësie a embelly l'age doré et toutes le inventions à feindre une heureuse condition d'hommes, mais encore la conception et le desir mesme de la philosophie." Nearly the same praise in La Mothe Le Vayer, *Dialogues* ("De l'opiniâtreté"), 370.
48 *Leviathan*, XIII, 62/186.
49 On this see Vittorio Frajese, *Sarpi scettico. Stato e Chiesa a Venezia tra Cinque e Seicento* (Bologna: Il Mulino, 1994).
50 Anna Maria Battista, *Politica e morale nella Francia dell'età moderna*, ed. Anna Maria Lazzarino Del Grosso (Genoa: Name, 1998), chapt. VIII "Psicologia

e politica nella cultura eterodossa del Seicento," 221–48. This chapter is full of insightful hints about Hobbes; it suffers however from two limits: not considering the chronological evolution of Hobbes's thought, and not appreciating the existence of a major divide between *Leviathan* and skeptical psychologies (on this see below § 5).

51 By contrast, in *De cive* this anthropological or psychological prologue is missing altogether.

52 On the contrary, the chapter "Of religion" (*Leviathan* XII) seems to have been widely indebted to the French libertine debate. See Paganini, "Hobbes et les libertins."

53 We have showed elsewhere the novelty of human psychology in *Leviathan* in comparison to the previous works. See Paganini, "'Passionate Thought': reason and the passion of curiosity in Thomas Hobbes," in *Emotional Minds. The passions and the limits of pure inquiry in early modern philosophy*, ed. Sabrina Ebbersmeyer (Berlin: Walter De Gruyter, 2012), 227–56.

54 Cf. Paganini, "Thomas Hobbes e la questione dell'umanesimo," in *Le origini dell'umanesimo scientifico dal Rinascimento all'Illuminismo*, ed. Lorenzo Bianchi and Gianni Paganini (Naples: Liguori, 2010), 135–58.

55 *Leviathan*, introduction, 3/83.

56 Sextus Empiricus, *Pyrrhoniae Hypotyposes* I, 21.

57 *Leviathan*, introduction, 2/82–3.

58 Ibidem, introduction, 2/82.

59 Montaigne, *Essais*, III, 2, 805. About "l'avertissement à chacun de se cognoistre," see ibid., III, 12, 1075.

60 Charron, *De la Sagesse*, Title of the First Book, 44. On the analogy of the self to the book, see ibid., 177.

61 Such as obedience and observance of the laws (chapt. 8), behave well to others (chapt. 9), and be fair and wise in all kind of business (chapt. 10).

62 *Elements* I, VIII, 3, 34. Chapt. VIII precedes chapt. IX, which is devoted to the topic of the passions. On this change, yet without any hints about the skeptical milieu, cf. Arrigo Pacchi, "Hobbes and the Passions," *Topoi* 6 (1987): 111–19, reprinted in Pacchi, *Scritti hobbesiani (1978–1990)*, ed. Agostino Lupoli (Milan: Angeli, 1998), 79–95, esp. 87. Pacchi emphasizes instead the importance of the Cartesian model for the treatment of the passions in *Leviathan*.

63 *De cive* Libertas I, 5, 94

64 *De cive* Libertas I, 5, 94: "qua quidem nulla maior animi est molestia, neque ex qua laedendi libido maior oriri solet."

65 From this point of view, see above all Charron, *De la Sagesse*, 545–624, entirely devoted to prudence ("De la prudence premiere vertu").

66 *Leviathan* IX, 41/149.

67 *Elements,* xiv. Even if it is not sure that this chart is definitely Hobbes's work, it is highly probable because it closely mirrors the structure and the partitions of *Elements of Law.*

68 Montaigne, *Essais,* III, xiii, 1072: « Or les loix se maintiennent en credit, non parce qu'elles sont justes, mais parce qu'elles sont loix. C'est le fondement mystique de leur authorité ; elles n'en ont point d'autre. Qui bien leur sert. Elles sont souvent faictes par des sots, plus souvent par des gens qui, en haine d'equalité, ont faute d'equité, mais toujours par des hommes, autheurs vains et irresolus. » There are many other passages in the same vein. Cf. I, xliii, 270.

69 The best study on this general topic is still Arrigo Pacchi, *Convenzione e ipotesi nella formazione della filosofia naturale di Hobbes* (Florence: La Nuova Italia, 1965).

70 It is well known that in Hobbes's epistemology "science" is sharply distinguished from simple "prudence."

chapter four

Questionnements sceptiques et politiques de la fable : les « autres mondes » du libertinage érudit

JEAN-CHARLES DARMON

Remarques liminaires

Les apports de ce que l'on appelle communément le « libertinage érudit » à la pensée politique moderne ont été largement sous estimés par les grandes histoires de la philosophie. Pour qui essaie aujourd'hui de réfléchir sur les relations entre libertinage et politique aux temps de la monarchie absolue,[1] ils apparaissent à la fois comme extrêmement riches et comme difficilement synthétisables.

La diversité des figures et des usages du scepticisme chez les auteurs concernés n'est pas étrangère à cette situation. Ces « politiques sceptiques », ou plutôt inspirées par le scepticisme, affleurant dans le corpus libertin sous des formes diverses, semblent le plus souvent se dérober à toute interprétation uniforme et globalisante.

On a certes beaucoup glosé sur le « conservatisme » politique que certaines formes de scepticisme pouvaient, en terres libertines, contribuer à cautionner. Mais en quel sens peut-on considérer que le scepticisme aurait, *in fine*, pour effet de maintenir, voire de renforcer une adhésion sans réserve au pouvoir absolutiste qui ne cesse de se centraliser et de se renforcer ? Et jusqu'à quel point pourrions-nous continuer à soutenir par exemple, comme le faisait René Pintard à propos des « libertins érudits », que « c'est à l'avant-garde, à l'extrême pointe conquérante du mouvement absolutiste qu'il faut les voir, audacieux et décidés »[2] ? Dans la plupart des cas, il importe de savoir lire entre les lignes, et de mesurer, derrière ces jeux de langage usant et abusant volontiers des tropes sceptiques, ce que l'adhésion aux principes d'une monarchie *absolue* de droit divin peut avoir d'ironiquement *relatif* en pareil contexte.

En outre, en matière de scepticisme comme en tant d'autres, pour ces grands lecteurs de Michel de Montaigne, nous ne goûtons « rien de pur ». L'exégète moderne est souvent mal à l'aise devant la singularité des mélanges qui lui sont proposés, entre références explicites au scepticisme et références non moins explicites à des pensées de tout autres provenances. Mélanges foncièrement instables, et qui peuvent devenir détonants selon les mains qui s'en emparent !

C'est sur certains de ces phénomènes de voisinage et d'interférence que je souhaiterais m'attarder ici, en insistant sur deux types de questions.

1) Que se passe-t-il au juste quand des motifs sceptiques se trouvent associés, selon des modalités spécifiques, à des thèses, à des doctrines, à des parti pris de tout autre nature ? (Ces motifs sceptiques relèvent-ils alors surtout d'un « art d'écrire », au sens de Leo Strauss, visant à atténuer aux yeux du lecteur et du censeur ce que ces thèses, doctrines, parti pris peuvent avoir de radicalement hétérodoxe et dangereux ?)

2) Que se passe-t-il au juste quand ces voisinages entre scepticisme et naturalisme, par exemple, se trouvent eux-mêmes pris *dans un univers de fiction* ? Comment évaluer les rôles de la fiction narrative et de ses différents genres au sein de pareilles interférences ?

Un cas comme celui de Cyrano de Bergerac présente, de ce point de vue, me semble-t-il, un intérêt tout particulier. On ne reviendra pas ici sur ses affinités évidentes avec certaines grandes figures du « libertinage érudit » qui ont puissamment fait revivre le scepticisme sur la scène de la pensée des moderne : Gassendi et La Mothe Le Vayer, au premier chef – qui sont du reste explicitement cités dans *Les Etats et Empires de la Lune* comme deux « fréquentations » majeures du Démon de Socrate, le mentor du narrateur de Cyrano lors de son passage sur la Lune.[3] Le Bret, dans sa préface, réserve à la figure de Pyrrhon une place d'exception dans le Panthéon philosophique de Cyrano :

> « Démocrite et Pyrrhon lui semblaient, après Socrate, les plus raisonnables de l'Antiquité. Encore n'était-ce qu'à cause que le premier avait mis la vérité dans un lieu si obscur, qu'il était impossible de la voir, et *que Pyrrhon avait été si généreux*, qu'aucun des savants de son siècle n'avait pu mettre ses sentiments en servitude, et si modeste, qu'il n'avait jamais voulu rien décider (...)[4] »

La référence à Pyrrhon se trouve, très significativement, associée à la grande thématique de la *libertas philosophandi* ; à un *ethos* mis en relation avec l'indépendance sociale et politique de l'écrivain Cyrano ; à une éthique libre, pour ne pas dire libertine, de la « générosité » – le qualificatif de « généreux » appliqué à Pyrrhon serait, en l'occurrence, à rapprocher de l'usage que La Mothe faisait de ce terme au seuil de ses *Dialogues faits à l'imitation des anciens.*[5]

A la figure « généreuse » de Pyrrhon se trouvent associées :

- une posture permettant de démasquer les impostures de la raison dogmatique, à l'infini ;
- une posture, également, qui ne s'arrête pas à la critique et à la démystification des opinons et des croyances génératrices d'illusions, de superstitions et d'impostures, mais qui permet d'examiner toutes sortes de savoirs nouveaux et d'en jouir librement, en dehors de tout effet d'autorité.

« Néanmoins, il ne blâmait jamais un ouvrage absolument, quand il y trouvait quelque chose de nouveau ; parce qu'il disait que c'était un accroissement de bien, aussi grand pour la république des lettres que la découvertes des terres nouvelles est utile aux anciennes ; et la nation des critiques lui semblait d'autant plus insupportable, qu'il attribuait à l'envie et au dépit, qu'ils avaient de se voir incapables d'aucune entreprise (qui est toujours louable, quand bien l'effet n'y répondrait pas entièrement), la passion qu'ils font paraître à reprendre les autres » (A.486).

Sans revenir sur l'ethos d'inspiration « pyrrhonienne » attribuée par son ami Le Bret au personnage Cyrano, je voudrais plutôt m'interroger sur les figurations du scepticisme à l'intérieur même de l'œuvre, et sur leurs effets éthiques et politiques dans des fictions comme *Les Etats et Empires de la Lune et du Soleil.*

Il apparaît, en tout premier lieu, que le scepticisme n'est pas seulement ici une position philosophique parmi d'autres, une doctrine parmi d'autres, côtoyant atomisme épicurien, copernicianisme, pansensisme, naturalisme magique, cartésianisme, etc. : il intervient aussi et surtout comme une attitude fondamentale qui *modalise* le rapport à aux diverses doctrines activées successivement et tient à distance les savoirs sur la nature auxquels le lecteur sera tenté d'adhérer. A ce titre, le scepticisme participe très activement à l'invention d'une littérature de l'infini, sans centre ni point fixe, à la fabrique même du récit et à la constitution des paysages ontologiques de la fable.

La fiction, cependant, tout en étant nourrie en ses représentations de la Nature par la variation des modes sceptiques, permet l'expression de thèses foncièrement hétérodoxes bien connues dans la sphère du libertinage érudit. On s'attardera, dans un second temps, sur un exemple de « mélange » parmi tant d'autres : celui de la thèse de l'imposture politique des religions, qui est figurée de diverses manières. Mais tout en surgissant au fil du récit, cette thèse n'en est pas moins prise dans les variations inspirées par le scepticisme, et puissamment relativisée dans les mondes de la fiction. Une comparaison avec des utopies libertines où la question de l'imposture est politiquement centrale conduit à mettre l'accent sur tout ce qui déstabilise les interprétations dogmatiques que l'on pourrait en faire ; et à s'interroger, pour finir, sur le type d'expérience de pensée qu'une telle ironie, nourrie par certaines formes de scepticisme, put alimenter, en matière de politique comme en d'autres domaines.

I. Mise en récit des tropes sceptiques et poétique du voyage imaginaire

Dans un récit tel que *L'Autre Monde*, la diversité intrinsèque des images de la Nature se trouve démultipliée par un *art de la variation* tel que l'hétérogénéité des « effets naturels » semble primer sur toute « notion » ou « idée » de Nature préalable et unifiante. Sur la scène de la fiction, représenter la Nature, c'est d'abord explorer tout une gamme de possibles ouverts par le langage : la Nature, à l'image de cette matière grande comédienne qu'évoque le personnage Domingo Gonzales est à chaque fois ici et ailleurs en un inépuisable jeu de rôles. Le texte est alors susceptible d'engendrer chez le lecteur cette « épochè » sceptique, joyeuse et libre, que décrivait par exemple de façon saisissante La Mothe Le Vayer du dialogue sur l'opiniâtreté.[6]

Mais dans *L'Autre Monde* la prééminence du scepticisme en tant que position philosophique à part entière semble tout aussi aléatoire que celle d'autres doctrines (plus ou moins) concurrentes : atomisme épicurien, pansensisme, cartésianisme ... En fait, tout se passe comme si la tradition sceptique fournissait à l'écrivain *moins une identité philosophique* ultime qu'une *poétique de la variation* particulièrement fertile ; des techniques de démultiplication du point de vue permettant de créer au sein de la diversité des images d'intempestives turbulences : la nature se manifeste alors en ce mouvement imprévisible dont le « suivi » nous échappe. Aussi le lecteur de Montaigne, de La Mothe Le Vayer, du Gassendi des *Exercitationes* se sent-il à maints égards de plain-pied dans *L'Autre Monde.* Les grandes variations pyrrhoniennes, transmises de main en main, y trouvent d'incessants échos. A ceci près, toutefois, que ce qui est pour ainsi dire disposé verticalement dans l'argumentation sceptique traditionnelle sous forme d'accumulation d'arguments devient ici matière et matrice à récit, composante dynamique d'une trame narrative linéaire. Tel exemple de la diversité de la nature ou des coutumes, qui figure ou eût pu figurer dans les variations de Sextus Empiricus ou de Gassendi reprenant les modes de Sextus, se trouve développé en épisode singulier, métamorphosant ce qui n'était qu'un argument parmi une infinité d'autres possibles en choix narratif unique. La topique pyrrhonienne, par une série de transformations ponctuelles et de mises en situation aléatoires (à l'exemple des pères punis par leurs enfants, à celui des emblèmes phalliques affichés comme marque de distinction, Cyrano aurait pu en ajouter d'autres, puisés dans les énumérations sceptiques transmises par Sextus, le chapitre XXI des *Essais* etc ...) devient ainsi une composante essentielle de *l'invention* de la Nature dans *l'Autre Monde* : elle procure toutes sortes de matériaux hétérogènes alimentant une esthétique de la surprise et permettant précisément de faire en sorte que les Mondes de la fiction soient vraiment Autres.

Les textes prégnants de la tradition sceptique, en particulier les *Hypotyposes* de Sextus qui, comme l'avait montré notamment Charles B. Schmitt, ont servi de référence centrale à partir des années 1560 (au détriment d'autres sources comme les *Académiques* de Cicéron) livrent à l'écrivain par leurs tropes et leurs classifications bien plus qu'une série d'exemples extrêmes ou exotiques : les Massagètes dévorant les corps de leurs parents en signe d'honneur, tel rite funéraire où aux larmes certains ont substitué joie et festins-motif du festin qui peut du reste se combiner avec celui du suicide.[7]

Les tropes (ou modes) d'Aenésidème peuvent aussi fonctionner implicitement comme des sortes de topiques permettant de classer ces exemples dispersifs – ils ne le sont pas tous au même titre – et d'indiquer les diverses opérations possibles entre ces séries, de façon à accroître l'impact corrosif du questionnement : « oppositions mutuelles » à l'intérieur d'une même série d'exemples (opposer telle coutume à telle coutume, telle loi à telle loi ...), « oppositions réciproques » entre séries d'exemples disjoints (opposer telle croyance à telle coutume, telle coutume à telle loi, telle loi à tel mythe ...).[8] Le questionnement sceptique tel que Sextus l'a popularisé fournit potentiellement, en maintes occasions, au récit de voyage et à la rhétorique du « monde renversé » toute une série de lignes qui s'entrecroisent en de multiples points – et dont les 10 modes nous permettent d'avoir une vue d'ensemble :

Bien des argumentations et des situations imaginaires de *L'Autre Monde* sont alimentées par une amplification du 10ème mode fondé sur les morales, les lois, les coutumes, les croyances légendaires et les convictions dogmatiques (ce qui était devenu en soi assez commun en terres libertines dès lors que l'on abordait des questions politiques, religieuses et morales[9]) ; mais ces mêmes argumentations et situations imaginaires sont aussi surdéterminées par des variations sur le 1er mode, fondé sur la diversité des animaux ; sur le 2ème mode, fondé sur la différence entre les hommes ; sur le 3ème mode, fondé sur la disposition des organes sensoriels ; sur le 4ème mode, fondé sur la diversité des impressions affectant le même organe sensoriel ; sur 5ème mode, fondé sur la diversité des positions, des intervalles et des lieux ; et même, dans une moindre mesure, par des affleurements de questions liées au 6ème, fondé sur la diversité des mélanges ; au 7ème mode, fondé sur la quantité et composition des substances externes ; 9ème mode, fondé sur la fréquence et rareté des rencontres. L'ensemble des discours et des jeux de langage relativistes faisant de la terre une lune inversée et vice versa étant lui-même enveloppé par une activation sans cesse renouvelée du 8ème mode fondé sur la relation. Mode que Pierre Gassendi, pour sa part, dans son commentaire de la « logique » des pyrrhoniens,[10] avait caractérisé comme « le plus général » (« Le huitième mode est celui qui se fonde sur la relation, puisqu'il n'existe aucun objet qui ne soit relatif à quelque chose ; par conséquent ce mode est le plus général »).

Autant de champs de variations « eidétiques » sur ce qui fait pour nous un monde, et sur ce dont on se fait, comme on dit, « tout un monde », moralement et politiquement, en « notre » monde, autant de croyances et de dogmes relativisés puissamment par le grand jeu de la fiction. Cette matrice de variations, cette grande rhétorique pyrrhonienne passées de main en main depuis Montaigne a été relativement peu étudiée *en ses transpositions narratives.*[11] *L'Autre Monde* pourrait constituer à cet égard un objet d'étude fort riche.

Le premier mentor du narrateur sur la Lune, le Démon de Socrate – qui en tant qu'être solaire figure à sa façon l'unité des deux voyages – dès ses premiers discours, jouera simultanément sur plusieurs lieux communs de cette topique pyrrhonienne et en particulier sur ceux gravitant autour du premier mode. Il condense à lui seul toute une rêverie sur la diversité des animaux : diversité des organes et des sens, diversité des modes de génération, diversité des instincts.

Souvent le questionnement lié au troisième mode (différence de disposition des organes des sens) vient prolonger le motif général du « monde renversé », les différences « naturelles » entre les divers sens et organes se redistribuant constamment au fil du récit.

Certains développements des *Hypotyposes* – tel le célèbre passage sur la pomme, qui a inspiré Gassendi lui-même à maintes reprises – pourraient trouver ici bien des échos :

> que d'un autre côté cette pomme puisse renfermer plus de qualités que celles dont témoignent les représentations, voici comment je l'infère. Imaginons un homme, sourd et aveugle de naissance, et ne disposant que du toucher, du goût et de l'odorat : pour lui, il n'existera nul objet visible ou audible et son univers se bornera aux trois sortes de qualités qu'il est capable d'appréhender. Or, ne se peut il justement que moi, qui n'ai que cinq sens, je ne perçoive, des qualités propres à cette pomme, que celles que je puis sentir ; et que celle-ci renferme encore d'autres qualités susceptibles d'affecter d'autres organes sensitifs, dont la privation m'empêche actuellement.[12]

Ce « plus de qualités » qui échappe à l'humain et marque ses limites dans la nature, le Démon de Socrate lui les sent et il apprend au narrateur qu' « il y a dans l'Univers un million peut-être de choses qui pour être connues demanderaient en nous un millions d'organes tous différents. [...] vous autres ne sauriez donner jusques à ces hautes conceptions, [...] non plus qu'un aveugle-né ne saurait s'imaginer ce que c'est que la beauté d'un paysage, le coloris d'un tableau, les nuances de l'iris, ou bien il se les figurera tantôt comme quelque chose de palpable, tantôt comme un manger, tantôt comme un son, tantôt comme une odeur » (A.64–5).

Dans une semblable perspective, par toute une série d'amplifications, d'inversions, de translations, l'imagination cyranienne fait du texte de fiction une sorte de multiplicateur d'organes : à chaque détour du récit l'humain rencontre des figures de la nature sentant et jugeant autrement ; rendant immédiatement perceptibles surtout les limites d'un narrateur destitué de toute prééminence ontologique.

Les grands animaux qu'il rencontre sur la lune évaluent immédiatement leur posture comme plus conforme à la nature que la sienne – et le narrateur, à la réflexion, adhère à leur point de vue. Mais ces animaux eux-mêmes, que sont-ils relativement au Démon et à ses facultés de réincarnation qui les font à leur tour crier au miracle ? Par ce type d'effet relativiste renvoyant virtuellement chaque point de vue supérieur à d'autres qui l'englobent et l'excèdent, les effets de la Nature apparaissent comme infiniment multiples – pareils aux musiques de cet instrument qu'évoquait Montaigne après Sextus et bien d'autres : « l'air n'étant qu'un, il se fait, par l'application à une trompette, divers en mille sortes de sons ».

Sans cesse dans *L'Autre Monde* se juxtaposent les motifs liés au 1er mode (différence des animaux, des organes ...) et ceux qui se rattachent classiquement au 10ème (mœurs, coutumes ...) dont l'amplification constitue l'une des démarches privilégiées de la littérature sceptique. Du reste, dès les origines de la parole sceptique le dixième trope fut en affinité avec l'économie et la poétique du récit de Voyage.[13]

Les effets que Sextus eût nommés « oppositions mutuelles » (opposant deux à deux une coutume à une coutume, une opinion dogmatique à une autre, etc.) surabondent dans le récit. Cyrano opère parmi les possibles un choix ostensiblement aléatoire et ludique. A aucun moment n'apparaît dans la façon de construire l'ailleurs lunaire – et surtout les mœurs de ses habitants – une systématique des choix ; un souci réel que l'ensemble de coutumes imaginées reflète ou révèle *une* Nature commune, enfin transparente à tous. Sur la lune les oppositions mutuelles entre coutumes demeurent aussi vivaces (codes musicaux pour les uns, gestuels exclusivement pour d'autres) et les variations pyrrhoniennes aussi opératoires. Tantôt de façon explicite : sur la lune même la coutume A est ouvertement opposée à la coutume B, A tire sa pertinence de B, de n'être pas B. Tantôt l'autre terme de l'opposition reste implicite, tel rite lunaire conteste tel rite terrestre qui n'est pas nécessairement nommé et il revient au lecteur complice de remplir cette case blanche à sa guise et éventuellement de décider quelle coutume semble plus conforme à la nature.

Mais la gamme des oppositions « réciproques », entre termes d'ensembles *a priori* différents (à telle coutume on oppose telle loi, à telle opinion dogmatique, telle créance, à telle loi tel mythe, etc.) offre des virtualités encore plus riches peut-être, rendant plus dispersives et hétérogènes les images de la Nature qui en résultent. Si bien qu'on en arrive à une érosion des catégories initiales : la philosophie ici est-elle envisagée sous l'angle des « opinions dogmatiques », des coutumes, des lois, des rites, des mythes ? Du fait du jeu des oppositions réciproques où les différents discours sur la Nature se trouvent pris, Cyrano obtient, par croisement de diverses séries, maints effets burlesques. Ainsi quand, lors de l'interrogatoire visant à définir son être, sa « nature » (question relevant du 1er mode), les juges lunaires demandent au narrateur de faire état de ses opinions en matière de physique (question relevant du 10ème mode): « Cependant, il fallait bien que quelqu'un eût réchauffé les *querelles de la définition de mon être*, car comme je ne songeais plus qu'à mourir en cage, on me vint quérir encore une fois pour me donner audience. Je fus *donc* interrogé en présence de force courtisans, sur *quelque point de Physique*, et mes réponses, à ce que je crois, satisfirent aucunement » (A.97). Tout se passe comme si ce que Sextus eût nommé « opinion dogmatique », relevant du 10ème trope, valait, – telle est la saveur logique du « donc » – pour définir la nature d'un être !

La nature représentée est d'autant moins unitaire que ces variations sont elles-mêmes perçues par un narrateur qui ne les saisit que de façon partielle, incohérente, essayant sans cesse de les interpréter à la lumière de son expérience terrestre propre et d'un « référentiel » inadéquat – Cyrano nous rappelant constamment les limites de la « puissance d'être affecté » de son narrateur, ce que la tradition sceptique répertorie comme les « modes du sujet » entre alors en résonance avec ceux de l'objet, voire avec les modes dits mixtes, fortement représentés également (variations sur les distances, les positions des lieux, les mélanges externes et internes, et surtout la relation).

On a souvent remarqué le peu d'affinité entre Cyrano et l'Utopie. Cela tient entre autres raisons à cette amplification narrative de diverses topiques sceptiques si peu conformes à l'élaboration d'une utopie stable, centrée, comme la *Civitas Solis* de Campanella où le système des *relations* enveloppe et reflète une vérité sur la Nature et sur l'Homme.

Dans *L'Autre Monde* la poétique de la variation multiplie les effets centrifuges des images de la Nature. D'où un certain malaise parfois des commentateurs face à cette dissémination critique, si peu « constructive », malaise dont Erica Harth par exemple témoigne.[14] Des segments d'Utopie flottent ici et là dans le décentrement général des images de la Nature – ainsi celles du Royaume des Amoureux, dont des envoyés surgissent dans le second voyage, face à Campanella, lui offrant en quelque sorte un reflet déformant et burlesque de sa propre pratique de l'utopie. Après l'énonciation d'une série de lois et de coutumes, le discours de l'utopie se dissout progressivement dans la rhétorique paradoxale et joueuse de l'écriture « pointue » – celle de certaines lettres satiriques – et apparaît tout à coup, comme un *deus ex machina* la figure matricielle qui présidait à l'engendrement de cette histoire : l'hyperbole – sans nul doute l'un des « nerfs » rhétoriques les plus actifs de la variation d'images chez Cyrano.

Pourtant, au sein de ces déplacements sceptiques surgissent des thématiques libertines extrêmement virulentes, qui semblent devoir emporter le lecteur « déniaisé » bien au-delà d'une suspension du jugement quant à ce qui serait plus ou moins conforme à la nature en matière de politique ou de morale. On concentrera l'attention, à titre d'exemple symptomatique, sur l'une des thèses les plus caractéristiques qui, ici et là, affleurent au fil du récit fictif : celle de l'imposture politique des religions. Si le scepticisme apparaît par ailleurs comme un instrument permettant de mettre en lumière les impostures de la raison dogmatiques, comme se conjugue-t-il, localement, avec une doctrine de ce type, qui renvoie à des présupposés sur la nature qui n'ont rien de « sceptique » ?

II. Entre motifs sceptiques et utopie naturaliste: Nature et Imposture d'un monde à l'autre

La thèse de l'imposture politique des religions instituées, que Gabriel Naudé reprend sous la forme d'une typologie d'« inventions » bien connues de tous les « législateurs et politiques » depuis la nuit de temps,[15] et dont on ne cesse de redécouvrir la fécondité entre Age Baroque et Lumières,[16] constitue, sans nul doute, « l'une des constituantes majeures du libertinage ».[17] En réalité, on pourrait avancer que la question de l'imposture fut pour le libertinage bien plus qu'une thèse locale (celle, récurrente, des *Trois Imposteurs*) ; et qu'elle offrit un point de vue critique sur l'histoire politique dans son ensemble, un prisme pour l'analyse de tout pouvoir et des croyances lui conférant fondement et légitimité.

D'où toute une série de déplacements périphériques du motif de l'imposture, où la doctrine centrale de l'origine politique des religions n'est plus directement sollicitée, et où elle vaut plutôt par analogie, en des contextes où il s'agit par exemple d'examiner l'imposture du médecin, de l'homme de loi, du philosophe, du pédant, du magicien, du sorcier, et aussi simultanément parfois l'imposture de ceux qui dénoncent les magiciens et brûlent les sorciers.

Cette dissémination donne lieu à des approches mouvantes, polyphoniques de l'imposture. Une relecture de l'ensemble du corpus « libertin » de l'Age Baroque et de l'Age Classique laisse entrevoir une solidarité profonde entre ces impostures, grandes et petites, comme si elles s'emboîtaient les unes dans les autres ainsi que des poupées russes ; ou plutôt comme si elles étaient *autant de variantes d'un même trait anthropologique*, rendant intelligible une part essentielle de l'histoire politique de l'humanité, depuis que l'homme est sorti de l'état de nature et s'est donné des lois et des Maîtres.[18] Au point que certains textes, tel ce *Theophrastus Redivivus* qui apparaît comme une somme du libertinage du premier XVIIème siècle, donnent à penser que l'humanité a connu deux Ages : un Etat de Nature, dont il revient au *Sapiens* de retrouver l'innocence, et un Etat d'Imposture, avec lequel il faut apprendre à composer, et hors duquel le Peuple serait ingouvernable.

On trouverait sans peine, dans les œuvres de Cyrano, des éléments identiques ou voisins à ceux qu'une utopie libertine comme la *République des Philosophes* attribuée à Fontenelle permettrait d'énumérer. Mais les figurations de l'imposture dans les Autres Mondes de Cyrano de Bergerac sont bien loin de donner à imaginer une séparation aussi radicale, une ligne de partage aussi « claire et distincte » entre les mondes incluant l'imposture et ceux qui l'excluraient à jamais. Ici et là clignotent des indices, des potentialités d'imposture, chez ceux-là mêmes qui la dénoncent en l'homme, et en stigmatisent violemment les effets parmi les peuples de la terre.

Soit un affleurement particulièrement symptomatique de cette grande thématique libertine. Il prend place dans une sorte de fragment d'utopie inséré dans le second voyage, *Les Etats et Empires du Soleil* (et il convient de souligner « une sorte de », tant les déviations que Cyrano imprime aux structures topiques de l'imaginaire u-topique sont importantes, au point d'en suggérer la critique parodique). On se souvient que le narrateur, fait prisonnier par le Peuple oiseau, est accusé d'être homme et condamné à mort. Dans le procès qui précède cette condamnation, le simple fait d'être un homme équivaut en soi à un crime, au pire d'entre tous. Et parmi les chefs d'accusation qui motivent ce jugement sans appel, l'imposture figure en bonne place.

L'homme incarne l'imposture par excellence dans l'ordre de la nature. L'homme est, pour ainsi dire, *un « être-pour-l'imposture »*, notamment parce qu'il est un « être-pour-la-mort » : comme dans les grandes tirades libertines de Séjanus, le lien entre imposture, crainte des dieux et crainte de la mort constitue la nervure la plus forte de l'argumentaire athée. Et le thème épicurien selon lequel « la mort n'est rien pour nous », que les oiseaux, et tout particulièrement les « oiseaux de paradis », s'approprient, est présenté comme l'antidote le plus « naturel » dans la thérapeutique de la crainte qu'ils proposent à Dyrcona, en guise d'ultime consolation :

> (...) Encore est-ce un droit imaginaire que cet empire dont ils [les hommes] se flattent ; il sont au contraire si enclins à la servitude, que de peur de

> manquer à servir, ils se vendent les uns aux autres leur liberté. C'est ainsi que les jeunes sont esclaves de vieux, les pauvres des riches, les princes des monarques, et les monarques mêmes des lois qu'ils ont établies. Mais avec tout cela ces pauvres serfs ont si peur de manquer de maîtres que, comme s'ils appréhendaient que la liberté ne leur vînt de quelque endroit non attendu, ils se forgent des dieux de toutes parts, dans l'eau, dans l'air, dans le feu, sous la terre ; il en feront plutôt de bois, qu'ils n'en aient, et je crois même qu'ils se chatouillent des fausses espérances de l'immortalité, moins par l'horreur dont le non-être les effraie, que par la crainte qu'ils ont de n'avoir pas qui leur commande après la mort. (A. 266)

Apparemment, on est ici au plus près du type d'argument mobilisé plus tard par les Ajaoïens de l'utopie de Fontenelle, à propos de l'âme comme invention politique et comme dispositif imaginaire destiné à perpétuer la crainte et la culpabilité parmi les hommes. On assiste même à un « tour d'écrou » supplémentaire, qui rend ces oiseaux plus radicaux encore que ne le seront les athées vertueux de Fontenelle : l'âme immortelle, comme fiction au service de l'imposture, n'est pas seulement imposée aux hommes par ceux qui veulent en être les maîtres. Elle procède aussi plus fondamentalement d'un *désir d'être dominé* inscrit en chaque sujet, même après sa mort. L'imposture est un phénomène à double face, et l'analyse des « coups » de l'imposteur doit être complétée par un « discours de la servitude volontaire ». Obscur objet du désir à l'œuvre dans l'imposture qui vaut analogiquement pour les relations jeunes-vieux (on y reviendra), pauvres-riches, princes-monarques, monarques-lois, hommes-dieux, homme-âme immortelle. (« C'est ainsi que les jeunes sont esclaves des vieux, les pauvres des riches, les princes des monarques, et les monarques mêmes des lois qu'ils ont établies. »). Impostures en cascade, solidaires les unes des autres, et qui conduisent jusqu'aux oracles, en des enchaînements thématiques d'une grande rapidité qui n'ont pu laisser le Fontenelle de l'*Histoire des oracles* indifférent :

> (...) Voilà le bel effet de cette fantastique monarchie et de cet empire si naturel de l'homme sur les animaux et sur nous-mêmes, car son insolence a été jusque-là. Cependant, en conséquence de cette principauté ridicule, il s'attribue tout joliment sur nous le droit de vie et de mort ; il nous dresse des embuscades, il nous enchaîne, il nous jette en prison, il nous égorge, il nous mange, et, de la puissance de tuer ceux qui sont demeurés libres, il fait un prix à la noblesse. Il pense que le soleil s'est allumé pour l'éclairer à nous faire la guerre ; que Nature nous a permis d'étendre nos promenades

> dans le ciel, afin seulement que de notre vol il puisse tirer de malheureux ou favorables auspices ; et quand Dieu mit des entrailles dedans notre corps, qu'il n'eut intention que de faire un grand livre où l'homme pût apprendre la science des choses futures. (A. 266)

Mais, encore une fois, il importe simultanément de mesurer ce qu'a de relatif – au sens fort – cette dénonciation de l'imposture par les oiseaux de Cyrano.

1) Ces oiseaux qui stigmatisent anthropocentrisme et anthropomorphisme comme deux traits essentiels de l'homme imposteur dans la nature, ressorts inusables de sa volonté de puissance, tendent à lui substituer – on l'a déjà remarqué – un « ornithocentrisme » qui en est comme la réplique inversée ; eux-mêmes se situent au-dessus des autres animaux, tout en parlant en leur nom contre l'homme. Ils dénient à ce dernier le plein usage de la raison, dont ils jouissent, et le définissent à partir des représentations qu'ils ont d'eux-mêmes, le définissant comme une sorte d'oiseau monstreux, un « oiseau plumé », variation ludique sur la définition aristotélicienne de l'homme comme « bipède sans plumes » *etc.*

2) L'argumentation de style épicurien censée neutraliser une fois pour toutes crainte des dieux et crainte de la mort dégénère : tout en ne concédant à l'homme qu'une âme matérielle et mortelle, ces arguments lucrétiens sont mis à contribution par des locuteurs ailés qui postulent, eux, *in fine*, l'immortalité de leur propre âme (« Je parle à toi ainsi, *a cause que ton âme n'étant pas immortelle comme la notre,* tu peux bien juger quand tu meurs, que tout meurt avec toi. »). Ce qui brouille singulièrement au passage le sens et l'effet de la cellule idéelle « la mort n'est rien pour nous » mobilisée dans la thérapie de la crainte source d'imposture.

3) Si le concept de Nature est sollicité en cette République des oiseaux pour penser ce que serait une politique sans imposture, une politique enfin transparente à tous, les lois, les rites, les coutumes qui régissent cette république ont bien peu de rapport avec ce qui relèverait d'un « droit naturel » régénéré, ils apparaissent bien plutôt comme des variations imaginaires sur le dixième mode sceptique, dans le prolongement de ceux que l'on trouvait dans la Lune, se réclamant eux aussi de la nature. (L'idée même d'un droit naturel – dont on connaît la crise en ces années – est renvoyée à un *autre monde* précisément, à un monde non-humain, les hommes tels que les oiseaux solaires les décrivent en étant par nature incapables.)

4) L'animalité elle-même, si souvent convoquée dans la tradition libertine sur un mode primitiviste, comme ce « miroir de la nature » qui montre à l'homme ce que veut la nature est ici un miroir brouillé. On est loin, fort loin de l'utilisation primitiviste du thème épicurien de l'animal « *speculum naturae* » que l'on trouvait développée dans le *Theophrastus*, nous montrant ce que put être un Age d'Or de l'humanité d'avant les Lois, c'est-à-dire d'avant l'Etat d'Imposture qui succède à l'Etat de Nature. Et même quand certains thèmes semblent philosophiquement communs (ainsi, on l'a vu, l'égalitarisme que voudrait la Nature, toute monarchie étant par essence une imposture), la configuration même du monde-oiseau et la structuration de son discours en relativise ironiquement la portée.

5) Autre source de « clair-obscur » pour le moins équivoque en cette Nature critiquant l'imposture : le statut ambigu de la référence au Peuple. Dans *La Mort d'Agrippine*, le Peuple était cette instance qui, à l'horizon de l'action des protagonistes, mérite l'imposture, nécessite la duperie (qu'elle vienne de Tibère, d'Agrippine, ou de Séjanus lui-même). Dès les premiers moments de l'emprisonnement de Dyrcona dans l'Histoire des Oiseaux, il apparaît que d'un monde l'autre, la scission entre Peuple crédule et esprits éclairés, déjà mise en scène sur la Terre (épisode de Toulouse) et sur la Lune (écart entre la société des philosophes et celle des sélénites ordinaires), subsiste, telle une structure récurrente avec laquelle on n'en aura jamais fini. La « charitable pie » qui sert de truchement au narrateur dans ce monde-oiseau l'en avertit dès l'abord :

> Entre autres choses, il me souvient qu'elle m'avertit que *la populace des oiseaux* avait fort crié de ce qu'on me gardait si longtemps sans me dévorer ; qu'ils m'avaient remontré que j'amaigrirais tellement qu'on ne trouverait plus sur moi que des os à ronger. (A. 254 ; je souligne)

Or la « nature » est précisément, en l'occurrence, ce référentiel qui sert au Peuple-oiseau pour légitimer ses croyances et son intolérance :

> La rumeur pensa s'échauffer en sédition, car, ma pie s'étant émancipée de représenter que c'était un procédé barbare de faire ainsi mourir sans connaissance de cause un animal qui approchait en quelque sorte de leur raisonnement, ils la pensèrent mettre en pièces, alléguant que cela serait bien ridicule de croire qu'un animal tout nu, que la nature même en mettant au jour ne s'était pas souciée de fournir des choses nécessaires à le conserver, fût comme eux capable de raison. (A.254–5)

Mais surtout, par un déplacement caractéristique de l'ironie cyranienne, au Peuple de ce monde 2 se trouvent désormais attribués des types d'arguments qui revenaient aux esprits éclairés dans un monde 1 (critique des illusions de l'anthropocentrisme etc.) :

> Encore, ajoutaient-ils, si c'était un animal qui approchât un peu davantage de notre figure, mais justement le plus dissemblable et le plus affreux ; enfin une bête chauve, un oiseau plumé, une chimère amassée de toutes sortes de natures, et qui fait peur à toutes : l'homme, dis-je, si sot et si vain, qu'il se persuade que nous n'avons été faits que pour lui ; l'homme qui, avec son âme si clairvoyante, ne saurait distinguer le sucre d'avec l'arsenic (...) ; l'homme qui soutient qu'on ne raisonne que par le rapport des sens, et qui cependant a les sens les plus faibles, les plus tardifs et les plus faux d'entre toutes les créatures ; l'homme enfin que la nature, pour faire de tout, a créé comme les monstres, mais en qui pourtant elle a infus l'ambition de commander à tous les animaux et de les exterminer. (A.255)

Si bien qu'on ne sait plus vraiment qui est le sujet de l'énonciation, en ce réquisitoire au nom de la nature : de la « populace » des oiseaux, on passe au « ils », puis on apprend, à la ligne suivante, que ces propos étaient tenus « par les plus sages » :

> Voilà ce que disaient les plus sages ; pour la commune, elle criait que cela était horrible de croire qu'une bête, qui n'avait pas le visage fait comme eux, eût de la raison.
> – Hé, quoi ! murmuraient-ils l'un à l'autre, il n'a ni bec, ni plumes, ni griffes, et son âme serait spirituelle ! Ô dieux ! quelle impertinence ! (A.255–6)

Dans la République des Ajaoïens subsistera certes cette distinction, récurrente dans le discours libertin, entre le Peuple, vulnérable à toutes les impostures, et le type du Sage, capable d'y résister en les démasquant au nom de la nature et de la raison. Cette bipartition topique s'accuse notamment dans le moment dialogique le plus fortement dramatisé, celui qui suit le discours du narrateur sur l'existence de Dieu :

> Mon beau-père, à qui j'avais communiqué mon discours comme je l'ai dit, en avait gardé une copie à mon insu, & comme la matière lui paraissait aussi délicate qu'extraordinaire, il l'avait communiqué à ce Pu-ki-haï qui passait pour le Socrate de l'île ; [...] Puki-haï *se doutant de l'effet qu'aurait mon discours sur l'esprit du peuple, naturellement amateur de la nouveauté, en avait*

préparé un autre pour réfuter le mien. [...] Il eut tout le succès qu'il avait espéré : il ne renversa pas mes preuves, mais il persuada à ses concitoyens la nécessité de vivre comme avaient vécu leurs Pères[19] ; chacun lui applaudit, et on lui donna le titre de *défenseur de la liberté.* Cela n'empécha pas que je ne gagnasse l'estime de tous les Adoë-Rezi et même de Pu-ki-hai. Mais le Souverain Magistrat me pria de ne jamais parler à l'avenir du Dieu que je leur avais annoncé ni de son culte, ni en public, ni en particulier : je le promis et j'ai exactement tenu ma promesse.[20]

Cependant l'opposition entre Peuple et esprits éclairés, radicalisée dans le *Theophrastus*, sans cesse rejouée et déplacée dans les mondes de Cyrano, demeure dans *La République des philosophes* extrêmement discrète. Et pour cause : ici se manifeste la croyance que l'éducation publique, prise en charge par un Etat rationnel, peut amoindrir l'écart entre Sages et non-Sages.[21] Croyance inexistante, ou frappée d'ironie, dans les fragments d'utopie que Cyrano mêle à ses voyages imaginaires.

La question qui pourra se poser au lecteur « déniaisé » d'une œuvre comme celle de Cyrano dès lors aussi celle-ci : dans quelle mesure et jusqu'à quel point faudra-t-il considérer en pareil contexte qu'une autre conception de la « nature » peut ou doit investir la place laissée vacante par les « impostures » du politique fondé sur la religion et sur ses « fables » – ainsi, une conception néo-épicurienne de la la nature, anti-finaliste et anti-théologique, indéfiniment ouverte sur un infini immanent ?

Ce type de questionnement diffus, s'il semble éloigné de l'univers politique résolument artificialiste du Séjanus de *La Mort d'Agrippine*, sollicitera à diverses reprises l'imagination du lecteur de *L'Autre Monde.* Ce sera le cas, précisément, en cette République des oiseaux, où Cyrano désigne, comme au passage, ce que pourrait être une « utopie naturaliste » où l'ordre politique trouverait son fondement ultime en une pensée de la nature régénérée, inspirée notamment par la lecture de Lucrèce, échappant aux catégories stérilisantes de l'aristotélisme scolastique et aux griffes des inquisiteurs.

Mais la place d'un discours utopique de ce type n'est désignée que comme une virtualité qu'il reviendra à la *phantasia* du lecteur de reconfigurer et d'évaluer – ou de ridiculiser par avance comme le germe d'un nouveau dogmatisme en puissance, source à son tour de nouvelles impostures. Dans un cas comme dans l'autre, l'articulation entre un nouveau savoir sur la nature et un nouvel ordre politique et social est prise dans les jeux baroques du « monde renversé » d'une part, dans la démultiplication sceptique des points de vue sur la nature d'autre part. Non que toutes les images de la nature invoquées pour fonder tel rite, telle loi, telle coutume, telle croyance fussent également présentées comme des jeux de langage sans consistance.

Si certaines renvoient manifestement à ce que j'ai pu nommer ailleurs une « nature de papier » produite par jeux de mots, métaphores réalisées, greffes de fables hétérogènes revisitées par une plume burlesque (songeons aux longues variations généalogiques des chênes de Dodone qui font songer à la nature fabulatrice, voire, à l'occasion, burlesque, de certaines lettres), d'autres ont une portée essentiellement critique éclairant ce qui dénature la nature dans les institutions terrestres, ou une fonction ouvertement heuristique en contraignant l'esprit à se mouvoir hors du vieux référentiel aristotélico-thomiste pour juger de ce qui est naturel et de ce qui ne l'est pas.[22]

Il serait donc assez naïf – et passablement anachronique – de voir là un quelconque militantisme pédagogique de Cyrano en faveur d'un idéal démocratique qui serait, *in petto*, le sien, réclamant *hic et nunc* pour tous les sujets, et en particulier pour ce « peuple » dont *L'Autre Monde* ou diverses *Lettres* (*Contre les Frondeurs, Contre les Sorciers* ...) donnent une idée si défavorable, la liberté naturelle dont les oiseaux solaires se font l'incarnation.[23]

L'éthique de la liberté s'exprime en ses fictions sur le mode de l'évasion individuelle vers des lieux apparemment plus libres, mais dont le narrateur devra s'évader encore, en une échappée sans fin.

Dès qu'une parole de « liberté » est proclamée au nom du « peuple », le démon de l'ironie refait surface, mêlant la tentation d'un discours utopique avec sa parodie grimaçante. Et quel que soit le monde envisagé, les distinctions entre le « peuple » (par nature « niais » et crédule) et le héros « déniaisé » (capable d'une liberté supérieure eu égard aux superstitions du vulgaire) se répètent et se reflètent. Comme si les « lieux communs » de la duperie politique et les formes de la croyance ne faisaient, d'un monde l'autre, que se déplacer ; comme si la croyance était un ingrédient structurellement irréductible pour tout corps socio-politique et pour toute institution – aussi « éclairés » fussent-ils ; comme si, enfin, avec la violence produite par ces mécanismes d'inclusion et d'exclusion propres aux croyances de chaque peuple, le rêve d'évasion de l'esprit fort n'en avait jamais fini.

III. Démons du scepticisme et politique de l'ironie : pouvoirs relativistes de la fiction libertine

Pareils effets de sens peuvent faire penser, à divers titre, à ce que Richard Rorty disait de la figure de l'ironiste. L'ironiste est quelqu'un qui « passe son temps à s'inquiéter de la possibilité qu'on l'ait initié dans la mauvaise tribu, qu'on lui ait appris à jouer le mauvais jeu de langage. Il craint que le processus de socialisation qui a fait de lui un être humain en lui donnant un langage lui ait donné le mauvais langage et ait fait de lui un être humain d'un mauvais genre ».[24] Figure-type de l'ironiste à laquelle s'oppose foncièrement celle du métaphysicien sur la scène de la pensée, ce dernier accusant l'ironiste d'être relativiste :

> (…) Le métaphysicien réagit à ce type de discours en le taxant de « relativisme » et en déclarant avec force que ce qui importe, ce n'est pas le langage employé, mais ce qui est *vrai.* (…) Ainsi les métaphysiciens pensent-ils qu'il y a là, données dans le monde, des essences réelles qu'il est de notre devoir de découvrir et qui sont disposées de manière à concourir à leur propre redécouverte. Ils ne croient pas que l'on puisse faire paraître quoi que ce soit bon ou mauvais en le redécrivant : ou s'ils le croient, ils le déplorent et s'accrochent à l'idée que la réalité nous aidera à résister à de pareilles séductions.[25]

La tension entre deux figures majeures, celle de l'ironie d'inspiration sceptique, celle de l'utopie d'inspiration naturaliste, fut d'une fécondité rare, et sans doute sous-estimée par l'histoire des idées. J'ai essayé de m'attarder ailleurs sur les usages intrinsèquement relativistes de l'ironie en terres libertines. Il faudrait analyser plus longuement comment, chez Cyrano, les pouvoirs de « redescription » de la fiction (au sens où Rorty utilise ce terme) se conjuguent avec ceux de l'ironie pour engendrer de nouvelles formes de relativisme.

Ce bref parcours en terres libertines peut conduire à formuler, pour finir, trois types de remarques à caractère plus général.

1) A suivre ainsi le déplacement complexe des relations entre ironie et imposture, on comprend peut-être mieux les jeux d'ombre que Cyrano fait subir en permanence au genre de l'utopie. Modèle possible, dont la tentation est souvent figurée (*via* la référence à *La Cité du Soleil* de Campanella surtout), pour être aussitôt déjouée, déstabilisée par une « ironie à l'infini ». Il n'y a pas d'utopie possible dans

les mondes renversés de Cyrano. Même en négatif. On n'y trouve aucun monde qui donne à imaginer de façon stable, par un système d'inférences cohérent, ce qui pourrait être un « monde à l'endroit », un monde ayant enfin trouvé son endroit. Par exemple, un monde vivant entièrement selon des principes dérivés de la loi de nature (telle qu'on la trouve exprimée dans le *Theophrastus redivivus*, et telle qu'elle est invoquée dans le discours des oiseaux solaires).

Paradoxe ultime de l'ironie libertine de Cyrano, qui l'éloigne de celle que l'on trouve chez Gracian ou chez Quevedo par exemple – on trouverait sans peine dans les mondes renversés de Quevedo les traces d'un « misonéisme foncier »[26] qui ne peut exister dans les univers de fiction de Cyrano. Paradoxe, si l'on ose le formuler ainsi, d'un *envers sans endroit*, du moins d'un « endroit » qui remît enfin l'axiologie sur ses pieds une fois pour toutes.[27]

Les figures du monde à l'envers de *L'Autre Monde* conspirent à souligner, par analogie et par différences, les impostures de notre monde. Mais l'ironie (et l'auto-ironie) mise en mouvement par les « imaginations pointues » de Cyrano conspirent aussi à relativiser ce *que L'Autre Monde* (Lune ou Soleil) instaure en lieu et place des impostures stigmatisées.

Les procès lunaires et solaires, hantés par la mémoire des procès de Vanini, de Théophile, et de Galilée, suggèrent que, d'un monde l'autre, avec l'imposture on n'en a jamais fini, quelles que soient les conventions adoptées, fussent-elles jugées plus « naturelles » que les nôtres ; et que les impostures, telles des Phœnix, renaissent inlassablement comme relatives à chaque monde, dès lors que celui-ci se configure, dans les paysages ontologiques de la fiction, en un ordre légitimé par nature et par raison.

2) L'ironie libertine qui s'exprime notamment dans la rhétorique des mondes renversés, mais aussi dans les indéterminations axiologiques de *La Mort d'Agrippine*, ou encore de certaines *Lettres*, participe dès lors plus largement, d'une conception de *la lecture comme « expérience de pensée » relativiste sans fin* – désignant en creux le bon lecteur, le lecteur déniaisé, comme celui qui sait jouir de la fable sans jamais y adhérer pleinement – ce qui implique, dans le corpus libertin plus qu'en tout autre, une *dialectique des rapports entre lecture et croyance* d'une extrême subtilité si on la suit d'un genre à l'autre et d'un auteur à l'autre (des comparaisons entre Sorel, Naudé, La Mothe, Cyrano, un certain La Fontaine, Fontenelle et cela jusqu'à Sade seraient riches d'enseignement à cet égard). Ce qui ne signifie pas que dans cette

expérience de pensée, toutes les croyances se valent, et que dans cette ironie une ligne de sens ne prédomine sur les autres ; que tout dépende du lecteur, libre d'infléchir le texte dans les sens les plus contradictoires et de considérer, par exemple, dans la gamme des interprétations possibles, entre les thèses les plus hétérodoxes et les interprétations les plus conformistes, il y aurait en définitive « match nul ».

Un petit détour par la théorie par la théorie littéraire et par l'*ethical theory* contemporaine, faisant le procès de l'indéterminisme en matière d'interprétation pourrait être, de ce point de vue, utile pour spécifier les types d'expérience de pensée que l'on qualifie souvent de « relativistes » – mais en quel sens ?

Martha Nussbaum, dans un intéressant chapitre de son livre récent *Love's knowledge*, intitulé « Sophistry About Conventions », s'emploie à rabattre toute une part de la théorie littéraire contemporaine (indéterministe) sur le paradigme sophistique dénoncé par Platon : de l'analyse platonicienne de l'imposture sophistique à celle du relativisme conventionnaliste d'un Stanley Fish, il y aurait plus qu'une analogie : tout un continuum de présuppositions axiologiques unirait le sophiste antique et le critique moderne, quant aux rapports entre convention et vérité.[28]

Dans ce contexte, Martha Nussbaum cite ce passage des *Nuées* d'Aristophane (1399 ff) où le fils, sortant d'un cours de sophistique, en disciple zélé de Protagoras, appliquant ses préceptes relativistes (sur le mode d'un « ma loi est aussi fondée que la tienne, et même davantage »), passe à l'acte : il battra son père au nom de cette nouvelle convention. Le plus drôle est qu'en l'occurrence le père se prête complaisamment au jeu.[29]

Pour le lecteur de Cyrano, la tentation de rapprocher pareil passage d'Aristophane de celui de *L'Autre Monde* où une convention similaire est introduite dans *Les Etats et Empires de la Lune* sera évidemment très forte. Au-delà de la question des sources et des influences (Cyrano a-t-il en tête Aristophane en imaginant cet épisode du récit lunaire ?), il serait surtout intéressant de s'interroger sur la nature des effets produits :

- effets relativistes faisant apparaître les lois, coutumes, dogmes, rites etc. comme de pures conventions (les conventions lunaires « conventionnalisent » les lois terrestres, les déplacent, leur dérobent leur fausse naturalité) ;
- effets ironiques également, affectant les fondements et le statut même de la nouvelle convention « argumentée », « prouvée »,

défendue par le jeune homme comme plus naturelle et plus juste que celles qu'elle conteste et inverse.

(Étrange lecteur que celui pour qui, quelque soit le monde, universellement et de toute éternité, il reviendrait sérieusement aux fils de battre les pères, aux jeunes de juger et de punir les vieux – dans le texte d'Aristophane, cette dimension auto-ironique du point de vue est renforcée par le fait que le père se montre d'autant plus docile qu'il reçoit l'assurance de pouvoir battre à son tour sa femme en vertu des même principes conventionnalistes !)

- Mais cette ironie à l'égard de la valeur absolue de la nouvelle convention n'invalide pas pour autant la portée critique du déplacement relativiste, la fonction d'éveil ou de réveil des argumentations paradoxales qu'il permet de mettre en œuvre, quels que puissent être leurs sophismes latents. Le lecteur pourra ironiser sans peine sur les fondements et la portée universelle d'une maxime comme « il est plus naturel et juste que les fils jugent et punissent leurs pères », il restera néanmoins sensible à l'effet critique « déniaisant » des arguments qui la sous-tendent :
  a) La maxime inverse, vénérée sur terre et ayant force de loi, n'en reste pas moins une pure convention susceptible de variations ;
  b) Les arguments latents qui fondent cette « loi » respectée sur terre sont eux-mêmes sophistiques ;
  c) Leur « naturalité » n'est qu'une imposture diffusée en nous par la puissance de la coutume ;
  d) A ces trois types d'effets critiques s'en ajoute un autre que l'on pourra juger plus spécifique de l'approche libertine et excédant en cela la topique d'un relativisme conventionnaliste de type sceptique : la dénonciation de l'imposture politique des religions en tant que telle, qui vient se joindre aux motifs burlesques de ce monde à l'envers où les fils battent les pères :

> – Mais, direz-vous, toutes les lois de notre monde font retentir avec soin ce respect qu'on doit aux vieillards. Il est vrai, mais aussi tous ceux qui ont introduit des lois ont été des vieillards qui craignaient que les jeunes ne les dépossédassent justement de l'autorité qu'ils avaient extorquée, *et ont fait comme les législateurs aux fausses religions un mystère de ce qu'ils n'ont pu prouver.* » (A.104 ; je souligne)

Bref, si l'on peut songer à des formes très anciennes de dénonciation de l'imposture contemporaines des polémiques entre Platon et les sophistes (le démon de Socrate de Cyrano ferait-il écho aux arguments de Calliclès dans le *Gorgias* ?), il est évident que l'argumentaire relativiste conventionnaliste entre ici en résonance avec toute une analytique de l'imposture politique des religions, qui en a fait l'un des *leitmotive* de la littérature des déniaisés.

3) D'où une troisième remarque, portant sur la nature du « relativisme » si souvent associé au « libertinage érudit ». Le relativisme libertin n'est pas en soi une thèse, parmi d'autres ; ni une position doctrinale ; ni une posture figée. C'est bien plutôt un *paradigme de déplacement de la pensée*, une exigence de mouvement la rendant toujours autre, toujours surprenante pour elle-même.

En bien des sens, le relativisme ainsi conçu est, par son potentiel critique, non pas « mou », mais extrêmement tranchant : par la critique radicale qu'il permet d'instaurer, il sape toute prétention à fonder durablement quoi que ce soit, fût-ce le matérialisme ; fût-ce le scepticisme lui-même. (Et que dire, en politique, du « républicanisme » que certaines lectures récentes attribuent à Cyrano ?)

C'est en ce sens que le Démon de Socrate, par exemple, devient, sous la plume de Cyrano, la figure par excellence d'une ironie fondamentalement relativiste. Non pas seulement parce que le Démon serait intrinsèquement *fait* de motifs sceptiques et nominalistes, inscrits dans la fabrique malicieuse de certaines de ses argumentations, où l'on peut lire autant de variations cyraniennes sur Sextus Empiricus relus par Pierre Gassendi à l'occasion de sa polémique anti-scolastique. Mais aussi, plus profondément, parce que le Démon de Socrate, en tant que personnage conceptuel, a une façon éminemment relative d'habiter les mondes de la fiction : toujours ici et toujours ailleurs, le Démon « fréquente », au passage, des philosophies, bien plus qu'il ne les habite :

> J'ai fréquenté pareillement en France La Mothe Le Vayer et Gassendi : ce second est un homme qui écrit autant en philosophe que ce premier y vit. J'y ai connu aussi quantité d'autres gens, que votre siècle traite de divins, mais je n'ai rien trouvé en eux que beaucoup de babil et beaucoup d'orgueil. (A. 58–9)

Le verbe « fréquenter », dans la présentation que le Démon de Socrate fait de lui-même au narrateur, a toute son importance. Il renvoie à une série de figures et de pensées qui ressemble à un habit d'Arlequin, mais dont l'aspect presque bouffon ne peut dissimuler la dominante hétérodoxe qui les réunit à des titres divers : celle d'une *libertas philosophandi* polymorphe et ubiquitaire, dont le commun dénominateur est une méfiance foncière à l'égard du vulgaire. Mais « fréquenter » suggère aussi, en l'occurrence, une position particulière, étrangère à toute adhésion doctrinale : l'accord du Démon avec tel ou tel, ne peut être que ponctuel et transitoire.

Cet accord s'auto-désigne avec une ironie dont il est difficile de mesurer le « poids » exact : il peut impliquer, du reste, aux yeux d'un déniaisé, de fort mauvaises « fréquentations », du côté des fables, des chimères, des impostures. Et que l'on ait pu voir dans le Démon de Socrate un travestissement imaginaire de Pierre Gassendi (hébergé par l'Hôte, Lhuillier, dans une scénographie où la figure impétueuse du Fils de l'Hôte correspondrait, elle, à celle de Chapelle) ne donne que plus de sel à cette ironie.

Or, il est remarquable que le verbe « fréquenter », en cette image de la pensée démonique qui nous est proposée par Cyrano, va de pair avec un certain lexique de la « souplesse » :

> Un jour, entre autres, j'apparus à Cardan comme il étudiait ; je l'instruisais de quantité de choses, et en récompense il me promit qu'il témoignerait à la postérité de qui il tenait les miracles qu'il s'attendait d'écrire. J'y vis Agrippa, l'abbé Tritème, le docteur Faust, La Brosse, César, et une certaine cabale de jeunes gens que le vulgaire a connus sous le nom de chevaliers de la Rose-Croix, à qui j'enseignai *quantité de souplesses et de secrets naturels,* qui sans doute les auront fait passer pour de grands magiciens. Je connus aussi Campanella ; ce fut moi qui l'avisai, pendant qu'il était à l'Inquisition de Rome, de styler son visage et son corps aux grimaces et aux postures ordinaires de ceux dont il avait besoin de connaître l'intérieur, afin d'exciter chez soi par une même assiette les pensées que cette même situation avait appelées dans ses adversaires, parce qu'ainsi il ménagerait mieux leur âme quand il la connaîtrait. (A. 57. Je souligne)

« Quantité de souplesses » ... Loin, très loin assurément du « relativisme » que nous qualifierions de « mou » dans notre langage ordinaire, le relativisme « démonique » ainsi pratiqué se présente comme un jeu de rôles inaccessible au vulgaire, et comme un exercice de pensée d'une invraisemblable plasticité, capable de mimer de l'intérieur toutes les « postures », jusqu'à celles de l'imposteur se faisant passer pour « grand magicien » : au-delà des aspects *défensifs* de cette « politique de la grimace » que le Démon enseigne à Campanella pour affronter la persécution inquisitoriale,[30] on sera sensible au *caractère prodigieusement heuristique et inventif* de l'ironie ainsi conçue, dont l'esthétique de la simulation me fait irrésistiblement songer à un texte presque inconnu, mais fort beau en son genre : l'article « Souplesse » que l'on trouve dans les *Sorberiana* :

> SOUPLESSE: Les Badaux qui voient les tours de passe-passe, les jeux de cartes, et les autres adresses surprenantes des Bâteleurs croient que le Diable s'en mêle, et qu'ils ne peuvent pas concevoir qu'il n'y ait en tout cela que de la souplesse, et qu'un prompt mouvement de la main. Je ne pouvois me persuader en mon enfance, que les Danseurs de corde n'eussent fait pacte avec le Démon, et non seulement je trouvois des femmeletes qui tomboient dans mon sens ; mais si l'on eût recueilli les avis de toute la ville, le mien eût prévalu sur celui des personnes bien sensées. On aime naturellement la Dogmatique, et le Peuple qui est toujours fort ignorant, ne veut point être Pyrrhonien. Il aime mieux rendre quelque raison, vaille que vaille, que d'avouer qu'il ne l'a pas encore trouvée, et le Diable est un agent qu'il emploie en toutes occasions, quoi qu'il ne lui donne aucune idée de la manière en laquelle se font les choses dont l'on ignore les veritables causes. Les personnes sages n'en usent pas ainsi, et aiment mieux dire franchement qu'ils ne sçavent par particulierement comment les choses arrivent, que d'en rendre des raisons frivoles, ou dont ils connoissent la fausseté. Je crains que ce procédé des Badaux ne se puisse apliquer à quelques Philosophes, qui veulent rendre raison de toutes les choses, en appellant à leur secours les Métaphysiques.[31]

NOTES

1 Voir notamment, sur ces questions, *Libertinage et politique au temps de la monarchie absolue*, *Littératures classiques*, n°55, sous la direction de J.-Ch. Darmon et G. Molinié, été 2005.

2 René Pintard, *Le libertinage érudit dans la première moitié du XVIIème siècle*, Paris, 1943, p. 560.

3 « J'ai fréquenté pareillement en France La Mothe Le Vayer et Gassendi : ce second est un homme qui écrit autant en philosophe que ce premier y vit. J'y ai connu aussi quantité d'autres gens, que votre siècle traite de divins, mais je n'ai rien trouvé en eux que beaucoup de babil et beaucoup d'orgueil. » (Cyrano de Bergerac, *Les Etats et Empires de la Lune et du Soleil*, éd. M. Alcover, Champion classique, 2002, p. 58–9 ; Les références à cette

édition seront par la suite désignées dans le corps du texte par A., suivi du numéro de page.) Le thème de la philosophie comme manière de vivre est ici associée à par le Démon au sceptique La Mothe le Vayer, sans que l'opposition entre écrire en philosophe, à la manière de Gassendi, et vivre en philosophe, à la manière de La Mothe, soit réellement éclairée. Ces affinités libertines et sceptiques se manifestent aussi de manière fort explicite, sur un terrain proprement politique, dans la Lettre « Contre les Frondeurs », où La Mothe le Vayer et de Naudé sont loués pour leur soutien à Mazarin.

4 Sur ces aspects, voir J.-Ch. Darmon, *Le Songe libertin : Cyrano de Bergerac d'un monde à l'autre*, Klincksieck, p. 13 et suivantes.

5 Cette conception « libertine » de la « générosité » intervenait sous la plume de La Mothe dans un contexte où, sous les « caprices » des « fantaisies » énoncées, s'affirme une plume raison souveraine, ne devant de compte qu'à elle-même, "affranchie", "indépendante" – d'où son affinité pour les "paradoxes" – ... et l'énonciation de "veritez ou vraisemblances naturelles" (le présupposé étant que la divulgation de la vérité – ou de la vraisemblance naturelle – est toujours risquée, toujours dangereuse) : « Pour le moins suis-je seur que vous me trouverez hors les termes serviles de ceux qui ne taillent leur plume que par commandement, ou par interest, et pour en profiter ; incapables par ce seul dessein de rien faire qui puisse durer, et indignes d'une plus grande recompense que celle qu'ils se sont proposez. *Ma main est si genereuse, ou si libertine, qu'elle ne peut suivre que le seul caprice de mes fantaisies* ; et cela avec une licence si independante et si affranchie, qu'elle fait gloire de n'avoir d'autre visee, qu'une naïve recherche des veritez ou vraisemblances naturelles, ny plus important objet, que ma propre satisfaction, qui se trouve dans cet innocent entretien. » La Mothe Le Vayer, "Lettre de l'autheur" (*Dialogues faits à l'imitation des Anciens, par Orasius Tubero* (1632 ?), rééd. Arthème Fayard, 1988, p. 15. Je souligne).

6 Cf. La Mothe le Vayer. *Dialogues faits à l'imitation des anciens. De l'opiniâtreté.* Ed. Fayard, 1988, p. 386.

7 Voir par exemple Pierre Gassendi, *Exercitationes adversus Aristotileos*, édition et traduction B. Rochot, Vrin, p. 456, «[…] mais c'était au contraire la coutume chez les locriens et dans l'île de Cos d'emporter les morts au milieu de la joie et d'organiser un festin. […] Les gens de Cos, quand ils se sentaient parvenus à l'extrême vieillesse, avaient coutume de s'inviter comme pour un festin solennel ou un sacrifice, et alors de boire la ciguë, couronnés de fleurs ».

8 Sur cet usage traditionnel des oppositions mutuelles et réciproques, cf. Sextus Empiricus, in *Les Sceptiques grecs*, traduits par J.P. Dumont, PUF, p. 73 et suivantes.

9 « Fortifier et amplifier le dernier précepte de notre Décalogue, je veux dire le dernier des dix moyens de notre inestimable Epochè », tel était le souci de La Mothe Le Vayer dans *Le Banquet sceptique* et tant d'autres textes. Voir notamment Joseph Beaude : « Amplifier le dixième trope ou la différence culturelle comme argument sceptique », *Recherches sur le XVIIème siècle*, V, Editions du CNRS, 1982, p. 21–9.

10 On trouvera le commentaire gassendien des modes sceptiques au seuil des développements importants qu'il consacre aux signes et aux critères de la vérité. Voir *Syntagma Philosophicum*, première partie (« Logique »), livre 2 (« De la fin de la logique »), chapitre 3 (*Modi Epoches Scepticorum circa Veritatem, ipsiusque Criteria*). Rappelons le rôle essentiel de Gassendi dans la diffusion savante non seulement de l'épicurisme, mais aussi du scepticisme, comme le rappellera notamment Pierre Bayle dans plusieurs articles de son *Dictionnaire*.

11 Il serait intéressant de comparer les effets de cet usage des tropes sceptiques combinés entre eux sur des modes fort inventifs par Cyrano au sein d'un univers de fiction avec ceux qu'en fait La Mothe Le Vayer dans ses dialogues ; usages privilégiant le 10ème trope abordés notamment par Joseph Beaude dans l'article mentionné précédemment. Mais lorsqu'à la fin de son propos l'auteur esquisse cette comparaison, c'est pour minorer aussitôt (et de manière à mon sens très contestable) les effets critiques d'une fiction comme celle de Cyrano : « (…) Peut-être les inventions d'autres peuples ou d'autres mondes, comme dans les Etats et Empires de la Lune et du Soleil de Cyrano sont-ils à mettre en relation avec cette amplification du dixième trope. Pourquoi au fond ne pas augmenter encore la variété constatée par une variété imaginaire, pourquoi ne pas créer par imagination une humanité tout à fait autre. (…) Mais il apparaît vite à la lecture que les différences inventées ne sont pas aussi grandes que les différences réelles. Cela tient au fait que les différences inventées ne le sont qu'à partir de notre propre système culturel. L'autre monde n'est alors que notre monde renversé, régi par une raison dissemblable mais comparable à la nôtre, et la « sélénité » inverse seulement notre propre humanité. Les autres mondes ne permettent en somme qu'une critique de notre monde ». (Article cité, p. 27–8.)

12 Sextus Empiricus, H.P., I, p. 94–5. Traduction de Jean-Paul Dumont, dans *Les sceptiques grecs*, Paris, PUF, 1966, 3ème éd., 1992.

13 On trouve par exemple chez Sextus : « Chez nous l'adultère est défendu, alors que chez les Massagètes la coutume se montre à son égard indifférente, ainsi que le relate Eudoxe de Cnide, dans le premier livre de son *Voyage autour du monde* ». *Les sceptiques grecs*, éd. citée, p. 74.

14 Voir à ce sujet *Cyrano de Bergerac and the polemics of modernity*, en particulier p. 192 et suivantes.

15 Gabriel Naudé, *Considérations politiques sur les Coups d'Etat, Paris*, Les Editions de Paris, 1988, p. 161 et 163–4. Pour une mise en perspective de ce texte dans l'histoire de la problématique des Trois Imposteurs, voir, par exemple, Françoise Charles-Daubert, *Les libertins érudits en France au XVIIème siècle*, Paris, PUF, 1998, p. 87 et suivantes.

16 A l'occasion d'une enquête collective récente consacrée relations entre libertinage et politique au temps de la monarchie absolue, on a pu mesurer, une fois de plus, la richesse et la plasticité extrêmes du motif de l'imposture, qui ne se cesse de se déplacer et de se transformer dans bien des textes de philosophie et de fiction. Cf. *Libertinage et politique au temps de la monarchie absolue, Littératures classiques*, n°55, sous la direction de J.-Ch. Darmon et G. Molinié, été 2005, 307 p.

17 J-P. Cavaillé, « Imposture politique des religions et sagesse libertine », *op.cit.*, p. 28

18 Sur le thème du « *Leges mentiuntur et fingunt* » et son histoire depuis les utilisations libertines d'Averroès, je renvoie à la belle et riche étude de Gianni Paganini, « *Legislatores* » et « *impostores* ». Le *Theophrastus redivivus* et la thèse de l'imposture des religions au milieu du XVIIe siècle ». *Sources antiques de l'irréligion moderne*. Ed.par D. Foucauld et J.-P. Cavaillé, Collection de l'E.C.R.I.T, n°6, Toulouse, 2001, p. 181 et suivantes.

19 Fontenelle, *Histoire des Ajaoïens*, édition citée, p. 66 ; je souligne.

20 *Ibid.*, p. 66–7.

21 Il serait d'un grand intérêt de mettre en regard certaines propositions de *La République des philosophes* avec les principes que formulera Fontenelle ultérieurement, notamment dans les dix-neuf fragments de sa République. « Ici encore, commente Jean Dagen, on se projette au-delà du machiavélisme libertin. On ne saurait davantage apercevoir dans ces fragments l'esquisse d'une utopie. Ils représentent une manière directe et logique de faire pièce aux institutions de la monarchie française, auxquelles ils opposent une image inversée. (...) Pour en connaître la portée véritable, il faudrait comparer ces dispositions non seulement aux conceptions d'un La Mothe Le Vayer, mais aussi à celles du « Petit Concile ». Les analyses et recommandations de Fontenelle l'éloignent autant de la résignation à l'irrationnel que de l'abandon à l'idéalisme ; il préfère à l'idéologie, mystique de la loi, credo naturaliste ou caution religieuse, l'idée d'une amélioration par des mesures concrètes d'un système dont la nocivité est historiquement vérifiée et dont les défauts connus signalent les réformes indispensables. Appliqué au politique, vers lequel il conduit logiquement,

le rationalisme critique engendre optimisme relatif, exempt de tout historicisme, porté par la certitude de calculer toujours mieux les lois d'un équilibre politique, mais tributaire des conditions historiques. » (Jean Dagen, « Fontenelle et l'invention du politique », *Libertinage et politique au temps de la monarchie absolue, Littératures classiques*, n°55, sous la direction de J.-Ch. Darmon et G. Molinié, 2005, p. 141–2.)

22 Sur ces trois types d'images de la nature (que j'ai proposé de caractériser comme « images-télescope » (dévoilant un nouveau savoir sur l'ailleurs), « images-miroirs » (donnant à penser de manière critique sur l'ici) et images « coups de dés » (affichant leur caractère ludique, léger, voire gratuit, sous le signe de la pointe, des jeux intertextuels etc.) interféant constamment dans les voyages imaginaires de Cyrano, Cf. mon étude « Cyrano de Bergerac et les images de la nature », dont divers éléments sont repris dans le chapitre IV de *Philosophie épicurienne et Littérature.*

23 Les paradoxes du monde renversé en ce qui concerne le choix et les pouvoirs du roi, dans la République des oiseaux, très sévèrement contrôlé par le « peuple » qui le choisit faible et pacifique, le juge et le remplace régulièrement peuvent faire songer à une extrapolation ironique dérivant de certains arguments libertins que consignera l'auteur du *Theophrastus.* Ainsi, on pourrait rapprocher ces épisodes du *Soleil* avec le passage suivant : avant que les vices ne s'insinuent et que la royauté ne tourne à la tyrannie, « les premiers rois étaient plus esclaves que maîtres de leurs sujets, puisque les sujets avaient tous les pouvoirs sur eux et eux, en revanche, aucuns sur leurs sujets. Solin (chapitre XXV) rapporte qu'on trouve chez les habitants des îles Hébrides pareil régime politique, qui serait souhaitable pour l'ensemble des nations (si d'aventure un régime politique est souhaitable). Leur roi ne possède rien en propre ; tout appartient à tout le monde ; il est contraint à l'équité par certaines lois et, pour que l'ambition ne le détourne pas du vrai, il apprend la justice par la pauvreté, en tant que personnage dépourvu de biens personnels et entretenu sur le denier public. [...] Dans le choix du roi, ce n'est pas la noblesse qui prévaut, mais le suffrage recueilli. [...] Les Scythes observent à l'égard de leur roi une coutume plus cruelle mais plus sûre, comme le rapporte Pomponus Mela. Ils choisissent les rois par une élection, en présence du peuple, les tiennent enchaînés et sous la plus étroite surveillance, et quand les rois se sont rendu coupables de faute à cause d'un mauvais commandement, ils les condamnent à être privés de nourriture pendant toute une journée. Enfin, chez toutes les nations qui autrefois ont mis un roi à leur tête, les sujets étaient beaucoup plus heureux que les rois eux-mêmes, auxquels ils refusèrent toujours d'exercer librement et selon leur gré un pouvoir héréditaire, pour éviter

que, installés au faîte de ce genre de dignité, ils n'aient l'insolence de s'exalter au-dessus des autres et n'oublient tout à fait l'égalité naturelle. » (Ed.cit., p. 305–6.)

24 Richard Rorty, *Contingence, ironie et solidarité*, traduit de l'américain par Pierre-Emmanuel Dauzat, Armand Colin, p. 113.

25 R. Rorty, *op.cit.*, p. 113–14.

26 Voir notamment Augustin Redondo, « Monde à l'envers et conscience de crise chez Gracian » (in *L'image du monde renversé et ses représentations littéraires et para-litttéraires de la fin du XVIème siècle au milieu du XVIIème*, Paris, Vrin, 1979, p. 83–97). Après avoir montré les liens entre la thématique du monde renversé et la conscience d'une crise de la société espagnole déplorée par Gracian, d'une société « en proie à la confusion » où « chacun veut monter », l'auteur remarque que Gracian « ne peut admettre ces nouveautés. Il veut maintenir les structures qui ont fait la structure passée de son pays ; il veut retrouver l'ordre préexistant derrière ce désordre, mettre à l'endroit ce monde à l'envers. » Michèle Gendreau-Massaloux, dans une autre étude du même volume, montre comment « les écrits quévédiens sont souvent marqués d'une tension qui dévoile un misonéisme sans espoir. C'est lui qui fonde le renversement du Songe de l'Enfer : fait implicitement partie d'un monde à l'envers tout ce qui empêche le monde du Vrai, de l'Ordre, de la Loi, de rester figé, immuable, éternel. » (« Le Gaucher selon Quevedo », *op.cit.*, p. 80.)

27 Il revient à un personnage d'un autre grand genre subverti par Cyrano, la comédie, d'ironiser, dans *Le Pédant Joué*, sur le geste naïf qui consisterait renverser ce qui est « à l'envers » pour que tout aille enfin pour le mieux. Au pédant Granger qui pense que le monde « s'en va renverser », son valet Paquier répond : « Tant mieux : car autrefois j'entendais dire la même chose, que tout était renversé. Or, si l'on renverse aujourd'hui ce qui était renversé, c'est le remettre en son sens. » Cyrano de Bergerac, *Le Pédant Joué*, acte I, sc.2. *Œuvres complètes*, Tome III : *Théâtre*. Textes établis et commentés par André Blanc. Paris, Champion, 2001. Cf. à ce propos J. Lafond, article cité, p. 139.

28 M. Nussbaum, *Love's Knowledge: Essays on Philosophy and Literature*. Oxford University Press, Oxford, New York, Toronto, 1990, p. 220–9.

29 Voici un passage caractéristique de cette séquence : "[...]STREPSIADE. Mais nulle part la loi n'exige qu'un père subisse ce traitement.

PHIDIPPIDE. N'était-il donc pas homme, comme toi et moi, celui qui a, le premier, établi cette loi, dont la parole a convaincu les anciens ? Pourquoi donc me serait-il moins permis, à moi, d'établir une loi nouvelle qui permît aux fils de battre leurs pères à leur tour ? Tous les coups que nous avons reçus avant l'établissement de cette loi, nous vous en faisons grâce et nous vous accordons d'avoir été impunément battus. Mais vois les coqs et les autres animaux, comme ils se défendent contre leurs pères. Cependant en quoi diffèrent-ils de nous, sinon qu'ils ne rédigent pas de décrets ?[…] ». (Trad. Eugène Talbot.)

30 Cf. à ce propos J.-Ch. Darmon, "Rhétorique du songe, fictions heuristiques et politique de la « grimace » : Cyrano sur les traces de Quevedo, de Kepler et de Campanella." *Cyrano de Bergerac. Les États et Empires de la Lune et du Soleil. Littératures classiques,* numéro 53, Octobre 2004, p. 173–208.

31 *Sorberiana, ou bons mots, rencontres agréables, pensées judicieuses, et observations curieuses de M.Sorbière,* A Paris, Chez la Veuve Marbre-Cramoisy, M.DCCXXII, article « Souplesse », p. 205–6.

chapter five

Obeying the Laws and Customs of the Country: Living in Disorder and Barbarity. The Powerlessness of Political Skepticism According to the *Discours sceptiques* (1657) of Samuel Sorbière

SYLVIA GIOCANTI

As the title suggests, the *Discours sceptiques* of Samuel Sorbière follows in the tradition of skepticism, more precisely in the libertine conception of the tradition, by its composition and its presentation of texts.[1] Alétophile sustains paradoxes, indulges in "Saturnine" opinion for the sake of exercise, makes use of the mobility proper to the skeptical spirit, and of the practice of retraction (palinode) in order to foil the opponent's or the censor's thrusts.[2]

Presented as entertainment, the argumentation is not, however, a purely rhetorical game. It is, rather, an opportunity to test one's judgment by measuring it against the criteria of likelihood, by practising the "art of conferring" borrowed from Montaigne, in which one may take pleasure in being refuted (60). Therefore, even though Alétophile shrouds his subversive comments in skeptical language, it is quite possible that the positions discussed bear genuine philosophical substance.

I will attempt to show that political skepticism is implicitly criticized in *Discours I*, and explicitly subverted in *Discours II* and *III*: in his *Discours sceptiques*, Sorbière proposes his thoughts on obedience to the political order in skeptical terms as a self-regulating disorder, based on the observation of its practical consequences: the "barbarity" that reigns in the European monarchies, and especially in France (*Discours I*). Barbarity, redefined according to skeptical relativism, as applied by Montaigne in the chapter "Of Cannibals," runs counter to the skeptical conception of politics, since it serves to justify despotism in *Discours II* and since the "supposed wisdom of our skeptic" (94), and the ethics of flexibility that it requires (99), are transformed into the unlimited practice of villainy in *Discours III.*

Yet, to arrive at this conclusion, it was first necessary to consider that Montaigne's exhortation – itself derived from Sextus Empiricus's tenth mode – to obey the laws and customs of the country, implies acceptance of a fundamental disorder, the disastrous result of which is the ineffectiveness of political decrees and thus the inability to achieve their aims, in particular the keeping of public and private peace.

Since it is from a critique of the political order as disorder that Sorbière proposes in his *Discours sceptiques* to bring the skepticism of Montaigne's *Essais* to its ultimate conclusions – in order to contradict him – we will begin with a review of *Discours I* (*Discours sceptique à Philotime*).

The Skeptical Political Order Criticized as the Reign of Disorder

In the introduction to her edition of *Discours sceptiques,* Sophie Gouverneur insists that, for Sorbière, obedience to the political order is necessary and that in this sense he agrees with Hobbes and the tradition of Reason of State, according to which man is subject to passions that must be kept in check. We might add that he thus inherits from the skeptical tradition, which holds that, given the instability of passion and reason, we must find a framework larger than ourselves, the framework of laws and customs, capable of combating the forces of deregulation by wielding rules and regulations.[3]

The manner of imposing order is, however, not the same from one tradition to another: according to Hobbes, it is possible to produce a rational political order provided that it is backed by force. In the concept of Reason of State, political order necessarily relies on ruse and violence. For a skeptic like Montaigne, order, though arbitrary (because it is not based on a distinction between justice and injustice) and fortuitous, does not necessarily require the use of force since it is all the better accepted if it is born of customary behaviour established over time or, perhaps, if it is part of a movement for self-organization immanent to the society. This skeptical conception of order can be clarified from Montaigne's metaphor of men thrown together in a sack by chance, with no particular design (by nature nor by reason), all of whom must find their place, based on their respective dispositions: "The society of men is maintained and held together at what price whatsoever; in what condition soever they are placed, they will still close and stick together, moving and heaping upon themselves; as uneven bodies, that, shuffled together without order, find of themselves means to unite and settle, often better than they could have been disposed by art."[4] In Renato Lessa's analysis, the fortuitous way in which societies police themselves is in fact one of the main distinctive features of political skepticism from Montaigne to Bayle.[5] This is the key difference from Sorbière, who does not share Montaigne's theory of self-regulation of societies by custom, and for whom the arbitrary nature of the order established by laws and customs that one must obey points to nothing more than disorder. For Sorbière, disorder no longer designates, as it does for Montaigne, the arbitrariness of order, which basically remains fortuitous, but is nonetheless regulated by "plis accoutumés" [acquired habits].[6] Disorder refers rather to that which resists all forms of order, and reflects the powerlessness of the law to exert any influence on behaviour.

The example of this is Paris, capital of France and, by metonymy, the expression of all France: rather than producing a fortuitous gathering of people who manage to find a mutual agreement, though nothing predisposes them to such an agreement, the result is a "tumultuous gathering of people" (62), and "drunks rising and stumbling into each other" (77). It is also quite likely that Sorbière was thinking of Montaigne's praise of Paris in skeptical terms ("great and incomparable in variety and diversity of commodities, the glory of France"), when he insists on the incommodities the capital inflicts on us.[7] A product of chance, Paris is unfavourably compared with more orderly cities where we find the result of some reasoning. Worse still, unlike other European cities, Paris gives the impression that we are dealing with "several cities, one on top of the other" (62), i.e., cities that overlap without having a clear place in relation to each other.

Sorbière replaces Montaigne's metaphor of self-organization of the society of men thrown together in the same sack with the metaphor of the vain and therefore incommodious superposition of the different parts of the city, taking up in his own words the famous Cartesian metaphor of the two models for building a city.[8] If Paris is not conceived of as built or governed with all the civility and reason we imagine or observe elsewhere (69), it is because Sorbière has in mind a model of order for cities that is quite rigid, drawn along geometric lines, rather than the cities built haphazardly according to the historical model advanced by the skeptical tradition from Montaigne to Bayle.[9] By socio-political extension of this Cartesian architectural criterion, Sorbière believes that, insofar as political "order" is built haphazardly, it is unlikely that it can be bent to a principle of order, a posteriori, and it is necessarily disorderly, irregular, and therefore a failure.[10]

Equating irregularity with imperfection evokes the skeptical experience of the world while refuting the charms the skeptics found in it, which Sorbière mocks: "There is little doubt that the greatest inequality, the most inconvenient and ordinary incommodities, disorder and all that I call barbarity concur into making Paris the sweetest and the most charming place to stay in the world."[11]

True, the skeptical position is defended, or at least represented in the text, in the form of objections, recalling several chapters of *The Essays.*[12] The variety or contrariness of reality that the skeptic experiences, and which indeed constitutes his experience of the world itself, entertains the senses, feeds the imagination, and prevents boredom, just as an obstacle enhances pleasure through the difficulty of overcoming it (70). But these suggestions, in keeping with skeptical aesthetics and ethics, serve in the composition of Sorbière's *Discours sceptiques* as a counterpoint; they in no way temper the author's critique of the skeptical conception of political reality. Sorbière analyses (76) the disorder reigning in France in terms of irregularity – an irregularity identified as a political confusion made all the more regrettable in that it cannot be corrected – and he finds no charm in the variety and dissimilarity of the world. And while irregularity – the target of his critique – is deliberately associated by Sorbière with adjectives that, in Montaigne's writings, reflect the skeptical experience of the world's disorder ("unequal" and "disorderly," "misshapen," "indistinct," "monstrous," "discordant," "mismatched"), they now disqualify Paris and the French political reality.[13]

The skeptical experience of the world, analysed since Sextus Empiricus in terms of *anomalia,* i.e., irregularity that cannot be reduced to unity (which prevents decision and forces a suspension of judgment), is associated by Sorbière with the experience of *anomie,* the absence of political laws, which cannot be applied to concrete reality nor have any effect on it.[14]

This may surprise us since, in skepticism, the experience of *anomalia* does not prevent the organization of political reality into certain forms, based on customs. "Necessity reconciles and brings men together; and this accidental connexion afterwards forms itself into laws."[15] For Montaigne in particular, laws formalize customs, no matter how contingent, so, contrary to Descartes's assertion at the beginning of part II of *Discours de la méthode,* they are as valid as anything that more rational principles might offer. Rational principles are not only unfit for policing a society, they raise the risk that the lawmaker will view his personal opinion as the universal truth. Of course, for a skeptic, customs are discordant from one society to another. For Sextus Empiricus, therefore, listing the various customs is the same thing as listing socio-political irregularities, as he demonstrates, more clearly than in other modes, in his 10th mode (devoted to laws, customs, beliefs, myths, and opinions).[16] It is nonetheless true that they provide a form of regularity in a given society, which may then be transformed into law. *Anomalia* is compatible with laws, unlike *anomie*, which, put in the skeptical context of Montaigne's *Essais*, reflects the powerlessness of laws to shape and to police social reality. This powerlessness is the sign of an interventionist desire to uselessly multiply laws, in an attempt to encompass the infinite diversity of human actions, rather than to wait patiently for the history of a people to prescribe its practices and enshrine them.[17]

In his *Discours sceptiques*, when Sorbière puts *anomalia* in the same category as *anomie*, he is challenging the skeptical tradition in a provocative manner in order to mark a break with it. In particular, he implies that political skepticism is capable of supporting barbarity, which is not the opposite of civilization but, rather, a product of it. True, it is not new to contrast barbarity with order, since, in Furetière's dictionary, the word "police" – "the laws, order and conduct to be followed for the subsistence and maintenance of states and societies" – is given as opposite to barbarity. What is newer is the critique of skepticism in the name of the political meaning of "barbarity," knowing that the definition of barbarity as "mitigated" also evokes in the *Discours sceptiques* (as, indeed, in the definition of "barbarity" in Furetière's dictionary) this moral asset of the skeptical critique: the relativism applied to that concept by Montaigne in his chapter "Of Cannibals." Montaigne's relativism on the matter of barbarity from the perspective of civilization is turned against itself on another level, since that which leads to barbarity is a certain skeptical conception of political order as being compatible with disorder.

To clarify this point, we must come back to what Montaigne and Sorbière, respectively, mean by *obeying* the laws and customs of the country, by showing that the skeptical socio-political model of self-regulation is "corrected" by the requirement of unconditional obedience that eliminates private interest, with despotism presenting itself as a remedy to widespread disobedience, which, in corrupted monarchies, destroys the public interest.

Sorbière's Subversion of Skeptical Obedience to Laws and Customs of the Country: No Distinction between Private and Public

In the skeptical tradition of Montaigne, obedience to laws and customs is not unconditional, precisely because it must first be feasible for a given community, i.e., it must be possible to obey them and, second, because obedience must protect, or at least not endanger, the community. As concerns the first point (the feasibility of obedience), as indicated in the reference to the place where one lives in the wording of the precept, this comes down to saying that laws are applicable only if they reflect pre-existing mores and derive from local customs that have become mandatory rules.[18] Laws must be obeyed to the extent that they are likely to be accepted – as we note in the title of chapter I, 23: "Of custom and that we should not easily change a law *received.*" They are not made acceptable by judgment but because they already correspond to customary practice and because there is tacit social consent, so that people obey of their own accord. According to A. Tournon, Montaigne does not view the constraint of laws in terms of absolute submission, but as a discipline acquired through the trust of a social group in its mores and the autonomy gained thanks to its mores.[19] This is made possible by a customary conception of the law, which itself implies a conception of custom as a regulatory power, all the more efficient if it is not perceived as a constraint.

Sorbière does not hold with irrational conception of training based on custom considered by Montaigne as a flexible force that enables a society to police and regulate itself; therefore, he challenges the idea that a skeptical vision of the world could make it acceptable (disorder as a product of variety) by associating it with political powerlessness: that which escapes the law cannot be considered as coexisting with a certain order, but as ruining that order or preventing it from becoming effective. Without acknowledgment of the effective existence of a regulation by custom, in a world where reason never triumphs over passions, but tends rather to propagate them by finding reasons to obey them, obedience, when it is not disavowed out of pique (as in *Discours III*), must then be unconditional, absolute, to overcome disorder, as Sorbière recommends in *Discours I.* Obedience cannot be obtained by consent, but it must be imposed by force in the context of an absolutist regime of the despotic type, something which the skeptical justification for obeying laws and customs of the country does not demand, since it is assent obtained by common practice, the compliance of laws with mores, which gives obedience its legitimacy.

We could of course object that a tendency towards a stiffening in the relationship between the people and the law is perceptible in Montaigne's *Essais*, in reference to the historical context of recording customs in the sixteenth century that imparted an obligatory character tending to demand obedience in an authoritarian way, even though the religious conflicts had made the already very hierarchical society downright repressive.[20] However, this did not give obedience a sacred character leading to a religious obedience that would prevent people from daring to object to injustice. On the contrary, Montaigne's political skepticism has the singularity of recommending both obedience and a detachment from customary manners of judging, which prevent an assessment of the obedience we owe to laws:

> There is nothing so much, nor so grossly, nor so ordinarily faulty, as the laws. Whoever obeys them because they are just, does not justly obey them as he ought. Our French laws, by their irregularity and deformity, do in some sort lend a helping hand to the disorder and corruption which is manifest in their dispensation and execution. The command is so perplexed and inconstant, that it in some sort excuses both disobedience and defect in the interpretation, the administration and the observation of it.[21]

The laws are so deficient (poorly made and incomprehensible) that they foster disorder and corruption, so that we are, in a way, excusable for not obeying. We must therefore obey, says the skeptic, but, when the laws are unacceptable, we must be ready to denounce them and be tolerant towards those who disobey them, and even demand a form of independence in the application of the laws and penal justice.

Sorbière thus proceeds as if he were taking political skepticism to its logical conclusion, after excising both the decisive role Montaigne's skepticism assigns to custom in the incorporation of laws and the prerogatives of judgment: if we must submit to order, and if obedience is no longer seen as the condition of freedom, to call for obedience means calling for servility without reserve, all the way to despotism (*Discours II*). Conversely, since the laws are not the expression of customary practice, when they become impracticable because inaccessible or contrary to our personal interest, Sorbière sees no other solution than to secretly avoid them by steering around them to our private ends (*Discours III*). But it is remarkable that he refers to Montaigne's critique of excessive precepts that foster corruption in the moral domain (90), and subverts the ethic of flexibility found therein (98–9). He does not use the political argument whereby laws may not comply with the practices of a society and are unsuited to its customs, an argument we find in the *Essays*, for example, at the end of I, 23 (122), while Montaigne is ready to admit that laws make allowances for circumstance and, because of this, we no longer obey them, we do not resist innovation, if the body politic is defective.[22] Precisely, Sorbière differs from the skeptical politics of Montaigne in so far as, faced with the disorder of the body politic and the perversion of mores, it is never a question of disobeying the laws in order to adapt them to new public practice. The only alternative to absolute obedience (*Discours II*) is a return to one's own personal interest (*Discours III*). Be it rhetorical or sincere, the immorality of *Discours III*, like the authoritarianism of *Discours II*, is a disavowal of skeptical politics, which in the *Essays* espoused a construction based on custom, leading the individual to articulate properly the public and the private.

The Subversion of the Skeptical Relationship between Public and Private (*Discours II and III*)

It is by nuancing the rather conventional remarks on political skepticism, and especially the relationship between the private and the public, that were supposedly launched in *The Essays*, that we are able to gain new insight into the skeptical inheritance of Sorbière in his *Discours sceptiques.* In Montaigne's skepticism, custom is what shapes our lives and allows us to construct ourselves simultaneously as private and social beings. Because of this social construction of the self, we are all likely to cooperate with our own subjugation and with that of others, and so we must not only obey the laws and customs, we must fight against subjugation out of a duty to independence.[23] Accepted customs and laws can be understood not only as a constraint to which we must submit, but also as a condition for the construction of individual freedom, the forms of subjugation (all social conditions) being the origin of claims for freedom. To the extent that the individual constructs himselfas a private person away from the public space, the distance he maintains in his "backroom" ("arrière-boutique") allows him not to break away from relations with others, but rather to reflect on them and to create the critical distance necessary for the public role we play not to be assimilated with the private person. In this way, "being above the vices of one's trade," as Montaigne advocates, does not mean the refusal to participate in political life in order to remain one's own master. As a matter of fact, to become one's own master, one must commit oneself to others and contribute to civil society. Consequently, "being above the vices of one's trade" means preserving a space for judging political life by distinguishing between what is detrimental to others and oneself, without sacrificing personal interest to public interest, nor public interest to personal interest.[24]

Blind obedience prescribed by Sorbière in the *Discours sceptique II*, whereby individuals sacrifice themselves and their relations to the community, is explicitly excluded by the political skepticism of Montaigne: "Let us not fear to believe [...] that the common concern ought not to require all things of all, against private interest, [...] and that all things are not lawful to an honest man for the service of his prince, the laws, or the general quarrel."[25] But what Sorbière prescribes conversely in his *Discours sceptique III*, that individuals avoid obedience and pursue their own interests to the detriment of others, is equally excluded. For Montaigne, not everything is permitted, not even against enemies, and the public good may reasonably require that we risk our lives, if we deem it necessary, private interest not being in itself superior to the public interest.[26]

Sorbière subverts the skepticism of Montaigne because unconditional submission of the people to the law, or its contrary, i.e., the total liberty of the private individual (who could evade the law through ruse), would imply the elimination of a separation between the private (space of freedom and frankness) and the public (space of submission and cunning), which Montaigne supposedly introduced in favour of the private.[27] Sorbière subverts skepticism because he does not take into account what is implied in the skeptical construction of social ties by *linking* (and not separating) public and private spheres. Consequently, he preserves neither of them, and indeed eliminates both in turn.

Even in the *Discours sceptique III*, the idea is no longer to transpose the maxims of Reason of State, whose value is public, to the private Montaignian sphere.[28] That would imply a cleavage between the two spheres, quite frequent of course in libertine thought – being the condition in which the wise man gives the appearance of obeying the laws and customs of the country, but disobeys them in private – but non-existent in Montaigne's skepticism. The idea is to eliminate the distinction between the two spheres, the linking of which was, in the skeptical tradition, the condition for socializing the individual, making his existence as a social being his entire existence. It is in fact a return of the individual to an asocial and apolitical freedom that imposes no commitment, and a total submission to the ruler whereby private interests are quashed and relationships between individuals prevented, or a situation such as described in *Discours III*, where individuals reduce everything to their private sphere.[29]

According to the skeptic, we must therefore obey the laws and customs on the twofold condition that this obedience damages neither our personal interest nor the public interest. These interests are distinct for Montaigne – contrary to Cicero, who believed that individual interests must be identified with general interests – but they are impossible to satisfy separately, or in a relationship of opposition, because the individual is bound to others by ties of honesty, including in the public exercise of his trade.[30] "The knot that binds me by the laws of courtesy pinches me more than that of legal constraint."[31] And in public negotiations, Montaigne says he prefers losing a deal to breaking his word, whether betraying a prince in favour of an individual or betraying an individual in favour of a prince.[32]

An "honnête homme" [gentleman; well-bred man] is indeed, therefore, according to the skepticism of Montaigne, an "homme mêlé" [composite man].[33] When Sorbière suggests, with explicit reference to chapter I, 26 (167), that in the exercise of this flexibility, the desire to do the right thing is more important than the ability to do evil (which the body must acquire but which the soul must know how to reject), he is referring to a comment by Montaigne on education that has little importance on the socio-political level since, for Montaigne, one may very well collectively wish evil without causing damage to the social order, since the social order does not depend on the moral order.[34] Sorbière thus sets aside the political aspect of the "compound man": "the mind of various stages,"[35] the virtue "of many wavings," which in the *Essays* enhance flexibility in both public and private life, as an aptitude for adapting to others, rather than "to the times," a Machiavellian impersonal expression significantly favoured by Sorbière (98).[36] Sorbière neglects the qualities which, according to Montaigne, allow men to open up to others, with the dual meaning of turning to them and speaking to them frankly. So, whereas for Montaigne, "living for others" was the condition for "living for oneself," the skeptical ethic of flexibility and the idea of serving oneself are subverted by Sorbière to mean a withdrawal into oneself (97).[37]

More generally, we may conclude that Sorbière subverts the skeptical exhortation to obey the laws and customs of the country in that it goes hand in hand in Montaigne with a duty to independence that maintains the link between private and public (from the backroom). But Sorbière nonetheless breaks away from the libertine tradition of his time, which separates and subordinates the public sphere to the private sphere and bases the tranquillity and liberty of the country's subjects on duplicity. By eliminating the distinction between private and public spheres in two different manners, first by sacrificing the private sphere to the public sphere in *Discours II*, and then by sacrificing the public sphere to the private sphere in *Discours III*, he paradoxically praises two forms of servile attitude: submission to the despot in *Discours II*, broad suspicion of the subjects in *Discours III*.

This makes us wonder if there is not a subversive intention in his sanctification of obedience to the laws and customs, which then leads to the abandonment either of all public values, or of all private values.

Disobey the Laws and Customs of the Country in Favour of Naturalism?

It is hard not to see the irony when reading this declaration on Oriental despotism: "All subjects deem themselves honoured by the title of slaves to their king, and would never disobey him" (85). Does such servility of a people, supposed to represent an improvement over European monarchies, not refer back to the unreasonable acceptance of the socio-political order? The despotic regime indeed corresponds – as Sorbière mentions in passing (76–7) – to what Aristotle, in *The Politics* (III, 14 [1285]), classes among the hereditary tyrannical monarchies that are only suitable to barbarians, servile people who do not see that the laws they obey do them disservice and that, therefore, they should not feel bound by them. We note that in classical culture, which is not disavowed by Montaigne, there is "no social bond between the tyrant and ourselves," which thus legitimizes his assassination.[38] Aristotle adds that one of the means used by the tyrant to stay in power consists of spreading mistrust among the subjects, debasing their souls, making them incapable of handling public affairs, knowing that tyranny can be toppled if certain citizens build a mutual trust.[39]

What is notable throughout the *Discours sceptiques* is that man is characterized by the baseness of his soul (99), treachery, the lack of resolve and selflessness (74), the need to stay on his guard (87), and that in *Discours III* especially, as in Aristotle, men have the distrustful characteristics of tyrannized subjects. This is quite the opposite of what Montaigne's skepticism recommends: trust, based on word of honour (to be distinguished from language or reason[40]), constitutes the social tie. Even in a society of wicked men, trust among members of society must be preserved. "Skeptical wisdom" (to which Sorbière refers [94]) is based on trust among the subjects in their effort to serve society, and rules out cowardice, betrayal, and villainy. Far from imagining the elimination of social relations, as in Sorbière, this skeptical wisdom presupposes them and takes its strength from them against the surreptitious thought that accompanies the breakdown of social ties.

When individuals do nothing but simulate and dissimulate, widespread distrust provokes a return to a state in which each person pursues his natural liberty. This is the situation assumed by Sorbière in *Discours III*: man fending for himself becomes not only asocial but apolitical.[41] We might then ask if Sorbière's twisting of the skeptical conception (based on custom and word of honour) of socio-political ties aims in fact to prove that the social tie is unthinkable, that the individual, because of his egoism, is incapable of obeying the law – be it the law of reason or the law of state – unless forced to do so. This comes down to supporting, against skepticism, that man is an animal doomed to three forms of barbarity: the disorder of civilisation (the "mitigated" barbarity of European monarchies in *Discours I*), the violence of absolute state power (the barbarity of tyrannical despotism in *Discours II*), and the anarchic disorder specific to civil war (the barbarity of savages who eat each other in *Discours III*). In the first case, the skeptical outlook on order is turned against skepticism; in the second case, the skeptical meaning of obeying the customs and laws is turned against skepticism; in the third case, the skeptical meaning of the private sphere is subverted.

But we need not conclude on this pessimistic hypothesis, to the extent that – as Sophie Gouverneur rightly claims in her introduction to the *Discours sceptiques* – the tacitly restored natural liberty is not systematically assigned only to the state of war by Sorbière, but also to the state of beasts or "the savages of America" (Canadians and Brazilians) who follow the laws of nature, and therefore do not harm each other, but help each other, even living in a state of happiness (*Discours II*, 85). This allows us to propose another hypothesis as to the interpretation of the *Discours sceptiques*: on the ruins of political order, by referring to regulation by natural laws, Sorbière is replacing a skeptical model of self-regulation by a naturalist model, in which liberty is based on natural rights, very loosely inspired (from a naturalist idealization) by Montaigne's "Of Cannibals."

Obeying the laws and customs of the country does not therefore make any real political sense to Sorbière, after the destruction of the socio-political ties resulting from the subversion of Montaigne's skepticism. The polemical critique of the skeptical exhortation may have served as a pretext to make a clean sweep and rethink new forms of society, based perhaps, as Sophie Gouverneur suggests, on a naturalist framework in which the exercise of political reason would be redefined very differently from the skeptical approach.

NOTES

1 In his *Dialogues faits à l'imitation des Anciens* (Paris: Fayard, 1988), 365, La Mothe Le Vayer defines the skeptical game as consisting of adopting different opinions, one after the other.
2 Sorbière, *Discours sceptiques*, ed. S. Gouverneur (Paris: Honoré Champion, 2002), 89, 97, and 102, 63, and 66, respectively. Hereafter cited in parentheses in the text.
3 Hobbes himself inherited ideas from the skeptical tradition. See the article by G. Paganini in this volume.
4 Montaigne, *The Essays*, trad. William Hazlitt (London, 1842), book III, chapter 9, 442. Hereafter cited as *The Essays.*
5 Renato Lessa, "Montaigne's and Bayle's Variations: The Philosophical Form of Skepticism in Politics," in *Skepticism in the Modern Age*, ed. J.R. Maia Neto, G. Paganini, and J.C. Laursen (Leiden: Brill, 2009), 225: "an image of social life through which a myriad of local and circumstantial behaviours cluster together into a global outcome not foreseen by any of the parties."
6 *The Essays*, 296: "For that which our reason advises us to, as the most likely, is generally for every one to obey the laws of his country [...] and by that, what would it say, but that our duty has no other rule but what is accidental?" About "acquired habits," cf. III, 9, p. 441.
7 *The Essays*, III, 9, p. 972.
8 Descartes, *Discourse on the Method of Rightly Conducting the Reason*, part II [Edinburgh, 1850], 12.
9 Montaigne, *The Essays*, II, 12, p. 583; Bayle, *Oeuvres Diverses*, vol. III: *Pensées diverses sur la comète*, Trévoux, 1727 (reprints 1964–9), Hildesheim, G. Olms, 262, 158b. See the analysis by F. Brahami, in *Le Travail du scepticisme* (Paris: PUF, 2001), 78–9, and that of Renato Lessa, "Montaigne's and Bayle's Variations," 224.
10 Descartes continues his comparison of two manners of building cities (one geometric, the other historic) with this political comparison: "In the same way I fancied that those nations which, starting from a semi-barbarous state and advancing to civilisation by slow degrees, have had their laws successively determined, and, as it were, forced upon them simply by

experience of the hurtfulness of particular crimes and disputes, would by this process come to be possessed of less perfect institutions than those which, from the commencement of their association as communities, have followed the appointments of some wise legislator" (*Discourse on the Method of Rightly Conducting the Reason* [Edinburgh, 1850], 55).

11 71. Cf. also 59: "I had the intention of saying in praise of Paris, that she seemed to me the most charming among barbaric cities."

12 For example, I, 38 (*That we laugh and cry for the same thing*) or II, 15 (*That our desires are augmented by difficulties*).

13 See respectively pp. 71, 62, 64, 70, 78, and p. 70: "One never sees in it the same thing twice."

14 *Discours sceptiques*, I, 64: "It is quite useless for us to have books of rules where all things are perfectly ordered, far from being a testimony to our politeness and humanity, they show our irresistible inclination towards the vices which we have intended to correct." Cf. Sextus Empiricus, *Esquisses pyrrhoniennes*, I, 12 (29), Montaigne, *The Essays*, III, 13, p. 1065.

15 Montaigne, *The Essays*, III, 9, p. 956, translation Hazlitt, p. 442.

16 *Esquisses pyrrhoniennes*, III, 24 (198) and I, 163, respectively.

17 *The Essays*, III, 13, p. 1066, trans. Hazlitt, 419: "What have our legislators got by culling out a hundred thousand particular cases, and annexing to these a hundred thousand laws? This number holds no manner of proportion with the infinite diversity of human actions."

18 I, 23, p. 118, Hazlitt, 46: "For it is the rule of rules, and the general law of laws, that every one observe *those of the place wherein he lives*" (author's italics).

19 See A. Tournon, *Routes par ailleurs, le nouveau langage des Essais* (Geneva: Slatkine, 2006), 223: "Montaigne applies to what he calls 'laws' the antiquity of customs and their 'credi'" (a term which replaces that of authority, and assumes trust rather than submission). (...) In the eyes of the jurists of the time, how long a practice has been in existence precisely secures collective assent." And 226: "Because he considers civic discipline according to the custom model, Montaigne is drawn to conclude that ancient rules must be kept intact, and that one 'should not easily change a law received.'"

20 Tournon, *Routes par ailleurs*, 232 and 248.

21 III, 12, p. 1072, Hazlitt, 497. In this sense, we cannot agree with Stéphan Geonget, who, by not distinguishing between obedience to religious laws and civil laws, believes that obedience to laws according to Montaigne is absolute. See *La Notion de perplexité à la Renaissance* (Geneva: Droz, 2006), 296: "There is no obedience but unconditional obedience."

22 Here we must nuance what is too often called the conservatism of Montaigne, an opinion that L. Bianchi supports when he claims in "Absolutism and

despotism in Samuel Sorbière: Notes on Skepticism and Politics," in Maia Neto, Paganini, and Laursen, *Skepticism in the Modern Age*, 206) that the separation between politics and ethics is expressed "with formal support for the monarchy and the resigned acceptance of established power (...)." Not only, as J.C Laursen rightly points out (*The Politics of Skepticism in the Ancients, Montaigne, Hume and Kant* (Leiden: Brill, 1992), chapt. 4, "Montaigne and the politics of skepticism," 127), is this supposed conservatism never based on nature or reason, but is it not wielded against the reign of fortune, since it is subject to it. True, in II, 17, p. 655, Montaigne, against the instability of things, expresses the wish to "put something under to stay the wheel and keep it where it is"; but it is because the regime in question is not out of touch with the mores or events. If, however, it has done its time, one mustn't oppose the passing to a new order of things (see I, 23, p. 122). Hence, Montaigne's support for the monarchy is not unshakeable: it depends on the circumstances.

23 See III, 9, p. 968, trans. Hazlitt, 448: "I have nothing mine but myself; and yet the possession is in part defective and borrowed."

24 About being above the vices of one's trade, see III, 10, p. 1012, trans. Hazlitt, 495: "An honest man is not accountable for the vice or the folly of his business, and yet ought not to refuse to take the calling upon him; 'tis the custom of his country, and there is money to be got by it; a man must live by the world, and make the best of it, such as it is. But the judgment of an emperor ought to be above his empire." It does not signify the refusal to participate in political life. The wise man must withdraw to his backroom, not to flee the world but to preserve "his power to judge freely of things" (I, 23, p. 118). This is how we should interpret what Montaigne writes about kings: "all reverence and submission is due to them, except that of the understanding" (III, 9, p. 935; trans. 433). In her introduction to *Discours sceptiques* by Sorbière, S. Gouverneur maintains, with reference to III, 10, 1004: "to obey without taking part is to remain one's own master, while political activity removes us from ourselves and thus enslaves us" (p. 47).

25 III, 1, p. 802, trans. Hazlitt, 396.

26 III, 1, p. 802: " Let us not fear to believe that there is something unlawful, even against an enemy."

III, 10, p 1007, trans. Hazlitt, 466: "I would not that men should refuse, in the employments they take upon them, their attention, pains, their eloquence, and their sweat and blood, in time of need."

27 Lorenzo Bianchi, in "Absolutism and despotism in Samuel Sorbière," claims that "Sorbière's political path thus differs from that of other skeptics such as Montaigne or Charron, where the separation of politics from ethics expresses

itself in the search for personal wisdom and private equilibrium" (205–6). D. Taranto also claims that Montaigne's skepticism and his conception of the self make him see private reason as that which "removes all ability to coincide with the public." See "La métamorphose du privé," *Libertinage et philosophie au VIIe siècle, 3 – Le public et le privé,* 1999, 50. This thesis of the separation between the private and public spheres being introduced for the first time in *The Essays,* perhaps came from a reading of Hugo Friedrich, *Montaigne* (Paris: Gallimard, 1968), 195. On the relation between the public and private spheres in early modern philosophy, see A.M. Battista, "Appunti sulla crisi della morale comunitaria nel Seicento francese," *Il pensiero Politico* II (1969): 187–223; D. Gobetti, "Privato/Pubblico," *Teoria Politica* no. 3 (1986): 3–20; D. Goodman "Public Sphere and Private life: towards a synthesis of current historiographical approaches to the Old Regime," *History and Theory* 31 (1992): 1–20. For a more general discussion, see J. Habermas *The Structural Transformation of the Public Sphere: An Inquiry into a Category of Bourgeois Society* (Neuwied, 1962; English translation Cambridge, MA: MIT, 1989).

28 S. Gouverneur interprets Sorbière's position this way, in Sorbière, *Discours sceptiques,* 43: "How can one retain natural liberty within an absolutist State? The answer lies in the distinction between the private sphere and the public sphere. (...) In his third skeptical discourse, Sorbière will suggest a private use of the reason of State; the individual making his own the State's techniques of deceit in order to protect himself from the impingement of power." In fact, there is no longer a political power in the situation described by Sorbière, but a struggle between individuals who have become apolitical.

29 Indeed, as Cicero says in *De officiis* (III, 6–26) – to which Sorbière refers on two occasions to refute him, in *Discours sceptique III*: "By bringing everything back to oneself, one dissolves the community of men."

30 Ibid.: "One must have but one goal: to make one's particular interest at one with the general interest."

31 III, 9, p. 966, Hazlitt, 447.

32 III, 1, p. 791.

33 III, 9, p. 986, Hazlitt, 457: "Tis truly said that a well-bred man is of a compound education."

34 See *Discours sceptique* III, p. 99: "Wisdom must make us pliable and limber enough for all sorts of moves [...] An honest man must know how to do all things, including the bad ones, but he must find pleasure only in the good ones, says Michel de Montaigne, after asking the Ambassador of the King to Switzerland how often he had gotten drunk for His Majesty's service." Sorbière is referring precisely to the *The Essays* on pp. 166–7 of I,

26. See also *Essays*, III, 9, Hazlitt, 443: "King Philip mustered up a rabble of the most wicked and incorrigible rascals he could pick out, and put them all together into a city he had built for that purpose, which bore their name; I believe that they, even from vices themselves, erected a government amongst them, and a commodious and just society. "

35 III, 3, p. 821, trans. Hazlitt, 379: "I should commend a mind of various stages, that knows both how to extend and to slacken itself; that finds itself at ease in all conditions of fortune; that can discourse with a neighbour about building, hunting, or any little contest betwixt him and another; and that can chat with a carpenter or a gardener with pleasure."

36 III, 9, p. 991, trans. Hazlitt, 459: "the virtue that is assigned to the affairs of the world is a virtue of many wavings, corners, and elbows, to join and adapt itself to human frailty; mixed and artificial, not straight, clean, constant, nor purely innocent."

37 III, 10, p. 1003, trans. Hazlitt, 405: "Tis my opinion that a man should lend himself to others, and only give himself to himself," but "Who does not in some sort live to others, does not live much to himself" (p. 1007).

38 Montaigne does not condemn tyrannicide under any circumstances. It is even a duty to assassinate the tyrant if he endangers the survival of the society. On this topic, see S. Geonget, *La Notion de perplexité*, 295. Cf. Cicero, *Des devoirs*, III, VI, 32.

39 *Politics*, V, 11, 1314.

40 Cicero, *Des devoirs*, I, XVI, 50: "The social tie of this society (of the human kind) is reason and the language."

41 98: "In the State we think of, there is a kind of natural liberty, tacitly restored." Cf. also 94.

chapter six

Bernard Mandeville's Skeptical Political Philosophy

RUI BERTRAND ROMÃO

Bernard Mandeville (1670–1733), one of the most famous and controversial pamphleteers, satirists, and thinkers of his time, was seriously opposed by most of his contemporaries, including George Berkeley, George Bluet, and Francis Hutcheson, and only posthumously recognized as a remarkable political and moral philosopher by, among others, David Hume and Adam Smith.[1] After a period of relative oblivion generally corresponding to the nineteenth century, Frederick Kaye generated a Mandeville revival. His critical edition of *The Fable of the Bees*, first published in 1924, remains today a landmark of Mandeville studies.[2] In the second half of the twentieth century Mandeville's work and theories became the focus of special attention from economists and sociologists who proposed him as a forerunner of conceptions developed only much later.[3]

At present, most scholars accept that late Renaissance and early modern philosophers like Montaigne and Charron, as well as the French moralists of the seventeenth century, including the "erudite libertines"[4] and the "divines" attached to Port-Royal (like Pascal and Nicole) and figures related to the Dutch Enlightenment (such as Spinoza and Pierre Bayle), exerted some kind of influence over Mandeville.[5] We can thus find among this group of influences in the background of his thought a considerable number of philosophers related to the early modern skeptical tradition. Early on, two years after the publication in 1723 of the much-enlarged and successful third edition of *The Fable of the Bees*, Bluet stressed Mandeville's links to the ancient Pyrrhonians as well as to Montaigne and French thinkers influenced by them: "From this *Pyrrho*,

Scepticks were called Pyrrhonians, or Pyrrhonists; and from hence that treatise of *Sextus Empiricus* [...] had its name; in one part of which he endeavors to overturn the Certainty of Right and Wrong, Virtue and Vice, by collecting a great many monstrous Opinions and Customs of People contrary to the common ones. From hence, or rather from *Montaigne* [...], who has borrowed it from hence, has our Author again borrowed what he has given us to the same Purpose, and in the Pursuit of the same laudable End."[6] Bluet here clearly declares that Mandeville belongs to the skeptical tradition, at least regarding ethical issues. For him, this tradition, conferring an overwhelming importance on the notion of custom and obfuscating the differences between values, leads to a radical moral relativism. In spite of its biased nature and its oversimplifications, this testimony has the merit of showing a contemporary author correctly identifying an important part of Mandeville's "borrowings" and seeing them as tied to a specific philosophical tradition.

Two centuries later, Kaye explicitly called Mandeville a Pyrrhonist, though what he meant by this designation does not necessarily coincide with what the majority of scholars now understand as such.[7] He emphasized the link between Mandeville's anti-rationalism and a similar element in the skeptical tradition and asserted that "[...] the Sceptics were among the intellectual grandparents of Mandeville."[8] More recently, other commentators have related Mandeville either directly or indirectly (especially through his kinship with the foremost undeniably skeptical philosophers like Pierre Bayle, for instance) to skepticism. Notwithstanding this, there still seems to be no consensus about the exact nature of the relation of his thought to skepticism. In the present chapter I am trying to clarify this relation, focusing on some crucial elements of skepticism that permeate his philosophy in general, and his moral and political philosophy in particular.

Before entering into the core of my subject, I shall present a few preliminary remarks on the hypothesis that there was a scission between two kinds of skepticism precipitated by the Cartesian attack on traditional skepticism. In spite of its heterogeneity and its historical discontinuity since antiquity, some common traits can be used to identify a skeptical philosophical tradition. Among them are (1) that it is a philosophy that uses certain kinds of argumentation, (2) that it claims an attitude of searching for truth, (3) that it stresses antitheses and antilogies, and (4) that it possesses practical aims, seeking a sort of wisdom of which the main element is *ataraxia*. Traditional skepticism thus seems not only livable but propitious to wise living.

What we may claim to be the most relevant branch of the early modern skeptical tradition in moral and political philosophy arguably derives from the reinvention of Pyrrhonism carried out by Montaigne.[9] The Cartesian skeptical tradition inaugurated what Anglophone philosophers commonly call modern skepticism, basically concerning epistemological and strictly theoretical issues. In fact, we may consider Descartes's approach to skepticism as aimed at dissociating the skeptical posture from any practical standpoint, turning it into an unlivable challenge both to common sense and to the findings and theories of mainstream philosophy. When he created his version of skepticism, based upon an instrumental reduction of *skepsis* to universal doubt, capable of becoming hyperbolic, he did not conceive it as a philosophical attitude but as a problem that carried along with itself its own overcoming. Such a conception of *skepsis* as a purely hypothetical and absurd stance cannot be properly understood except as originating in the context of a refusal of any previous kind of skepticism. Descartes can thus be considered to have really belonged to an ancient tradition parallel to skepticism: the anti-skeptical tradition.[10] As a consequence of this way of fabricating a version of skepticism that allowed him to deal with doubt and incertitude by eradicating them completely by rational means, Descartes eventually provoked the aforementioned splitting in the early modern skeptical tradition between two kinds of skepticism, which often crossed paths with each other: one was a theoretical skepticism conceived in the moulds fashioned by Descartes, and the other was a livable and moderate skepticism.

Thus, the early modern thinkers who continued to consider the skeptical posture compatible with everyday life and common sense focused primarily upon political and moral issues and, generally speaking, avoided classifying themselves as skeptics. They felt free to accept Descartes's claims against theoretical nihilistic doubt, while characterizing this doubt as a preposterous position not seriously adopted by any philosopher. Most of them did not eschew dealing with epistemological and other theoretical problems, but they always dealt with them from a point of view related to a moderate form of skepticism.[11] Before Descartes, one could find those two types of skepticism joined together, in several versions, as a livable and somewhat coherent albeit unorthodox philosophy.[12] Jonathan Barnes and Myles Burnyeat maintained in celebrated articles a different view, claiming a separation, since antiquity, between two kinds of Pyrrhonian skepticism: a rustic Pyrrhonism and an urbane Pyrrhonism. For them, Montaigne is a typical representative of the latter subspecies of Pyrrhonism in the sixteenth century.[13] This artificial distinction, based upon a somewhat free interpretation of observations made by Galen, a thinker who was an adversary both of the Pyrrhonist school of philosophy and of the empirical school of medicine, is one that only became perfectly conceivable after Descartes. Barnes and Burnyeat also seem to misunderstand Montaigne's reinvention of ancient Pyrrhonism. Indeed, they tend to present it as a forerunner in many aspects of the conception of skepticism imposed by Descartes.[14]

The two most important arguments of the adversaries of ancient skepticism were the *apraxia* and the *self-refutation* claims, both of them also held against many other schools of philosophy. The first type of argument asserts the impossibility of living strictly according to the tenets of the professed philosophy. The other kind refutes a specific philosophy as self-contradictory. One can easily see that anti-skeptics, in using these two arguments or others derived from them, followed a strategy of *reductio ad absurdum* of the position the skeptics put forward. The Pyrrhonists, in distinct periods, seem to have replied to their adversaries in different ways. As to the first objection, we do not know for sure the exact reply given to the adversaries by Pyrrho of Elis himself and by his direct disciples. We can, however, interpret the earliest, most complete reliable testimony on Pyrrho's philosophy, that of Aristocles cited by Eusebius, as providing a kind of program of action, albeit an original one. Later, Sextus explicitly addresses the issue in the *Outlines of Pyrrhonism*, namely, when he presents the fourfold criterion of the Skeptics: "Thus, attending to what is apparent, we live in accordance with everyday observances, without holding opinions – for we are not able to be utterly inactive."[15] This observation shows Sextus's unequivocal concern in stressing that Pyrrhonists avoid inactivity. Regarding the second objection, we may say generally that avoiding self-contradiction is a central concern to them.

In fact, all skeptical traditions may be envisaged as trying to find a way out of the reach of the attacks of their adversaries.[16] And curiously, the ancient skeptics, as well as late Renaissance figures like Montaigne, Charron, or Sanches, conceived of skepticism as a therapeutic philosophy and used against their opponents some form of those two same objections. Nonetheless, the adversaries of several sorts of skepticism systematically have kept using variants of these two arguments throughout the ages since antiquity and up until the present. For instance, contemporary philosophers like Jules Vuillemin and Martha Nussbaum refer to them when criticizing ancient pyrrhonism.[17] Descartes, with his instrumental version of *skepsis*, implicitly combined these two kinds of arguments, adding to them a new nihilistic dimension.

This reading of ours can be somehow conciliated with Richard Popkin's brilliant account of Descartes's struggle with skepticism, in spite of involving a slight revision of certain elements of it. Popkin emphasized that the French philosopher "saw that only by admitting the full and total impact of complete Pyrrhonism, could one be prepared"[18] to overcome the *crise pyrrhonienne* of his time.[19] Putting the stress on Descartes as part of a tradition of philosophy antagonistic to skepticism from the start, as I am here doing, carries as a consequence that he could not really admit a "complete Pyrrhonism,"[20] but, instead of it, only a distorted one associated with his invented hyperbolic doubt. The anti-skeptics always took Pyrrhonism as having to be overcome by an exaggeration of their main elements, such as *epoché*, *metriopatheia*, *isostheneia*, and *arrepsia.* Cartesian skepticism, as we have above suggested, seems to stem from this anti-skeptical tradition. Descartes's innovation resides essentially in conflating arguments used as leading to *epoché* and in exaggerating them to the extreme point of transforming them into a *nihilistic* stance, which could be employed against itself as part of a methodical procedure designed to provide absolute certainties upon which a dogmatic building of philosophy and science could be erected. Thus, in a way, he tried to take advantage of the Pyrrhonian use of *peritrope.*[21] This manoeuvre was eventually self-defeating, as Popkin demonstrated in the chapter of *The History of Scepticism* titled "Descartes, sceptique malgré lui."[22] Nevertheless, Descartes's way of perceiving and trying to defeat skepticism from an anti-skeptical trend was effective in influencing the later skeptical tradition, obliging it to transform itself. An aspect of that transformation consisted in the aforementioned splitting of skepticism; another is that skeptical philosophers afterwards had to accept some of Descartes's claims.[23]

In Mandeville's philosophy two families of thought related to ancient skepticism converge. One, as mentioned above, corresponds to the early modern currents of thought that stemmed from the reinvention of Pyrrhonism by Montaigne and other thinkers who followed his trail, independently from being directly or indirectly influenced by him. We can precisely name among them two philosophers whose reading recognizably marked Mandeville's thought: La Rochefoucauld and Pierre Bayle. But one should not ignore Montaigne himself as having exerted an important and direct influence on Mandeville.

The other family of skeptical thought to which Bernard Mandeville belongs is the medical one.[24] The specific medical outlook that he endorsed, which he himself described as akin to that of the sect of the "Empiricks," is striking in Mandeville's moral and political theory.[25]

The criss-crossings of skepticism and medicine have been so frequent throughout history since the inception of philosophical skepticism in Ancient Greece till now that they cannot but be considered important. Mandeville outstandingly illustrates in the early modern age this relation between skepticism and medicine, of which the most remarkable example in antiquity is none other than the philosopher and doctor to whom we owe the most complete account of ancient Pyrrhonism, Sextus Empiricus, a leader of the school of the Skeptics or Pyrrhonists in the second century A.D., and also a physician related to the empirical school of medicine. In what we can classify as Mandeville's most ambitious and important work besides *The Fable of the Bees*, titled *A Treatise of the Hypochondriack and Hysterick Passions [...]*,[26] he calls the character that admittedly represents his own views Phylopirio, a direct reference to his empiricism: "In these Dialogues I have done the same as Seneca did in his *Octavia*, and brought my self upon the Stage; with this difference, That he kept his own Name, and I changed mine for that of *Philopirio*, a Lover of Experience, which I shall always profess to be."[27] In this book he amply shows his profound knowledge of the history of medicine, his engrained anti-rationalism, and his distrust of speculative theories such as hypotheses made up to plausibly explain the symptoms of a distemper and not to examine its real causes,[28] as opposed to knowledge by "Use, Practice and Experience."[29]

The influence of Cartesianism in Mandeville's writings strikes its readers as extremely strong.[30] The enormous impact of this influence, especially marked in strictly medical sections, should not however hinder us from envisaging Mandeville's independence towards it.

Concerning explicitly epistemological passages (which are rare in Mandeville's medical and other works), we may compare the Dutch physician's different ways of expressing his endorsement of the first two truths of Descartes's metaphysics in the 1711 edition of *A Treatise of the Hypochondriack and Hysterick Passions [...]* and in the 1730 enlarged and corrected edition of it published under the title *A Treatise of the Hypochondriack and Hysterick Diseases in Three Dialogues*.[31] In the 1711 edition Mandeville alludes to Descartes's *cogito* in a rapid and matter-of-fact way: "The Metaphysical Principle of Monsieur Descartes, *Cogito, ergo sum*, is a very good one, because it is the first Truth, of which a Man can well be sure, and we all agree, some few Atheists excepted, that matter it self can never think, how elaborately fine soever it may be supposed."[32] The passage correspondent to this relatively brief reference is much more important in the enlarged version:

> But then it is to be consider'd, that human Knowledge can only come *a posteriori.* You'll give me Leave to trace it from the Beginning; and I'll be content to start with Monsieur *Descartes,* and at my first setting out to doubt of every thing. Now as Doubting must always imply Thinking, and it is impossible that I should perceive the first without being confident of the latter, I take his Metaphysical Principle, [...] *Cogito, ergo sum,* to be a very Just one; because it is the first Truth of which a Man be well sure: and if from our being conscious that we think, we may not falsely conclude that we exist, then we can be certain of nothing.[33]

Whereas the first edition, taking an apparently anti-materialistic perspective, just declares the Cartesian *cogito* a Metaphysical Principle, the 1730 edition situates it in an epistemological context that seems to follow Descartes more to the letter while keeping distance from his philosophy by the implicit conciliation it prompts of it with a moderate empiricist and skeptical philosophy. We have to stress that if Mandeville seems to adopt the *cogito* as well as the consequences immediately drawn from it by Descartes as metaphysical principles, he just does it because those principles enable men to have certitude enough upon which they may cautiously ground their own observations derived from experience. Furthermore this endorsement should be articulated with Mandeville's insistence on the imperfection of our scientific knowledge and on "the greater use of observation than reasoning in Physicks,"[34] an insistence extensively confirmed in *The Fable of the Bees.*

Most likely Mandeville's medical training (like that of so many skeptics), associated with his experience as a citizen involved in political affairs in Rotterdam, also contributed to the shaping of the pessimistic anthropological conceptions he developed. For the Dutch author, human nature is flawed and imperfect. On his account, man cannot be considered naturally sociable. Human will and human reason are deemed incapable of achieving what we want, mere chance being far more potent than both of them. Indeed, in his moral and political writings Mandeville intertwines anthropological pessimism with moderate anti-rationalism just as he did concerning medical issues. According to his views, reason, though subject to the superior force of the passions, does play a role of some importance as such in guiding human behaviour.

The core of Mandevillian philosophy seems to be essentially ambiguous and ambivalent and for that reason particularly open to varied and new readings.[35] His contemporaries, such as Hutcheson, already highlighted this characteristic. It can be understood as very aptly prolonging the early modern skeptical tradition and Pyrrhonian procedures of opposing notions, theories, opinions, facts, and points of view.[36]

Another trait characterizing the early modern skeptical tradition in moral and political philosophy that we find in Mandeville has to do with literary form. Even when they do not expressly follow Montaigne's sophisticated and quite difficult to imitate example, most authors linked to that tradition tend to write in a fashion compatible with an unorthodox, open-ended, and unsystematic doctrine. Though Mandeville's relatively coherent and compact philosophy presents some systematic features, we can hardly call it a system comparable to Hobbes's, Locke's, Spinoza's, or Leibniz's. It is true that he more than once uses the term "system" to refer to his doctrine, but I take it that he does so by analogy with the philosophies he opposes and that he simply means by that term a cogent philosophical whole centred on one or two principles and not really an organic set of coordinated theories. Anyhow, he adopts for the exposition of his thoughts forms that are clearly preferred by skeptical philosophers: small, relatively digressive essays, commentaries, and dialogues, even when he calls a collection of them a treatise. We can include among those forms his verses constituting the original *Grumbling Hive.* The open-ended character of the ever-expanding *Fable of the Bees,* built on that initial poem, augmented from edition to edition like Montaigne's *Essais* or Bayle's *Dictionnaire,* forms a clear example of the skeptical inconclusiveness related to *zetesis* and to the ceaseless quest for truth. If in some places, such as, for instance, "Part Two" of the last edition of *The Fable of the Bees,* he occasionally adopts a less skeptical tone, even there, the frequent humorous touches, the judicious use of irony, and a quite ingenious way of using dialogue devices prevent the work from showing a dogmatic style.

Although, as we have seen above, some of Mandeville's contemporaries highlighted the kinship of his thought with Montaigne's, and many present-day scholars confer importance to the relation between the two authors, it seems to me that even their accounts underestimate too much that relation. The very subtitle of *The Fable of the Bees* is based upon a correlation of private and public, vice and virtue, which bears some resemblance to remarks in the *Essays.* Mandeville could not perhaps make central to his philosophy the distinction between self-liking and self-love without having studied Montaigne's passages on *philautia*, on self-knowledge, and on the self-preservation instinct in men and animals.

We have also to remark that some important features of Montaigne's Pyrrhonism can be found in Mandeville's philosophy. We may list, besides those already mentioned, the following ones among others: the combination of a pessimistic anti-anthropocentric *Weltanschauung* with moderate anti-rationalistic conceptions and arguments; an unorthodox form of political conservatism; a mitigated epistemological skepticism; diffidence towards unattainable ideals such as those of stoicism or some Christian or other religious ascetics (in both philosophers we find expressions of the refusal of self-denial); a quite crucial role imparted to passions as springs of human behaviour; a curious blend of pragmatic realism and rigorous moralism; the constant use of paradoxes; the valorization of contingency; some kind of attenuated naturalism; the observation of the intertwining of good and evil in almost every human action; and enormous attention to perverse effects.

These traits, which show themselves as striking affinities between both authors, are far more important than signs of mere influence. They reveal that each of these two authors, developing an original and innovative philosophy, works out his ideas within a common framework that envelops them, that of the skeptical moral and political philosophical tradition.

Most early modern skeptical authors in the wake of Montaigne share the consideration that passions subdue reason and will and that they fundamentally govern human action and conduct. Mandeville, exploring similar views, develops a rather sophisticated theory of passions founded on the valorization of the self.[37] Mandeville also emphasizes that his viewpoint is descriptive rather than normative.

Joining together self-examination with the study of the passions and of human behaviour, Mandeville conceives the former as a kind of therapeutic procedure possessing some similarities with the role played by self-knowledge in Montaigne's neo-Pyrrhonian philosophy or in the philosophy of other skeptical thinkers of the seventeenth century like La Mothe Le Vayer or La Rochefoucauld. For Mandeville, self-study constitutes the background against which his analysis of human nature and his discussion of the interplay of vice and virtue are set. Without duly observed self-examination, which could almost seem an end in itself for the pleasure it gives, a man falls prey completely to the empire of the passions and to the power of social games of dissimulation. So Mandeville's valorization of the individual has two complementary traits: the free individual, having to be considered as such, becomes the most important asset of a free society; men, as they are unwillingly driven by passions, must recognize their role and understand their functioning as springs of action and guides to conduct in order to overcome their power.

The valorization of contingency, along with expressions of anti-rationalism, form an essential part of what we could call the pattern of early modern skepticism in relation to moral and political philosophical issues. Renato Lessa has explored the idea that the "Sceptics established a form of thinking about sovereignty as grounded on accidents, traditions and beliefs."[38] This idea and the related notion of "operators of circumstance, circumscription and finitude" as characteristic of skeptical philosophers are inspired by St Anselm's ontological argument and Bodin's conception of sovereignty as brilliantly developed by the Portuguese philosopher Fernando Gil.[39] A belief in "limits and circumscription" replaces the Anselmian and Bodinian belief in the unbound.

I do not fully endorse this interpretation, despite its fecundity and the brilliance with which Lessa defends it. It seems to me that the undeniable importance conferred by the early modern skeptical tradition in moral and political philosophy upon contingency and circumstances is better construed as corresponding to a rejection of belief in finitude.

An important issue in the interpretation of Mandeville's thought concerns his alleged foreshadowing of modern liberal capitalism. According to a quite common view he defended some form of spontaneously ordered free market. The famous subtitle of *The Fable of the Bees*, namely, *Private Vices, Publick Benefits*, forms an appropriate summary of his basic notion that if people pursue their own self-interest (which he calls "vices") a sort of harmonious equilibrium producing benefits for society as a whole will eventually turn up as an unexpected result (due to more or less complicated chance mechanisms). The most important point here seems to consist in the circumstance that the uncoordinated single efforts pursued by individuals pursuing their own interests and following their own "vicious" inclinations are paradoxically beneficial to the whole. And analogously, according to Mandeville, the coordination of those very efforts made willingly in order to achieve a common good is far less efficient than that later called "spontaneous order." This view seems to imply that a planned large-scale human intervention is doomed to fail due to chance and to the interplay of factors that cannot be controlled by human reason. But that does not mean that spontaneity magically begets order, either.

We see here at work a clearly paradoxical effect. It seems rather unlikely that Mandeville would in truth dream of straightforwardly sustaining any economic and social system like modern capitalistic ones. In the first place, there is not a single known form of modern capitalism that really renounces some kind of rational order and deliberate interference with what the ancients called the whims of Fortune and the Christians called the mysterious designs of divine Providence. In the second place, there has never been any government that really endorsed the kind of realism claimed by Mandeville. Moreover, no historical known system officially sustains the objectives ascribed by Mandeville to his "grumbling hive." To the objection that forms of government that are really guided by such a set of values have prevailed throughout history though people in power hypocritically proclaimed other public objectives, while in reality pursuing those aims, one may reply that if that is true it does not apply to liberal systems only but also (albeit in perhaps a somewhat more recondite way) to other sorts of systems, including socialist ones. The point is that if we base our reading of society entirely upon the assumption of hypocrisy or dissimulation, we are at a loss because we will lack an adequate criterion to distinguish dissimulated statements from sincere ones.

That does not mean however that we have to put aside interpretations of Mandeville's economic and political thought such as the famous one sustained by Hayek in 1951 (which was followed by many others in its wake) somehow claiming the Dutch physician and philosopher as a forerunner of liberal economics.[40] Those interpretations have legitimacy as long as they limit themselves to admitting that they are expressing a conception of Mandeville that foreshadows future conceptions that he could not have conceived because they are based upon realities that had not yet come completely to form in his own time. I would like to emphasize that those interpretations are only partially true, disclosing just one among many other contradictory aspects of Mandeville's philosophy. As Keynes himself (among others) pointed out, Mandeville can also be seen as a forerunner of interventionist theories like his.

Independently of the particular kinds of influence exerted by some thinkers on others, one can find in some authors more or less strong affinities of thinking. Thus, to find in author traces of his partaking of *peritropical* thought or at least elements that connect him with it does not mean that they are the product of direct influence. I believe Mandeville to be such a case. He certainly read Montaigne's *Essais* and seems to have held them in the highest esteem, as we have seen above. However, one cannot infer from that circumstance the exact nature and extent of the influence he received from the French philosopher. We may suggest that the sum of the elements and features these two authors share with each other may suffice to consider them somewhat akin. In addition to the other elements I have referred to above, the one to which I would like to call your attention consists precisely of a variant of a basic element of *peritropical* thinking. This is the use Mandeville makes of perverse effects as a ground for a theoretical construction trying to explain complex structures and institutions.

The central paradox of Mandeville's masterpiece *The Fable of the Bees* in any of its editions is epitomized in the subtitle of the work: *Private Vices, Publick Benefits.* A first hint of this famous formula appears also as a subtitle qualifying the original poem (published for the first time in 1706, and reprinted in all editions published during the life of the author): *The Grumbling Hive, or Knaves Turned Honest.* In this case, two sorts of individuals are contrasted: the knavish ones and the honest ones. The author puts here the stress on the passage from one condition to the other through the past participle of the verb "turn." An operation of metamorphosis makes a bridge between the two opposed qualities, one seen as a point of departure, the other envisaged as the arrival point. Mandeville thus gives relevance to the process of change itself. Interestingly enough, he observes the alteration as unilateral and not as reciprocal: while knavish individuals become honest, honest people do not become knaves. And the contrast alluded to in the subtitle has two faces, so to speak. The first one, which performs only a circumstantial function, is that the author shows in the poem the bees engaging in knavish conduct and behaving honestly. The second one, the most impressive and important one, is that individuals acting as rogues may form a strong and wealthy collective, thus becoming elements of a sound society and consequently honest as long as they are taken as parts of a whole.

The poem itself explores the intertwining of this famous Mandevillian thesis, expressed as a paradox, with its similarly paradoxical counterpart: a hive stocked with corrupt and vicious bees was prosperous and powerful; once the hive, because of a divine intervention, became free of fraud and the bees acquired virtuous habits, it lost its prosperity and power. According to the first part of the paradox, when the insects followed their vices (or, as we normally translate Mandeville's use of that term, self-interest) and behaved knavishly, business flourished and thrived, instead of decaying. As Mandeville says: "Thus every Part was full of Vice, / et the whole Mass a Paradise."[41] In spite of this flourishing, hypocritical bees, simulating love for virtue, display discontent: "[...] all the Rogues cry'd brazenly, / Good Gods, had we but Honesty!"[42]

Mandeville's depiction in the fable of the hive turned honest after Jove answered prayers asking for a complete moral reform has to our modern ears clear dystopian overtones. In fact, the author in the often-quoted verses of the conclusion of the poem openly declares that the wish to entirely banish from society the vices that constitute an integral part of it and that may contribute to its prosperity is a rationalist utopian desire:

> [...] Fools only strive
> To make a great an honest Hive.
> T'enjoy the World's Conveniencies,
> Be famed in War, yet live in Ease
> Without great Vices, is a vain
> Eutopia seated in the Brain.
> Fraud, Luxury, and Pride must live
> Whilst we the Benefits receive.[43]

Note that he does not say that the mentioned vices will always entail beneficial consequences for the societies, only that we have to endure them and be contented with their role in society *as far as* they turn into benefits.

I have thus far spoken of the first presentation of his paradox by Mandeville in 1705. I must here insist that though the later editions of *The Fable of the Bees* (of which the most important are those from 1714, 1723, and 1729) are much bulkier than the original one, containing the addition of long comments and essays, and even in the case of the last edition published during the life of the author, an entirely new second part, they actually reprint the poem as it was initially published.

The readings Friedrich Hayek made of Mandeville's theorizing on social sciences issues since the 1940s constitute a landmark in the modern appreciation of the thought of the author of *The Fable of the Bees*, having much contributed to the revaluation of it. Hayek's famous "Lecture on a Master Mind" of 1966 is his last word-synthesis on the subject. There we can read that the poem "gives yet little indication of his [Mandeville's] important ideas" and that "The idea that 'The worst of all the multitude / Did something for the common good' was but the seed from which his later thought sprang."[44]

For Hayek, "[Mandeville's] main original thesis emerges only gradually and indirectly, as it were a by-product of defending his initial paradox that what are private vices are often public benefits."[45] That gradual process had begun with *The Grumbling Hive* and, after the important landmarks constituted by the first and second editions of *The Fable of the Bees*, culminated in the 1729 publication of the second part.

The paradox itself would not then have been immensely original. Hayek expressly says so. The most important Mandevillian innovation, according to him, resides in the theoretical developments concerning the spontaneous ordering of complex social institutions it gave rise to. Explaining the evolutionary processes by which language and the laws were formed from the time of the origins of society is Mandeville's remarkable feat. The fact that his highly imaginative and plausible hypotheses and theories are, as we have already hinted, made out of a single principle seems even more admirable.

Hayek's interpretation of Mandeville highlights two important aspects of his thought: the enormous development it shows from the first to the last text of the author, and the circumstance that the bulk of the original contribution by him to the posterity of the social sciences lies in the exploration that essentially takes part along the six dialogues of the second part of *The Fable of the Bees.* Yet the most innovative feature of Hayek's rereading of Mandeville consists in shifting the emphasis from the famous paradox to an explanation of the formation of complex social institutions through a naturalistic evolutionary process. We can observe, however, in both these notions (the paradox and the process) an unchanging element that somehow binds them together: the use for theoretical purposes of the consideration in a more or less large scale of a mechanism involving *perverse effects.*

A striking example of the use Mandeville makes of that mechanism is a passage of the Fourth Dialogue of Part Two of *The Fable of the Bees,* where Cleomenes, the character the author mainly speaks through, presents an analogy between the long-sought-after perfect happiness and the philosopher's stone that leads him to the observation of curious and precious side effects of the pursuit of some unsuccessful searches:

> It is with complete Felicity in this World, as it is with the Philosopher's Stone: Both have been sought after many different Ways, by Wise Men as well as Fools, Tho' neither of them has been obtain'd hitherto: But in searching after either, diligent Enquirers have often stumbled by Chance on useful Discoveries of Things they did not look for, and which human Sagacity laboring with Design a priori never would have detected.[46]

Readers of Sextus Empiricus's *Outlines of Pyrrhonism* may easily recall a somewhat similar story told by Sextus about Apelles. The famous painter was looking for a special effect, a naturalistic depiction of foam in a horse's mouth. After having for some time tried in vain to produce it, he quit, giving up on his goal. In despair he threw his sponge at the painting, and by chance that achieved the effect he wanted.

That story is crucial to the Pyrrhonians. By an analogy with it Sextus explained the purpose or end of their philosophy, for they claimed suspension of judgment (*epochê*) was first attained in a similar way – only after having expressly renounced the attainment of their aim, they eventually attained it in fact through the suspension of judgment: "So, too, the Skeptics were in hopes of gaining quietude by means of a decision regarding the disparity of the objects of sense and of thought, and being unable to effect this they suspended judgment; and they found that quietude, as if by chance, followed upon their suspense, even as a shadow follows its substance."[47]

In spite of the paramount importance he confers to this analogy, Sextus does not specify the details of the passage from *epoché* to *ataraxia*. He also does not reveal who was the first skeptic who observed that consequence. Was he Pyrrho himself? If yes, according to which tradition? As there is no confirming trace in ancient testimonies on the philosopher from Elis about anything that could be interpreted in a similar way, that hypothesis seems quite unlikely. In the case that the quietude following suspension did not correspond to a symbolic historical occurrence, how should one interpret the emphasis put by Sextus on the episode but as stressing the paradoxical hazardous process itself?

Let us return to Mandeville to conclude. His description of perverse effects processes so well and accurately emphasized by Hayek as to *The Fable of the Bees* stands as one of the most innovative features of this unique book. It confers on his understanding of society and politics a characteristic tone that we would not refrain from considering akin to skepticism as outlined in modern times since Montaigne and his intellectual seventeenth-century heirs. It apparently did not strike his contemporary readers as the most shocking or even "skeptical" notion Mandeville's books purported, for they seemed mainly interested in trying to refute him on a different ground.

NOTES

1 For a concise and well-informed account of Mandeville's reception, with updated bibliography, see M. Simonazzi, *Le Favole della Filosofia. Saggio su Bernard Mandeville* (Milan: FrancoAngeli, 2008), 19–28.

2 See F.B. Kaye, "Introduction," in B. Mandeville, *The Fable of the Bees: Or Private Vices, Publick Benefits*, ed. F.B. Kaye (Oxford: Clarendon Press, 1924), LXVIII–CXIII. Among known nineteenth-century exceptions, also referred to by Kaye, we have to mention Karl Marx and Leslie Stephens. Arthur Lovejoy's addiction to Mandeville should be associated with this revival, as his correspondence published by Kaye as an appendix shows: see ibid., vol. 2, 451–3. Lovejoy's most important contribution to Mandevillean scholarship corresponds to the 1941 lectures eventually published in 1961: see A.O. Lovejoy, *Reflections on Human Nature* (Baltimore: Johns Hopkins University Press, 1961).

3 Nevertheless, the first book entirely devoted to Mandeville published since the eighteenth century was Hector Monro, *The Ambivalence of Bernard Mandeville* (Oxford: Clarendon Press, 1975).

4 This is the famous expression coined by the French scholar René Pintard in the 1940s and since then almost unanimously consecrated: see R. Pintard, *Le Libertinage Érudit dans la première moitié du XVIIe siècle* (Paris: Boivin, 1943).

5 See, especially, J. Lafond, *L'Homme et son image; morales et littérature de Montaigne à Mandeville* (Paris: Honoré Champion, 1996).

6 G. Bluet, *An Enquiry whether a General Practice of Virtue tends to the Wealth or Poverty, Benefit or Disadvantage of a People* (1725), collected in *Private Vices, Publick Benefits? The Contemporary Reception of Bernard Mandeville*, ed. J. Martin Stafford (Solihull, UK: Ismeron, 1997), 298.

7 Kaye, "Introduction," lxi–lxii, lxxvii–lxxxvii, lxxix, cxxxii.

8 Kaye, "Introduction," lxxixn1.

9 See, especially, Rui B. Romão, *A Apologia na Balança. A Reinvenção do Pirronismo na* Apologia de Raimundo Sabunde *de Michel de Montaigne* (Lisbon: Imprensa Nacional, 2007).

10 See, especially, Rui B. Romão, *Caminhos Caminhos da Dúvida – cepticismo, protomodernidade e política* (Lisbon: Vendaval, 2010). What I call the anti-skeptical tradition should not be simply taken as dogmatism in general. Instead, it is a tradition developed around a core of arguments used by the adversaries of skepticism and perfected as well as updated to face the evolution of the skeptical positions.

11 The expression "mitigated skepticism" is only conceivable after Descartes, referring to these skeptical attitudes.

12 There was indeed before Descartes a kind of theoretical skepticism, in spite of its not being extreme, for it was conceived as a sort of philosophy guiding life and not made up as an untenable position..

13 Cf. J. Barnes, "The Beliefs of s Pyrrhonist," in *Proceedings of the Cambridge Philological Society* N. S. 28 (1982): 1–29; M. Burnyeat, "The Sceptic in

his Place and Time," in *Scepticism from the Renaissance to the Enlightenment*, ed. R.H. Popkin and C.B. Schmidt (Wiesbaden: Olms, 1987), 13–43.

14 See Romão, *Caminhos Caminhos da Dúvida.*

15 Sextus Empiricus, *PH*, I, XXXII, 226.

16 See Romão, *A Apologia na Balança.*

17 Cf. J. Vuillemin, "Une morale est-elle compatible avec le scepticisme?" *Philosophie* 7 (1985) 21–51; M. Nussbaum, *The Therapy of Desire: Theory and Practice in Hellenistic Ethics* (Princeton: Princeton University Press, 1996), 313–15.

18 Richard H. Popkin, *The History of Scepticism. From Savonarola to Bayle* (Oxford: Oxford University Press, 2003), 142.

19 The notion itself of *crise pyrrhonienne*, independently from its historical justification, should be taken *cum grano salis*, for it derives from an anti-skeptical conception, according to which pyrrhonism should never be envisaged but as a crisis that has to be overcome.

20 The Pyrrhonism of the skeptics Descartes fought against was, considered as such, complete in itself.

21 The *peritrope* is an ancient Greek term that signifies the very same kind of argument used by anti-skeptical philosophers when accusing their skeptical adversaries of self-refutation whenever they present their philosophical attitude. I have been upholding for some years now a theory according to which ancient Skeptics of all tendencies developed in varied forms and degrees a kind of thinking I call *peritropical* thinking, involving simultaneously debating techniques and a sort of intellectual *ascesis* grounded on a complex process that has as its centrepiece the exploration of what can be construed as a perverse effect device (cf. Romão, *A Apologia na Balança*, 200–2, 485–92). A crucial point of this theory is precisely that better than any other element what explains the continuity of the skeptical tradition is the assimilation of self-contradiction as part of the dynamics of skepticism. Montaigne perfected *peritropical* thinking, giving it a larger scope than that conferred on it by the ancient skeptics. In the "Apologie de Raimond Sebond," the openly philosophical chapter of the *Essais*, and in many ways its centre, the structure, as I have analysed elsewhere, follows a progression that reveals a characteristic conceptual figure of skeptical thought: what I called the *peritropical metamorphosis.* Its presence in Montaigne's *Essais* (in general, and not only in the Apologie) is more striking and more complex than its previous presence in any other skeptical writing.

22 Popkin, *The History of Scepticism*, 43.

23 Until recently (perhaps fifteen or twenty years ago), most philosophers and historians of philosophy studied the theoretical branch of early modern skepticism by preference. Even Richard Popkin and his first disciples,

such as Charles B. Schmitt or Craig Brush, did not greatly (at least at the beginning of their research) counter that traditional tendency. They took ethical issues into due consideration, but they seemed to perhaps overplay the purely theoretical interpretation. The pioneering work of John Christian Laursen, *The Politics of Skepticism in the Ancients, Montaigne, Hume and Kant* (Leiden: Brill, 1992), directed our attention to the ethical and political aspects. See Laursen, *The Politics of Skepticism*, where Mandeville is said to be at "the roots of a number of Hume's ideas" (p. 174).

24 Discontinuity characterizes the history of skepticism both in antiquity and in the Renaissance and early modern age. But we can still refer to it (and to the ties between ancient skepticism and its renewal) as a tradition, albeit varied and many-sided. We can hardly say the same about what I have called the family of medical skeptical thought. Though tied to the skeptical tradition, it does not seem to constitute a tradition. The members of this "family" produced extremely personal and idiosyncratic versions of skepticism. They include neo-Galenists and anti-Galenists. The most outstanding members of it in the late Renaissance and early modern period are, perhaps, Francisco Sanches, Robert Burton, and Mandeville, to whom we could add the Spanish thinker Martín Martínez, studied by Laursen: J.C. Laursen, "Medicine and Skepticism: Martin Martinez (1684–1734)," in *The Return of Scepticism: From Hobbes and Descartes to Bayle*, ed. G. Paganini (Dordrecht: Kluwer, 2003), 305–25.

25 Mandeville, *A Treatise*, 48–50; 2nd ed., 1730, 56–8.

26 The complete title of the first edition of this treatise in three dialogues is *A Treatise of the Hypochondriack and Hysterick Passions, Vulgarly call'd the Hypo in Men and the Vapours in Women; In which the Symptoms, Causes and Cure of those Diseases are set forth after a Method intirely new. The whole interpreted, with Instructive Discourses on the Real Art of Physick itself, And Entertaining Remarks on the Modern Practice of Physicians and Apothecaries: Very useful to all, that the Misfortune to stand in need of either* (London: David Leach, 1711). The title of the second edition is *A Treatise of the Hypochondriack and Hysterick Diseases. In Three Dialogues* (London: J. Tonson, 1730).

27 Mandeville, *A Treatise*, 1711, xi.

28 Cf. Mandeville, *A Treatise*, 105–6. See, also, e.g., 139–40.

29 Mandeville, *A Treatise*, 68.

30 See, for a recent and informed contextualization of Cartesianism in the University of Leiden in particular and in the Netherlands in general when Mandeville studied and lived there, with bibliographical references, M. Simonazzi, *Le Favole*, 36–50; R. Donati, *Le Ragioni di un pessimista: Mandeville nella cultura dei Lumi* (Firenze: Edizioni ETS, 2011), 86–90.

31 Mandeville, *A Treatise,* 1st ed., 124.

32 Mandeville, *A Treatise,* 1st ed., 124.

33 Mandeville, *A Treatise,* 2nd ed., 154.

34 Mandeville, *A Treatise,* 32. See also 37, 47, 51.

35 The classic study of Mandeville's ambivalence still remains Hector Monro's *The Ambivalence of Bernard Mandeville.*

36 See, e.g., Sextus Empiricus, *PH,* I, iv, 8–10; I, xiii, 31–4.

37 The following passage, taken from the "Introduction" of the 1732 edition of *The Fable of the Bees,* shows perfectly how Mandeville sees man as completely subject to passions: "[...] I believe Man (besides Skin, Flesh, Bones &c. that are obvious to the Eye) to be a compound of various Passions, that all of them, as they are provoked and come uppermost, govern him by turns, whether he will or no." Mandeville, *The Fable of the Bees,* 39.

38 R. Lessa, "Montaigne's and Bayle's Variations: The Philosophical Form of Skepticism in Politics," in *Skepticism in the Modern Age,* ed. J.R. Maia Neto, Gianni Paganini, and John Christian Laursen (Leiden: Brill, 2009), 211–18.

39 See F. Gil, *La Conviction* (Paris: Flammarion, 2002).

40 Cf. F.A. Hayek, *New Studies in Philosophy, Politics, Economics and the History of Ideas* (London: Routledge & Kegan Paul, 1978).

41 Mandeville, *The Fable of the Bees,* 24.

42 Mandeville, *The Fable of the Bees,* 27.

43 Mandeville, *The Fable of the Bees,* 24.

44 Hayek, *New Essays,* 251.

45 Hayek, *New Essays,* 252.

46 Mandeville, *The Fable of the Bees,* II:179.

47 Sextus Empiricus, *Outlines of Pyrrhonism,* tr. R.G. Bury (Cambridge, MA: Harvard University Press, 1976), 21.

chapter seven

David Hume: Skepticism in Politics?

ANDREW SABL

Among this volume's distinguished scholars of skepticism, I must start by admitting that I am not one of those. In fact, I have just completed a book on David Hume's political thought, with particular attention to his *History of England*, without saying much at all about his skepticism.[1] Some of this is due to my background as a political theorist of "realist" sympathies, not trained primarily in philosophy. Since I have never harboured either an aspiration to model politics on rationalist lines or a belief that this was possible, I have felt little need to wonder whether philosophical skepticism is true or false. But my neglect of skepticism, up to now, is also justified by the subject matter. Hume's political writings, and above all his *History*, are *empirical* enquiries modelled at least loosely on modern science. (The title page of Hume's *Treatise* famously proclaimed it "An Attempt to introduce the experimental Method of Reasoning into Moral Subjects," and it would be perverse to describe the *Essays* and *History* as *less* empirical than the *Treatise.*) Modern science, which posits hypotheses and tests them against observation, can be seen as an attempt to gain adequate knowledge even if metaphysical skepticism be true; and Hume's historical writings have been read as part of such a program.[2] On the other hand, empirical science is also compatible with various forms of dogmatism, e.g., Newton's deism, which asserted a cosmos designed and harmonized by God, or Spinoza's materialism, which denied such providentialism.[3] Careful factual enquiry in politics is also consistent with quite a different agenda that would have less to do with systematic knowledge as such than with portraying political situations accurately so that practitioners can draw lessons for practical conduct – lessons grounded either in an intellectual virtue, whether ancient prudence or an updated version, or in something less intellectualized and moralized, akin to

Machiavelli's *virtù*.[4] In short, the empirical student of politics can adopt any number of positions regarding skepticism, or stay agnostic. Hume's goal is to describe, through the weighing of testimony and sources, how people act in politics and how societies develop. Metaphysical doubt about Reason and its ability to describe reality seems possibly suited to justifying such a project – a Humean believes that we need not establish the truth of metaphysics before studying politics – but not relevant to carrying it out. Once one accepts that empirical enquiry is legitimate, as we mostly now do, the fact that what it can find is merely probable, not demonstrable, is no longer very interesting.

Here I will argue, however, that skepticism is very helpful for understanding not the content of Hume's political work but its form, its style, and its intended effect. In fact, the general themes and outlooks of the skeptical tradition pervade Hume's work in politics and history. I hope in this chapter to contribute, as a scholar of what seem to be Hume's least skeptical writings, a new appreciation of how aspects of skepticism can appear in places where we would not normally seek them.

It was once thought, and asserted by many of Hume's annoyed critics, that Hume's politics were quietistic and conservative because that was the only kind of politics a skeptic could have.[5] However one assesses Hume's politics, it is no longer respectable to accept this particular piece of reasoning. On a conceptual level, John Christian Laursen has pointed out that skepticism as such gives no grounds for any politics, conservative or otherwise: "If on the one hand skeptics could not challenge the status quo on the basis of knowledge, on the other hand they had no reason to accept its legitimacy on that basis either." From a different angle, Petr Lom has argued that every skeptic has, in addition to skepticism, a "non-skeptical intent" or commitment and that this commitment may lead in all sorts of directions besides a conservative one: to Richard Rorty and Judith Shklar's liberalism of fear, or to Nietzsche's nihilism, involving not quietism but contemptuous rejection of existing norms and practices.[6] If it's a matter of Hume himself, scholars in recent years have presented abundant evidence that his politics were, if perhaps conservative with regard to constitutional forms and some other matters, hardly quietist in general. They have rediscovered the fact, which would hardly have surprised Hume's contemporaries, that Hume was very happy to plead reason and evidence – without capital letters – in direct opposition to reigning myths of his time regarding economic policy, history, party politics, and, of course, religion.[7]

Laursen has argued that Hume's skepticism reveals itself in a political theory based on opinion, custom, and manners. These are obviously crucial elements of Hume's political thought. But to stress these elements is to stress things that make Hume perhaps very *relativist* (with respect to some things, like the proper form of social and political conventions) but not particularly *skeptical* in the metaphysical sense. For one thing, Hume can only express confidence that all government rests on opinion, and pretty much all of life on custom, because he believes he has a sound theory of human nature (or "science of man") under which it is always and everywhere the case that our convictions rest on mental habits, the product of repeated experience, rather than reason. Though Hume stipulates that he only believes this out of mental habit himself,[8] and that his own hypotheses are tentative rather than certain, he clearly believes in a substitute for truth – call it universal satisfaction of calm philosophical sentiments – that will allow for systematic philosophical conclusions. Once we get rid of "hypotheses" that are "embrac'd merely for being specious and agreeable" (more on these later), "we might hope to establish a system or set of opinions, which if not true (for that, perhaps, is too much to be hop'd for) might at least be satisfactory to the human mind, and might stand the test of the most critical examination."[9] In a letter some years later, Hume repeated this sentiment. *"That Caesar existed, that there is such an Island as Sicily,"* were propositions for which we have "no demonstrative nor intuitive Proof," but Hume did not therefore deny "their Truth, or even their Certainty": "There are many different kinds of Certainty; and some of them as satisfactory to the Mind, tho perhaps not so regular, as the demonstrative kind."[10] Thus by assuming the level of "certainty" appropriate to empirical examinations, Hume could and did write a systematic treatise on the science of man – something that early modern skeptics, with their attachment to forms like letters, dictionaries, and essays, hardly attempted.[11]

But if Hume's work on politics and history does not rest on metaphysical skepticism (except in the sense of avoiding or transcending it), it does partake of classic skeptical styles and methods. It is in Hume's *Essays* and *History* that we find the reporter of all sides, the doubter of exclusive claims, the distruster of systems, the person determined to find some possible truth in a variety of viewpoints and exclusive and absolute truth in none. We also find, to a surprising degree, someone who both aspired to and hoped to evoke in others the Pyrhhonian elements that have precisely been noted as absent in Hume's *Treatise:* suspension of judgment (*epoché*) and tranquillity (*ataraxia*). Hume prized these ideals not in personal life – where Hume claimed the former was impossible, since "[n]ature ... has determin'd us to judge as well as to breathe and feel," and the latter, if achieved, would result in death through inactivity[12] – but in politics. In the *Essays* and *History* Hume used the tropes of skepticism to combat social and psychological barriers to the proper operation of both empirical judgment and the moral virtues in politics. Those barriers involved, above all, a problem unfamiliar to those who wrote about skepticism in a context of absolutism: faction, which Hume saw as the unwelcome cousin of political liberty.

I. The Targets of Hume's Skepticism: Factions, not (Merely) Sects

A. The Meaning of Moderation

One goal of Hume's political thought was to undermine partisan fervour and pave the way towards universal appreciation of Britain's constitutional arrangements. This is widely known.[13] Less often noted is that the language Hume employed in doing this was skeptical, in the ancient sense, and aimed at therapy. Hume calls for "moderation" in our party quarrels. This is so obvious and prominent a theme of his work, including his historical work – his *History* regularly pauses for imagined speeches by each side of a debate, followed by Hume putting his own judgment in the mouths of unspecified "men of sense" – that Sheldon Wolin has called Hume "temperamentally averse to taking sides."[14] That would not be accurate if taken to mean that Hume never adopted the position of one party or the other. He did so all the time (for instance, defending something like the Court/Whig position on corruption, the Country/Tory position on the national debt). His moderation, rather, lay in his determination to erode a particular, partisan mode of pervasive side-taking and partial identification that had pernicious effects on morals. Men, Hume said, should be supposed knaves in politics but in no other realm. This is because while a regard for praise and blame would in ordinary life (as Bayle stressed too[15]) motivate good action, in politics the partisan actor who through some vicious act succeeds in harming the opposing party only enhances his reputation among his own party, which is the only reputation he cares about.[16] It is this parochialism of sympathy, with its devastating effects on the quiet virtues of attachment to laws and social customs, that Hume sought to undermine. He telegraphs his method. Speaking of his hoped-for "coalition" or alliance among prevailing parties, Hume writes:

> There is not a more effectual method of promoting so good an end, than to prevent all unreasonable insult and triumph of the one party over the other, to encourage moderate opinions, to find the proper medium in all disputes, to persuade each that its antagonist may possibly be sometimes in the right, and to keep a balance in the praise and blame, which we bestow on either side. The two former Essays, concerning the *original contract* and *passive obedience*, are calculated for this purpose with regard to the *philosophical* and *practical* controversies between the parties, and tend to show that neither side are in these respects so fully supported by reason as they endeavour to flatter themselves. We shall proceed to exercise the same moderation with regard to the *historical* disputes between the parties, by proving that each of them was justified by plausible topics; that there were on both sides wise men, who meant well to their country; and that the past animosity between the factions had no better foundation than narrow prejudice or interested passion. ("Of the Coalition of Parties," italics in original, underlining added)[17]

I have underlined the portions of the passage that bespeak a characteristically skeptical method. Hume intends to balance praise and blame – for its own sake, not just because a particular case may demand it – so as to defuse each party's impression of certainty. He intends to disabuse both sides of their self-flattering impression that they are fully supported "by reason" (a striking phrase, not required by the flow of the prose, and one that seems quite deliberately inserted). With regard to history in particular, Hume intends to tell a story that will reveal that the parties of his time are largely based, not on principles demanded by reason, nor on the kind of calm passions of social sympathy that motivate attachment to salutary social conventions, but on *narrow* prejudice and *interested* passion. Under the influence of partisan fervour, such prejudices and passions are able to dress themselves up as reasons. Hume, through skepticism, aims to strip off the disguise.

B. Anti-rationalism vs. Ideology

Mandeville's editor F.B. Kaye has coined the term "anti-rationalism" to describe a central aspect of Mandeville's outlook. Kaye portrays anti-rationalism as having many components, many of which Mandeville borrowed from Bayle and some, via Bayle, from a wider Pyrrhonist tradition. But for our purposes most relevant is the doctrine "that men do not act from principles of reason or from regard for abstract morality, but from the reigning desires of their hearts."[18]

The idea of a reigning desire (Kaye astutely flags Bayle's *passion dominante* from the *Pensées Diverses*[19]) was a favourite of Hume's. The phrase "ruling passion," which I believe Hume helped popularize in Commonwealth English, appears a dozen times in Hume's work (though never in the philosophical *Treatise* and *Enquiries*: twice in the essay "My Own Life" and ten times in the *History of England*). Glossing human motivations in anti-rational terms, as the product of dominant passions, is more radical and subversive than it seems. Hume is saying that to understand human actions we should study not Providence, nor even people's subjective religious beliefs, nor certainly their political and moral opinions, which probably ape those current in their time, but something in their temperament that provides no easy or general lessons to those who have a different temperament. In fact, the more we see history as a story of dominant passions, the more we will have to draw the skeptical lesson that those who do have a different temperament probably will not act as the historical figure in question did – and possibly should not. The history that results may provide moral lessons, and may be the occasion for sound moral judgments. But it will not, in fact due to its anti-rationalism *cannot*, encourage the facile moral-exemplar reasoning – "what would [insert saintly figure here] do?" – that pervades so much religious ethics, and for that matter popular history.

When it comes to each political party's doctrines of authority – doctrines that Hume considers the most dangerous of all party doctrines and the least amenable to coalition and compromise, since they bear on "the essentials of government"[20] – Hume does not use the language of dominant passions, partly because he wants to make a point about human beings' uniformity rather than their diversity. But the essentials of his argument are anti-rationalist. Regarding the Tory doctrine of Passive Obedience (which he dismisses in a short essay since he thinks nobody, including its supposed partisans, seriously believes it), Hume recaps his own theory that authority is based on mutual advantage, and ceases when it no longer promotes that end. But rather than arguing that point thoroughly, he cuts quickly to the psychological chase:

> *Salus populi suprema Lex*, the safety of the people is the supreme law. This maxim is agreeable to the sentiments of mankind in all ages: Nor is any one,

> when he reads of the insurrections against NERO or PHILIP the Second, so infatuated with party-systems, as not to wish success to the enterprize, and praise the undertakers. Even our high monarchical party, in spite of their sublime theory, are forced, in such cases, to judge, and feel, and approve, in conformity to the rest of mankind. (italics in original, underlining added)[21]

Hume is not merely mocking the Tory theory of government. He is mocking, sweepingly, *any* theory. No "sublime theory" that would vainly try to flout human sentiments on such a clear point will succeed in driving actual feelings and judgments.

If natural sentiments that justify rebellion render the Tories' theory of Passive Obedience ridiculous, they also render the Whigs' contract theory of government superfluous. For reasons both fairly familiar and beyond this paper's scope, Hume thinks Lockean contract theory makes no sense. But he goes on to say that it does not matter. Once again, Hume writes in the essay "Of the Original Contract" (which is deliberately and openly paired with "Of Passive Obedience"), a theory that crosses universal sentiments will lack "authority." Hume's intended point, I suggest, is something like this: given that government is everywhere very useful, people will obey authorities even in the (likely) case that there is not and has never been a contract on which to found it. Therefore Whig Original Contract theory is not only false – no modern government was founded on a contract – but irrelevant; people will act the same way whether it is philosophically "true" or not.[22]

When discussing this question in the *Treatise*, Hume hastens to add that the Whigs are functionally correct (for the wrong reasons) regarding their central tenet of the right to rebellion: people always will always abandon their allegiance to a government that practices insufferable, egregious tyranny.[23] In "Of the Original Contract," perhaps because he is about to make this point in the "Passive Obedience" essay addressed to Tories, he instead makes a *different* skeptical (though in this case not as clearly anti-rationalist) point. He suggests that one can derive from the Whigs' favourite theory a range of equally plausible consequences, including the one opposite to their favourite one: "The only passage I meet with in antiquity, where the obligation of obedience to government is ascribed to a promise, is in PLATO'S *Crito:* where SOCRATES refuses to escape from prison, because he had tacitly promised to obey the laws. Thus he builds a *tory* consequence of passive obedience, on a *whig* foundation of the original contract."[24] (If he had really wanted to twist the knife, Hume could have cited Hobbes instead of Plato.)

To sum up, nature provides a practical disproof of the Passive Obedience thesis. It does so, ironically, in much the same way as it renders irrelevant Pyrrhonian skepticism: by determining us to act regardless of what we believe. On the other hand, nature also renders the Original Contract thesis obsolete, by ensuring that people will recognize authority with or without a contract, and will engage in rebellion with or without a judgment that a contract has been violated. Meanwhile, it doesn't matter much which theory we adopt, as we will find ways of twisting any theory's minor premises so as to result in the conclusion that our temperament would like to find in the first place.

On this reading, the very naturalism that saves Hume from metaphysical skepticism should also, he thinks, save the parties from political partisanship. If nature forces us to judge against our ideologies, it makes no sense to get as worked up as we do over those ideologies. Because theories of obligation are irrelevant for practice, their only purpose is to set citizens at odds, to make our factional struggles bitter and immune to compromise. Hume deploys his naturalism and anti-rationalism – not precisely consequences of skepticism, but positions acquired through struggles with skepticism – to instil the lesson that both parties' ideologies can only make politics worse, but not better.

C. The Protestant Succession: The Coolness of Distance

The words "skeptic" and "skeptical" (or "sceptic" and "sceptical," in Hume's spelling) barely appear in Hume's historical and political writings. "Skeptic" appears only three times in the *Essays, including* the title of the essay "The Sceptic," and one of them is a variant reading eliminated from the final editions (though an interesting one).[25] "Skeptical" appears only twice, once in the area of aesthetics (in a passage that those who attribute Pyrrhonian skepticism to Hume would do well to note, since he seems to describe a skeptical attitude towards taste only to reject it[26]) and once in a variant reading where Hume, in self-deprecating fashion, is really calling himself fallible, not skeptical.[27] In the *History* "skeptic" appears not at all and "skeptical" only *once*, in discussing a passing religious heterodoxy.[28] In other words, religious skepticism is a relevant question in philosophy, not in politics.

The absence of this fairly common word in the *History* is remarkable in a voluminous work containing 1.3 million of them. (The word "beef" appears six times as often.) It suggests, again, that skepticism is irrelevant to empirical investigations. It also suggests its irrelevance to the kind of moral evaluation in which Hume in the *History* freely engages: observations regarding what people might have done differently in particular circumstances, which require no absolute certainty on ultimate measures of right and wrong. Finally, it suggests that "skeptical" or "skeptic" are not useful labels when describing figures *in* history. After all, any sometime or self-styled skeptic who acts on the stage of history will be doing so in spite of that actual or alleged skepticism, i.e., in pursuit of goals and beliefs that he or she cannot keep from having in spite of being unable to rationally justify them all the way down.

But there's just one little thing. "Skeptical" does appear in a political context in a fairly famous letter that suggests that Hume might be practising skepticism even when not speaking of it explicitly. In a letter to Henry Home in February 1748, Hume, referring to his essay "Of the Protestant Succession," writes, "I treat that subject as coolly and indifferently, as I would the dispute between Caesar and Pompey. The conclusion shows me a Whig, but a very sceptical one. Some people would frighten me with the consequences that may attend this candour, considering my present station, but I own I cannot apprehend any thing."[29] A few days later Hume, having taken further counsel and received conflicting advice, writes to another friend describing his essay exactly the same way, but with more worry as to its possible effects:

> I suppose a Man to deliberate, before the Establishment of that Succession, which Family he shou'd adhere to, & to weigh the Advantages & Disadvantages of each. I hope I have examin'd this Question as coolly & impartially as if I were remov'd a thousand Years from the present Period: But this is what some People think extremely dangerous, & sufficient, not only to ruin me for ever, but also throw some Reflection on all my Friends, particularly those with whom I am connected at present.[30]

Hume was not wrong to think it dangerous to take a cool and impartial approach to the Protestant Succession. The question was, after all, combustible. Three years earlier, in 1745, a Stuart (Catholic) claimant to the throne, violently opposing the reigning Hanoverian (Protestant) dynasty, had landed in Scotland, taken Edinburgh, and struck fear into the English that he would march straight to London. Hume's friend agreed that this was not the time to publish an even-handed essay on the subject; on Hume's authority he suppressed this essay until a later edition of Hume's essays, in 1754. But it was not just a matter of bad timing. The question of the Protestant Succession was *the* major constitutional question of English politics, involving questions not just of monarchy but of religion and constitutional authority (the Hanoverians held their title through parliamentary authority, not strict heredity). Tacit pro-Stuart tendencies continued to be attributed to the Tory party, including by Hume.[31] In this context, to write an "indifferent" essay on the matter, one taking the same perspective as one would take one or two thousand years in the future, was, even a few years after the rebellion of "the '45," extraordinary.[32] It was akin to writing an essay in Philadelphia in 1785 treating the American Revolution as one would the Punic Wars, or an essay in 1972 weighing the relative claims of the Civil Rights movement and segregation in the same tone one would discuss a passage in Gibbon about how the Romans treated some ethnic minority long since forgotten. Hume was right to fear – and frankly odd not to realize until advised of the fact – that people might consider such thinking eccentrically philosophical, a sign that he lacked strong civic commitment. Hume here resembles no one more than Socrates, philosophizing silently in the middle of a camp preparing for battle.

This is a sign that Hume's skepticism in politics was more profound than it may seem, *provided* that we understand the objects towards which his skepticism was directed. These were not metaphysical questions, which affect politics barely if at all, nor religious questions, regarding which Hume did his best, with little success, to keep his own "skepticism" (a euphemism for disbelief in Christianity) a secret, but *party* questions. By seeking a coalition between parties with large and potentially very dangerous ideological disagreements on basic constitutional questions, and doing so through the skeptical methods of even-handed interrogation, ceaseless dialogue and dialectic, and something close to a suspension of judgment, Hume was playing just as thoroughly a skeptical game, and almost as dangerous a game, as Bayle was playing in casting doubt on all sides of religious questions. The only reason we find it hard to recognize this now is that the party positions Hume was treating skeptically have now disappeared – largely due to Hume's own efforts, leading Nicholas Phillipson to call Hume "author of his own neglect"[33] – whereas religious sectarianism, as would have much dismayed Hume, has not.

The radical implications of Hume's coolness also suggests that we should look for Hume's skepticism under borrowed cloaks: in the language not of skepticism as such but of cool thought, of independence from partisan extremes, of attention to facts that provide insulation from party prejudices.

II. Skepticism in History: Preliminary Theses

In claiming there are skeptical tricks or tropes in Hume's political and historical works, I will not claim to have final answers. But I hope to have found some fruitful places in which others (and I) might look further.

A. History as Skeptical Mean: Special-Purpose Epoché *and* Ataraxia

In "Of the Study of History" (an early essay, though later withdrawn) Hume portrays history as good for virtue because it involves a sentimental mean between the extremes of philosophical indifference and partisan engagement:

> When a man of business enters into life and action, he is more apt to consider the characters of men, as they have relation to his interest, than as they stand in themselves; and has his judgment warped on every occasion by the violence of his passion. When a philosopher contemplates characters and manners in his closet, the general abstract view of the objects leaves the mind so cold and unmoved, that the sentiments of nature have no room to play, and he scarce feels the difference between vice and virtue. History keeps in a just medium betwixt these extremes, and places the objects in their true point of view. The writers of history, as well as the readers, are sufficiently interested in the characters and events, to have a lively sentiment of blame or praise; and, at the same time, have no particular interest or concern to pervert their judgment.[34]

History, in this description, embodies not just a salutary but a "true" point of view (this truth explicitly being a matter of sentiment, not reason: presumably like the "satisfactory to the human mind" standard mentioned above). It would seem that historians are not only the "true friends of virtue"[35] but also the virtuous friends of truth. When Hume in the "Protestant Succession" essay adopts, and recommends, approaching present-day questions as if they are historical, he is practising what he preaches: the best way to approach topical questions calmly and truthfully, caring about their outcome but disregarding as much as possible partisan and ideological opinions regarding them, is to approach them as if they are not topical but historical.

In judging a difficult, controversial question, in this case the legitimacy of the Hanoverian dynasty, Hume counsels something very like *epoché*. "[A] philosopher ... who is of neither party," putting "all the circumstances in the scale," will realize that "all political questions are infinitely complicated"; the consequences of every choice are "always" unforeseen and rarely all good or all bad; "[h]esitation, and reserve, and suspence, are, therefore, the only sentiments he brings to this essay or trial."[36] But if Hume praises *epoché* (as well as, by implication, its constant companion *ataraxia*) as good for political judgment, he also condemns it as bad for morals. In his essay "The Sceptic," Hume explicitly doubts that *ataraxia* would be good for virtue. Skeptics' "refined reflections" "commonly ... cannot diminish or extinguish our vicious passions, without diminishing or extinguishing such as are virtuous, and rendering the mind totally indifferent and unactive."[37] An attitude that leaves us disengaged leaves us free from troubling excitement but also free from the sentiments that lie at the root of social virtues; leaves us better able to tolerate others' vices, *qua* part of the natural order, but also our own.[38] On the other hand, as we have seen, partisan attachments, the fruits of a distorted and partial sympathy, drag us passionately towards political knavery while removing the checks of social reputation.

Under the circumstances, we may conclude, we would best cultivate an attitude of modest engagement: enough to enlist the sentiments that are the source of virtue, not enough to make us feel that we are on a side whose triumph matters more than the public good. At stake is not a complacent, difference-splitting moderation but a delicate balance between two extremes, either of which saps virtue. Hume fully recognizes the salutary effects of skeptical *ataraxia* but is afraid that it might work too well. The historical attitude that he hopes to cultivate is meant to achieve, one might say, a limited-purpose *ataraxia* that leaves us indifferent towards parties but still attached to virtue.

John Immerwahr has claimed that the project of promoting "calm" or "tranquil" passions over violent ones runs through much of Hume's oeuvre, moral and political as well as epistemological.[39] This is true, but with a qualification. We need passions that are tranquil but not too tranquil. Hume calls his own attitude towards the Protestant Succession "cool," but that word in his *History* has a double-edged meeting. On the one hand cool "judgments" or "reflections" are what we might think they are: considered, sober, not distorted by passions or attachments that we would regret in calmer moments. On the other hand, "cool blood" is a state divorced from the human sympathies that would check vicious acts. When people are described as acting in cool blood – we would say cold blood – they are typically engaged in killing someone. And religious or partisan "bigotry" is typically the cause of their cold blood; it hardens them to the suffering of adversaries or even makes them regard it as an active good.[40] Hume's reflections on Philip II of Spain, the tyrant paired above with Nero in the "Passive Obedience" essay, make the point with particular clarity:

> Philip II. of Spain, though he reached not any enlarged views of policy, was endowed with great industry and sagacity, a remarkable caution in his enterprizes, an unusual foresight in all his measures; and *as he was ever cool and seemingly unmoved by passion,* and possessed neither talents nor inclination for war, both his subjects and his neighbours had reason to expect justice, happiness, and tranquillity, from his administration. *But prejudices had on him as pernicious effects as ever passion had on any other monarch;* and the spirit of bigotry and tyranny, by which he was actuated, with the fraudulent maxims which governed his counsels, excited the most violent agitation among his own people, engaged him in acts of the most enormous cruelty, and threw all Europe into combustion. (emphasis added)[41]

This is why Humean history is so important. At its best, it allows us to reach a state that is skeptical in all the right places: indifferent to party but morally engaged.

B. The Politics of Fact-Checking

One aspect of Bayle's writing that Richard Popkin notes when writing about Bayle himself but seems to slight in his wider reflections on skepticism (perhaps unable to shake the philosopher's conviction that the only topic of real interest is the relation of concepts to other concepts) is the element of obsessive fact-checking.[42] Philosophers who study Hume often slight it too. Yet it pervades his essays – consider especially "Populousness of Ancient Nations" – and his *History,* and is a key component of his skeptical method.

When it comes to method and epistemology, Hume in the *History* certainly seems a complete empiricist. He weighs sources carefully, examines controversies scrupulously, and was very upset when he heard second-hand (and inaccurately, it turned out) that a clerk of Parliament had caught him in serious mistakes.[43] Hume's empiricism is not merely pedantic but has moral purpose. For one thing, Hume could hardly have traced the psychic delusions resulting from religious bigotry, factional prejudice, and, rarely, other collective passions without having true facts against to which to compare these delusions. For another, there is no better way to undercut a lazy historical myth than to embarrass its holders into admitting that it commits them to beliefs that are demonstrably false. (I mean literally that there is no better way, not that this way is always effective, in either Hume's time or ours.)

But Hume also names a third purpose. Apropos of a fool who, based on ridiculous and inadequate evidence, tried to vindicate Mary Queen of Scots – the fool's book is, alas, still read by some in Scotland – Hume writes: "There are indeed three events in our history, which may be regarded as touchstones of partymen. An English Whig, who asserts the reality of the popish plot, an Irish Catholic, who denies the massacre in 1641, and a Scotch Jacobite, who maintains the innocence of queen Mary, must be considered as men beyond the reach of argument or reason, and must be left to their prejudices."[44] Again, this is "argument" and "reason" in loose senses of those words, the offspring of impressions and calm sentiments. Hume does not create what Jean-François Lyotard called a metanarrative, a story of Empiricism's permanent and epic purpose meant to justify the importance of his type of work to those unable or unwilling to judge the work itself.[45] Rather, the empirical attitude itself, the equation of facts with appearances, is meant to undermine the "false philosophy" that is Hume's label for superficially philosophical method allied with dogmatic religion (though Donald Livingston has astutely broadened its application to include what we call ideology).[46]

I submit that in the passage discussing the "touchstones of partymen" Hume intends both to advise and to shame. If you want to find people worth talking to seriously about politics, you may safely neglect people who think that President Obama was born in Kenya or that all the Jews left the Twin Towers just before they were destroyed. Similarly, Hume wants to change the standard for being taken seriously in politics away from the traditional ones (skill at metaphysics or theology) towards the test of whether one is prepared to take a "skeptical" attitude towards controverted facts – or on the contrary is inclined to believe them without evidence and in the fact of contrary evidence, merely because they fit one's personal prejudices.

To be sure, fact-checking as such, a critical attitude towards the source of empirical knowledge and its reliability, in no way logically entails philosophical skepticism. But psychologically, the link is very strong, and the two share many common enemies. Those who do not bother to check the facts will remain comfortable in the false belief that a sufficiently developed ideology provides certainty about the world. And those who reject the high rationalist belief that philosophizing gives certain knowledge of the world will be more comfortable with the contingent knowledge to which careful historical investigation and its present-tense equivalents give rise. Though not all fact-checkers are skeptics, those threatened by the checking of facts – or worse, unaffected when presented with the results of factchecking – are almost always dogmatists. Hume has a more chastened attitude than Bayle in this respect. Bayle hoped that fact-checking would cure dogmatists. Hume is content to detect them.

C. The Progress of Appearances

In *Hume's Politics* and other works[47] I portray Hume as having, among other things, a technological attitude towards politics: political conventions arise by accident but will persist based on their usefulness, and will even travel from one society to another because they are so useful. Political technologies Hume identifies in his own time include the rule of law; religious toleration; freedom of the press (at least up to a point); the intricate rules of hereditary monarchy; the office of prime minister, which separates competence in governing from the formal source of authority; and modern, well-ordered armies. I would claim that a contemporary Humean could identify further political technologies based on a long set of experiences that Hume lacked: universal public education and other public goods, but also constitutional refinements like caretaker governments, electoral commissions, and so on – as well as parliaments, which Hume considered optional but which now seem necessary for including and accommodating the diverse interests of a modern polity.

This is an approach, not a full-blown theory or an ideology. Hume did not write a treatise expounding his political outlook (which might have tempted people into trying to fit facts into the template when they didn't belong). There is no necessity to any particular step in the process. We cannot predict what will prove useful in the future (in fact, the above conventions are revealed as useful after the fact, seeming unproven and probably unwise *ex ante*). And one cannot tell whether something really is useful without a specific enquiry into its consequences. Hume's account of political progress is therefore consistent with skepticism. But it avoids the haphazardness sometimes attributed to Bayle's attitude towards human history[48] because Hume thinks he has observed regularities – of course contingent rather than logically necessary, yet observable everywhere – in human nature.

One such regularity is the universal science of psychological custom already mentioned, which leads people to stick with familiar institutions if they work fairly well. Another is a regularity in human desires: people are "so much the same" on a very general level that we can assume they will have *some* combination of the same passions and desires in every age, in spite of radical variation in which mixtures predominate in each time and place.[49] Because of these regularities, institutions that serve a great variety of human desires and interests – e.g., the rule of law, some system of property, and a constitutional rule of authority that prevents civil wars on the death of every ruler – will be attractive everywhere once perceived, and durable once established. This is consistent with the possibility that these institutions will, quite legitimately, take very different forms given local circumstances and historical accident. It is also consistent with the possibility, in fact the likelihood, that powerful actors who lose out under such institutions, like barons who prefer anarchy to law and bishops who prefer religious monopolies to toleration, may well resist these institutions and may do so for a very long time.

D. Irony vs. Intimation

Current attacks on the so-called Whig view of history, a view that (allegedly) posits inevitable progress and reads intimations of current practices back into the past, are not skeptical. They substitute for an old story of perennial problems addressed ever more wisely and adequately over time, a contrary dogma that denies the existence of perennial questions and of progress in human affairs. This counter-dogma seems neither analytically plausible, let alone demonstrable, nor capable of being grounded on empirical evidence.

Hume, the original opponent of the original Whig theory of history,[50] took a different tack. The original Whig theory asserted, in order to vindicate the party line, that certain assertions about the past were true. A dogmatic response to this – e.g., the Tory response – would be to declare them all false. Hume's more skeptical response had two components.

One was to ask why it mattered what had happened hundreds or thousands of years ago. If the Whigs' favoured institutions, such as a strong parliament, the rule of law, religious toleration, and a limited monarchy, were good in Hume's own time, his contemporaries' approval of them should rest on the grounds that they *were* good in Hume's own time, that they promoted the current advantage.[51] Using Clifford Geertz's language, one might say that Hume mustered against ideological thinking, which provides roadmaps and speaks through metaphor, an early version of literalist, information-gathering, cause-tracing social science. Social science – and Hume was one of the first to hope, as one of his essay titles put it, "that politics may be reduced to a science" – simultaneously operates on a different plane from that of ideology and provides a check on ideology to the extent that the latter starts to take its metaphors too seriously, mistaking them for literal statements of fact, or of cause and effect.[52]

The other aspect of Hume's response to Whig history was simply to question the mythical-historical assumption that all the things his contemporaries were for historically went with, and mutually caused, one another. Fact-checking was, and still is, part of this; but so was, and still is, a kind of conceptual anarchism that relentlessly interrogates the (ideological) view that the things we think are good must go together, either historically or logically. Contemporary political scientists who study ideology often describe it as "issue constraint": the process by virtue of which we come to believe that those who take a "progressive" position on one issue, say, taxing the wealthy, should take a predictable stance on another issue that logically has nothing to do with it, like abortion.[53] Hume's *History* systematically sought to undo the bonds of Whig and Tory ideologies by showing that history combines values in ways neither party would expect.

Thus while the Tory party in Hume's time came out for authority and the Whigs for liberty, Hume argued that there was no real liberty without authority, for without authority the weak were subject to arbitrary violence from the strong. While the Whigs simultaneously called for parliamentary privilege and personal liberty as if they were the same thing, Hume showed that Parliament often spent a great deal of energy defending the former while doing nothing to vindicate the latter; meanwhile, kings often defended the rights of unpopular minorities when parliaments bayed for their blood. The Whigs in Hume's time asserted that the Anglo-Saxon kings had been elected; the Tories, that they were hereditary. Hume demonstrates a third possibility that is obvious after one has substituted factual investigation for myth: the kings were neither hereditary nor elective but typically gained their thrones through violence. To multiply the subversive irony, the Whigs of Hume's time, on his portrayal, had reason to wish their theory had been wrong: if kings *had* been hereditary, as they later became, it would have gone much better for ordinary people. As it was, the Anglo-Saxons saw, as the result of weak and contested authority, centuries of stagnation with regard to the economic, legal, and cultural improvements that make people's lives better.[54]

Such arguments aim to combat mythical and magical thinking through a sense of contingency. It is common and easy, especially in politics, to proclaim a pragmatic attitude that cares only about results (perhaps with certain moral side-constraints, certain means that few or no ends can justify). But it is much harder, under partisan and ideological pressures, to apply this approach consistently. Human beings love a story with heroes and villains. When studying history, we are prone to make sense of what's happening, to endow it with meaning and interest, by convincing ourselves that the battles of the past are just the same as those that excite us in the present. If we advocate the right to revolution in the present, we convince ourselves to cheer on revolutionaries of the past, to rejoice when they succeed and be disappointed in their failure. The same goes for whatever we want to vindicate: the rule of law, executive authority, religious dissent. The people who advocate these things in the past become our friends, their enemies our enemies, regardless of whether the people who advocated them in the past wanted to bring about what we value, and regardless of whether their achieving their superficially similar goals in the very different circumstances of the past would have had the same good effects then as we take the contemporary equivalents to have now. To ask strictly causal questions about history – why people did things, in what circumstances they did them, what alternatives they faced, what the results of their success or failure actually were (or would have been) – is to train ourselves out of the human tendency to root for human types and familiar symbols rather than analysing, with evidence, actual human actions. Demystifying the past is a tonic meant to treat, though it can never cure, our tendency to magical and symbolic thinking in the present. In both cases, the partisan or ideological tendency to make sense of things by quickly picking a side is meant to yield to the analytic demand for a specific, fact-based question, and to the skeptical interrogation, "how do you know?"

In this context, Hume's personal and "moralizing" tendencies, which those who wrote about Hume in the age of social history tended to find rather anachronistic and to treat with some condescension,[55] make perfect sense and are perfectly consistent with a neo-skeptical program. If we are to read history without rooting for what we falsely take to be our own partisan or ideological team, we have to have some other object for our imaginative engagement. Hume focuses on individuals, whom he invites us to regard as admirable or despicable (or almost always, in good skeptical style, a mix) because of what they actually did to further permanent human interests, in circumstances that do not resemble our own and regardless of the partisan side or tendency that they putatively represent.

Hume wrote in a letter to a friend, "My views of *things* are more conformable to Whig principles; my representations of *persons* to Tory prejudices." He claimed that this led him to be misunderstood but in particular to be taken for a Tory, for "men commonly regard more persons than things."[56] As this comment implies, the quest to accurately represent personal character was not easily calculated to maximize popularity. Nor did it represent a non-scientific approach to politics. It was precisely scientific – provided, again, that one means by science a skeptical activity that sticks close to judgments that can be backed by empirical evidence in specific cases, rather than a project of seeking in history world-hysterical patterns that aren't there.

Conclusion

There may be no overall, synoptic lesson to be drawn. Unlike philosophical hedgehogs, foxes like Hume (and Bayle) have a high ratio of examples and insights to theses and laws. Perhaps the best conclusion is to be practical and ask what a Humean approach would mean today and whether the disciplines we are familiar with – history, philosophy, political science – can be said to have adopted it.

Hume's kind of skeptical history is not at all easy to sustain. Put more strongly, his approach to history, which combined a history of political development and social trends with attempts at accurate and instructive moral evaluation,[57] has all but disappeared. Those who pursue a large-scale, "macro" history of social trends often adopt a dogmatic myth of social progress (or, if conservative, regress) or else the dogmatic desire to debunk such myths at all points – even if this means failing to note particular cases, which often last a century or more, in which things really do get better in identifiable respects.[58] Their history is either progressive or anti-progressive, not (like Hume) agnostic on the question. There continue to be competing partisan histories of the same period that root unequivocally for the success of one past party over another.[59] Meanwhile the evaluation of particular historical figures has become the province of a popular history determined to make past heroes avatars for present causes and to discuss their acts without a careful regard for evidence and context. I would claim that Hume's kind of history, combining macro and micro, is not accidental, that a rejection of mythical thinking requires it. We cannot free ourselves from ideological myths unless we drill down into particular decisions so as to illuminate the specifics that our ideological shortcuts do their best to obscure. And we cannot learn from past actions unless we are prepared to be surprised by what past actors did and the historical context that explains why they did it, and prepared as well to re-evaluate our dogmatic belief that the people we take as our heroes merit our taking them as such.

Many historians are at least attempting a skeptical approach to these matters. Philosophers and political theorists, judged by Humean standards, may fare much worse. To step back from social and political philosophy is to see a field permeated by easy ideology: lifelong animal-rights activists writing books claiming that sound philosophy entails animal rights, socialists writing books on distributive justice, libertarians coming up with ever more ingenious defenses of unlimited property rights and minimal government regulation.[60] I see no sign that political theorists and philosophers are wiser in our political judgments than the general educated voter. In fact, our education tends to make us *more* predictable in our ideologies than less educated citizens are. (Many voters who have relatively low political information are dissatisfied with the parties because their own opinions are opposed to legal abortion but in favour of more social spending, or opposed to foreign wars but in favour of tax cuts for the wealthy. Among the educated, such dissent from conventional ideologies is much less common. The melancholy mechanism is, to oversimplify only slightly, that almost all voters in a mass democracy are prone to adopt the ideological lines laid down by party elites, but only the well-informed know enough about what elites think to fall in line as predictably as people like us are observed to do.[61]) It is not clear that we are more skeptical regarding ideological myths than the average educated voter. Worse, it is not clear that we have any interest in becoming more skeptical. Our obsession with ideas makes us easy prey for false philosophy and for ideological shortcuts that save us from having to dig into the facts about the past (history) or about the present (policy).

Empirical social scientists, especially political scientists, may fare better. They imbibe a strong ethos of impartiality. This does not mean that they lack social and political opinions; all the data suggest that their political beliefs resemble those of philosophers and political theorists. It means something like Humean mitigated skepticism: a determination to put ideological and partisan assumptions to the test, to compare them against facts. The flip side of this is being relatively uninterested in abstract moral and political ideas (except to the extent that they generate hypotheses that can be tested against data, or, conversely, are hobbies that have nothing to do with the study of politics).[62]

This brings up the question of whether a Humean skeptic ought to cultivate a certain anti-intellectualism (just as Laursen has claimed that the skeptical tradition in philosophy is more anti-philosophical than philosophical).[63] The kind of anti-intellectualism I mean is something very specific: a distrust of systematic reflection concerning ideas, a distrust in particular of abstract reflection regarding the proper connection of one moral idea with another, or of moral ideas to political reality. A skeptic might suspect that intellectualizing politics will always entail constructing myths, to the detriment of both the truth (which requires fact-checking) and the good of our fellow citizens (which requires, if we are to avoid partisan corruption, an ironic attitude towards the adequacy of all myths). The unofficial motto of the so-called behavioural revolution in political science, namely "learn how to count," could after all also have been Hume's motto:

> When we run over libraries, persuaded of these principles, what havoc must we make? If we take in our hand any volume; of divinity or school metaphysics, for instance; let us ask, *Does it contain any abstract reasoning concerning quantity or number?* No. *Does it contain any experimental reasoning concerning matter of fact and existence* No. Commit it then to the flames: for it can contain nothing but sophistry and illusion.[64]

My fellow sophists and illusionists, if such we be, have long worried about so-called foundations and relativism. We may have been looking for worry in all the wrong places. Skeptical worries about ultimate truth need worry only dogmatists. Stipulating that we are all arguing about mere appearances, political theorists can practise attention to the particular appearances that interest us – including moral and political opinions – and can claim to serve our fellow human beings by observing patterns in such opinions more reliably or creatively, in this limited realm, than others do. (If metaphysical skepticism is false, we can do even better; but we do not need to.)

But the kind of Humean skepticism *in politics* outlined above suggests that our professional habits may in fact make us worse than other people: worse politically, not metaphysically. If the task, or at least one task, of political theory is to remove partisan and ideological blinders, we may instead be systematically prone to reinforcing them.

NOTES

I would like to thank for their invaluable comments the participants in the "Skepticism and Politics" conference, especially Chris Laursen, as well as Tom Merrill.

1 Andrew Sabl, *Hume's Politics: Coordination and Crisis in the* History of England (Princeton, NJ: Princeton University Press, 2012).

2 Richard Popkin, *The History of Skepticism from Savonarola to Bayle* (Oxford: Oxford University Press, 2003), 112f., portrays Mersenne and others as developing something akin to the contemporary "scientific outlook" as a response to skepticism. David Fate Norton argues that Hume's self-proclaimed "science of man" had this project of pursuing "an adequate level of certainty ... with regard to appearances" in mind. Norton, "History and Philosophy in Hume's Thought," in *David Hume: Philosophical Historian*, ed. David Fate Norton and Richard H. Popkin [Indianapolis: Bobbs-Merrill, 1985], xxxvii).

3 See Jonathan I. Israel, *Enlightenment Contested* (Oxford: Oxford University Press, 2006). While Israel does not describe Spinozism as dogmatic, his account of it abundantly justifies that label.

4 I thank Tom Merrill for alerting me to the former possibility. Frederick G. Whelan, *Hume and Machiavelli: Political Realism and Liberal Thought* (Lanham, Md.: Lexington Books, 2004) explores the latter.

5 John Stuart Mill was the first of many to render this critical view popular – as it still is in many quarters, but not among Hume scholars. See the literature review in John B. Stewart, *Opinion and Reform in Hume's Political Philosophy* (Princeton, NJ: Princeton University Press), 3f.

6 John Christian Laursen, *The Politics of Skepticism in the Ancients, Montaigne, Hume, and Kant* (Leiden, The Netherlands: E.J. Brill, 1992), quotation at 5; Petr Lom, *The Limits of Doubt* (Albany: SUNY Press, 2001), quotation at 79.

7 In addition to Stewart, *Opinion and Reform*, see Neil McArthur, *David Hume's Political Theory* (Toronto: University of Toronto Press, 2007).

8 David Hume, *A Treatise of Human Nature*, ed. David Fate Norton and Mary J. Norton (Oxford: Oxford University Press, 2000), 1.4.7.11–12 (henceforth *Treatise*).

9 Hume, *Treatise*, 1.4.7.14. For a stress on this passage, see John P. Wright, "Hume's Academic Skepticism," *Canadian Journal of Philosophy* 16, no. 3 (September 1986): 407–35, p. 417.

10 Letter from Hume to John Stewart, February 1954; in *The Letters of David Hume*, ed. J.Y.T. Greig (2 vols., Oxford: Clarendon Press, 1932), 1:187.

11 Bayle, in addition to writing in the form of "diverse thoughts" (in epistolary form), repetitive and badly organized treatises like the *Philosophical Commentary*, and a huge *Dictionary*, described his kind of philosophy as resembling a kind of history or reportage rather than advocacy, his own role closer to that of journalists covering a trial than that of attorneys arguing one side of it. See Renato Lessa, "Montaigne's and Bayle's Variations," in *Skepticism in the Modern Age*, ed. José R. Maia Neto, Gianni Paganini, and John Christian Laursen, (Leiden, The Netherlands: Brill, 2009), 224–5.

12 See Wright, "Hume's Academic Skepticism," 415, citing *Treatise* 1.4.1.7 and Hume's *Enquiry Concerning Human Understanding* (of which the standard edition is now ed. Tom L. Beauchamp [Oxford: Clarendon Press, 2000]), 12.23.

13 Duncan Forbes, *Hume's Philosophical Politics* (Cambridge: Cambridge University Press, 1975); Nicholas Phillipson, *David Hume: The Philosopher as Historian* (New Haven, CT: Yale University Press, 2012).

14 Sheldon Wolin, "Hume and Conservatism," *American Political Science Review* 48, no. 4 (December 1954): 999.

15 Pierre Bayle, *Various Thoughts on the Occasions of a Comet*, trans. Robert C. Bartlett (Albany: State University of New York Press, 2000), especially §137.

16 Hume, "Of the Independency of Parliament," in David Hume, *Essays Moral, Political, and Literary*, rev. ed., ed. Eugene F. Miller (Indianapolis: Liberty Fund, 1987), 42–3. For more on this, see Andrew Sabl, "Hume's Moral Psychology of Party," paper presented before the Annual Meeting of the Hume Society, Koblenz, Germany, 7–10 August 2006.

17 Hume, "Of the Coalition of Parties," *Essays*, 494.

18 F.B. Kaye, Introduction to Mandeville, *Fable of the Bees* (2 vols., Oxford: Clarendon Press, 1924; reprint, Indianapolis, Liberty Fund, 1988); 1.civ.

19 Bayle, *Various Thoughts*, §137.

20 Hume, "Of the Coalition of Parties," *Essays*, 493.

21 Hume, "Of Passive Obedience," *Essays*, 489.

22 Hume, "Of the Original Contract," *Essays*, 487. There are many ways of interpreting Hume's apparently odd claim that "the general practice of mankind" (ibid.) should trump "so refined and philosophical a system" as only philosophers would invent (470); as well as the following odd concession to vulgar opinion: "New discoveries are not to be expected in these matters. If scarce any man, till very lately, ever imagined that government was founded on compact, it is certain, that it cannot, in general, have any such foundation" (487). In the current context, one should remember that the contract theory would posit the *absence* of legitimate government wherever no consent took place. Yet government

being necessary to human existence everywhere, except (Hume stipulates) in subsistence societies, and consent being uncommon, no human society will in practice live by the anarchic consequence of such a theory. We might say that this renders that theory "false" for practical purposes; not "satisfactory" to actual humans.

23 Hume, *Treatise*, 3.2.9.1. For a detailed discussion, see Sabl, *Hume's Politics*, 104–7.

24 Hume, "Of the Original Contract," *Essays*, 487.

25 In a passage in "Of the Rise and Progress of the Arts and Sciences" that appeared in many editions, Hume mentions skepticism in the course of noting the arrogant structure of Cicero's dialogues, in which Cicero's close friends, and extremely eminent Romans, are given subordinate parts. He writes: "And 'tis remarkable [i.e., noteworthy], that CICERO, being a great sceptic in matters of religion, and unwilling to determine any thing on that head among the different sects of philosophy, introduces his friends disputing concerning the being and nature of the gods, while he is only a hearer; because, forsooth, it would have been an impropriety for so great a genius as himself, had he spoke, not to have said something decisive on the subject, and have carried every thing before him, as he always does on other occasions. There is also a spirit of dialogue observed in the eloquent books *de Oratore*, and a tolerable equality maintained among the speakers: But then these speakers are the great men of the age preceding the author, and he recounts the conference as only from hearsay" (*Essays*, 623). Hume seems to be saying that a skeptic with good manners might present opposing sides and then hesitatingly and with a due acknowledgment of his or her own fallibility express an uncertain opinion. This is precisely his own practice in the *Essays*. In the *History*, as noted, Hume puts his own opinions in the mouths of "men of sense," "men of cool judgment," and the like.

26 Hume, "Of the Standard of Taste," *Essays*, 230.

27 Hume, "Populousness of Ancient Nations," alternate reading, *Essays*, 639. Hume is essentially saying that by not making his conclusions in that essay more certain than doubtful evidence could justify, he left himself able to respond to criticism by making corrections rather than losing his side of the argument altogether. He says much the same thing in a letter to Montesquieu (26 June 1953: Greig, *Letters*, 1.178).

28 In that passage Hume notes how the outbreak of the Reformation led precisely one person to make a speech proclaiming the difficulty of knowing the full truth about religion and the permissibility of holding any belief that acknowledged a supreme being and preached good morals. Hume quickly notes that these principles, which we might compare to those of Rousseau's

Savoyard vicar, "would be deemed latitudinarian, even in our time, and would not be advanced, without some precaution, in a public assembly." He goes on to say that religious controversy produced skeptical reflections in a very few of studious dispositions but was much more likely to lead most people to choose religious sects and stick with them. David Hume, *The History of England from the Invasion of Julius Caesar to the Revolution in 1688*, 6 vols., ed. William B. Todd (Indianapolis: Liberty Fund, 1983; cited by volume and page number), 3.187.

29 Hume, letter to Henry Home, 9 February 1748, Greig *Letters* 1.111.

30 Hume, letter to Charles Erskine, Lord Tinwald, 13 February 1748, Greig *Letters* 1.111.

31 Hume, "Of the Parties of Great Britain," *Essays*, 64–72.

32 At the time "indifferent" more often meant "impartial" than "uncaring." The second meaning was, however, also in use and apparently derived, in good skeptical fashion, from the former since someone with no strong prejudice on either side was unlikely to display strong passions on either side. OED "indifferent" 1, 2.

33 Phillipson, *David Hume*, 133.

34 Hume, "Of the Study of History," *Essays*, 568.

35 Hume, "Of the Study of History," *Essays*, 567

36 Hume, "Of the Protestant Succession," *Essays*, 507. I thank Tom Merrill for pointing out the relevance of this passage.

37 Hume, "The Sceptic," *Essays*, 173.

38 "It will be easy, by one glance of the eye, to find one or other of these defects in most of those philosophical reflections, so much celebrated both in ancient and modern times. *Let not the injuries or violence of men,* say the philosophers, *ever discompose you by anger or hatred. Would you be angry at the ape for its malice, or the tyger for its ferocity?* This reflection leads us into a bad opinion of human nature, and must extinguish the social affections. It tends also to prevent all remorse for a man's own crimes; when he considers, that vice is as natural to mankind, as the particular instincts to brute-creatures.

> "*All ills arise from the order of the universe, which is absolutely perfect. Would you wish to disturb so divine an order for the sake of your own particular interest? What if the ills I suffer arise from malice or oppression? But the vices and imperfections of men are also comprehended in the order of the universe:*
>
> *If plagues and earthquakes break not heav'n's design,*
> *Why then a BORGIA or a CATILINE?*
>
> Let this be allowed; and my own vices will also be a part of the same order.

"To one who said, that none were happy, who were not above opinion, a SPARTAN replied, *then none are happy but knaves and robbers.*" Hume, "The Sceptic," *Essays,* 173–4; internal citations omitted.

39 John Immerwahr, "Hume on Tranquillizing the Passions." *Hume Studies* 18, no. 2 (November 1992): 293–314.

40 For cool judgments or reflections, see Hume, *History* 1.212; 3.446–7, 5.460. For "cool blood," see *History* 1.56, 200 (with religious bigotry as the cause); 6.435 (an alleged cool-blooded murder by others wrongly attributed by Lord Russel to religious bigotry); 1.63, 2.66; 2.450.

41 Hume, *History* 4.52–3.

42 On Bayle himself, see Popkin, *History of Scepticism,* 296–9. Interestingly, the context is Bayle's attempt to dissuade people from uncritical hero-worship of Spinoza as a person, even as Bayle honoured him as a thinker (while mis-portraying his ideas). Bayle's fact-checking mania of course extended much further. In addition to citing almost every page of the *Dictionary* one could mention more systematically the *Various Thoughts,* §49, "How Ridiculous It Is to Seek Out the Causes of What Is Not," which recommends settling whether something exists before asking what it is, and asking whether something is done before asking how it works. Bayle cites Montaigne here: the "Apology for Raymond Sebond" and "Of Cripples."

43 For particular examples of Hume's empiricism, see *History* 6.295 and 6.412, as well as Norton, "History and Philosophy." For the clerk episode, see Greig, *Letters,* 1.354–6.

44 Hume's *History* 4.395, note M.

45 Jean-François Lyotard, *The Postmodern Condition: A Report on Knowledge,* trans. Geoff Bennington and Brian Massumi (Minneapolis: University of Minnesota Press, 1984): xxiv and passim. We often neglect Lyotard's argument that "grand narratives" of emancipation or philosophical progress are employed by empiricists to justify their own importance to audiences who cannot appreciate their specialized scientific work. Hume did not need a metanarrative because his actual narrative was so engaging. The social scientists who have thumped the tub loudest on behalf of Social Science and its aspirations to Progress have rarely been good writers.

46 Donald W. Livingston, *Philosophical Melancholy and Delirium: Hume's Pathology of Philosophy* (Chicago: University of Chicago Press, 1998).

47 See especially Andrew Sabl, "When Bad Things Happen from Good People: Hume's Political Ethics of Revolution," *Polity* 35, no. 1 (Fall 2002): 73–92, and "The Last Artificial Virtue: Hume on Toleration and its Lessons," *Political Theory* 37, no. 4 (August 2009): 511–38.

48 See Lessa, "Montaigne's and Bayle's Variations," 224–5.

49 Hume, *Enquiry Concerning Human Understanding*, 8.7. Sabl, "When Bad Things," contains a discussion of this passage and reviews the literature rebutting the view that Hume's portrait of human nature is "uniformitarian" and ignores deep diversity.

50 The Whig position in Hume's time was not, however, progressive, as "Whig" history was later said to be. On the contrary, Whigs in Hume's day claimed that the constitution had been most perfect in the distant past.

51 Things are actually far from this simple. For Hume argues that conventions of authority do require ancient roots in order to serve their fundamental role and that other conventions gain force, consistent with the habit theory, the longer they operate (see Sabl, *Hume's Politics*). But this Humean proviso also flouts the Whig theory – which posited ancient roots for the English constitution because it pretended that that constitution had been *purer* in the past, that England had fallen away from its original virtues. Against this, Hume gathers overwhelming evidence that whatever liberty and law the English constitution contains were crude at first and grew stronger over time.

52 Clifford Geertz, "Ideology as a Cultural System," in *The Interpretation of Cultures* (New York: Basic Books, 1973), 193–233. For interpretations of Hume as proto-social scientist, see Stewart, *Opinion and Reform*, and McArthur, *David Hume's Political Theory*.

53 Philip E. Converse, "The Nature of Belief Systems in Mass Publics," in *Ideology and Discontent*, ed. David Apter (Glencoe, IL: Free Press, 1964): 206–61.

54 See Sabl, *Hume's Politics*, chapter 4.

55 See Forbes, *Hume's Philosophical Politics*, chapter 9.

56 Greig, *Letters*, 1.237. For more on this, see Sabl, "When Bad Things."

57 See the discussion in Sabl, *Hume's Politics*, 15–16, and accompanying notes.

58 Though I cannot quote her by name, an extremely eminent contemporary American historian recently told me in conversation that debunking progress-oriented histories, especially popular ones, was "the goal" of her historical colleagues.

59 See, most conspicuously, Sean Wilentz's pro-Democratic Party history of the early nineteenth-century United States, *The Rise of American Democracy* (New York: Norton, 2005) and Daniel Walker Howe's pro-Whig Party *What Hath God Wrought* (Oxford: Oxford University Press, 2007) on the same period.

60 Gerald Gaus, "Should Philosophers Apply Ethics?" *Think* 3 (Spring 2005): 63–7.

61 See John Zaller, *The Nature and Origins of Mass Opinion* (Cambridge: Cambridge University Press, 1992).

62 Based on purely anecdotal evidence, I would say that empirical political scientists, like economists, are admirably serious about brainy hobbies (music, art, film, literature) while remaining totally uninterested, on principle, in what we do – political and moral philosophy, social theory, the history of ideas – which they regard as involving empty words, or else assertions about the state of the world that are clear but demonstrably false.

63 Laursen, *Politics of Skepticism*, 1.

64 Hume, *Enquiry Concerning Human Understanding*, 12.34, p. 165.

chapter eight

Denis Diderot and the Politics of Materialist Skepticism

WHITNEY MANNIES

What is the connection between Diderot's skepticism and his political thought? Diderot's skepticism is not the *pyrrhonisme outré* that suspends judgment even about external reality and sense perception; he thinks this radical notion only devolves into absurdity. But while some see his affirmation of external reality and sense perception as signalling only the *limits* of Diderot's skepticism, it is in fact also its origin: his skepticism is best understood as the logical consequence of his materialism. Though materialism is often equated with a mechanical, predictable view of nature that is inimical to skepticism, this is not Diderot's view. In the first part of this paper, I argue that Diderot is situated within a materialist tradition that includes, among others, Democritus, Epicurus, Lucretius, and Montaigne, and which posits an eternally dynamic, imperfectly knowable universe and fallible sense perception. This Epicurean materialist tradition is thus compatible with and even implies a form of skepticism. His political thought reflects these skeptical materialist assumptions: for example, his rejection of "benevolent despotism" follows from his belief in the fallibility and limitations of our knowledge. In the second part of this paper, I consider the problem for free will and morality posed by materialism, and I argue that Diderot draws on the skeptical materialist tradition to suggest how we might create our own freedom and morality through our own conscious reflection. Finally, I demonstrate that Diderot uses a naturalistic writing style to communicate his materialism, realize its skeptical implications, and provoke self-conscious reflection.

First, what does Diderot say about skepticism, and what do we know about his knowledge of skepticism? His entry in the *Encyclopédie,* "Pyrrhonism or Skepticism," is a long article notable for Diderot's considerable commentary. It contains a genealogy of skeptics, and at least from

Pyrrho through Huet, it is largely a summary of Johann Jacob Brucker's genealogy in the *Historia critica philosophiae* (1742). Brucker, in turn, identifies Sextus Empiricus as his main source for skeptical doctrine.[1] As for Diderot, he implies a familiarity with Sextus: "We will say nothing of Sextus Empiricus: Who does not know his *Hypotyposes*?"[2] Elsewhere we are told that Sextus pales in comparison to Bayle. Diderot departs from his summary of Brucker in the second half of the article, where he devotes a long paragraph to unalloyed admiration of Montaigne; his work "will be read as long as there are men who love truth, strength, and simplicity."[3] Above all, Diderot's article lavishes attention on Bayle, whose skepticism is said to result in tolerance and freedom of thought. Ironically, it was precisely these passages that were most severely censored, along with any suggestion that Bayle's detractors erred, or that church and state be separate. The bowdlerized passages were recovered in 1933 when what is likely the publisher Le Breton's own copy of *L'Encyclopédie* surfaced, including, serendipitously, the proofs of the censored articles.[4] The reconstituted text reveals that "Pyrrhonism or Skepticism "was one of the most aggressively censored entries, testifying to the risk Diderot was willing to take to praise Bayle – a very dangerous thing to do at the time.

For all his admiration of the skeptics, Diderot rejects unmitigated skepticism on moral as well as materialist and empirical grounds. First, such skepticism has the deleterious effect of rendering all moral knowledge uncertain and of thus undermining the basis of moral and political action: "But if goodness and badness are nothing in themselves, then there remain no rules or principles either for manners and morals or for life."[5] Here, Diderot's answer is simply to "no longer listen" to skeptical denials of a distinction between true and false, good and bad, just and unjust. Though it is true that Diderot was never content to accept skeptical moral conclusions, his published and unpublished works, as well as his private correspondence, imply that he could never rest easily with its uncritical rejection.[6]

Second, he rejects skeptical suspension of judgment regarding the existence of external reality and the integrity of our sense perception: "What shall I say to one who claims that although he sees, touches, hears, and perceives, he nevertheless never perceives anything but his own sensations …? I will recognize instantly the absurdity and the profundity of this paradox, and will guard myself well from losing my time destroying in someone an opinion that he does not have and to which I have nothing to oppose that is more clear than what he denies."[7] Skepticism can serve useful ends, but if it does not begin by assuming the integrity of our empirical experience, it descends into absurdity. Radical skepticism – the *pyrrhonisme outré* that suspends judgment about the existence of the external world – paradoxically undermines the empirical basis of the skeptic's own questioning. Perhaps most critically, such questioning is a waste of time that could be better spent napping "to aid our digestion."[8] In addition, his *Philosophical Thoughts* (1746) argues that the skeptical pretention to find equal reasons on each side of an issue is itself dogmatic, since it assumes the ability to accurately weigh the worth of those reasons.[9] On this point, Diderot's critique of skepticism is that it is not skeptical enough.

Though Diderot does not deign to respond to the most extreme skeptics, he thinks a moderate skepticism may challenge dogma, increase tolerance, and temper our passions. Moreover, he develops a less radical path to skepticism: skepticism as the logical consequence of his view of nature:

> On our part, we conclude that everything in nature is interconnected, and that properly speaking there is nothing of which man has perfect, absolute, complete knowledge, not even of the most evident axioms, because that would require that he had knowledge of everything.
>
> Because everything is connected with everything else, it is necessary that in all discussions one will arrive at something unknown. Thus when one arrives at this unknown, one will have to conclude with respect to it either ignorance, obscurity, or uncertainty concerning the preceding point, and of the point preceding it, and thus all the way back to the most evident principle.[10]

In this article, then, Diderot identifies with a materialist view of nature that is compatible with, and indeed implies, elements of skepticism. That "everything in nature is interconnected" does not mean that we can thereby trace causal connections, but the opposite: such varied and infinitely complex interconnections mean that we cannot presume to be certain of anything. In his *Thoughts on the Interpretation of Nature* he writes, "Phenomena are endless; their causes are hidden and their pattern is, perhaps, transitory."[11] This leaves us to our own powers of observation and reflection, but unfortunately our powers are dwarfed in comparison with nature: "When we compare the infinite number of phenomena in nature with the limitations of our own intelligence and the frailty of our organs, how could we ever expect to discover ...

anything but a few broken, isolated parts of the great chain which links everything together."[12] This is a view Diderot repeats in all of his works on natural philosophy and in his fictional *D'Alembert's Dream* and *Jacques the Fatalist.*

The interconnected chaos of the universe extends even to the mind. Our thoughts, being material, are determined, but they are linked by causal chains too complicated to enable prediction. Thus the causal connections of thought are not linear but labyrinthine, not mechanistic but meandering. He begins his *Thoughts on the Interpretation of Nature,* "I shall let my thoughts flow from my pen in the order in which things occur to me, to give a better picture of the workings of my mind."[13] Diderot makes a similar observation of Montaigne: "The contradictions in his work are faithful images of the contradictions in the human understanding."[14] On the other hand, a patina of randomness may simply conceal the enigmatic interrelations of matter, just as Montaigne's loose starting and stopping of essay topics is not entirely unrestrained: "It is only a subtle appearance that one stops and begins again without a cause. There is a necessary connection between any two thoughts, even the most disparate. This liaison is either in sensation, in words, in memory, either within or outside a man."[15] The mind's web of cause and effect is loosely, complexly interconnected.

Diderot's materialism also entails the primacy of sense perception, though it does not thereby establish its infallibility: sense perception is both limited and inherently subjective. His *Thoughts on the Interpretation of Nature* states that while the senses are the source of all our knowledge, "the senses cannot observe, nor the memory retain, everything."[16] Typical of this attitude is the assertion of the skeptical interlocutor in his *Philosophical Thoughts* (1746): "[T]he degree of certainty we can obtain through the senses is not very extensive. There are many things which we think we learn through their medium and of which we have not a full assurance."[17] The subjectivity of the senses impresses upon us the need to check our knowledge through repetition and through our experience with others, hence his championing of the experimental method and the desire to pass on knowledge to posterity – a kind of collective memory of facts, so we might approximate truth over the course of generations.[18]

Diderot's *Letter on the Blind* (1748) argues that the intrinsic subjectivity of sense perception prompts divergent reasoning; because the blind Dr Saunderson's empirical experience differs from that of the sighted, he arrives at different evaluations of beauty, morals, and religion.[19] Furthermore, sense organs vary – albeit minutely – from person to person, therefore we can never presume to have exactly equivalent experiences. Each person's reasoning will vary accordingly. This is complicated by the fact that "the mutual aid our senses lend each other stands in the way of their perfection."[20] Diderot does not think the senses are radically incommensurable, however; they can be reconciled after a process of careful reflection.[21] Ultimately, however, the incommensurability of experience and reason between individuals (and *within* individuals) is not so extreme as to preclude meaningful (if inexact) communication.

Richard Popkin argues that Diderot avoids the excesses of a *pyrrhonisme outré*, not by conclusively answering the Pyrrhonist's critiques, but "by refusing to take the sceptical questions seriously, though admitting that they cannot be resolved."[22] He sees this wilful refusal as stemming from Diderot's overweening desire to positively resolve questions. I do not believe this to be the case: Diderot does not arbitrarily limit his skepticism when it threatens his own positive moral and political principles. Rather, the scope of his skepticism follows from his materialist assumptions.[23]

Diderot's is not a novel position. In fact, he is working in an Epicurean tradition of materialism that actually begins with Democritus, and it has some skeptical consequences. Brucker's *Historia critica philosophiae* describes how Pyrrho arrived at skepticism via Democritean atomism: "Having learned, from [Democritus], to deny the real existence of all qualities in bodies, except those which are essential to primary atoms, and to refer every thing else to the perceptions of the mind produced by external objects, that is, to appearance and opinion, he concluded, that all knowledge depended upon the fallacious report of the senses, and consequently, that there can be no such thing as certainty."[24]

Democritus's cosmology consists only of matter (atoms) in eternal flux and void. There is no freedom or agency, only the determined courses of atoms, infinitely connected through webs of causation. This determination, however, does not equate to a mechanistic view of nature because the motion propelled by infinite atomic collisions is so chaotic as to defy predictability. Moreover, though sense perception is our only basis for knowledge, he argues that the senses only inform us of our experience of properties of objects and not of the properties themselves. Hence his dicta, "cold by custom, hot by custom; atoms and void in truth."[25] Democritus's atomism yields a determined universe with neither freedom nor knowledge.

Though he adopts Democritus's atomism, Epicurus cannot accept these pessimistic consequences. Instead, he argues that subjective sense perception *can* yield knowledge of properties since subjectivity may be double-checked through repetition and through the comparison of our own experience with others'.[26] While Epicurus is undoubtedly more optimistic about the possibility of knowledge than Democritus, it is still the case that the subjectivity of sense perception recommends an epistemological caution. In addition, Epicurus seems to think that we are not so perspicacious as to be able to discern *the* truth about nature, nor does this trouble him. It is enough that we can discern several possible natural explanations for phenomena, so long as we are freed from religious explanations. Diderot's entry "Epicureanism" emphasizes the chaos and vastness of the Epicurean universe, which renders knowledge limited, fallible, and fleeting: "Le monde n'est qu'une petite portion de l'Univers, dont la foiblesse de nos sens a fixé les limites; car l'Univers est illimité"[27] [The world is but a small portion of the universe, to which the weakness of our senses has fixed the limits, for the universe is unlimited]. And: "Le monde est l'effet du hasard, et non l'exécution d'un dessein. Les atomes se sont mûs de toute éternité. Considérés dans l'agitation générale d'où les êtres devoient éclore dans le tems, c'est ce que nous avons nommé *le chaos*"[28] [The world is the effect of chance, and not the execution of a design. Atoms move for all eternity. Considered in the general agitation where beings hatch in time, this is what we called *chaos*]. Chaos, in Epicurus's view, may yield order given infinite time, an idea Diderot repeats in his *Philosophical Thoughts.*[29]

Lucretius is the most influential expositor of Epicurus's natural philosophy, and he is often asserted to be the most influential, and perhaps the earliest, source of Diderot's materialism.[30] Diderot read Latin well and he had certainly read Lucretius's *De rerum natura* in the original; he even made some original connections between Virgil and Lucretius.[31] He was editor-at-large of Nicolas La Grange's and Naigeon's 1768 translation of *De rerum natura* into French.[32] In all likelihood he had also read and liked Creech's English translation, since La Grange identifies that edition as a useful resource throughout the translation process, and because Diderot was a capable English-to-French translator.[33]

Lucretius is a faithful expositor of Epicurus's materialist cosmology. Like Epicurus, he is optimistic about the possibility of knowing, but he is arguably more conscious of the limitations of knowledge. Lucretius emphasizes that matter is so infinite, its motion so chaotic, and its atomic operations so tiny and imperceptible that the universe cannot be predicted with certainty. Though some trails of knowledge may be discerned, we will always be in the dark about more minute details:

Malitious Nature grants not Pow'r to see.
Lastly: Not ev'n the sharpest Eye e'er sees
What Parts, to make Things grow by just Degrees
Nature does add; nor what she takes away ...
'Tis certain then, that much which Nature does,
She works by Bodies, undiscern'd by us.[34]

Book IV contains an extended consideration of the myriad ways in which our sense perception can be easily led astray when the variable conditions of our environment manipulate our sense perception: distance, darkness, echoes, or air pressure are each enough to cause us to perceive incorrectly or not at all. Lucretius recommends a simple experiment (similar to one elucidated by Sextus Empiricus)[35] to demonstrate the senses' manipulability: "If any presses underneath his Eyes, / Straight all the Objects Doubled seem to rise: / Two Lamps appear, when only one is brought."[36]

Furthermore, the vast operations of nature escape our attention, whether because they are so many and so fast,[37] or because they are so small: "So num'rous are they, and so swift they move. / But since these Forms are subtile, and refin'd, / They are too thin to be perceiv'd by Mind."[38] Also, knowledge is limited because focusing our attention on one thing causes other things to fade from view: "Besides; the Mind oft thinks small Objects great, / And thus she leads her self into a Cheat."[39] Lucretius also points out the various ways in which the different material composition of the sense organs will necessarily yield different subjective experiences, though he, like Epicurus, denies that the senses can conflict with each other. This view follows in the Epicurean tradition of subjective perception, but the frequency with which Lucretius points out the limitations of the senses suggests that he is more concerned than Epicurus about the limitations of the senses. Interestingly enough, Diderot diverges from Epicurus and Lucretius on this point, joining Sextus Empiricus in affirming the potential for contradictory sense perception.[40]

The limitations of such skepticism, however, are suggested by its materialist assumptions. Lucretius repeats the Epicurean judgment that there is ultimately no other reasonable basis for knowledge than sense perception, despite its limitations. If we do not accept the information given us by our sense perception, then the foundation of our reasoning, or even our skeptical questioning, is dissolved:

He, that says Nothing can be known, o'erthrows
His own Opinion: for he Nothing knows.

So knows not that: What need of long Dispute?
These Maxims kill themselves, themselves confute.[41]

This is the criticism of skepticism that Diderot echoes, both in his entry on skepticism in the *Encyclopédie* and, mockingly, in his *Philosophical Thoughts*: "The Pyrrhonist was convinced by a stick that he was wrong in doubting his own existence."[42] This acceptance of the existence of external reality and of sense perception – limited and flawed though it may be – separates the disingenuous Pyrrhonist from the *sincere* skeptic "who believes what a legitimate use of his reason and his senses has proved to him to be true."[43]

Perhaps no one understood the depth of the connection between Lucretian materialism and skepticism as well as Montaigne – one of Diderot's favourite writers. Montaigne cited Lucretius more than any other author save Horace. Significantly, he invokes Lucretius seventy times in his *Apology for Raymond Sebond* alone. In the section "The Senses Are Inadequate," Montaigne cites Lucretius several times to bolster his position that "all knowledge makes its way into us through the senses; they are our master."[44] He also, however, uses Lucretius nine more times to illustrate the senses' uncertainty and fallibility. Thus Montaigne concludes, "When the compass, the square, and the ruler are off, all the proportions drawn from them, all the buildings erected by their measure, are also necessarily imperfect and defective. The uncertainty of our senses makes everything they produce uncertain."[45] Philip Ford draws an awkward conclusion from Montaigne's use of Lucretius: though Montaigne first uses Lucretius to *support* his faith in sense perception, he then turns Lucretius's own examples *against* him, using his illustrations of the fallibility of the senses to make a skeptical argument for the *limitations* of our sense perception.[46] Ford thinks these skeptical elements are a *distortion* of Lucretius's thought, and so he finds it contradictory that Lucretius could be employed to support Montaigne's skeptical conclusions. Montaigne's elegant adoption of Lucretius, however, clearly perceives that, far from being a contradiction, Lucretius's materialist and empirical commitments *entail* skepticism. If we are reluctant to perceive the skepticism implied in this materialist world view, we will be forced to resort to a Byzantine logic to explain its skeptical outcomes.

This is the skeptical materialist tradition within which Diderot works. The material universe is arranged in an infinitely complex and dynamic web of causation. In comparison, our faculties of perception are both pitifully limited and inherently subjective. The infinitely complex causal relationships that propel the materialist universe render our knowledge no more certain, our senses no less biased and fickle. This conceptual overlap between Epicureanism and skepticism is a challenge to those who would force a strict separation of the Hellenistic schools. It also reveals that Epicurean materialism is a complex tradition that admits of different interpretations: Hobbes and Helvétius drew systematizing conclusions while Montaigne and Diderot drew skeptical ones.[47]

Emita Hill rightly discerns that Diderot's "materialistic hypothesis leads to no scientifically ordered and predictable universe."[48] Diderot himself emphatically rejects the rationalizing, systematizing tendencies of other materialists. In his entry "Hobbism," Diderot has nothing but disdain for the systematizing tendencies of Hobbes, who demonstrates the fault of systematic thinkers, "that is, of generalizing from particular facts and skillfully bending them to fit his hypothesis." Diderot warns his readers, "Take care not to go beyond his first principles, if you do not wish to follow him everywhere he cares to lead you."[49] While Diderot may have approved of Hobbes's materialist first principles – principles rooted in an Epicurean world view – he rejects the amoral, authoritarian, and systematized politics that Hobbes deduces from those first principles. Diderot also differentiates his own materialism from that of Buffon in his entry "Animal." Though he summarizes Buffon's thoughts with sophistication, he does not conclude, like Buffon, that nature is static material, externally ordered.[50] Rather, Diderot portrays nature as a dynamic disorder punctuated by spontaneous creation. His most conspicuous rejection of another materialist's work is undoubtedly his *Réfutation d'Hélvetius*. Helvétius had argued in his *De l'homme* that, "*juger* est *sentir*" ("*to judge* is *to sense*," emphasis in original).[51] Because man is superior to other organisms in physical organization and sense perception, argued Helvétius, he is thus a superior thinker. For Diderot, however, *juger* does not automatically result from *sentir*, but requires the intervention of conscious reflection guided by sociability.[52]

Despite such self-differentiation, Diderot is sometimes assumed to share the systematizing materialism of some of his *philosophe* coevals. Petr Lom typifies this line of reasoning connecting Diderot's materialism and politics: "The thoroughgoing determinist would deny that human nature is free, thus find political freedom incoherent, and so instead propose absolute rule. If people are not free, then the only way to change their behavior is through laws dictated by the absolute sovereign."[53] This logic lumps Diderot in with the *philosophes* who are portrayed as an undifferentiated mass of rationalizing, systematizing tendencies advocating a centralizing, benevolent despotism. Writers like Edmund Burke and Alexis de Tocqueville were crucial in elucidating this vision.[54] More recently, Michael Oakeshott's "The New Bentham" and Jacques Proust's seminal *Diderot et L'Encyclopédie* (1962) have served to perpetuate it.[55] Though some thinkers did desire to refound politics on rational principles, such a picture is at best an oversimplification and at worst a misrepresentation of the *philosophes*' diverse perspectives.

That Diderot endorsed benevolent authoritarianism is a particularly widespread misconception. Oakeshott's essay, "The New Bentham," for example, lumps Diderot, Helvétius, Voltaire, and d'Alembert together as "the last of the believers in Benevolent Despotism" who believed "that what is made is better than what merely grows, that neatness is better than profusion and vitality." One struggles to find support for such a hypothesis in Diderot's texts, however. Nor can we find support for Diderot's endorsement of benevolent despotism in his additions to the Abbé Raynal's *Histoire des deux Indes* (1777), where he declares unequivocally, "People say that the most fortunate kind of government would be that of a just, resolute, and enlightened despot. What nonsense!"[56] Nor do we find Diderot endorsing benevolent despotism in his early entry "Political Authority" (1751), where he argues explicitly for limited government, nor in his private correspondence.[57] Despite the dearth of textual support for Diderot's benevolent despotism, however, the myth continues to be repeated as a foregone conclusion by commentators unwilling to appreciate that materialism can entail skepticism. Lom implies that Diderot's materialism would have led him to share Helvétius's praise of Catherine II and Frederick II in his introduction to *De l'homme.* But it is precisely this work that provoked Diderot into writing his *Réfutation d'Helvétius,* a vigorous attack on Helvétius's mechanistic conception of man and society. Because Diderot is somewhat bizarrely identified with a type of materialism that he explicitly opposed, he is thus assumed to support a benevolent despotism that he emphatically rejected. Unfortunately, his *Réfutation d'Helvétius* remains unpublished in English, depriving anglophone perspectives of a source of nuance in Diderot's materialism.

Diderot is also quite skeptical about the unbounded ability of a powerful state to rationally direct its affairs. Dennis Rasmussen points out that Diderot does not advocate radical, revolutionary politics so much as he recommends reform, and he does not have unmitigated faith in reason and politics, but desires limited government.[58] His *Observations sur le Nakaz* (1774) excoriates his benefactress Catherine II for Russia's extant serfdom, among other things. The *Observations* is a clarion call for limited government, the separation of church and state, and the sovereignty of the people, as well as the idea that laws should be malleable and suited to the particular character and circumstance of a people. This is the basis for his anti-colonialism.[59] One of his contributions to Raynal's *Histoire de deux Indes* reads, "The state is a very complicated machine which one can neither assemble nor set in motion without knowing all the pieces. You cannot press nor loosen a single one without disturbing all the others ... All innovations should be gradual, born from need, inspired by a kind of public clamor, or at least in accord with general wishes. To create or destroy suddenly is to corrupt the good and make the evil worse."[60] Here Diderot exhibits an inclination towards limited government and organic, spontaneous reform – not a rationalizing, technocratic state. He is always opposed to physiocratic pretensions that are overconfident in their ability to know and oversimplify the complexity of society. Typical is his advice in the *Observations sur le Nakaz*: "Put in good order two or three important things, and leave the rest to the self-interest and taste of individuals."[61] Thus when Lom speculates that Diderot's hopes for benevolent despotism can be explained by the influence of material determinism on his thought, he is wrong on two counts. First, the idea that Diderot is optimistic about a benevolent despotism in fact does not reflect Diderot's thought, but rather the mythology that has grown up around other rationalizing, systematizing French *philosophes*. Second, Diderot's materialism has skeptical – not technocratic or authoritarian – consequences.

In addition to suggesting the limitations of sense perception and the unpredictable complexity of society, materialist skepticism inclines Diderot towards limited government as a result of its Epicurean recognition of the inevitability of decline and death. Epicurus thought material explanations could make us content with our mortality, and Brucker even tells us that Epicurus admired Pyrrho for exhibiting such contentment.[62] The death-obsessed Montaigne seizes on the Lucretian themes of mortality and decay, especially in his essay "To Philosophize Is to Learn to Die," where Lucretius is cited fifteen times. In his *Salon de 1767*, Diderot echoes a Lucretian claim, observing, "Le destin qui règle le monde veut que tout passe. La condition la plus heureuse d'un homme, d'un État, a son terme. Tout porte en soi un germe secret de destruction"[63] [The destiny that rules the world wills everything to pass. The happiest condition of man, of a State, has its term. Everything carries within it the secret germ of its destruction]. Clearly, Diderot was not optimistic about the unbounded ability of a rational politics to yield perpetual improvement. This organic, evolutionary conception of politics does not support linear growth, but rather eternal cycles of destruction and creation, within which progress is possible but neither permanently sustainable nor inevitable. Hence, "The law of nature, which wills that every society should gravitate towards despotism and dissolution, that empires should be born and die, will not be suspended for any exception."[64] Anthony Strugnell interprets this as a foreshadowing of the Hegelian historical dialectic, but Diderot's history is not linear but circular, and it lacks a notion of inevitable progression.

Strugnell attempts to connect Diderot's materialism to his politics in *Diderot's Politics* (1973). Following Proust, he reasons that in a materialist universe, political principles must proceed directly from material, physiological foundations. Diderot's materialism logically entails the indivisibility of sovereignty that, combined with his "mistrust of the people," convinces Diderot of the need to locate power in a Leviathanesque absolutist ruler who, being physiologically superior to the common people, is more inclined to rule benevolently.[65] The same assumptions that motivate Diderot's purported early endorsement of absolutism, however, later motivate him to "reject reformism" and become "the first effective advocate in the modern world of social and political reconstruction through violent revolution."[66] In this reading, Diderot's monolithic materialism admits of no division; sovereignty must either be entirely wielded by an enlightened despot or a single revolutionary movement.

The political conclusions Strugnell traces from Diderot's materialism are unjustified, however. A materialism that posits an eternally dynamic, infinitely complicated universe could not feasibly lend itself to the direction of one individual. Yet Strugnell concludes that Diderot's materialism reduces man "to the same inexorable laws that govern the rest of the universe," and reduces the brain to a basically passive role, amenable to enlightened manipulation.[67] This flawed perspective commits Strugnell to misinterpret Diderot as either endorsing absolutism or violent revolution because "inexorable laws" mean that reformism and pluralism are ineffective political options compared to a benevolent unitary power. The *Voyage de Bougainville*, for example, makes the anti-colonialist argument that laws should be malleable and suited to the character and situation of a people, not dictated from a distant government. Strugnell, however, reads it as an endorsement of a universal moral law to be applied everywhere.[68]

Finally, Strugnell misunderstands the role of physiology in moral knowledge. The *Lettres on the Blind* does not equate perfect physiology with *superior* moral guidance, as Strugnell argues. True, the blind Dr Saunderson reaches different moral conclusions than the sighted, but his conclusions are not therefore *less* moral, and they are sometimes *more* creative and instructive, as when Diderot notes Dr Saunderson's gift of hitting upon illuminating algebraic examples. The moral variance between the sighted and the blind indicates that morality is always mediated by sense perceptions that inevitably introduce subjectivity, but not superiority. This precludes the possibility of a universally applicable moral code discernible by an absolute ruler or physiocrats. In addition, as his *Réfutation d'Helvétius* points out, Diderot does not think that morality and judgment proceed directly from sense perception, but rather that this process is mediated by consciousness.[69] Strugnell's example demonstrates that we are likely to draw flawed conclusions about Diderot's politics if we fail to appreciate the skeptical facets of his materialism.

Thus far I have outlined how Diderot's materialist skepticism can point us towards principles such as limited government and freedom of thought. Crucially, however, it falls short of elaborating the *normative* content of politics. Even if materialism leaves room for skepticism, it is not clear how it leaves room for morality, for any contingent moral conclusions that we *do* manage to articulate are still only the determined outcomes of material causes. Without freedom, choice, or responsibility, there can be no genuine morality – whether certain or contingent. Skepticism merely renders moral knowledge uncertain, but materialist determinism threatens to render it *impossible* by eliminating freedom altogether. Diderot was disturbed by this. His *Lettre à Landois* (1756) suggests an early preoccupation with and pessimism about the disastrous moral consequences of materialism: "Mais s'il n'y a point de liberté, il n'y a point d'action qui merite la louange ou le blame; il n'y a ni vice ni virtue, rien dont il faille recompenser ou châtier"[70] [But if there is no freedom, there is no action that merits praise or blame; there is no vice or virtue, nothing which must be rewarded or chastened]. In the entry "Natural Right," he repeats the materialist objection to morality: If man is not free because his decisions spring from some material source, then there can be no moral good or evil; thus we see how important it is to establish the reality of both free will and liberty. A materialist skepticism, then, does not leave a basis for normative political action, only the imperative that we be cautious as to what kinds of political action we take. Without free will, our knowledge and actions can have no moral quality and thus cannot provide a normative basis for politics.

Perhaps it is possible to derive notions of right and wrong, of just and unjust, directly from nature itself? But Diderot rejects this possibility. He writes in *D'Alembert's Dream*, for example, that "man is merely a common phenomenon while a monster is only a rare phenomenon, but both are equally natural."[71] This prompts Lom to observe that for Diderot, science succeeds in description but not morality. In the same vein, Hill notes that Diderot's frequent allusions to monsters represent the inability of nature to provide a basis for morality because they imply that "[n]ature is blind and indiscriminate in her creations."[72] Alasdair MacIntyre points out that Diderot was alone among the *philosophes* in recognizing the limitations of nature as a guide to morality: nature by itself offers no guiding teleology, only raw material.[73]

Diderot is not content to accept this nihilistic conclusion of materialist determinism, but neither can he easily dismiss it. He agonizes over the contradiction between materialism and morality more than many of his materialist contemporaries. In his letter to Mme de Maux, for example, he is obviously aggrieved at the irreconcilability of the contradiction between determinism and morality: "J'enrage d'être empêtre d'une diable de philosophie que mon esprit ne peut s'empêcher d'approuver, et mon coeur de dementir"[74] [I am enraged to be entangled by a devil of a philosophy that my mind cannot help but approve, and my heart deny]. Throughout his career, Diderot remained occupied by the problem materialism entailed for free will and moral responsibility, and it is a central theme in his later fictional works: *Rameau's Nephew*, *D'Alembert's Dream*, and especially *Jacques the Fatalist*. Diderot's politics, then, depends on our resolving the question: How might we have moral knowledge to guide our political action in a universe where there exists neither certainty nor freedom?

Diderot locates a place for freedom in the material universe by altering the Epicurean concept of the "swerve" – a minute movement caused by an innate atomic consciousness. The ability of the atom to swerve represents the possibility that matter can break the bonds of its own inexorable causal chain. Similarly, Diderot argues that humans have "sensibilité," or consciousness, which endows them with the ability to reflect and to will. *This* is the "real miracle of life," and the way in which "All beings participate in the existence of all other beings."[75] By introducing consciousness, Diderot does not mean to introduce an immaterial element to his thought; he remains committed to the materialist world view. Rather, consciousness is an emergent property of the material mind reflecting back on its material existence. Through consciousness one can rise above the bonds of fate, thus establishing the freedom by which one can achieve a moral existence.[76]

Because political agency is predicated on freedom, one becomes a political agent only in the wake of conscious reflection. Only "matter that possesses active consciousness" can reflect on and intervene in its own causally determined existence. "Sensibilité" means that humans are not only objects in a determined universe, but determiners of that universe. David Coward notes that moral action is possible in Diderot because, "we can enter the chain [of materialist consequences] and affect outcomes," and, "by tapping into nature's processes we can begin to harness them."[77] In this way, our conscious reflection becomes the assertion of our self-determination through which we realize our own freedom and create our own moral possibilities. The reflection by which we become *causes* has no necessary content, but the action of reflection itself lends moral significance to our existence. Thus the possibility of moral knowledge exists because we *create* moral knowledge by intervening in the material universe through our own reflection. Dena Goodman's "Diderot's *Supplément au Voyage de Bougainville*" argues that Diderot's use of dialogue facilitates the process of conscious reflection, thereby becoming a medium for political reform: "[M]en have consciousness, they are able to reflect upon their actions. It is not actions in themselves that are vicious or virtuous, but actions informed by consciousness."[78] Dialogue connects the reader to facts, but it invites the reflection that Diderot believes endows the facts with moral and political significance.

Thus, individual conscious reflection transforms us into political agents who have the moral power to confer political legitimacy on government. Diderot describes this political origin story in his *Histoire de deux Indes*: the state of nature is bereft of natural law, humans congregate in order to better survive, and society progresses from simple to complex social arrangements – all purely physical developments. Then, fortuitously, democracy dawns: "Then for the first time the sacred name of *patrie* is heard. Then the humbled man lifts up his head and shows himself in all his dignity."[79] Legitimate political obligation – *patrie* – can only arise in the individualistic condition of democracy, because only through the operation of *individual* consciousness can humans exercise political agency. Furthermore, this is a choice that we must continually make to maintain political legitimacy, frequently revising the laws to better reflect our particular character and circumstance. When politics ceases to be the product of individual consciousness, legitimacy ceases.

This explains Diderot's radical advice in the *Observations sur le Nakaz* that "The decisions of courts should never be printed": if political legitimacy depends on conscious reflection, society must guard against magistrates who would forfeit their own interpretive ability in order to uncritically adopt that of another.[80] On one hand, this is not skeptical: it is a rejection of tradition as a possible source of moral knowledge and political guidance. Furthermore, Diderot seems to make the more profoundly anti-skeptical claim that each magistrate's reason is inherently capable of accessing universal justice. Yet this second claim cannot be sustained in light of the whole of the text. It would be wonderful if laws could be based on the natural order, "but," Diderot skeptically enquires, "when will such an order be discovered? Who will introduce it?"[81] The most often repeated refrain in the *Observations sur le Nakaz* is that the law should vary according to circumstance.[82] To rely on tradition is to surrender to our predetermined existence and cede our freedom, and without freedom there can be no knowledge that is specifically *moral* in character; as a result there can be no legitimate guidance for politics. The prohibition on printing legal opinions is not an endorsement of a universally accessible eternal law. Rather, it is the recognition that the use of reason itself is the source of freedom and moral knowledge.

Geoffrey Bremner argues that Diderot's state emerges organically from a natural disorder and would dissolve into disorder again if not for the efforts of the elites to weave an artificial illusion of freedom and political authority.[83] My own evaluation is more optimistic: individuals do not weave an illusion so much as they establish values through their active consciousness. This evaluation better comports with Diderot's insistence that laws remain dynamic and malleable. Bremner's elites want to manufacture a unitary order, but in fact Diderot's political authority rests not on the maintenance of any monolithic artifice but on the action of many different consciousnesses. This situation would not descend back into disorder, as Bremner suggests, because reasoning, while different, will not differ so radically as to make society impossible.

Diderot's prohibition of the publication of legal opinions suggests that, because moral knowledge is a result of the individual's *experience* of reason, it cannot be completely communicated through writing. Indeed, writing itself determines what the reader thinks, and as a result seems to undermine the very possibility of freedom and moral knowledge. But Diderot hoped that literature might evolve to keep pace with developments in knowledge and morality.[84] Specifically, he thought a more naturalistic literary style could connect the reader to empirical reality, confront her with its skeptical consequences, and leave the reader to exercise her own conscious reflection.[85]

Diderot's naturalistic style reflects his materialism by situating the reader in "the raw data of experience."[86] Truth, though, is not sterile empirical description but rather the little details of social life, the contingencies that impinge on and thwart our expectations instead of establishing or confirming to our expectations.[87] Diderot's disconnected anecdotes and quotidian minutiae have the effect of creating an uncertain and unpredictable world without a system – not because he departs from empirical reality, but because he adheres so faithfully to it. The woman with a wart on her nose is both more real and more surprising than the archetype of perfection.[88] In this way, Diderot's writing expresses the assumptions of his dynamic materialist universe and its skeptical consequences.[89]

One way Diderot accomplishes this is through the rambling, "natural" flow of his work, which thwarts the reader's expectations and provokes reflection. A literature that reflects life should proceed episodically, unconnected by thematic appropriateness. *Jacques the Fatalist*, for example, is "a tasteless mishmash of things that happen, some of them true, others made up, written without style and served up like a dog's breakfast."[90] This choppiness is intended to jar the reader out of her predetermined thought; her past experience with novels cause her to expect a romantic entanglement or a wacky adventure to an exotic place, but her expectations only expose her lack of freedom. Diderot subverts the reader's expectations by confronting her with meandering, anticlimactic plots, awkward dialogue, and multiple perspectives – in a word, reality. Anything less ordinary would confirm the reader's novelistic expectations and thus forfeit the potential for conscious reflection. Constantly subverting the reader's expectations thwarts her attempts to impose a framework on reality, opening up aporia that might allow for the reader's *sensibilité*. In this view, fiction becomes potentially epistemologically superior to other genres of philosophical writing, which may overdetermine the reader's conscious reflection and fail to cause the reader to make a conscious intervention in her own causality.[91]

Bourdin argues that Diderot introduces skeptical literary elements in order to challenge the linearity of academic forms of writing and to critique the scientific pretensions of dialogue. These skeptical literary tropes allow Diderot to remain somewhat detached from his materialist theses, the rhetorical distance always reminding the reader of the limitations of our knowledge. Skepticism does not encourage us to throw out our scientific knowledge, but "encourage plutôt à une prudence epistemologique accrue et nourrit une confiance mesurée dans les progrés des sciences"[92] [encourages instead an increased epistemological prudence and nourishes a measured confidence in the progress of sciences]. Diderot's use of skeptical literary elements challenges the epistemic pretensions of linear, logical forms of academic writing; they make room for our positively conjectural activities that work alongside rational, experimental forms of thought; and they nourish our philosophical imaginations. Bourdin thinks Diderot employs skeptical literary elements as a check on materialism, and as an *other* that reanimates our calcified thought. I would modify this conclusion, though, to point out that Diderot's skepticism actually emerges from *within* his materialism.[93]

I have argued that Diderot embraces a materialist skepticism that leads him to endorse ideas such as limited government, reform, tolerance, and freedom of thought. His materialist skepticism is also reflected in his naturalistic writing style, where the portrayal of protean reality and fallible perception causes the reader to confront the limits of her knowledge. Thus, Diderot's writing provokes a skeptical experience by foregrounding its materialist assumptions. Skepticism is not the end, however, but the beginning: it is the aporia that provokes the reader into the *sensibilité* by which she becomes free, thereby establishing herself as a moral and political agent. An ability to be skeptical is thus the first condition of freedom and conscious reflection, and in this way the most important political implications of skepticism are realized.

NOTES

1 Johann Brucker, *Historia Critica Philosophiae* (Leipzig: Bernhard Christopf Breitkopf), 6 vols., 1742–4. Hereafter cited from William Enfield, *The History of Philosophy, from the earliest times to the beginning of the present century; drawn up from Brucker's Historia critica philosophiae* (London: J. Johnson, 1791), vol. 1, 488.

2 Denis Diderot, "Scepticisme, ou Pyrrhonisme," in *Oeuvres complètes*, ed. Herbert Dieckmann, Jacques Proust, and Jean Varloot (Paris: Hermann, 1975–2004), vol. 8, 150; cited from Denis Diderot, "Pyrrhonian or Skeptic," in *Skepticism: An Anthology*, ed. Richard Popkin and Jose R. Maia Neto (New York: Prometheus Books, 2007), 251.

3 Diderot, "Scepticisme, ou Pyrrhonisme," in *Oeuvres complètes*, vol. 8, 152; cited from Diderot, "Pyrrhonian or Skeptic," in *Skepticism: An Anthology*, 252.

4 Douglas H. Gordon and Norman L. Torrey, *The Censoring of Diderot's Encyclopédie and the Re-Established Text* (New York: AMS Press, 1966).
5 Diderot, "Scepticisme, ou Pyrrhonisme," in *Oeuvres complètes*, vol. 8, 159; cited from Diderot, "Pyrrhonian or Skeptic," in *Skepticism: An Anthology*, 250.
6 See for example his *Promenade du Sceptique* (1747), *Rameau's Nephew* (c. 1761), *Jacques the Fatalist* (c. 1771), *Lettre à Landois* (1756), and *Lettre à Mme. Maux* (1769?).
7 Diderot, "Scepticisme, ou Pyrrhonisme," in *Oeuvres complètes*, vol. 8, 160; cited from Diderot, "Pyrrhonian or Skeptic," in *Skepticism: An Anthology*, 257.
8 Denis Diderot, "Scepticisme, ou Pyrrhonisme," in *Oeuvres complètes*, vol. 8, 160; cited from Diderot, "Pyrrhonian or Skeptic," in *Skepticism: An Anthology*, 257.
9 "The true sceptic has counted and weighed his reasons. But it is no easy matter to weigh arguments. Which of us knows their value with any exactness? ... If we dispute about their intrinsic value, how shall we agree upon their relative? Tell me how many moral proofs are needed to balance a metaphysical conclusion?" In Denis Diderot, *Pensées philosophiques*, in *Oeuvres complètes*, vol. 2, 31; cited from Diderot, *Diderot's Early Philosophical Works*, ed. Margaret Jourdain (Chicago: Open Court Publishing, 1916; reprinted Bibliolife, 2012), section XXIV, 41.
10 Diderot, "Scepticisme, ou Pyrrhonisme," in *Oeuvres complètes*, vol. 8, 159; cited from Diderot, "Pyrrhonian or Skeptic," in *Skepticism: An Anthology*, 257.
11 Denis Diderot, *Pensées sur l'interprétation de la nature*, in *Oeuvres complètes*, vol. 9, 41; cited from Denis Diderot, *Thoughts on the Interpretation of Nature and Other Philosophical Works*, ed. David Adams (Manchester: Clinamen Press, 1999), 44.
12 Diderot, *Pensées sur l'interprétation de la nature*, in *Oeuvres complètes*, vol. 9, 32; cited from Diderot, *Thoughts on the Interpretation of Nature*, 37–8.
13 Diderot, *Pensées sur l'interprétation de la nature*, in *Oeuvres complètes*, vol. 9, 27; cited from Diderot, *Thoughts on the Interpretation of Nature*, 35.
14 Diderot, "Scepticisme, ou Pyrrhonisme," in *Oeuvres complètes*, 152; cited from Diderot, "Skepticism or Pyrrhonism," 252.
15 Diderot, "Scepticisme, ou Pyrrhonisme," in *Oeuvres complètes*, vol. 8, 153; cited from Diderot, "Skepticism or Pyrrhonism," 252.
16 Diderot, *Pensées sur l'interprétation de la nature*, in *Oeuvres complètes*, vol. 9, 86; cited from Diderot, *Thoughts on the Interpretation of Nature*, 69.
17 Diderot, *Pensées philosophiques*, in *Oeuvres complètes*, 46; cited from Diderot, *Philosophical Thoughts*, in *Diderot's Early Philosophical Works*, 60.
18 Diderot, *Pensées sur l'interprétation de la nature*, in *Oeuvres complètes*, vol. 9, 86; cited from Diderot, *Thoughts on the Interpretation of Nature*, 69.
19 Denis Diderot, *Lettre sur les aveugles*, in *Oeuvres complètes*, vol. 4; Diderot, *Letter on the Blind*, in *Diderot's Early Philosophical Works*.

20 Diderot, *Lettre sur les aveugles*, in *Oeuvres complètes*, vol. 4, 22; cited from Diderot, *Letter on the Blind*, in *Diderot's Early Philosophical Works*, 76.

21 In his *Letter on the Blind*, Diderot considers "Molyneaux's Problem," which asks whether or not a person blind from birth, upon receiving sight, would be able to recognize a cube without first touching it. Diderot argues that this person would not recognize the cube, that there is no essential interdependence between the senses, and that sensations are only linked or de-linked through reflection. Diderot, *Lettre sur les aveugles*, in *Oeuvres complètes*, vol. 4, 56.

22 R.H. Popkin, "Scepticism in the Enlightenment," in *Scepticism in the Enlightenment*, ed. Richard H. Popkin, Ezequiel de Olaso, and Giorgio Tonelli (Dordrecht: Kluwer, 1997), 10.

23 Another passage that seems to mitigate against Popkin's conclusion is section XXXIV of Diderot's *Philosophical Thoughts*: "A half-hearted skepticism is the mark of a feeble understanding which reveals a pusillanimous reasoner who permits himself to be alarmed by consequences." Truth, he explains, has nothing to lose by examination. Denis Diderot, *Pensées philosophiques*, in *Oeuvres complètes*, vol. 2, 34; cited from Diderot, *Philosophical Thoughts*, in *Diderot's Early Philosophical Works*, 46.

24 Enfield, *The History of Philosophy*, 486.

25 Diogenes Laertius, *Life of Pyrrho*, in *Hellenistic Philosophy*, trans. Brad Inwood and L.P. Gerson (Indianapolis: Hackett, 1997), 288. Note that Sextus Empiricus rebuts those who think this adage makes Democritus a skeptic: Democritus wants to deny knowledge of properties while skeptics want to suspend judgment on the matter. See Sextus Empiricus, *That the Sceptical Approach Differs from Heraclitean Philosophy*, in *Hellenistic Philosophy*, 309.

26 Plutarch argues that the Epicureans' reliance on subjective sense perception – and their unconcern with the actual properties of things – amounts to an irrational skepticism. Plutarch, *Against Colotes*, in *Hellenistic Philosophy*, 272–3.

27 Denis Diderot, "Epicurisme," *Oeuvres complètes*, vol. 7, 273.

28 Diderot, "Epicurisme," *Oeuvres complètes*, vol. 7, 273–4.

29 Diderot favours the atheist's explanation, "that the possibility of fortuitously creating the universe is very small but that the quantity of throws is infinite." Denis Diderot, *Pensées philosophiques*, in *Oeuvres complètes*, vol. 2, 28; cited from *Philosophical Thoughts* in *Diderot's Early Philosophical Works*, 39.

30 See Johan Werner Schmidt, "Diderot and Lucretius: the *De rerum natura* and Lucretius's legacy in Diderot's scientific, aesthetic, and ethical thought," in *Studies on Voltaire in the Eighteenth Century*, 208:1, 1982. Lucretius was by no means Diderot's only materialist influence. Through the Parisian salons and his editorship of the *Encyclopédie*, Diderot knew personally many of

his scientific contemporaries and was exposed to a wide range of scientific observation. Lamarck, Hilaire, Buffon, La Mettrie, D'Holbach, Haller, Bordeau, Maupertuis, and Shaftesbury were notable influences.

31 Denis Diderot, "Decouverte sur Virgile et Lucrèce," *Oeuvres complètes*, vol. 13, 10–11.

32 The extent of Diderot's participation is not fully known, but Grimm's first-hand accounts of the excitement attending the translation of *De rerum natura* in Baron D'Holbach's salon suggest that its translation was somewhat collaborative. Diderot had both the interest and skill to be useful in the translation process. Even though La Grange is the credited translator, he died before it was completed and Naigeon took up the task in his stead.

33 Lucretius, *De la nature des choses*, 2 vols., trans. Nicolas La Grange (Paris: Bleuet, 1768), 6–7. Hereafter referred to as La Grange, trans. I use Creech's translation because of Diderot's proximity to that text.

34 Lucretius, vol. 1, 33; cited from Lucretius, *Of the Nature of Things*, 2 vols., trans. Thomas Creech (London: Warner and Walthoe, 1722), Book I, ll. 372–5, 379–80, 31–2. Hereafter referred to as Creech, trans.

35 Sextus writes, "And when we press one side of our eye the forms, shapes and sizes of visible things appear long and narrow." Sextus Empiricus, *The Modes*, P.H. 1.47, in *Hellenistic Philosophy*, 326.

36 La Grange, trans., vol. 2, 28; cited from Creech, trans., Book IV, ll. 460–2, 340–1.

37 La Grange, trans., vol. 2, 81; cited from Creech, trans., Book IV, ll. 796–803, 375.

38 La Grange, trans., vol. 2, 83; cited from Creech, trans., Book IV, ll. 801–3, 375.

39 La Grange, trans., vol. 2, 57; cited from Creech, trans., Book IV, ll. 820–1, 377.

40 Though they be separate, Lucretius argues that the senses confirm each other: "Thus Heat, and Cold, and other Qualities/Affect the Touch, while Colours strike the Eyes;/Odours the Smell, Savours the Taste; but none/Invades another's Right, usurps his Throne;/All live at Peace, contented with their own./Therefore, from what the other Senses shew,/In vain we seek to prove one Sense untrue." La Grange trans., 53; cited from Creech trans., Book IV, ll. 505–11, 346. Sextus, on the other hand, holds the senses to be sometimes incompatible. See Sextus Empiricus, *Outlines of Pyrrhonism*, in *Hellenistic Philosophy*, 1.43, 326.

41 La Grange, trans., vol. 2, 53; cited from Creech, trans., Book IV, ll. 4807, 343–4.

42 Denis Diderot, *Pensées philosophiques*, in *Oeuvres complètes*, 23–4; cited from *Philosophical Thoughts in Diderot's Early Philosophical Works*, 34.

43 Diderot, *Pensées philosophiques*, in *Oeuvres complètes*, 35; cited from *Philosophical Thoughts in Diderot's Early Philosophical Works*, 45. Lom argues

that it is the intention of the questioner that Diderot is most concerned with – Diderot disapproves of the destructive Pyrrhonist, but approves of the skeptic who intends to use questioning for an ultimately constructive end. A consideration of Diderot's materialism, however, reveals that the dividing line between an acceptable and unacceptable skepticism hinges not on subjective intention, but on the acceptance of sense experience as the foundation of all questioning. Peter Lom, *The Limits of Doubt: The Moral and Political Implications of Skepticism* (Albany: State University of New York Press, 2001).

44 Michel Montaigne, "Apology for Raymond Sebond," in *The Complete Essays of Montaigne*, trans. Donald M. Frame (Stanford, CA: Stanford University Press, 1976), 443.

45 Montaigne, "Apology for Raymond Sebond," 454.

46 Philip Ford, "Lucretius in early modern France," *The Cambridge Companion to Lucretius* (Cambridge: Cambridge University Press, 2007), 257.

47 Though Diderot portrays Hobbes as thoroughly unskeptical, Paganini (this volume, 55–82) demonstrates that Hobbes had a fruitful engagement with skepticism through Montaigne, Gassendi, and Charron. Like Hobbes, Diderot is discontented by the idea that a skeptical politics might end in mere "prudence," but unlike Hobbes, who desired a scientific basis for politics, Diderot's politics is based in the work of individual reason. For a nuanced consideration of the Epicurean tradition in Hobbes, see Gianni Paganini, "Hobbes, Gassendi and the tradition of political Epicureanism," in *Der Garten und die Moderne: Epikureische Moral und Politik vom Humanismus bis zur Auflkärung*, ed. Gianni Paganini and Edoardo Tortarolo (Stuttgart: Frommann-Holzboog, 2004), 113–37.

48 Emita Hill, "Materialism and Monsters in 'Le Rêve de D'Alembert," *Diderot Studies* 10 (1968): 67–93.

49 Denis Diderot, "Hobbisme," in *Oeuvres complètes*, vol. 7, 406; cited from Diderot, "Hobbism," in *Political Writings*, ed. John Hope Mason and Robert Wokler (Cambridge: Cambridge University Press, 1992), 27.

50 Schmidt, "Diderot and Lucretius," 226.

51 Claude Adrien Helvétius, *De l'homme: de ses faculties intellectuelles & de son education* (London: La Société Typographique, 1773), 93.

52 Denis Diderot, *Réfutation suivie de l'ouvrage d'Helvétius intitule L'Homme*, in *Oeuvres complètes*, vol. 24, 479–761.

53 Peter Lom, *The Limits of Doubt*, 72.

54 See Alexis de Tocqueville, *The Old Regime and the Revolution*, trans. John Bonner (New York: Harper and Brothers, 1856), 189–90. Tocqueville describes Diderot and the *philosophes* as "men of the Revolution" who "had a

robust faith in man's perfectibility and power ... They had no doubt but that they were appointed to transform society and regenerate the human race."

55 Michael Oakeshott, "The New Bentham" in *Rationalism in Politics and Other Essays* (Indianapolis: Liberty Fund, 1991 [1932]); Jacques Proust, *Diderot et l'Encyclopédie* (Paris: Armand Colin, 1962) 137, 139.

56 Guillaume-Thomas Raynal, *Histoire philosophique et politique des Établissemens et du commerce des Européens dans les deux Indes* (Geneva: Jean-Leonard Pellet, 1780), vol. 10, 40; cited from Diderot, *Political Writings*, 207. For a comprehensive catalogue of Diderot's contributions to Raynal's *Histoire*, see Michèle Duchet, *Diderot et l'Histoire des Deux Indes ou l'Ecriture Fragmentaire* (Paris: Nizet, 1978).

57 Arthur M. Wilson, "Why Did the Political Theory of the Encyclopedists Not Prevail? A Suggestion," *French Historical Studies* 1 (1960): 285.

58 Dennis C. Rasmussen, "Burning Laws and Strangling Kings? Voltaire and Diderot on the Perils of Rationalism in Politics," *The Review of Politics* 73 (2011), 77–104. Rasmussen is not alone in his more nuanced, liberal evaluation of Diderot and Voltaire. He echoes previous rejections of the benevolent despotism hypothesis, notably those of Diderot's biographer A.M. Wilson (1960; 1972), Jonathan Israel (2011), Peter Gay (1954, 385), Eric Steel (1941, 189), and J. Chapman (1889).

59 See Sankar Muthu, *Enlightenment against Empire* (Princeton, NJ: Princeton University Press, 2003).

60 Raynal, *Histoire philosophique et politiques*, vol. 10, 148; cited from Diderot, *Political Writings*, 209.

61 Diderot, *Oeuvres politiques*, ed. Paul Vernière (Paris: Garnier Frères, 1963), 446; cited from Diderot, *Political Writings*, 155–6.

62 Enfield, *The History of Philosophy*, vol. 1, 486.

63 Denis Diderot, *Oeuvres complètes de Diderot*, 20 vols., ed. Assèzat (Paris: Garnier Frères, 1875), vol. 11, 93.

64 Raynal, *Histoire philosophique et politique*, vol. 10, 25; cited from Diderot, *Political Writings*, 207.

65 Anthony Strugnell, *Diderot's Politics: A Study of Diderot's Political Thought After the Encyclopédie* (The Hague: Martinus Nijhoff, 1973), 210.

66 Strugnell, *Diderot's Politics*, 228.

67 Strugnell, *Diderot's Politics*, 3, 22. One of Strugnell's main sources for this view is Proust's *Diderot et l'Encyclopédie*, which largely neglects the Epicurean tradition. Instead, Proust identifies a stoic physiology at the foundation of Diderot's political thought: "L'encyclopédiste avait encore appris chez les stoïciens qu'on ne peut s'interroger sur la fin de l'homme sans considerer la place qu'il a dans l'univers. Parce que l'homme n'est qu'une partie du

'grand tout,' sa fin 'doit être de conformer sa conduit aux lois de la nature'" [The encyclopedist had also learned from the stoics that one cannot question the end of man without considering his place in the universe. Because man is but a small part of the "grand whole," his end should be to conform to the laws of nature'"]. Proust argues that such a physiology leads to an anti-individualistic, universalizing brand of politics. Jacques Proust, *Diderot et L'Encyclopedie* (Paris: Armand-Colin, 1962), 406.

68 Strugnell, *Diderot's Politics,* 38–9.

69 Denis Diderot, *Réfutation suivie de l'ouvrage d'Helvétius intitule l'Homme,* in *Oeuvres complètes,* vol. 24, 479–761.

70 Denis Diderot, "Lettre à Landois" [29 June 1756], *Correspondance littéraire,* ed. Jean Varloot et al. (Paris: Hermann, 1976), vol. 9, 257.

71 Denis Diderot, *Le Rêve de D'Alembert,* in *Oeuvres complètes,* vol. 17, 138; cited from Diderot, *D'Alembert's Dream in Rameau's Nephew and Other Works,* trans. Jacques Barzun and Ralph H. Bowen (Indianapolis: Hackett, 1956), 124.

72 Emita Hill, "Materialism and Monsters," 74.

73 Alasdair MacIntyre, *After Virtue* (London: Gerald Duckworth & Co., 1981), 46.

74 Denis Diderot, Correspondance, "Lettre à Mme. Maux" [1769?], vol. 9, Roth, ed. (Paris: Les Éditions de Minuit, 1955), 154.

75 Denis Diderot, *Le Rêve de D'Alembert,* in *Oeuvres complètes,* vol. 17, 138; cited from Diderot, *D'Alembert's Dream,* trans. Barzun and Bowen, 124.

76 This view is also reflected in the reasoning for Diderot's controversial choice to commission a statue of Voltaire as a naked representation of Seneca on the verge of suicide. By portraying the subject at the point of his conscious overcoming of material circumstance, the statue communicates that free will is the crux of morality. Tim Hochstrasser, "More long-lasting than Bronze? Statues, Public Commemoration and Representations of Monarchy in Diderot's Political Thought," in Monarchism and Absolutism in Early Modern Europe, Cesare Cuttica and Glenn Burgess, eds. (London: Pickering and Chatto, 2012), 213.

77 David Coward, in Denis Diderot, *Jacques the Fatalist and His Master,* ed. Coward (Oxford: Oxford University Press, 2008), xxi.

78 Dena Goodman, "The Structure of Political Argument in Diderot's Supplément au Voyage de Bougainville," *Diderot Studies* 21 (1983): 133.

79 Raynal, *Histoire philosophique et politique,* vol. 10, 24; cited from Diderot, *Political Writings,* 205–7.

80 Denis Diderot, *Oeuvres politiques,* 377; cited from Diderot, *Political Writings,* 106.

81 Diderot, *Oeuvres politiques*; cited from *Political Writings,* 96.

82 See especially sections V, XII, XIX, XXXVI, LII, LIII, CXXVII.

83 Geoffrey Bremner, *Order and Chance: The Pattern of Diderot's Thought* (Cambridge: Cambridge University Press, 1983).

84 Even early in his career, he hints at this naturalism in what is perhaps the unlikeliest of texts: his erotic novel, *The Indiscreet Jewels* (1748). Presiding over a refreshingly erudite harem, a woman argues that eloquence and poetry should experience progress just as the sciences have, adding, "Je n'entends point les règles ... et moins encore les mots savants dans lesquels on les a conçues; mais je sais qu'il n'y a que le vrai qui plaise et qui touche" [I do not understand the rules at all ... and less still the clever words in which we designed them; but I know that nothing but the truth pleases and touches]. Denis Diderot, *Les bijoux indiscrets*, in *Oeuvres complètes*, vol. 3, 163. This is an idea Diderot returns to in his entry "Encyclopédie" where he asserts that literary forms should change to adequately express changes in knowledge and morality: "Certain literary genres come to be neglected on account of their failure to reflect real life and current morality, thus losing their permanent poetic validity. Others remain, sustained by their intrinsic value, but only by taking an entirely new form." Denis Diderot, "Encyclopèdie," in *Oeuvres complètes*, vol. 7, 184; cited from Diderot, "Encyclopédie," in *Political Writings*, 23.

85 His evolving understanding of literature is perhaps most notable in his later philosophical fiction, notably *Jacques the Fatalist* and *Rameau's Nephew*, but it is also manifest in the natural flow of his *Thoughts on the Interpretation of Nature*, the dialogue form of *Voyage de Bougainville*, or the disjointedness of his *Ceci n'est pas un conte*.

86 Diderot, *Jacques the Fatalist and His Master*, ed. Coward, xv.

87 Diderot is deeply influenced by and has intense admiration for the novelist Samuel Richardson, whom he thinks succeeds spectacularly in rendering the raw details of human experience. See Denis Diderot, "Eloge de Richardson," *Oeuvres complètes*, vol. 13, 181–208.

88 He writes in *Les deux amis de Bourbonne*, "Je dirai donc à nos conteurs historiques: Vos figures sont belles, si vous voulez; mail il y manque la verrue à la tempe, la coupure à la lèvre, la marque de petite vérole à côté du nez qui les rendraient vraies" [I will say therefore to our storytellers: your figures are beautiful, if you wish, but they lack the wart on the temple, the cut on the lip, the smallpox on the nose that would make them real]. Denis Diderot, *Les deux amis de Bourbonne*, in *Oeuvres complètes*, vol. 12, 455–6.

89 Paolo Quintili argues that Diderot's aesthetic theory was an extension of his Epicurean and stoic materialism. Paolo Quintili, "La réception des materialists anciens chez Diderot," in *Materia actuosa: Antiquité, Âge classique, Lumières: Mélanges en l'Honneur D'Olivier Bloch*, ed. Antony McKenna, Miguel

Benitez, Gianni Paganini, and Jean Salem (Paris: Honoré Champion: 2000), 487–512.

90 Denis Diderot, *Jacques le fataliste et son maitre*, in *Oeuvres complètes*, vol. 23, 230, cited from Diderot, *Jacques the Fatalist and his Master*, 185.

91 This runs counter to Strugnell's (1973) view that Diderot's fiction has only limited philosophical value. In fact, Diderot is clear that his fiction is meant as more of a philosophical than an aesthetic venture. Strugnell's dismissal of the philosophical value of Diderot's fiction is baseless.

92 Jean-Claude Bourdin, "Matérialisme et scepticisme chez Diderot," *Recherches sur Diderot et sur l'Encyclopédie* (1999): 91.

93 It is not clear why Bourdin insists that Diderot is not a skeptic, or why he concludes that working outside of science "est intrinsequement pathologique" [is intrinsically pathological], 97. Bourdin alternately asserts that skepticism has (1) no role at all, (2) a positively conjectural role, and (3) a pathological role in Diderot's thought. Like Ford (2007), the reluctance to affirm the presence of skepticism leads to puzzling conclusions.

chapter nine

Rousseau: Philosophical and Religious Skepticism and Political Dogmatism

MARÍA JOSÉ VILLAVERDE

To take Rousseau's skepticism into consideration scholars focus unanimously on the "Vicar's Creed" included in *Emile.* Nevertheless there are many other works which also should be taken into account such as the *Lettres morales,* the *Lettre à Christophe de Beaumont,* the *Rêveries,* the *Lettre à Voltaire,* the *Discours sur les sciences et les arts, La Nouvelle Héloïse,* the *Lettre à M. de Franquières,* and the *Lettres écrites de la montagne.* According to Rousseau, all of his books breathe the same maxims but the creed of the author is expressed more freely in some of his writings than in the "Vicar's Creed."[1] In fact, as can be readily confirmed, Rousseau borrowed parts of his letters to Sophie to write the main part of the "Vicar's Creed."[2] Besides, in the *Lettres écrites de la montagne* he confesses that the creed of the Catholic Vicar correlates closely with the profession of faith of Julie, the devout character of *La Nouvelle Héloïse* (*Lettres ...,* OCIII, 694). If the author does not adopt them completely, he adds, he is quite in favour of them. I intend in this chapter to look at all of these books to pronounce on his skepticism. My thesis is that Rousseau is an academic skeptic in philosophy, a Pyrrhonian in theological matters, and a dogmatist in the remaining fields. First and foremost, he derides the vanity and futility of philosophy. Second, he believes in God with all his might but cannot say much about theological matters because they are beyond the capacity of his reason. Lastly, he is convinced of the goodness of his socio-political and moral model based on nature (simplicity, equality, and virtue), no matter whether or not the Enlightened and corrupted countries of his time are able to adopt it.

1. The *Philosophes*, between Skepticism and the Idea of Progress

It has been said recently that the eighteenth century represents the end of all certainties, the breaking down of the idea of progress and the end of the great hopes.[3] According to this approach, the claim in the 1960s of Richard Popkin ("there was, perhaps surprisingly, very little skepticism in the Enlightenment") has been described as untenable.[4] Although many other scholars from Ernst Cassirer to Pierre-André Taguieff endorsed it, the editors of *Skepticisme et modernité* insist on the great significance of skepticism in the eighteenth century. As they point out in the introduction to their volume, even the less skeptical members of the D'Holbach coterie – D'Holbach himself, Naigeon, and Grimm – were not so far from skepticism since they admitted the limits of reason and the finiteness of human nature.[5]

Other researchers such as Giorgio Tonelli, Keith Baker, and Ezequiel de Olaso have also contributed to the rehabilitation of skepticism in the eighteenth century.[6] According to Tonelli, if the Enlightenment symbolizes the age of reason, nevertheless it is a reason aware of its own limits. Sébastien Charles adds that even Condorcet, who represents the optimism of the Enlightenment, did not trust human capacities as much as has been said: "declamations against skepticism are the work of folly or quackery. A skeptic who would not admit different degrees of probability would be a fool; a skeptic who would admit them would differ from dogmatists only because he seeks to disentangle these different degrees with more subtleties."[7] Condorcet's skepticism is methodological; a critical instrument to revise knowledge that supposedly can offer an answer to all questions. And it is also moderate since he admits that knowledge is limited but within these limits certainties are possible.[8]

Véronique Le Ru also supports this approach.[9] Not only were the authors of the *Encyclopédie* not champions of progress, but in the *Discours préliminaire* of the *Encyclopedie* (DPE) they developed a clearly skeptical conception of the human understanding and its capacity to apprehend the universe. In effect, d'Alembert shows in the *Discours* the ambivalence of the *Encyclopédistes*' idea of progress: "barbarism lasts for centuries, it seems that it is our element, reason and good taste are just passing."[10] This sentence has great importance since it appears in the preface to the *Encyclopédie* and sets the guidelines to be followed in the whole work. As a matter of fact, the *Encyclopédie* was the product of a tension between the belief in progress and a pessimistic approach to history according to which the mind follows its way, takes a roundabout route, and from time to time gets lost. Even though d'Alembert and Diderot were aware of their contribution to human progress, they were also conscious of the weakness of knowledge. Man discovers himself as a historical animal who needs time to attain progress in the sciences and arts but at the same time his nature can degrade over the course of history. This is the ambiguity that the DPE expresses. But despite its ambiguity, d'Alembert, as the editor of the *Encyclopédie,* feels embarrassed about a contributor like Rousseau who denigrates progress.

To understand properly the context of the *Encyclopédistes'* thought, it is useful to remember that notions of progress and perfectibility were relatively recent in the eighteenth century but were nevertheless well integrated into philosophical discussions. In 1750, at the age of twenty-three, Turgot used the word "progress" for the first time. However, the absence of the word "perfectibility" in the *Encyclopédistes'* works and the brevity of the entry "Progress" can be explained by the relative distrust of the *philosophes* towards these ideas.

Rousseau promoted these notions both in his *Discours sur l'origine de l'inégalité parmi les hommes* and in his *Essai sur l'origine des langues* (written between 1754 and 1761). But for the first time, he enunciated the idea that man can make not only progress towards the good, but also towards evil, and that the history of mankind is synonymous with degradation. On the contrary, the *philosophes* followed Pascal, who, in the preface to the *Traité du Vide,* used the metaphor of the universal man who never stops learning and accumulates the knowledge of all previous centuries.[11] Fontenelle, for instance, in the *Digression sur les anciens et les modernes,* uses the same metaphor accompanied by the schema of the three ages, which will be taken up by Comte. Man is now in the age of virility, he says, where he argues more forcefully and has more intellectual capacity than ever. He will never degenerate since the sound views of all good minds that will follow will be always be added to each other. Rousseau read the *Digression sur les anciens et les modernes* by Fontenelle. He retained the points that there is no a priori superiority of the Ancients over Moderns, that there is no natural difference between men, and that inequality is a matter of institution or convention, but he did not accept the idea of progress.

2. Rousseau and Skepticism

Richard Popkin stated that "skepticism is a loose term that has been used to apply to any kinds of doubts, and particularly, doubts about certain aspects of the Judeo-Christian religion. It also applies to a rigorous epistemological doubt about the possibility of attaining knowledge."[12] If we accept this definition, Rousseau was indeed a skeptic. Most scholars from Pierre Burgelin to Robert Dérathé and from Marc-André Nadeau to Ezequiel de Olaso would certainly agree, even though Ezequiel de Olaso talks about two skepticisms in Rousseau, Pyrrhonism and academic skepticism, and Marc-André Nadeau refers to three, namely, the apparent skepticism of the *philosophes*, Pyrrhonism, and the involuntary skepticism of the Vicar.[13]

Nadeau points out that there is "certain skepticism" in Rousseau no matter how limited it may be (criticism of sciences and arts, of inequality, etc.).[14] This is a skepticism that is apparently quickly overcome since Rousseau presents, as it has been said, a purely affirmative doctrine. His affirmative doctrines have led to considering him as the spiritual father of Romanticism, Socialism, Totalitarianism, Primitivism, and other systematic and dogmatic doctrines diametrically opposed to skepticism. Nevertheless, according to Nadeau, Rousseau's fictions, such as the state of nature in the *Second Discours*, the ideal constitution of the *Social Contract*,[15] the education of Emile, or even the story of his own life offered in the *Confessions*, are not a dogmatic system but rather a way to conduct strictly philosophical research, and therefore skeptical about the nature of things.[16] In the last instance, Rousseau recognizes that "their truth is hold in abeyance."

However, in my opinion Rousseau was far from Diderot's political skepticism ("Enlightenment finishes at the suburbs"), which increased after Diderot's trip to Russia in the winter of 1773 and his relationship with Catherine the Great.[17] Instead, Rousseau believed that managing political power properly would lead to a society of free and equal men. "If I were a prince or a legislator, I would not waste my time on saying what should be done; I would do it" (CS, 351). Even though he was aware that his political ideal would not be followed in most European countries because of their corruption, at least it could be used as a political mirror. Thus he presents in *Du Contract social* a political model based on the Graeco-Roman republics. In his model a wise legislator like Solon or Lycurgus (or later Rousseau himself in his projects for constitutions for Corsica and Sardinia) would establish the appropriate framework of laws. Individuals would then be transformed into responsible and virtuous citizens, willing to be governed by the "volonté générale" and die for their fatherland.[18] Therefore, in political matters Rousseau was far from being a skeptic. His skepticism was philosophical and religious.

As Olaso recalls, in the "Vicar's Creed" Rousseau defines clearly his position on skepticism: "I am not a philosopher (...) I never intended to be one (...) I don't like philosophy at all (...) I have never boasted of being in the possession of a good philosophical faith, simply because I do not know one."[19] Therefore, he declares against the ordinary image of skepticism with which he was acquainted, the apparent skepticism of the *philosophes* that he rejects. But at the same time, Rousseau adheres to Pyrrhonism because philosophy and religion itself are full of incomprehensible aspects. Nevertheless, doubt with regard to what we need to know to behave properly in life is such a hard condition that it cannot be long endured; in spite of itself the mind decides one way or another. According to Olaso, ultimately his resort to sentiment due to the limits of reason unexpectedly makes him a member of the Pyrrhonian tradition.[20]

In "From Rousseau to Popkin," Sébastien Charles agrees that Rousseau seems at first sight to be totally opposed to skepticism since the modern skeptic is no longer seeking the truth by enquiry or investigation, like the zetetic in antiquity; his skepticism is not an act of doubt but of denial inasmuch as he considers it a merit to not believe in anything.[21] Therefore he is nothing more than a dogmatist. Hence Rousseau's phrase: "I do not know anyone as dogmatic as today's skeptics."[22] Indeed, an attitude such as that advocated by the skeptics, namely *epoché* or suspension of judgment, has no natural basis for Rousseau, who considers man a being of faith and not of doubt. As Charles states, we find in Rousseau's point of view the usual denunciation of skepticism as an intellectual posture.[23]

The connection between Rousseau and skepticism is thus complex, as Serguey Zanin stresses.[24] He indeed follows the skeptic tradition in criticizing the arts and sciences but moves away to build a moral system not based on relativism nor on doubt but on ancient virtues.

a. Rousseau's Itinerary: From Doubt and Uncertainty to Affirmative Doctrine. The Account of the Rêveries

In his literary and philosophical testament called *Les Rêveries du promeneur solitaire*, Jean-Jacques tells us that when he came to the age of forty (that is in 1752, at the time he was composing his opera, *Narcisse*), he accomplished a reform he had planned a long time earlier: "I left the world and its pomps, I gave up any adornment, no more swords, no more watches, no more white stockings, gilding, hair (...) and best of all (...) I began to submit my inside to a severe examination that could settle for the rest of my life."[25] Actually the plan was forced by his sickness or rather by the idea he had of it, as his letters of the winter of 1750–1 and the account of the *Confessions* prove. He was convinced that he had an incurable disease and that he would die soon. The intellectual reform followed the external one and pushed him to renounce the "gloriole littéraire" (vainglory) he had tried to reach for so long and which had turned into a literary poison, as he confesses in 1752, in the preface to *Narcisse* (OCII, 956). He also gave up his job as a cashier for M. Dupin and started making his living copying music.

But his reform also has to be considered in the context of his relationship with some of the *philosophes*, whom he describes as intolerant men, "ardent missionaries of atheism and very compelling dogmatists" who had shaken his beliefs without ever convincing him (*Rêveries*, 511). Their "distressing doctrine," instead of removing his doubts and resolving his irresolution, shook all certainty he still had. He is referring to D'Holbach, Grimm, and above all Diderot, who had published the *Lettre sur les aveugles* in 1749 and *Pensées sur l'interprétation de la nature* in 1753, and with whom he was very much in touch at the time. As he admits, even though he was sure from the bottom of his heart that they were wrong, he was disarmed by their thesis; he was not able to reply, he had no arguments to counter them.

It is possible, as Pierre-Maurice Masson suggests, that the straw that broke the camel's back can be located in 1754 between Shrove Sunday and June 1, the date of Rousseau's departure to Geneva to recover his citizenship, and that it happened at Mlle Quinault's house, during supper.[26] Some of the *philosophes* were chatting about religion and professing atheism. Rousseau could not prevent himself from getting up and exclaiming: "I believe in God (…) if you say one more word I will leave." At that moment, feeling himself intellectually unable to argue against the atheism and skepticism of his friends, Rousseau made a decision: instead of being eternally buffeted by the *philosophes'* "sophistry," he would seek his own philosophy and a fixed rule of conduct for the rest of his life.

His crusade against atheism probably began then. On 18 August 1756 Jean-Jacques wrote his *Lettre à Voltaire*, who, after the earthquake of Lisbon, had published his so-called Poem against Providence. Defending God's cause against Voltaire's doubts, Rousseau proposed politely to the poem's author, who he still considered a master, the drafting of the moral code he kept in mind at that time.[27] One year later, he pursued his crusade in writing the *Lettres morales* that he started in November 1757 (OCIV, 1081–118). In those letters addressed to Sophie d'Houdetot, he advised her to determine for good her opinions and her principles, a task he had undertaken himself. Mme d'Houdetot, with whom he was deeply in love at that moment, was in his imagination Julie de Wolmar, the character he was portraying in his novel *La Nouvelle Héloïse.* The so-called Lettres à Sophie predate "La profession de foi du Vicaire Savoyard," which forms part of *Emile* and was published in 1762. In both writings, Sophie's friend and the Vicar recommended to their protégés to undertake an examination of all their opinions and call into question metaphysical systems, as well as their cognitive faculties and their senses.

Between 1756 and 1758 Rousseau worked on *La Nouvelle Héloïse.* In the spring of 1758, after having read *De l'Esprit* by Helvétius, a violent attack against Christianity, he decided to expand his novel by adding two more parts to bear public witness to his religious beliefs.[28] A decade passed between the moral reform he undertook in 1750–1 and the final draft of the "Vicar's Creed."

Rousseau left Paris on 9 April 1756 and settled at the Ermitage, Mme d'Epinay's rural property, where likely his long meditations took place. As he says, he executed his project slowly and in several stages, probably from 1757 to 1762. The result of all his research, as he confesses in the *Rêveries* (512), was almost as he set later in the "Vicar's Creed." The narrative of the third promenade correlates closely with what he confesses many years later, towards the end of his life (15 January 1769), to M. de Franquières: "I examined all systems ... I pondered on those I could imagine. I compared them all to the best of my ability."[29]

For a long time he indulged in painful meditations and research.[30] As he recognizes in the *Rêveries* (512), at the beginning he was involved in such a whirlwind of doubts, impenetrable objections, and insoluble mysteries that it took him years to get rid of them. To refer to this time of distress, anguish, and anxiety, he uses repeatedly the words "labyrinth" and "maze" both in the *Rêveries* and in the *Lettres morales.*[31] He also compares his situation with a boat sailing across the sea, buffeted by storms, with no rudder, no compass, looking to an almost inaccessible lighthouse that showed no port (*Rêveries,* 512). Then he realized that these "insoluble objections" were common to everybody, since the human mind is too limited to solve them (*Emile,* 569). And he concluded that to get rid of this labyrinth, philosophy and knowledge were pointless. This point is repeated as a litany in many of his writings from the *Discours sur les Sciences et les Arts,* where the *philosophes* are called charlatans, to the *Lettres morales,* where he complains to Sophie d'Houdetot: "What have we learned from all this vain knowledge except quarrels, hatred, uncertainty, and doubt?" to the third *Rêverie,* where he stresses the futility of knowledge to reach what actually matters, happiness.[32] The more we delve, the more we find subjects of doubt, the more we learn, the more we lose the poor knowledge we have, he insists in the *Lettres morales* (OCIV, 2, 1091).

During this time of despair, doubt, and uncertainty, he was about to surrender to hopelessness, or so he confesses in the *Rêveries* (512). The difficulties in establishing his doctrines against his contemporaries constituted such a harsh task that he did not feel strong enough to complete it (*Rêveries*, 513). He realized that not only our senses but philosophy was unable to reach the truth, no matter what materialists tell us *(Lettres morales*, OCIV, 3, 1092, 1093, 1095). The only thing that forced him to persevere was the conviction that well-being in the afterlife was at stake.

Rousseau portrays the frightening life of a doubter who cannot support uncertainty and who needs to believe to release his anxiety: "The state of doubt is too violent for my soul and when my reason is indecisive, my faith cannot remain a long time in suspense, finally ... a thousand subjects of preference attract me towards the most comforting and join the weight of hope in the balance of reason" (*Lettre à Voltaire*, OCIV, 1070–1). Nevertheless, we can ask, did he really experience this state of doubt? And what kind of doubts did he experience? Were they religious? Actually they were not doubts concerning God since he denied such doubts twice. In his letter to Voltaire (OCIV, 1070–1) he writes: "I believe in God as strongly as I believe any other truth." And in his letter to M. de Franquières (OCIV, 1134) he admits that he cannot judge of the condition of a doubter because it was never his. The life of a doubter was indeed too painful for Rousseau: "How can we be skeptical bona fide? I cannot understand" (*Emile*, 567). As he confesses to M. de Franquières (OCIV, 1134): "I believed in my childhood by authority, by feeling in my youth, in my manhood by reason; now I believe because I have always believed." He makes up his mind one way or another and prefers to be wrong than not to believe (*Emile*, 567–8). As he writes to Voltaire (1070): "To believe and not to believe are things that do not depend on me."

b. The "Vicar's Creed"

The philosophical enterprise of the Vicar to determine his doctrine has been compared by scholars like Sébastien Charles and Henri Gouhier with Descartes's *Discours de la méthode* and has been characterized as a real cure of skepticism.[33] Nevertheless, the doctrines are quite different. On the one hand, Descartes's doubts are methodical and aim to establish the foundations of science, while Rousseau's are existential and only seek happiness. The clear and distinct notions of the Cartesian position play no role as a criterion of evidence for Rousseau. They are instead replaced by a different kind of evidence provided by the conscience, as we can easily perceive in the second and third letter to Sophie as well as in the "Vicar's Creed," the letter to Voltaire, the letter to M. de Franquières, etc. Instead of intellectual achievement, Rousseau seeks reliable principles that could get him out of despair. Moreover, to take apart religious beliefs and find a provisional morale is inconceivable for him, who is forced to philosophize by the lack of morality of the *philosophes*, by their atheism and their materialism. Hence the Vicar/Rousseau's comprehensive review and criticism of all his actions and opinions is aimed to "determine once and for all" his morality and metaphysics, and thereby put an end to the doubts and uncertainties into which he was constantly thrown (*Emile*, 570).

As Pierre Burgelin points out, the Vicar is undeniably a mask for Rousseau, like the pious Julie or the rationalist Saint-Preux, the characters of *La Nouvelle Héloïse*.[34] But if Julie and Saint-Preux were imaginary, the Vicar actually existed. We know that Jean-Jacques really met a certain abbé Gaime or/and abbé Gâtier who helped him in his difficult youth. In the "Profession de foi du Vicair Savoyard" there are two parallel stories and two of the characters represent Rousseau in one way or another; the Vicar, plunged into a religious crisis, symbolizes Rousseau at maturity, while the fugitive, forced to change religion to survive, is the alter ego of Jean-Jacques in his youth. On one hand, a Calvinist runaway tells a fellow citizen the story of his adolescence as well as the Vicar's. The Calvinist expatriates will soon get tired of his mask and will let us know that his story is Rousseau's (*Emile*, 563). On the other hand, the second story is the itinerary of the Vicar to overcome Pyrrhonism and it recalls Rousseau's own story.

The Vicar begins his confession by distancing himself from philosophy and the *philosophes*: "Do not expect from me any learned discourses or profound reasoning. I am not a great philosopher, and I do not care to be (...) I do not want to argue with you, or even try to convince you" (*Emile*, 565–6). Like Rousseau in the *Rêveries*, the Vicar also leaves philosophy aside because it provokes in him constant doubts and uncertainties. Besides, just as Rousseau, who calls himself "the friend of truth," has to move away from his friends the *philosophes* in order to seek his own path, the Vicar, in his search for truth, also denounces philosophy as an enemy of the truth.[35]

The Pyrrhonian crisis suffered by the Vicar is quite similar to the one that assailed Rousseau himself. The Vicar describes the times of trouble and anxiety, his wandering path from doubt to doubt, his uncertainty, his contradictions and the darkness that enveloped him (*Emile*, 567). And he uses, as Rousseau does in the *Rêveries*, the symbol of a sailor lost in the sea, with no rudder, no compass, and no other guide but an inexperienced pilot who disregards his way.

But the "Vicar's Creed" contains more than a description of a Pyrrhonian crisis. Rousseau clearly explains its meaning in the *Lettre à C. de Beaumont* (996–7). The Creed is composed of two parts. The first one, the most important as he says, is filled with striking truths and aims to oppose materialism, to establish both God's existence and natural religion as strongly as the author is able to. The second one proposes doubts and difficulties, above all concerning Revelation. The first part is decisive and dogmatic; the author does not doubt; his conscience and his reason determine him in an invincible way. He believes and he is highly assertive. In the other part, on the contrary, he offers his objections, his difficulties, and his doubts. As a result, he certainly establishes the essential dogmas while he keeps up a respectful skepticism towards other dogmas (*Lettres écrites de la montagne*, OCIII, 694–5).

In the first part of the "Vicar's Creed," the Vicar formulates the three dogmas that founded his faith: the movements of the universe require a principle that is a will; the order of the universe requires this will to be intelligent, and we call it God; and finally man is free, which distinguishes him radically from animals.[36] Thereby Rousseau takes sides in one of the great debates that separated materialists from traditional authors in the middle of the eighteenth century: the nature of matter. The new naturalists such as Diderot, La Mettrie, and D'Holbach argued against the static conception of nature and defended the thesis of an evolutionary and creative nature. Diderot, in *Pensées sur l'interprétation de la nature*, asks himself why not admit that matter is capable of movement, consciousness, feelings, passions, signs, gestures, speech sounds, language, law, science, and arts?[37] And between each of these changes million of years have elapsed and maybe in the future new transformations will occur. Matter seems to be endowed with a latent sensitivity and a hidden intelligence, and to be able, in certain circumstances, to coalesce and develop spontaneously. "Everything is in an eternal, perpetual, and necessary change" he writes in his comments on the *Lettre sur les hommes et ses rapports*, by Hemsterhuis.[38]

D'Holbach agrees.[39] The concept of nature, he says, necessarily involves the idea of movement. Nature is the cause of everything; it exists by itself, it will always exist, and it will always act; it is its own cause. Its movement ineluctably derives from its necessary existence: without movement, we cannot conceive nature. As matter is capable by itself of producing all observable phenomena, it is therefore futile to seek a cause external to it to explain its movement. The hypothesis of the creation of the universe is meaningless. Materialists in the second half of the eighteenth century deduce the non-existence of God. The new atheism is not based anymore on geometrical proofs as in Spinoza's times, but on experiments.

Jean-Jacques borrows Diderot's terms such as "dead matter," "great animal," and "living molecule," but he is far from sharing his conclusions.[40] Like Malebranche, Fénelon, or l'abbé Pluche, Rousseau asseverates that matter is dead and that its natural state is to be dormant: "The world is not a large animal that moves by itself. In its movements there is something alien to it" (*Emile*, 575). And he adds: "I made every effort to conceive of a living molecule, without being able to do it. The idea of matter feeling while having no senses seems to me unintelligible and contradictory" (*Emile*, 575, note). He points out also that the assumption that matter can think is a real absurdity (*Lettre à M. de Franquières*, OCIV, 1136).

The "Vicar's Creed" states that matter in motion, according to certain laws, proves the existence of an intelligence that he calls God (*Emile*, 578). This intelligence moves the universe and orders all things. Rousseau admits no doubts concerning the existence of God.[41] Finally, his third dogma is the immortality of the soul (*Emile*, 587). Even though Rousseau believes with all his heart in all three dogmas, he does not find rational arguments to demonstrate them. He realizes that his limited understanding conceives nothing boundless; everything called infinite escapes him. Dogmas and doubts are then mixed up in the "Vicar's Creed," no matter how affirmative Rousseau would like to be. Not only the immortality of the soul provoked his doubts, but Creation, the nature of God, the idea of eternity, eternal torments, the Gospel, and miracles did so.[42]

Concerning miracles, Rousseau seems at first sight to share the approach of Spinoza, Diderot, Voltaire, and D'Holbach, who states: "As for what we call miracles, i.e. effects contrary to the immutable laws of nature, such works are impossible because nothing could stop for an instant the course of events."[43] Jean-Jacques writes extensively about this subject in the *Lettres écrites de la montagne* (LEM), where, after defining miracles as real and visible exceptions to the laws of nature, he refuses to accept them: "even if they were thousands I will not believe in them."[44] In the *Lettre à Christophe de Beaumont* (990), he also rejects the obligation to believe in them in order to be a good Christian. But despite how affirmative he seems to be, he ultimately hesitates. Miracles do not indeed prove God's existence, although that is because they do not try to (LEM, 751). In effect they are only "acts of kindness, of charity" that God made for his friends and for his believers (LEM, 735). Far from wanting to give a proof of his divinity through them, Jesus Christ, on the contrary, asked to have the faith to make them. In any case, Rousseau asks, so what if they are true or false? They are useful for the common people (LEM, 729).

Even though Jean-Jacques lacks the proof to make a firm statement on this point, he is convinced that God has the power to make miracles, that is, to violate his own laws (LEM, 737). He cannot accept that God might be constrained by his own laws. This awful thought forces him to push backwards and find consolation in Descartes, who declares the freedom of Providence to change his own laws. Therefore, Jean-Jacques moves away from Spinoza and the determinism of the *philosophes* and comes close to the ideas of Malebranche, the abbé Pluche, and above all Fénelon, who declares God's absolute power over his Creation. Rousseau is nonetheless unable to be as affirmative as the archbishop of Cambrai: "It is the unalterable order of nature that best demonstrates the supreme being; if many exceptions occurred I would not know what to think, and I believe too much in God to believe in so many miracles so unworthy of him (...) If your miracles are made to prove your doctrine and need themselves to be proven, what are their purpose?" (*Emile*, 612). What to do in such cases? he asks himself. Come back to reason and leave miracles. Can we conclude that Rousseau trusts miracles? It is difficult to say, as he is really ambiguous. In any case he does not reject them out of hand (LEM, 747).

Unable to make up his mind on all these topics, Rousseau embraces an involuntary skepticism that do not affect moral life: "The first fruit I drew from these reflections was to learn to limit my research to what interested me immediately, to rest in profound ignorance of everything else, and to worry only about things important to know" (*Emile*, 569). He assumed ignorance on a number of religious matters that he considered "pointless questions (…) that transcend my reason" (*Emile*, 581).

Although Rousseau bases religion on two pillars, reason and Scripture, as he says in the *Lettre à C. de Beaumont*, neither reason nor Scripture can lead him to the religious truth: "I do not have the happiness of seeing in revelation the evidence they find, and if I decide for it, it is because my heart leads me there, since it has nothing but comfort for me (...) but it is not because I see it demonstrated, as very surely it is not for me" (*Lettre à C. de Beaumont*, 964).

Like Castellion, Calvin's critic who influenced the more liberal trend of Protestantism, Rousseau adopts a partial skepticism: "I do not have, it is true, that faith I hear so many people boast of (...) that strong faith that never doubts (...) and sets aside or hides objections it cannot solve" (*Emile*, 963–4). He calls this skepticism involuntary in the *Lettre à C. de Beaumont*, where he reiterates that to recognize insoluble difficulty in a doctrine does not mean to reject it.[45] And he depicts it in the *Lettre à M. D'Alembert*: "When a man cannot believe what he finds absurd, it is not his fault, it is his reason's fault; and how would I conceive God punishing him for not having attained an understanding that he has not received from him?"[46] Rousseau calls also his skepticism unintentional since it is based on invincible proofs on one side and on the other, which force reason to give up (*Emile*, 570). It is the kind of skepticism, as he says in the *Lettre à C. de Beaumont* (995), of "every reasonable Christian bona fide" who wants to know about heavenly topics only what he can understand. As for the maxims of conduct that everybody has to know to behave properly, Rousseau resorts to conscience. Indeed, reason can make us go wrong but conscience never deceives us. Hence his provocative sentence: it is reasonable not to be too rational.[47] As John S. Spink recalls, we are far from the intellectual evidence of Descartes (OCIV, 1519). In effect, Rousseau, like the abbé Pluche, claims the evidence of feeling.[48] Should we therefore talk about irrationalism?[49] At first sight the inner feeling does not oppose reason but guides it.

> "Conscience, conscience, divine instinct, immortal and heavenly voice, certain guide of an ignorant and narrow-minded being, but intelligent and free; infallible judge of good and evil, which makes man like God, it is you which make the excellence of its nature and the morality of his actions; without you I feel nothing in me that rises above the beasts but the sad privilege of wandering from error to error through an understanding without rule, and a reason without principle." (*Emile*, 600–1)

Conscience helps reason, which has limits. But does not the inner feeling, which is equivalent to conscience, replace reason in the long term? Does not Rousseau go too far? Julie, one of the masks of Jean-Jacques, suggests putting aside reason and giving up false philosophical principles, the origin of human pride.[50] And the Vicar seems also to reject reason in order to rest in detachment and conformity to the will of God (*Emile*, 628). Does not Rousseau approach too much to the mystics such as Mme de Guyon, Miguel de Molinos, or even Fénelon? Jean-Jacques confesses in the third *Rêverie* that during his youth he was about to become a devotee in the manner of Fénelon. But in his maturity he still loved the comforting spiritualism of the archbishop of Cambrai and his mystique of abandonment: "Feel your helplessness, humble yourself, be docile and trust the goodness of God who has not left us helpless to go to him. Let me do it, I will carry you in my arms."[51] These words can be equated to those of Rousseau, who requests "humbling oneself in front of the great Being who alone knows the truth" (*Lettre à C. de Beaumont*, 995).

Julie is also very close to that kind of quietism in spite of her efforts to distance herself from it: "I have blamed the ecstasies of the mystics. I still blame them when they detach us from our duties and keep away from the active life by the charms of contemplation, they lead us to this quietism that you think I am so close, and from which I think to be as far as you" (*La Nouvelle Héloïse*, 682). Even the other mask of Rousseau, the rationalist Saint-Preux, admits that he reads Fénelon and Muralt (*La Nouvelle Héloïse*, 695). And some of the sentences of the Vicar are reminiscent of the quietism of Julie and Fénelon: "O Supreme Being, merciful and kindhearted! Whatever your decrees are, I love them (…) I annihilate my feeble reason to your righteousness" (*Emile*, 592). But it is Jean-Jacques himself who, in the *Lettre à C. de Beaumont* (959), insists on the annihilation of reason: "I humble myself and told him: Being of beings, I am because you are (...) The more worthy use of my reason is to annihilate myself in front of you; my delight and the charm of my weakness is to feel overwhelmed by your greatness." And it is he who confesses in his letter to Mme. de Créqui that he would prefer to be a devotee than a philosopher.[52]

Pierre-Maurice Masson has shown the influence of Fénelon (above all of the *Introduction à la vie dévote* and *L'imitation*), Béat de Muralt (the Swiss mystic who wrote the *Lettres sur les Anglois* that Rousseau glosses), and Marie Huber, whose book *Lettres sur la religion essentielle à l'homme* Jean-Jacques owned since 1754.[53] Fénelon especially enjoyed great prestige in France, and Rousseau, as he confesses in the *Dialogues*, professed genuine admiration for him to the extent that he portrayed Emile's master with his features.[54] Jean-Jacques is also close to the Chevalier de Ramsay. In effect, "La Profession de foi de Daniel," contained in Ramsay's *Voyages de Cyrus*, published in 1727, correlates closely with the "Vicar's Creed." Indeed, Ramsay appeals to the heart to reach for the religious truths that reason is unable to attain. Like Rousseau, Ramsay's discourse tries to determine his behaviour and his doctrine to ensure peace of mind. According to Vernière (*Spinoza et la pensée française avant la Révolution*, 405), Ramsay talks in 1730 as Rousseau does thirty years later.

But Jean-Jacques does not always hide his bias in favour of quietism and ecstasies under the traits of the Vicar or Julie (*Emile*, 605). He expresses himself openly in the letters to Sophie d'Houdetot (OCIV, 1101): "Have not you felt these involuntary élans which capture a sensitive soul for the contemplation of beautiful morals and the intellectual order of things, this devouring passion that comes suddenly to engulf the heart of the love of heavenly virtues, these sublime wanderings which raise us above our being and bring us to the firmament next to God? Ah! If that sacred fire could last, if that noble delirium could animate our entire life!" Ecstasies, states of contemplation and abandonment, illuminations and mystical unions are present in Rousseau's writings from *Le Verger de Mme la baronne de Warens*, the "Lettre à Malesherbes," the "Fiction ou Morceau Allégorique sur la Révélation," to *Emile*, *La Nouvelle Héloïse*, *Les Rêveries*, etc.

Even though Jean-Jacques invokes conscience to help reason, in the end the balance leans towards faith. Indeed the "Vicar's Creed" finishes by an appeal to miracles. Like Rousseau, the Vicar keeps his faith relying on God who can turn stones into Abraham's children: "Whoever can read the bottom of my heart knows that I do not like my blindness (...) and if from stones God can get children to Abraham, every man has the right to expect to be enlightened when he makes himself worthy" (*Emile*, 631). Therefore, Rousseau like most skeptics accepted some kind of religious fideism. Although Montaigne does not reject specifically reason, he relegates it to the background, and assigns it the mission of supporting faith.[55] Charron also thinks that the nature and existence of God are unknowable due to the weakness of our understanding. Hence his belief in the authority of the Church in matters of faith as opposed to the unbearable pride of Calvinists. Indeed without the certainties provided by the Church, man would fall into doubt.

c. Skepticism and Dogmatism in Rousseau's Theory of Knowledge, Morals, and Politics

Thus Rousseau does not escape from religious skepticism. He does not hesitate to use it, although he rejects its most extreme conclusions and adopts a kind of dogmatism enabled by the existence of the "conscience." From his confrontation with skepticism, Rousseau retains the necessary limitation of human knowledge and the need to position himself in the world, no matter how uncertain it is, and to adopt principles even though they cannot provide certainty but only probability. Therefore, he shared a mitigated skepticism with many other authors. Like

Charron, Rousseau states that the only true knowledge and useful study for man is man himself.

Rousseau's critique of knowledge and philosophy was not new: he collected the ideas of Cicero in *De Finibus*, Agrippa, Montaigne, Pascal, and Charron, among others. When denouncing the evil and futility of knowledge in the preface to *Narcisse* (970), Rousseau repeatedly cites Charron, Montaigne's follower. This is quite unusual since, as we know, Jean-Jacques compiles materials from many different authors without bothering to report his sources. According to François Bouchardy, he was offered a copy of Charron's *De la Sagesse* by Mme Créqui, with whom he began a relationship in 1751.[56] He mentions Charron also in *Emile* (609), referring to this "good and wise priest," whose profession of faith is not very different from the Vicar's. Indeed the denunciation of science in Rousseau's *Discours sur les Sciences* reminds one of Charron. Both authors think that the practice of science is harmful since it sets aside virtue.[57] "I do not attack science, I defend virtue," Rousseau states in the *Discours sur les sciences et les arts* (5). In his reply to Stanislas of Poland's critique of his *Discours*, he insists: "I adore virtue" 39). Science is indeed the enemy of innocence, simplicity, and ignorance.[58] Moreover it is the root from which atheism, sects, and all kinds of errors in religion arise.[59] Rousseau, like Charron, praises ignorance. In his answer to Stanislas, Jean-Jacques commends a kind of "reasonable ignorance, that consists of confining curiosity to the extent of our faculties (...) (an ignorance) born of a great love for virtue and that inspires indifference to all things (...) which do not contribute to make him (man) better" (*Discours sur les sciences et les arts*, 54). Ignorance and happiness are synonymous. Therefore, in his *Discours*, Rousseau asks God to free men from the enlightened lights and arts and to restore ignorance, innocence, and poverty, which are "the only goods that can give them happiness" (*Discours sur les sciences et les arts*, 58). Indeed, when sciences and arts develop, happiness moves away.[60] Virtue, ignorance, and happiness are always linked in both of Rousseau's *Discours* and are opposed to progress and civilization: "luxury, dissolution and slavery have been (...) the punishment for the proud efforts we have made to overcome the happy ignorance granted to us by the eternal wisdom" (*Discours sur les sciences et les arts*, 15). Rousseau believes indeed that philosophy is at odds with virtue because its origin is pride (*Discours sur les sciences et les arts*, 46, note).

Rousseau sets two parallelisms. On one hand, he opposes the savage, ignorant, and happy man in the state of nature to the civilized man who exists side by side with pain and death.[61] On the other hand, in civil society he contrasts the courtier to the peasant; the peasant being a symbol of rusticity, simplicity, moderation, and virtue facing the courtier dressed in his impressive attire. Therefore Rousseau outlines an implicit critique of the luxury so reviled in the following pages. Next, there is an opposition between freedom and subjugation and between monarchies and republics (*Discours sur les sciences et les arts*, 6–7). Rousseau extols the ancient virtues when men were innocent, respected the gods, and experienced equality among them. But modern times have brought a baneful inequality: not enough peasants and too many philosophers: "We have physicists, astronomers, poets, musicians and painters; we do not have citizens anymore" (*Discours sur les sciences et les arts*, 26).

The apology for the natural and rustic life is a recurrent topic in Rousseau's works that culminates in the *Social Contract*, where his socio-political ideal is set out. It is a democratic system based on equality and liberty where groups of peasants resolve their issues by gathering in an assembly under a tree (*CS*, 437). It is the Graeco-Roman republican model that he confronts with monarchies ruled by "children, monsters, or fools" (*CS*, 410) but also with the prestigious English system so praised in France by Montesquieu and Voltaire. Rousseau's main thesis is that none of these regimes grant freedom. Therefore his critique of the "modern" idea of representation: the English people believe themselves to be free but once their representatives are elected, they become slaves (*CS*, 430). The ancient republics were not even familiar with this term; citizens were constantly gathered in assembly. However, modern countries value their profits more than their freedom.[62] As if he states in the *Discours sur les sciences et les arts* (19 and 20), if ancient citizens used to talk about customs and virtue, today people only talk about trade and money. They can attain everything through money except good customs and citizens. Therefore Rousseau confronts the virtue and patriotism of peasants (ancient Greeks as well as Swiss *montagnards*) with the greed for wealth of enlightened European nations (*CS*, 429), and he praises people such as Persians, Scythians, and Spartans, who managed to protect themselves from knowledge and remained virtuous, ignorant, and happy.[63] He especially considers Sparta a "Republic of demigods," "famous for its blissful ignorance" and exalted virtues where "men are born virtuous, and the air of the country itself seems to inspire virtue" (*Discours sur les sciences and les arts*, 11–12).

Rousseau holds modern philosophy responsible for keeping citizens away from their true duties and the *philosophes* responsible for undermining the foundations of faith and annihilating virtue with their "terrible paradoxes." Indeed, they attack, destroy, and vilify all that is holy among men and above all the sacred values of fatherland and religion. As he writes to Stanislas of Poland (*Discours sur les sciences et les arts*, 7–9, 40), the development of sciences and arts has had pernicious effects on customs; people do not dare to look like they really are anymore, a world of appearances and ornaments hides their deformities, and deceit and lack of transparency take over. Rousseau denounces the ideological role played by the sciences and arts for the benefit of political power: they conceal the iron chains suffered by the subjects of monarchies under garlands of flowers; they suffocate the feeling of men's original liberty; and they make subjects love their slavery. He concludes with a striking sentence: need has raised up the thrones and the sciences and arts continue to hold them up. Both his political ideal in *Du Contract social* as well as his two projects of constitutions for Corsica and Sardinia are attempts to defer those agricultural people from corruption.

But if there is a pernicious philosophy, there is also a "true" philosophy that relates to self-knowledge and a proper social behaviour; in short, moral knowledge.[64] According to Rousseau, as well as to Charron and Montaigne, the point is not to know everything but only what is useful for us from a moral standpoint. As Charron points out, the only study useful to man is man himself. Education should not therefore consist of the study of rules rather than the exercise of the will in order to be able to resignedly bear what life reports. The Stoic background is obvious.

Rousseau's ethic is opposed to the hedonism that prevails in the eighteenth century. Even though he thinks, like Helvétius, that the only motive of human behaviour is self-love, the meaning that Rousseau gives it is considerably different.[65] For Helvétius morality is based on self-interest (to enjoy maximum pleasure and avoid pain), which coincides with preservation. Men discover through reason the natural laws that lead them to safeguard their lives. Reason is therefore the foundation of morality. On the contrary, Rousseau refuses to base morality on interest. Indeed, in the *Discours sur l'origine de l'inégalité*,[66] he defines man in the state of nature as a compassionate and sensitive being, ruled not only by the instinct of conservation but also by piety towards other men. If men are good in the state of nature it is because they are not rational but sensitive.[67] Facing individualism and utilitarianism that preach self-interest as the only guide of human behaviour, Rousseau talks about two forms of self-love ("amour propre" and "amour de soi"). This distinction is based on moralists and mystics such as Marie Huber, Abbadie, and Vauvenargues.[68] According to Jean-Jacques, man is not only virtuous when he puts the interest of the soul before the interest of the senses (Augustinianism) but also when collective interests prevail over private interest (*Emile*, 635). Hence, his rejection of enlightened individualism and his attraction for republican virtue, synonymous with patriotism. Thus his political ideal is a *Cité* where the "volonté générale" dominates over the "volonté particulière" and where citizens would be willing to sacrifice their lives to the fatherland (*CS*, 376). The question he asks himself in *Emile* concerning education has an obvious answer: should a man be brought up for himself or for society? As he states in the two projects of constitutions for Corsica and Sardinia a man should be raised to become a citizen.[69]

Conclusion

Concerning religion, Rousseau is only skeptical in theological and therefore subtle topics, but he believes in God wholeheartedly. Regarding philosophy, understood as erudition, he thinks that it is vain and pointless, a merely cultural varnish to shine in the Parisian *salons*. Philosophy leads to corruption since it is synonymous with conceit and lies. Facing the futility and perversity of philosophical knowledge, Rousseau claims an ethical knowledge forgotten by his corrupted society that he designates as "the dregs of centuries." This ethical knowledge, based on ancient virtue, should lead to a proper social behaviour. Hence, Rousseau criticizes the *philosophes* for pursuing their private and petty interests concealed under the mask of virtue. They serve under powers that pay them not to teach or spread truth but to hide it, not to contribute to liberate people but to maintain them chained up.[70] According to Jean-Jacques, virtue can only be found in nature, among simplicity and ignorance.[71] Therefore his attempts to protect European countries still untouched by corruption like Corsica and Sardinia from progress and civilization. Indeed progress means for Rousseau love of oneself, selfishness, a desire to be preferred to others, and inequality and submission. In one word, corruption. Therefore, facing the enlightened but corrupt French society, where men were fettered by absolutism, Rousseau's ideal was the *montagnards*, the free and equal Swiss people who solved their problems in an assembly under a tree.[72] Their direct democracy reminded him of the political model of the Graeco-Roman republics. Those moral and political ideals were deeply inculcated since his childhood by his father, who taught him how to read using Plutarch's *Lives*.

Both his religious environment and republican upbringing marked him profoundly. Although his relationship with the *philosophes* shook all his beliefs and certainties later on, they were too solidly rooted to be removed. Concerning God, morality, and politics, his dogmatism does not succumb to doubt: virtue, fatherland, and God are the axes of his creed.[73]

NOTES

1 *Lettre à Christophe de Beaumont*, 933, in *Jean-Jacques Rousseau, Oeuvres complètes*, IV (Paris: Gallimard, 1969). Hereafter cited in the text by the initials OC and volume and page number. All the quotes have been translated by the author of this chapter.

2 In particular letters 5 and 6. See Henri Gouhier's introduction to *Lettres morales*, OCIV, CXCI.

3 M.A. Bernier and S. Charles, *Scepticisme et modernité* (Saint-Etienne, France: Publications de l'Université de Saint-Etienne, 2005), 12.

4 Richard H. Popkin, Ezequiel de Olaso, and Giorgio Tonelli, *Scepticism in the Enlightenment* (Dordrecht: Kluwer Academic Publishers, 1997), 1.

5 Pierre-André Taguieff, *Le sens du progrès* (Paris: Flammarion, 2004), 17.

6 Cf. Bernier and Charles, *Scepticism in the Enlightenment.*

7 Condorcet, *Notes sur Voltaire.* Cited by Sébastien Charles, "De Popkin à Rousseau: retour sur le scepticisme des Lumières," *Revue philosophiques* 35, no.1 (Spring 2008): 278.

8 According to the article "Evidence" of the *Encyclopédie*, probably by Quesnay, this term means "such a clear and evident certainty that the spirit cannot oppose to it." *Oeuvres de J.J. Rousseau*, OCIV, 1519, note.

9 Véronique Le Ru, "Le Scepticisme dans *L'Encyclopédie* de Diderot et de d'Alembert," *Revue de métaphysique et de morale*, 1/2010, no. 65, 75–92.

10 Le Ru, "Le Scepticisme dans *L'Encyclopédie* de Diderot et de d'Alembert," 28.

11 Le Ru, "Le Scepticisme dans *L'Encyclopédie* de Diderot et de d'Alembert," 77–8.

12 Popkin, Olaso and Tonelli, *Scepticism in the Enlightenment*, IX.

13 Pierre Burgelin, *La philosophie de l'existence de Rousseau* (Paris: PUF, 1952), 42: "Lecteur de Montaigne, il professe un certain scepticisme en face de la tradition philosophique." See also Robert Derathé, *Le Rationalisme de Jean-Jacques Rousseau* (Paris: PUF, 1948), 41–5; Yvon Belaval, "Rationalisme sceptique et dogmatisme du sentiment chez Jean-Jacques Rousseau," *Annales de la société J.J. Rousseau* 38 (1969): 7–24. Ezequiel de Olaso, "The

two scepticisms of the Savoyard Vicar," in Popkin, Olaso, and Tonelli, *Scepticism in the Enlightenment,* 131–46.

14 M.A. Nadeau, "Le scepticisme de Rousseau dans la Profession de foi du vicaire savoyard, " *Lumen: Selected Proceedings from the Canadian Society for Eighteenth-Century Studies / Lumen: travaux choisis de la Société canadienne d'étude du dix-huitième siècle,* vol. 25, 2006, 29–40.

15 Hereafter cited in the text by the initials *CS,* OCIII.

16 Nadeau, "Le scepticisme de Rousseau," 35.

17 Philip Blom, *A Wicked Company* (New York: Basic Books, 2010,) ch. 17.

18 *Discours sur l'economie politique,* OCIII, 254, 255, 261. See also *CS,* OC III, 351. Also in *Considérations sur le Gouvernement de Pologne,* OCIII, 957ff. About the legislator, see *CS,* 381ff.

19 *Emile,* OC IV, 565–6. Subsequent references are to this edition and will appear parenthetically in the text. Ezequiel de Olaso, "The Two Scepticisms of the Savoyard Vicar," in Popkin, Olaso, and Tonelli, *Scepticism in the Enlightenment,* 131–46.

20 Olaso, "Two Scepticisms," 132.

21 Rousseau, *Pensées d'un cœur droit* (LXV), OCII, 1312. Cited by S. Charles, "De Popkin à Rousseau," 284.

22 *Emile* (Manuscrit Favre), OCIV, 1283, cited by S. Charles, "De Popkin à Rousseau," 284.

23 Charles, "De Popkin à Rousseau," 284.

24 Serguey Zenin, "L'entremise du scepticisme. Jean-Jacques Rousseau et la composition du *Discours sur les sciences et les arts,*" in Bernier and Charles, *Scepticisme et Modernité,* 155–66.

25 *Les Rêveries du promeneur solitaire* (Paris: Seuil, 1967), OCI, 511ff. Subsequent references appear in the text.

26 Pierre-Maurice Masson, "Mme d'Epinay, Jean-Jacques ... et Diderot chez Mlle Quinault." Cited by Henri Gouhier, intro. to *Lettres morales,* CLXXXIV.

27 *Lettre à Voltaire,* OCIV, 1074. Subsequent references appear in the text.

28 In fact he wrote "Notes sur 'De l'Esprit,'" OCIV, 1121ff. In the *Lettres écrites de la montagne* (OCIII, 693, note) he states – without citing the author– that from its appearance in 1758 he resolved to attack its principles.

29 OCIV, 1134–5. M. de Franquières was a skeptic who, having studied the pros and cons of God's existence, remained in doubt, contrary to Rousseau.

30 It is not clear if his thinking was painful or peaceful, as in the *Rêveries* he says both. At p. 511 it is "peaceful" but at p. 512 it is "painful."

31 1112. Also in *Lettres morales,* 2, OCIV, 1088 and 1087.

32 *Discours sur les sciences et les arts,* OCIII, 27. Subsequent references will appear parenthetically in the text. *Lettres morales,* 2, 1088–9. *Rêveries,* 509ff.

33 Henri Gouhier's introduction to *Lettres morales,* CXCI. S. Charles, "From Popkin to Rousseau," 284.
34 See the introduction of *Emile,* OCIV, CXXXIV ff.
35 *Emile,* 569. Also in *Lettre à C. de Beaumont,* 967.
36 *Emile,* 576. On the contrary, materialists talk about "a blind force spread in all Nature." *Emile,* 577. Also 579–81 and 586–7.
37 *Pensées sur l'Interprétation de la nature* in *Œuvres de Denis Diderot (publiés sur les manuscrits de l'Auteur)* par Jacques-André Naigeon (Paris: Chez Deterville, An VIII), v.III, L. VIII, 2, 312–13.
38 *Lettre sur les hommes et ses rapports, (avec le commentaire inédit de Diderot)*, texte établi, présenté, et annoté par Georges May (New Haven, CT: Yale University Press, 1964; Paris: Presses Universitaires de France), 201.
39 *Système de la nature ou des lois du monde physique et moral (Notes et corrections par Diderot)* (Hildesheim: Georg Olms Verlagsbuchhandlung, 1966), v. II, 155.
40 In the letter to M. de Franquières (1140), Rousseau ridicules the materialists.
41 See, for instance, *Emile,* 581: "I know in all confidence that he exists."
42 *Emile,* see pages 581, 591, 593, 603. Also in *Lettre à C. de Beaumont,* 995.
43 According to Antoine Sabatier de Castres, Rousseau confessed to him that he had found his thesis on miracles on the *Theological-Political Treatise.* See Paul Vernière, *Spinoza et la pensée française avant la Révolution* (Geneva: Slatkine, 1979), 487. D´Holbach, *Système de la Nature,* T.I., cap. V, 72.
44 *Lettres écrites de la* montagne, OC III, 737.
45 Rousseau says that among so many contradictions, there is nothing to do except be "modest and cautious and respecting silently what can neither be rejected nor understood." *Lettre à C. de Beaumont,* 994–5.
46 *Lettre à M. D'Alembert sur son Article Genève* (Paris: Garnier-Flammarion, 1967), 59.
47 *Lettre à M. de Franquières,* 1138. *Emile,* 594–5 and 573: "My rule to trust feelings instead of reason is confirmed by reason itself."
48 *Lettre à M. de Franquières,* 1139.
49 One should not forget his anti-rationalistic statement in the *Discours sur l'origine de l'inégalité* (138): "Thought state is an unnatural state (...) man who thinks is a depraved animal." Diderot answered in the entry "Droit naturel" in the *Encyclopédie*: "Who does not want to use reason and renounces to the quality of man, has to be treated like an unnatural animal." Cited in OCIII, 1311.
50 *La Nouvelle Héloïse,* OC II, 358. Subsequent references appear parenthetically in the text.

51 Fénelon, *Lettres surs divers sujets de métaphysique et de religion,* lettre V. Cited by Spink, OCIV 1514.
52 *Correspondance Générale de J.-J. Rousseau (collationnée sur les originaux, annotée et commentée par Théophile Dufour* (Paris: Librairie Armand Colin, 1924), 16 vols, t. IV, 82.
53 Pierre-Maurice Masson, *La religion de Rousseau,* Hachette, Paris, 1916, 3 vols. Second volume: *La "profession de foi" de Jean-Jacques.* See OCII, 1315 ff.
54 *Rousseau, juge de Jean-Jacques. Dialogues,* deuxième dialogue, Seuil, OCI, 448.
55 Montaigne, *Apologie de Raimond Sebond,* T.II, ch.XII, 183 in *Œuvres complètes* (Paris: Seuil, 1967).
56 Introduction to the *Discours sur les sciences et les arts,* OCIII, 1278.
57 "Wisdom and science do not go ever together," *De la Sagesse,* par M. Pierre le Charron, Bourdeaus: Simon Millanges, 1606, l.III, ch.XIV, 20, 619.
58 "The study of the universe should raise man to his Creator, I know it; but it only develops human pride." Réponse à Stanislas de Pologne, OCIII, 41.
59 *De la Sagesse,* L.III, ch.XIV, 20, 619. See also L.III, ch.XIV, 15, 414 and L.1, ch.1, 1.
60 *Discours sur l'origine de l'inégalité,* 202, note IX.
61 *Discours sur l'origine de l'inégalité,* 203.
62 "Is there need to go into battle? they pay troops and stay home; is there need to go to the Council? they appoint deputies and stay home. Due to laziness and money they have soldiers to enslave the fatherland and representatives to sold it," *CS,* 428–9.
63 Rousseau regrets the decline of Rome, an ancient symbol of virtue, rusticity, simplicity, and restraint. But when Rome was interested in philosophy "everything was lost": wise men appeared and good men disappeared. "Rome became full with philosophers and orators, military discipline was neglected, agriculture was despised (...) and fatherland was forgotten." *Discours sur les sciences et les arts,* 14.
64 In the preface to the *Discours sur l'origine de l'inégalité* (122), Rousseau states that: "the most useful human knowledge seems to me to be man's (...)."
65 *Oeuvres Complètes d'Helvétius* (nlle. éd.) (Paris: Chez Mme. Ve. Le Petit, 1818), 18 v; t. I, discours second, ch.XXIV, 216ff. Concerning Rousseau, see *Emile,* 329.
66 *Discours sur l'origine de l'inégalité,* 154 and 126.
67 *Emile,* 602. In the *Discours sur l'origine de l'inégalité* (154), he defines piety as the "innate repugnance to see our fellow suffer."
68 It seems that in one of his notebooks Rousseau copied a paragraph from the *Introduction à la connoissance de l'esprit humain* by Vauvenargues. OCIII, 219, note 1.

69 “The good social institutions know how to denature man and deprive his absolute existence to give him a partial one,” *Emile*, 249.

70 *La Nouvelle Héloïse*, OC II, second preface, 24.

71 *Projet de constitution pour la Corse*, OCIII, 915.

72 *Lettre à M. D'Alembert sur son Article Genève*, 133ff. See also the sedication to the *Discours sur l'origine de l'inégalité*, 111ff.

73 *Discours sur les sciences et les arts*, 19.

chapter ten

Skepticism and Political Economy: Smith, Hume, and Rousseau

PIERRE FORCE

Skeptical arguments and a Ciceronian way of arguing in utramque partem *are at the core of Adam Smith's reflections on the foundations of political economy. David Hume had speculated on why utility pleases – against the "skeptics" (Bernard Mandeville and Jean-Jacques Rousseau), who had argued that the constitution of the social order was utility-based (artificial invention of clever politicians in order to turn asocial beings into social ones). According to Hume, the public utility of social virtues pleases (in other words, we like what is good for the public, irrespective of what's in it for us). Smith appropriates this argument and takes it further. Utility pleases for non-utilitarian reasons, as it were; it is good in itself, irrespective of its consequences. Rousseau criticized the modern economy as generating artificial needs and artificial ways of meeting these needs. This critique is true in a way, but in a different perspective the beauty of the modern economy is not about outcomes, it is in the goodness of the system itself. The skeptical critique of the social order is true. The critique of the critique is true as well. This, paradoxically, is the skeptical foundation of political economy, and this ambivalence is at the heart of Smith's entire system.*

Skepticism in Adam Smith has rarely been studied. When it has been analysed, the focus has been on cognition, natural philosophy, or religion.[1] There has been relatively little work on the function of skepticism in the moral and political philosophy of Smith.[2] I would like to argue here that skeptical arguments play a fundamental role in all discussions about justice and utility and suggest even further that skeptical arguments play a foundational role for political economy itself. My analysis of Smith will lead to a discussion of Hume and then will come back to Smith.

1. Smith on Why Utility Pleases

Let us begin with the famous chapter in *The Theory of Moral Sentiments* that includes the analysis of "the economy of greatness" and the invocation of an "invisible hand" that makes "nearly the same distribution of the necessaries of life, which would have been made, had the earth been divided into equal portions among all its inhabitants."[3] This analysis is itself part of a broader discussion of utility, or rather an enquiry into the reasons why utility, or the appearance of utility, is pleasing to us. Smith breaks down the reasons into three categories going from the most obvious to the least often observed. First, "the fitness of any system or machine to produce the end for which it was intended, bestows a certain propriety and beauty upon the whole, and renders the very thought and contemplation of it agreeable." This fact, Smith adds, "is so very obvious that nobody has overlooked it." Second, as Hume has observed, the pleasure generated by utility is contagious, so to speak, because we sympathize with it. When we see someone who owns a beautiful and comfortable house, we share the feelings of satisfaction of the owner: "The spectator enters by sympathy into the sentiments of the master, and necessarily views the object under the same agreeable aspect. When we visit the palaces of the great, we cannot help conceiving the satisfaction we should enjoy if we ourselves were the masters, and were possessed of so much artful and ingeniously contrived accommodation."[4] The third reason is the least obvious one, and Smith proudly stresses the fact that no one before him has ever mentioned it. What gives pleasure in the appearance of utility is not the contemplation of benefits or good outcomes. It is the contemplation of the very system that leads to these good outcomes: "But that this fitness, this happy contrivance of any production of art, should often be more valued, than the very end for which it was intended; and that the exact adjustment of the means for attaining any conveniency or pleasure, should frequently be more regarded, than that very conveniency or pleasure, in the attainment of which their whole merit would seem to consist, has not, so far as I know, been yet taken notice of by any body."[5]

In order to understand why this point is new and paradoxical, one should go back to the three classical categories: *utile, honestum, dulce* (the useful, the honourable, the pleasurable), which originated in Aristotle[6] and had broad currency in ancient moral philosophy. In the passage from *The Theory of Moral Sentiments* quoted above, Smith collapses *utile* and *dulce* into one category by referring to "conveniency *or* pleasure."

The paradoxical point of the passage concerns the relationship between the useful and the honourable. In *De Officiis*, Cicero, following the Stoics, had established a hierarchy between the useful and the honourable, and argued that the honourable should be sought for its own sake, even though its consequences are also beneficial.[7] He had further argued that there can be no conflict between the useful and the honourable, because what is honourable is always useful, while nothing truly useful can be dishonorable.[8] Here Smith argues that we like what is useful for the same reasons we like what is honourable. A machine that produces well-made objects is admirable not because of the objects it produces, but because it is perfectly suited for its end. From this point of view, the useful pleases us as the honourable does, because it finds its own end in itself. There is a way in which the useful and the honourable can be said to be the same, but this is different from the Stoic solution that subordinates the useful to the honourable. Here, there is a certain way of looking at the useful that makes it good absolutely. The useful is good in itself, and not simply for its consequences.

2. Hume's Refutation of "skeptics ancient and modern"

Smith's discussion of the reasons why utility pleases presents itself as the continuation of a discussion started by Hume: "The cause too, why utility pleases, has of late been assigned by an ingenious and agreeable philosopher, who joins the greatest depth of thought to the greatest elegance of expression."[9] In order to understand the meaning and implication of Smith's thesis we must therefore go back to Hume's argument. The chapter of the *Enquiry Concerning the Principles of Morals* entitled "Why utility pleases" is a refutation of the "sceptics both ancient and modern"[10] who saw in utility the only foundation of morality and politics:

> From the apparent usefulness of the social virtues, it has readily been inferred by sceptics, both ancient and modern, that all moral distinctions arise from education, and were, at first, invented, and afterwards encouraged, by the art of politicians, in order to render men tractable, and subdue their natural ferocity and selfishness, which incapacitated them for society.[11]

Who are these "sceptics ancient and modern"? The modern skeptic is clearly Mandeville, who famously ascribed the constitution of the political order to the ruse of politicians. In the chapter of *The Fable of the Bees* entitled "Origins of Moral Virtue," Mandeville had narrated the origin of society as the passage from a savage state to a semi-civilized state in which a small group of people used morality to organize and control others:

> This was (or at least might have been) the manner after which Savage Man was broke; from whence it is evident, that the first Rudiments of Morality, broach'd by skilful Politicians, to render Men useful to each other as well as tractable, were chiefly contrived that the Ambitious might reap the more Benefit from, and govern vast Numbers of them with the greater Ease and Security.[12]

Regarding the ancient skeptics, one may recall the famous speech by Carneades against justice. If we think about references Mandeville himself would have been very familiar with, we can mention the account of this speech by Bayle. In his article on Carneades in the *Dictionnaire historique et critique,* Bayle summarizes it in the following way:

> If there were such a thing as justice, it would be based either on positive right or on natural right. Yet it is not based on positive right, which varies according to time and place and is redefined by each nation according to its interests and benefit. It is not based on natural right either, because such right is nothing but an inclination given by nature to all kinds of animals leading them to seek what is useful to them.[13]

In other words, what we call justice, positive or natural, is always derived from utility.

Hume's discussion begins with an acknowledgment of the fact that utility plays a large part in our feeling of approbation of certain types of behaviour as opposed to others. In that sense, according to Hume, it is an error to try to exclude utility entirely from a definition of morality:

> But perhaps the difficulty of accounting for these effects of usefulness, or its contrary, has kept philosophers from admitting them into their systems of ethics, and has induced them rather to employ any other principle, in explaining the origin of moral good and evil. But it is no just reason for rejecting any principle, confirmed by experience, that we cannot give a satisfactory account of its origin, nor are able to resolve it into other more general principles.[14]

Because selfishness, or the drive towards private utility, seems inconsistent with the public good, many philosophers have invoked everything but utility when trying to identify the first principles underlying morality. This is an error, because we know from experience that utility plays a role, and we should make a greater effort to determine what exactly this role should be in the theory.

Some philosophers, on the other hand, namely, the skeptics, have taken the opposite stance, as we have seen, and made utility the sole explanatory principle. But even though the analysis of the skeptics contains a large part of truth, public utility is agreeable to us for reasons that are a combination of private utility and other, non-selfish motives. What Hume, in another passage, calls the "selfish hypothesis"[15] cannot be the whole story. This, according to Hume, is because we regularly sympathize with ends that have little or no connection with our private utility:

> In general we may remark, that the minds of men are mirrors to one another, not only because they reflect each others emotions, but also because those rays of passions, sentiments and opinions may be often reverberated, and may decay away by insensible degrees. Thus the pleasure, which a rich man receives from his possessions, being thrown upon the beholder, causes a pleasure and esteem; which sentiments again, being perceiv'd and sympathiz'd with, increase the pleasure of the possessor; and being once more reflected, become a new foundation for pleasure and esteem in the beholder.[16]

Hume describes human relations as an infinite game of mutual reflections. Private utility is the primary reason why a man enjoys his possessions, but this is only the beginning of a long chain of reflections. A beholder will sympathize with these feelings of enjoyment, and the owner will enjoy being looked at with sympathy:

> There is certainly an original satisfaction in riches deriv'd from that power, which they bestow, of enjoying all the pleasures of life; and as this is their very nature and essence, it must be the first source of all the passions, which arise from them. One of the most considerable of these passions is that of love or esteem in others, which therefore proceeds from a sympathy with the pleasure of the possessor. But the possessor has also a secondary satisfaction in riches arising from the love and esteem he acquires by them, and this satisfaction is nothing but a second reflexion of that original pleasure, which proceeded from himself. This secondary satisfaction or vanity becomes one of the principal recommendations of riches, and is the chief reason, why we either desire them for ourselves, or esteem them in others.

> Here then is a third rebound of the original pleasure; after which 'tis difficult to distinguish the images and reflexions, by reason of their faintness and confusion.[17]

What is interesting for Hume in this game of mirrors is that it is potentially infinite, and the connection with private utility becomes increasingly tenuous as the original pleasure is reflected, and reflected again, by the power of sympathy. In the end, it is virtually impossible to tell the difference between private utility and its images. Hume criticizes the "selfish hypothesis" as having been proposed by ancient and modern skeptics, but his refutation of such hypothesis is skeptical both in its spirit and its method. In the end, one must suspend judgment as to what role private utility plays in the feelings of approbation for public utility or the utility of others. One finds the same skeptical stance regarding first principles. Everyone wants to know to what degree human beings are selfish or selfless at the core. This, however, is a question that should be left open:

> It seems a happiness in the present theory, that it enters not into that vulgar dispute concerning the degrees of benevolence or self-love, which prevail in human nature: a dispute which is never likely to have any issue, both because men, who have taken part, are not easily convinced, and because the phenomena, which can be produced on either side, are so dispersed, so uncertain, and subject to so many interpretations, that it is scarcely possible accurately to compare them, or draw from them any determinate inference or conclusion.[18]

For Hume, therefore, it is important to have a skeptical take on the "selfish hypothesis"[19] in order to ground a science of morals and a political economy. The degree to which we act selfishly or selflessly has long been debated by philosophers, but it is not necessary to solve this riddle in order to understand how morality and society work. The question of first principles should be bracketed out.

3. Smith's Refutation of Modern Skepticism

Now I would like to show that Smith engages these issues in a very similar way. As we have seen above, in *The Theory of Moral Sentiments*, there is an extensive discussion of the reasons why utility pleases, which presents itself explicitly as a continuation of Hume's treatment of the matter. The discussion ends with the remark that we enjoy owning watches not because watches give time, but because watches are perfectly and exquisitely made objects. What follows, surprisingly, is a long and vehement tirade that contradicts what has just been said:

> How many people ruin themselves by laying out money on trinkets of frivolous utility? What pleases these lovers of toys is not so much the utility, as the aptness of the machines which are fitted to promote it. All their pockets are stuffed with little conveniencies. They contrive new pockets, unknown in the clothes of other people, in order to carry a greater number. They walk about loaded with a multitude of baubles, in weight and sometimes in value not inferior to an ordinary Jew's-box, some of which may sometimes be of some little use, but all of which might at all times be very well spared, and of which the whole utility is certainly not worth the fatigue of bearing the burden.[20]

From this point of view, watches are not perfectly made objects that we enjoy because of their perfection, but mere trinkets and baubles of highly dubious utility. Smith then generalizes the point he has just made: owning watches is frivolous, but the same can be said of the pursuits of private and public life, from which we derive little or no utility. What follows is the famous passage about "the poor man's son, whom heaven in its anger has visited with ambition," who, "when he begins to look around him, admires the condition of the rich."[21] This young man sees that the rich and the powerful seem to live comfortable lives because they never have to walk or ride a horse. In order to achieve the same status, "he submits in the first year, nay in the first month of his application, to more fatigue of body and more uneasiness of mind than he could have suffered through the whole of his life from the want of them."[22] The whole enterprise takes a toll not only on the body but also on the soul, and the young man debases himself as he tries to climb the social ladder: "For this purpose he makes his court to all mankind; he serves those whom he hates, and is obsequious to those whom he despises."[23] This passage clearly echoes Rousseau's satire of the "citizen" in the *Second Discourse*, not in some abstract way but literally. Here is the corresponding passage in Rousseau, translated by Smith himself:

> The citizen, on the contrary, toils, bestirs and torments himself without end, to obtain employments which are still more laborious; he labours on till his death, he even hastens it, in order to put himself in a condition to live, or renounces life to acquire immortality. He makes his court to the great whom he hates, and to the rich whom he despises.[24]

Using Rousseau's own words, Smith generalizes Rousseau's proposition. While Rousseau had written: "He makes his court to the great whom he hates, and to the rich whom he despises," Smith writes: "he makes his court to all mankind; he serves those whom he hates, and is obsequious to those whom he despises." The self-debasement that Rousseau had presented as a feature of the relation between the rich and the poor is here portrayed as a characteristic of all human relations.

What does this have to do with skepticism? The word "skepticism" is not mentioned in the chapter, but the passage rehearses precisely the same arguments that Hume had called arguments of "the sceptics both ancient and modern." In Hume's chapter, the modern skeptic is Mandeville, who argued that morality was invented by clever politicians to control the populace. In Smith, the part of the modern skeptic is, intriguingly, played by Rousseau. But precisely, according to Smith, Rousseau's narrative about the origins of the social order had been borrowed from Mandeville. Smith had made this point in a review article published shortly after the publication of the *Second Discourse*: "Whoever reads this last work with attention, will observe, that the second volume of the *Fable of the Bees* has given occasion to the system of Mr. Rousseau."[25] According to Smith, on the development of the arts and on the origin of justice, Rousseau's narrative and Mandeville's narrative are entirely similar:

> Both of them suppose the same slow progress and gradual development of all the talents, habits, and arts which fit men to live together in society, and they both describe this progress pretty much in the same manner. According to both, those laws of justice, which maintain the present inequality amongst mankind, were originally the inventions of the cunning and the powerful, in order to maintain or to acquire an unnatural and unjust superiority over the rest of their fellow creatures.[26]

From this point of view, alluding to Rousseau has the exact same function as alluding to Mandeville. Smith rehearses the argument (made by both Mandeville and Rousseau) about the artificiality of the social order and the artificiality of the needs created by it: "Power and riches" are "enormous and operose machines contrived to produce a few trifling conveniencies to the body," but they have little utility when it comes to the real needs and wants of a human being: "They keep off the summer shower, not the winter storm, but leave him always as much, and sometimes more exposed than before, to anxiety, to fear, and to sorrow; to diseases, to danger, and to death."[27]

Finally, after having rehearsed the Mandeville/Rousseau argument about the artificiality of the social order, Smith comes back to the earlier point about the pleasure we find in utility. The skeptical critique of the origins of the social order is an example of "splenetic philosophy, which in time of sickness or low spirits is familiar to every man," and "entirely depreciates those great objects of human desire."[28] However, "when in better health and in better humour, we never fail to regard them under a more agreeable aspect."[29] The implication here is that there is something misanthropic about the skepticism of Mandeville and Rousseau. Those who do not suffer from the same melancholy see utility in a different way:

> If we consider the real satisfaction which all these things are capable of affording, by itself and separated from the beauty of that arrangement which is fitted to promote it, it will always appear in the highest degree contemptible and trifling. But we rarely view it in this abstract and philosophical light. We naturally confound it in our imagination with the order, the regular and harmonious movement of the system, the machine or oeconomy by means of which it is produced. The pleasures of wealth and greatness, when considered in this complex view, strike the imagination as something grand and beautiful and noble, of which the attainment is well worth all the toil and anxiety which we are so apt to bestow upon it.[30]

It has been sometimes said (notably by the editors of the Oxford edition)[31] that in putting forward this argument, Smith decisively rejected Rousseau's critique of the origins of social order. I would argue that things are not so simple. Smith admits that Rousseau's critique of utility is at least plausible in theory, or, as he puts in, in an "abstract and philosophical light." The endeavours of modern commercial society seem entirely vain if, as Rousseau does, we relate them to a strict definition of utility. If, on the other hand, we put sympathy into the mix, we will have a much looser definition of utility, and the pursuit of images or phantoms of utility, rather than the thing itself, will be justified. This is not to say that there is true utility in the pursuit of power and riches, but the illusion of utility is necessary for the good order and prosperity of society: "And it is well that nature imposes upon us in this manner. It is this deception which rouses and keeps in continual motion the industry of mankind."[32]

The presence of skeptical arguments is quite remarkable here because this is a discussion about the very foundations of modern commercial society, which Smith and Hume take up in very similar ways. One could see it as an effort to overcome a skeptical critique of modern commercial society. However, and this is even more remarkable than the presence of skeptical arguments, the entire discussion is itself skeptical in its tone and in its method.

It has been shown by Thomas Olshewsky that, in his style of argument, Hume borrows from Academic skepticism, especially in its Ciceronian form. [33] The same could be said of Smith, at least in passages like the one I have just analysed.[34] So far I have focused on "the sceptics both ancient and modern," and their argument that private utility was the foundation of social order. This argument, in different contexts, has been associated with Rousseau, or Mandeville, or Carneades. What I have not yet mentioned is that the famous speech Carneades gave against justice was one of a set of two speeches, the first one being an encomium of justice. According to Cicero, what characterized Carneades and other Academic skeptics is that they philosophized by arguing on both sides of an issue. The purpose of this style of argument was not to make a final determination in favour of one side. Rather, it was to excite the mind to look further in the pursuit of truth.[35] If we keep this in mind, we can have a better sense of what Cicero was trying to accomplish in a dialogue like *De Officiis*. The main discussion is about the connection between the useful and the honourable. A hierarchy is established between the two categories, because only the honourable should be sought for its own sake. Cicero upholds, or seems to uphold, the Stoic theory that the conflicts between the useful and the honourable are only apparent, and what is truly honourable is also useful, while nothing truly useful can also be dishonourable. Or perhaps, as Walter Nicgorski suggested, Cicero's conclusions are more ambiguous, and contain an implicit critique of Stoicism and a suggestion that there are goods other than the highest good.[36] Common wisdom and the consideration of intermediate ends justify the pursuit of utility. These considerations offer a skeptical critique of a Stoic position that would bring philosophy into disrepute if held too strongly. According to this view Cicero would use skeptical arguments in order to put a check on the excessive claims of Stoicism regarding the value of the honourable. Pierre Bayle, in the *Dictionnaire historique et critique*, puts it in a slightly different way. According to him, Cicero was so afraid of Carneades's critique of justice that he never tried to rebut it, but addressed it only in oblique ways:

> He does not bother to account for the school of Epicurus, because it held that one should detach oneself from politics: thus he lets it have its retreat however it wishes, but he asks Arcesilas and Carneades for mercy. He fears

> that, if they were to attack him, they would open too many breaches in the building he thought he had constructed. He does not have the heart to repel them, thus he does not want to be subject to their wrath; he wishes to appease them; he wants no war with them.[37]

What these two interpretations have in common is the realization that Cicero's dialogue does not arrive at a univocal conclusion on the nature of the relationship between the useful and the honourable. This does not mean, however, that the dialogue is incoherent or futile. It can be an effective handbook on the duties and obligations of the statesman, even if some questions having to do with first principles or final ends are left pending. This is true of Smith as well. In the chapter of *The Theory of Moral Sentiments* that discusses utility, he argues on both sides of the issue. The skeptical critique of the social order is true. The critique of the critique is true as well. The question of what constitutes true utility is left pending. We are left with the notion that "the appearance of utility,"[38] rather than utility itself, provides a solid foundation for the social order. Similarly, in the chapter of *The Wealth of Nations* that discusses the origins of the division of labour (which is itself the cause of the increase in the wealth of nations), Smith deliberately sidesteps the consideration of first principles. The division of labour is ascribed to "the propensity to truck, barter, and exchange one thing for another."[39] As to whether such propensity is a first principle or whether there is a more fundamental principle behind it, like the skeptics, we have to suspend judgment. Smith suggests that a more fundamental principle might be "the faculties of reason and speech."[40] However, this is something that "belongs not to our present subject to inquire."[41] When the analysis reaches first principles, Smith typically resorts to a skeptical mode of argument. This is not to say that his political economy is without foundations. Rather, it is to say that Smith's political economy has skeptical foundations, and that ambivalence about the roots of modern commercial society is at the heart of his entire system.

NOTES

1 Ryan Patrick Hanley, "Scepticism and Naturalism in Adam Smith," *Adam Smith Review* 5 (2010): 198–212.

2 For an attempt to link Smith's epistemology to his political theory, see Sergio Cremaschi, "Adam Smith: Skeptical Newtonianism, Disenchanted

Republicanism, and the Birth of Social Science," in *Knowledge and Politics: Case Studies in the Relationship Between Epistemology and Political Philosophy*, ed. Marcelo Dascal and Ora Gruengard (Boulder: Westview Press, 1989), 83–110.

3 Adam Smith, *The Theory of Moral Sentiments, Glasgow Edition of the Works and Correspondence of Adam Smith*, vol. 1 (Oxford: Oxford University Press, 1976), IV.i.10. Henceforth cited as *TMS*.

4 *TMS*, IV.i.2.

5 *TMS*, IV.i.3.

6 *Sympheron* (the useful), *kalon* (the honourable), and *hedu* (the pleasurable). Aristotle, *Nicomachean Ethics*, tr. H. Rackham (Cambridge, MA: Harvard University Press, 1926), II.3.7.

7 Cicero, *De Officiis*, tr. Walter Miller (Cambridge, MA: Harvard University Press, 1913), book 3.

8 *De Officiis*, III.30.

9 *TMS*, IV.i.2.

10 Hume, *Enquiries Concerning the Human Understanding and Concerning the Principles of Morals*, 2nd ed. (Oxford: Clarendon Press, 1902), 214.

11 Ibid.

12 *The Fable of the Bees*, vol. 1, ed. F.B. Kaye (Oxford: Clarendon Press, 1924), 46.

13 "S'il y avait de la justice, elle serait fondée ou sur le droit positif, ou sur le droit naturel. Or, elle n'est fondée ni sur le droit positif, qui varie selon les temps et les lieux, et que chaque peuple accommode à ses intérêts et à son utilité ; ni sur le droit naturel, car ce droit n'est autre chose qu'un penchant que la nature a donné à toutes sortes d'animaux vers ce qui leur est utile." Bayle, *Dictionnaire historique et critique*, 5th ed. (Amsterdam: Brunel, 1740), vol. 2, art. "Carnéade."

14 *Enquiry Concerning the Principles of Morals*, 214.

15 *Enquiry Concerning the Principles of Morals*, 298.

16 Hume, *Treatise of Human Nature* II, 2, 5 (Oxford: Clarendon Press, 1896), 365.

17 Ibid.

18 Hume, *Enquiry Concerning the Principles of Morals*, 270.

19 *Enquiry Concerning the Principles of Morals*, 298.

20 *TMS*, IV.1.6.

21 *TMS*, IV.1.8.

22 Ibid.

23 Ibid.

24 Rousseau, *Discourse on the Origin of Inequality*, trans. Adam Smith, in *Letter to the Edinburgh Review, Works and Correspondence of Adam Smith*, vol. 3 (Oxford: Oxford University Press, 1980), 253. "Au contraire, le citoyen toujours actif sue, s'agite, se tourmente sans cesse pour chercher des occupations encore

plus laborieuses: il travaille jusqu'à la mort, il y court même pour se mettre en état de vivre, ou renonce à la vie pour acquérir l'immortalité. Il fait sa cour aux grands qu'il hait et aux riches qu'il méprise." *Discours sur l'origine de l'inégalité*, 192.

25 *Letter to the Edinburgh Review*, 250.

26 Ibid.

27 *TMS*, IV.i.8.

28 *TMS*, IV.i.9.

29 Ibid.

30 Ibid.

31 *TMS*, p. 183, note 1.

32 *TMS*, IV.i.10.

33 Thomas Olshewsky, "The Classical Roots of Hume's Skepticism," *Journal of the History of Ideas* 52 (1991): 269–87.

34 For an overview of Smith's use of Cicero, see Gloria Vivenza, *Adam Smith and the Classics. The Classical Heritage in Adam Smith's Thought* (Oxford: Oxford University Press, 2001).

35 "[Carneades] excitabat ... ad veri investigandi cupiditatem," Cicero, *De natura deorum*, I, II.

36 Walter Nicgorski, "Cicero's Paradoxes and His Idea of Utility," *Political Theory* 12 (1984): 557–78. Also see Douglas Kries, "On the Intention of Cicero's *De Officiis*," *Review of Politics* 65 (2003): 375–93.

37 "Il ne se met point en peine de l'école d'Epicure, car elle faisait profession de se tenir à l'écart de la politique: il la laisse donc dans cette retraite comme elle voudra mais il demande quartier à Arcésilas et à Carnéade. Il craint que, s'ils venaient l'attaquer, ils ne fissent de trop grandes brèches dans le bâtiment qu'il croyait avoir construit. Il ne se sent pas assez de courage pour les repousser, il souhaite donc n'être pas exposé à leur colère, il désire de les apaiser, il ne veut point de guerre avec eux. " *Dictionnaire historique et critique*, art. "Carnéade."

38 TMS, IV.i.1.

39 WN, I.ii.1.

40 Adam Smith, *An Inquiry Into the Nature and Causes of the Wealth of Nations, Glasgow Edition of the Works and Correspondence of Adam Smith*, vol. 2, I.ii.2.

41 Ibid. See Pierre Force, *Self-Interest Before Adam Smith* (Cambridge, MA: Cambridge University Press, 2003), 126–34.

chapter eleven

Can a Skeptic Be a Reformer? Skepticism in Morals and Politics during the Enlightenment: The Case of Voltaire

RODRIGO BRANDÃO

The rather rhetorical question in the title is intended to be a reformulation of a traditional problem addressed to skeptics, concerning the difficulties of coherently living skepticism. All those traditional caricatured narratives of Pyrrho's life actually address the problem of the criterion for action. How can a skeptic live his skepticism if his actions seem to depend on beliefs, which skeptics are not supposed to have? Life without beliefs or life without judgment? The debate on the ethical and political consistency of skepticism is rich.[1] However, my aim here is not to fully analyse that debate, but to contribute to thinking about how skeptics *could* live their skepticism and a skeptical politics, and indicating how skeptical perspectives could have contributed to certain aspects of modern politics, particularly those formulated during the Enlightenment. The goal is both philosophical and historical. I intend to show a particular presence and use of skepticism in the Enlightenment by the study of Voltaire's works, and by doing it, I would like to think about both the consistency and the limits of skepticism.

In order to do so in a more detailed manner, two preliminary aspects have to be taken into account. The first concerns the pertinence of the question, for a skeptical life and a skeptical politics are traditionally regarded as something rather difficult, or even impossible.[2] Skeptics are accused of incoherence and sometimes of being hypocrites, of not confessing that they do believe in something. Or the question is answered by claiming that skepticism must lead to moral and political conservatism.

A deeper analysis would require further consideration of that debate, but here I want to follow a different strategy, pointing out some aspects of Voltaire's thought that show a precise use of traditional skeptical topics and the possibility of a moderated skeptical as well as reformist attitude in politics, in spite of a *minimum* of moral beliefs.

The second aspect mentioned above concerns the rather difficult connections between skepticism and Enlightenment, particularly when it comes to Voltaire's works. I shall focus specially on this second aspect. As I have already pointed out in another article, those connections are richer and more profound than they have been considered until now.[3] It is interesting to evoke such aspects as the problem of the external world, the conflicts of philosophy, the relation between faith and reason, and the relation between the skeptical *epoché* and Enlightenment *raison libre* to show that the connections between Voltaire's thought and skepticism are deeper than they are usually considered. I can mention as well the substantial knowledge Voltaire had of the skeptical tradition, both ancient and modern: he read Diogenes Laertius, Sextus's *PH,* Cicero's *De natura deorum,* Pierre Charron, Montaigne, Bayle, La Mothe le Vayer, and Pierre-Daniel Huet's *Traité de la faiblesse de l'entendement humain.*

Here, I shall first present some elements of Voltaire's thought that are apparently opposed to skepticism. Then I shall present some apparently skeptical elements of Voltaire's works, followed by a reconsideration of the apparently anti-skeptical elements. Finally, I shall consider whether his politics are in complicity with the skeptical aspects of his thought.

Some Apparently Anti-Skeptical Elements of Voltaire's Thought

1) There is an attack on skepticism, particularly Pyrrhonism, in the *Traité de Métaphysique,* chapter IV. There we find Voltaire's criticism of what he considered an extreme and unsustainable form of skepticism, the one that doubts the existence of the external world. His criticism can be divided into three parts. The first is an attack on the skeptical attitude towards daily life showing its inadequacy to the world; an ironical attack on the possibility of coherently living radical skepticism.[4] The second is the rejection of the strength of the dream argument.[5] The third is a defence of Locke's perspective – according to which touch is the only sense that enables us to have access to the primary quality of things.[6] With the latter Voltaire wanted to avoid the skeptical consequences of the separation of qualities into two different classes, claiming that the essential properties of bodies are accessible by touch. For my purpose, the most remarkable aspect of Voltaire's refusal of radical skepticism is found in the examples he provides to attack the skeptical

attitude and its inadequacy to daily life: they all demand action, which would either turn the skeptic into a dogmatist or would make skepticism ineffective.

2) Voltaire's famous deism, which he sometimes characterizes as demonstrated and based on the proof of the argument from design.[7] That kind of claim about the existence of God would certainly be a mark of a dogmatic philosophy.

3) The defence of Newtonian science. Voltaire's belief in Newtonian physics and defence of the experimental philosophy are limits to his skepticism, apparently due to having some philosophical beliefs. The superiority of the history of the human soul provided by Locke compared to Descartes's romance and the superiority of the method of "analysis" compared to the fables of the *systèmes* are all signs of a non-skeptical philosophy.

4) Voltaire's moral universalism. The relativity of manners does not prevent him from finding some universal elements, such as the prohibition of lies.[8] The very topic of the variety of customs, which is Aenesidemus's tenth mode for the suspension of judgment, is used in order to reach universality: a natural capacity is developed by time and use like any other natural capacity. We must remember as well his numerous references to natural law and his criticism of Locke for his rejection of innate moral principles.[9]

Some Aspects Apparently Favourable to Skepticism

1) Voltaire's anti-metaphysical attitude. We should remember his well-known attacks on metaphysical systems, mainly those of Descartes and Leibniz, and the necessity of establishing the limits of human reason – which most of the time come together with a defence of Locke and Newton. The skeptical image of a blank book at the end of *Micromégas, une histoire philosophique* and the use of doubt in some texts such as the *Philosophe ignorant* (except for its apparent commitment to innate moral principles), in which the traditional index, "Table de matières" [Table of contents], is replaced by a "Table de doutes" [Table of doubts].

2) No political system. Voltaire does not seem to adopt any systematic politics. He had no particular passion for theoretical questions about power and sovereignty, for example, and he seems to not ground his political action on principles from which everything derives. His political texts are prominently contextual – motivated by special cases, the

well-known "affaires de Voltaire": Calas, La Barre, etc. Even texts such as *Idées republicaines par un membre d'un corps* are concerned with specific issues of his time, in this case the publication of Rousseau's *Du Contrat social* and all the *affaires* of both philosophers with Geneva. All political actions and considerations seem to depend on the comprehension of their singularity and circumstances.[10]

Beyond that, when we analyse Voltaire's comments on the tradition of political philosophy, we see that he is always critical. *L'A,B,C* begins with a critique of Grotius, Hobbes, and Montesquieu. Voltaire attacks political philosophers because of their abstractions, their lack of historical knowledge and historical accuracy (using skeptical arguments found in historical Pyrrhonism to attack them), and for their use of unimportant details to sustain their claims. Doubt, ignorance, and the impossibility of a theoretical political system are the most remarkable characteristics of some of Voltaire's political writings.

3) No positive anthropology, no deep knowledge of human nature, no dogmatic discourse on aspects of the human soul, the truth of man's destiny, etc. – man's soul is a closed book. For Voltaire the question of man depends on metaphysical questions, but they are mostly about the limits of metaphysical discourse. As examples, let me consider two questions that are part of the problem of theodicy, which much troubled Voltaire during his long life: human freedom and the existence of evil.[11] Concerning the existence of evil, Voltaire never adopted a definite philosophical response to it. At the beginning of his philosophical career, he was close to philosophical optimism, but after the Lisbon earthquake his hesitation turned into a virulent attack on that tradition. The several texts where he discusses the question of evil are composed of a myriad of different opinions on the subject, from the Hindus to Plato to Shaftesbury and Leibniz, and they always attack dogmatism and present a diaphonic history of the debate.[12]

Regarding human liberty, Voltaire moves from a defence of freedom of the will to determinism. In the 1730s, based on a position very close to that of Descartes, Voltaire defended liberty in the *Traité de Métaphysique*; and in his letters to Frederick on the freedom of the will, he adopts some of Clarke's perspectives against Anthony Collins in order to defend his belief on human freedom.[13] But the later Voltaire leaves Clarke for Collins, and in *Le Philosophe ignorant* and the *Dictionnaire philosophique* he adopts determinism, although he still strives to find a place for human liberty by distinguishing human action from natural determinism.[14]

4) The variation of opinion. His texts are full of conflicting perspectives, and many of them are structured on the basis of philosophical *diaphonia*: *Micromegas*, various entries of the *Dictionnaire philosophique*, and his numerous dialogues.[15]

5) Voltaire's nominalism. When he comments on the faculties of man, he stresses the fact that they are not separate entities, but names we give to certain actions we identify.[16]

Re-evaluating the Evidence

Now I am going to suggest a re-evaluation of the obstacles to understanding Voltaire as a skeptic mentioned above. In summary, except for the case of morals, all of them can be re-evaluated to show that they are consistent with a skeptical attitude, even if he clearly rejects an extreme form of it.

1) Both in the case of history and the existence of the external world, Voltaire does not consider seriously what he calls a "*pyrronisme outré*" [excessive Pyrrhonism]. It is too radical, and it would prevent man from living. Both radical epistemological skepticism and radical historical Pyrrhonism would demand too much of reason and they would be obstacles to historical and scientific knowledge. But as it is characterized in the *Traité*, for example, a kind of egoism, a radical solipsism, it is more an extreme theoretical possibility than a real livable philosophical option.

2) His deism. The first thing when it comes to Voltaire's deism is to take his language about proof and demonstration with caution, for in many texts, such as the *Dialogue entre Lucretius et Posidonius*, we see him drawing such a strong picture of atheism that one should hesitate to take the claims about the demonstration of the existence of God at face value. Here we have to consider the nature of the belief in God he expresses. In a text such as the *Traité de Métaphysique*, which was one of the few complete texts of Voltaire's not intended for publication, Voltaire is much less conclusive in his opinions about deism against atheism. Deism is only more probable, it has more verisimilitude than atheism, as he clearly states in his letter to Frederick of 17 April 17 1737, but that is all.[17]

In addition to that, what is Voltaire's deism? If we pay attention to his last texts about God, texts that he published under the pseudonym of abbé Tilladet, Voltaire is far too distant from the image of a wise and powerful God demonstrated by the design argument, or the a posteriori argument. Since the writing of *Le Philosophe ignorant*, and the *Tout en dieu, essai sur Malebranche*, we can follow a Voltaire more interested in the opinions of Malebranche and Spinoza on God. In his last texts on God, he replaces the metaphor of the clockmaker God with the image of the Sun.[18] No anthropomorphical image, no preoccupation with human evil, and the world is not the result of an impossible *ex nihilo* creation, but an emanation of the first principle, as the sun's rays come from the sun. But he still defends intelligence and matter, against just matter. Well, here, in his two-front battle, against *l'Infâme* and against atheism, we can grasp Voltaire's attitude, for what unites *l'Infâme* and the atheists is dogmatism, which is manifested both in the dogmas and in the attachment to them – a dogmatic content and a dogmatic attitude. Even if atheism is slightly better, Voltaire rejects Holbach's *Système de la nature* like any other pretentious systematic view of nature and man.

3) Voltaire's defence of Newtonian science can also be considered as being from a skeptical point of view, since for him Newton and Locke are mainly concerned with the limits of human knowledge.[19] The supporter of Locke in *Micromégas* is characterized as someone who limits his opinions to that which is observable by everyone; he is the author that established the limits of human knowledge. In the case of Newton, his science does not try to reveal the ultimate principles of nature. Gravitation is the cause of many phenomena and is used to explain them, but its own cause is unknown. Hence, it is highly probable that Voltaire regarded Newtonian physics in a phenomenalist manner. It explains the physical phenomena, but it does not give us the answer or the essence of matter, or the ultimate principles of the universe.

4) The case of morals is the most difficult, and perhaps here one finds Voltaire's most dogmatic claims. His defence of moral universalism, the natural capacity to distinguish evil from good, and his repeated references to natural law imply important political practices for modern times, toleration and the proportionality of crimes and punishments, separation of religious and state power, and so on, but they are certainly not skeptical.

However, we have to consider two different strategies to confirm the case of morals: (1) the first is to understand the consistency and the nature of Voltaire's universal moral beliefs, (2) and the second is to see if his politics depends upon his morals, and I mean by "politics" both his political texts and his political activity, which are not separate in an author such as Voltaire. In the first case, we should understand what Voltaire's universal moral beliefs are and how they are conceived before taking into consideration the variation of customs and laws. Second, we should check if Voltaire's politics is dependent on his moral conceptions.

Voltaire's Morals and Politics

After considering the presence of skeptical elements in Voltaire's works – that his thoughts on different subjects such as metaphysics and history are deeply connected to skepticism (sometimes "influenced" by it and sometimes a reaction to it, as in the case of morals and the problem of the external world), that his works are nourished by skeptical reflection – we can now move to his politics. Can it be considered in complicity with the skeptical elements of his thought? Apparently not, precisely because of the case of morals: his references to natural law and the defence of a universal human background for morality. He considers the traditional topic of the variations of customs in order to claim that there is a universal background.

Let's consider it in a more detailed way, paying special attention to the text of the *Traité de métaphysique*, where he develops a very interesting point of view against moral Pyrrhonism or what we would call today moral relativism. According to Voltaire, there is a universal definition of virtue and justice, and man has a natural capacity to distinguish evil from good. However, history is also a determinant, because that natural capacity must be developed. It is not properly an innate principle, so Voltaire strives to give an empiricist characterization of that capacity despite Locke's denial of innate moral principles, which is seen as Locke's only mistake. Actually, Voltaire's perspective seems to be a compromise between naturalism and conventionalism, for virtue and justice are defined in a formal way, whose contents are given by history and culture. It is a natural ability that is developed over time.

When it comes to consider the notion of virtue for any one society, this compromise also appears, for in every time and society, says Voltaire, we find that a virtuous action is the one that favours the common good, and vice what threatens it. But what is the common good? Well, that is also given by history and culture. Hence, there is no dogmatic postulation of what is good or bad for societies, and when he affirms that lying is bad he means only that, according to him, a society cannot be based on lies. And as for claims, for example, that respect for elders is a universal rule found in all societies, it is important to say that, according to Voltaire, this is not something truly based on reason or abstract reasoning, or on an abstract notion of human nature. It is a prejudice, and as Voltaire says, there are good prejudices, historically established "truths" that are not originally grounded on reason, but are justifiable by later philosophical reflection.[20]

Now let us consider Voltaire's politics, and see if it is dependent on his morals. What is Voltaire's politics? First of all, Voltaire's comments on politics do not constitute a systematic political corpus, which is something that we would expect from a philosopher with a skeptical attitude towards politics. There is no single text in which he expresses the whole of his opinions on politics in a coherent and systematic manner. His opinions are spread over different kinds of texts, from articles to dictionaries to tales, dialogues, and pamphlets.

Two major attempts to organize Voltaire's opinions and perspectives on politics were Peter Gay's 1959 book, *Voltaire's Politics: The Poet as Realist*, and René Pomeau's 1963 introduction to selected texts, *La Politique de Voltaire.*[21] Gay was not satisfied with the generally accepted view on Voltaire's politics, which reduced it to "enlightened despotism" and "literary utopianism," and defends the claim that Voltaire "was a realist, a practical hard-headed political man" who acknowledged human weaknesses, but claimed that "while reason is a weak reed, authority in whatever form is both weaker and less dignified."[22]

One special aspect of Gay's book for my purpose here is its chapter on Voltaire and natural law. The reiterated references to natural law, which transcends positive laws and enables their evaluation, would clearly be an obstacle to any attempt to identify a skeptical attitude in Voltaire's politics. However, Gay shows that Voltaire's references to the natural law tradition cannot be considered literal claims of truth, for 1) Voltaire rejected the theory of knowledge that could sustain natural law, 2) he attacked all the great authors of the natural law tradition, 3) he was never seriously interested in the notions of a natural state or an original contract, and 4) his defence of universal consent is both wrong and has little theoretical interest.

Pomeau also made some important comments for our purpose, despite starting with a rather traditional perspective on Voltaire's politics, dividing the *philosophe*'s choices and preferences into "enlightened despotism" that was weakened after his German experience, and English liberalism, which he eventually preferred, for in the English case freedom is both the end and the medium.[23]

Both Pomeau and Gay considered Voltaire's political opinions highly dependent on particular elements and singular aspects of eighteenth-century French politics, but at the same time far too important for the political ideas and practices of modern man, such as the defence of religious tolerance and of freedom for intellectual activity, for example. According to Pomeau, the absence of a system and the strong dependence on particular disputes and problems are not a lack of competence, but the fact that Voltaire was "convaincue que les systèmes de politique, plus que tous autres, faussent les faits et sont démentis par l'évènement" (convinced that political systems, more than others, are not based on facts and are refuted by events).[24] Voltaire's politics is characterized as a "pensée empirique" (empirical thought). In addition to that characterization, Pomeau makes another claim that is significant for my purpose here, saying that Voltaire's thought is "par nature politique" (by nature political), that is to say that every philosophical concern Voltaire had in some manner or other led him to politics. Here Pomeau stresses the point that Voltaire is usually concerned with the social results and uses of philosophical and metaphysical doctrines.

Despite the absence of a systematic political corpus, it is possible to find some important texts that present most of Voltaire's late views on politics. I will consider two of them, the dialogue *l'A,B,C* and the article "Gouvernement" from the *Questions sur l'Encyclopèdie.* The first is a mix of skepticism and pessimism, of attack on political authors such as Grotius, Hobbes, and especially Montesquieu, and a claim for reforms and separation of church and state. At the end, even with a strong appeal for republicanism, we are not able to decide which is the best form of government, or even if the pursuit of the best of all governments is something that should be attempted. The latter is a text that synthetizes most of Voltaire's political thought, revealing its most important aspects: his realism, a defence of the English system, criticism of Ancient Regime politics in France, and his anticlericalism. Actually, in all seven sections of the article, only the sixth, about the English government, is positive (but that does not mean at all that the English government could be transposed to other countries). All the rest of the article is composed either of criticism of political authors and their general political doctrines, as well as of religion, or by a skeptical and pessimistic view about the possibility of regulating political phenomena and of avoiding violence and war. Voltaire criticizes political authors such as Bossuet for lack of practical knowledge about public administration, authors such as Pufendorf for their inconsistencies, and also political maxims such as the one that affirms that the good of the people is the supreme law. Politics is not as regular as geometry, and since it is founded on human passions, there is no possible end for conflict, no recipes for political action: "comment faut-il faire? Ou risquer, ou se cacher" (what should one do? Either take a risk, or hide).[25]

In spite of all the negative aspects of politics and the skepticism towards the possibility of regulating conflict, Voltaire was deeply engaged in fighting for the defence of freedom and tolerance. His skepticism towards politics, both as theory and practice, did not prevent his actions on behalf of Calas, for example. Certainly, however, we find a positive aspect in that criticism of religion persecution, for what religious fanaticism and tyranny prevent is the development of human natural capacities, and of liberty. Voltaire's basic political beliefs are his anticlericalism, his demand for the complete separation of religion and worldly power, and liberty, which is connected to property and the freedom of speech, but they are always accompanied by skepticism about general political discourse and final answers to political conflict. Thus, it is clear that his moral and political beliefs are important to his political action, but they always come together with his skeptical considerations concerning violence, war, laws, and political theory, and they do not seem to determine the whole of his thought on politics. When it comes to political economy, we also find a mix of demands for change and better administration with a lack of belief in complete solutions or general systems.

As I have pointed out, in the domain of morals Voltaire refuses a radical skepticism, a "pirronisme outré" in his words, that is to say, he refuses a kind of skepticism that could lead to inaction. Voltaire's reflections are always connected to the moral results they can have. If reflections based on skepticism do not change anything in common life, they do not have any importance. The role of philosophy is to change daily life, not from an individualist point of view that would leave things as they are, like the different asceticisms attacked by the author, but to understand what is justifiable and what is not, what favours life in society and what does not. This is a practical approach, and Voltaire denounces the abuses and misuses of religion, of public administration, and of the powerful, such as the magistrates of his time.

Now, there is one thing we can already consider on the subject of skepticism and politics when it comes to Voltaire. If we consider that Voltaire defended a "mitigated skepticism," surely quietism or inaction is not the consequence of doubt, for Voltaire is, as we know, a militant philosopher, a philosopher of action, a proto-intellectual. In spite of the fact that "intellectual" was a term the Enlightenment was not familiarized with, Voltaire is said to be the first intellectual *avant la lettre.*[26]

Then, what is the criterion for action? How can we understand Voltaire's militant activity if he is supposed to not have access to how things really are? How can he struggle for reforms in law, customs, and religion? Here we find two rich aspects of his thought that can only be mentioned: his conception of belief and his considerations on the rapport between philosophy and common life.

Let's briefly consider the case of tolerance to guide us to my final words. For Voltaire, tolerance derives above all from human weakness. We cannot know the mysteries of man and the universe, and religious dogmas are based on those mysteries, so no religious dogma can be accepted as a guide common to human life. They can be a matter of private choices, we can go to heaven the way we want to, but social life must be ruled by things that can be understood in common, and such dogmas cannot be understood in common, but only by specific confessional groups.

What can then be understood in common? And what can guide man's action? I say beliefs can be understood in common and they can be a guide to man's action, not faith. Voltaire distinguishes belief from faith, saying that faith is obedience; it is a commitment to something that is absurd and incomprehensible, while belief has some degree of verisimilitude. But all beliefs are not based on demonstration and are not identified with scientific or theoretical knowledge. Very few beliefs can have the highest degree of certainty – these are the ones based on the principle of non-contradiction. But the others, the vast majority of the beliefs upon which we ground our actions, are just probable.[27] They can be strengthened or changed before further evidence, but they never are descriptions of how things really are. "Croire, c'est très souvent douter" [to believe is often to doubt], says Voltaire.

Finally, from everything I said, we can grasp an important aspect of Voltaire's thought. The difficulties of philosophy do not necessarily lead to the abandonment of philosophy in daily life. Of course it leads to the abandonment of philosophical systems, to sarcasm towards a dogmatic attachment to philosophical discourses, as well as to a blank book or to Candide's garden. But Candide's garden is not a place void of philosophical enquiry, or if it is, it is not Voltaire's garden, for we know how philosophical enquiry continued to be Voltaire's preoccupation. The skeptical *epoché* is just a moment of the continuous search for truth; the suspension of judgment does not prevent the philosophe's *raison libre* (free reasoning) from continuing its pursuit; on the contrary, it favours it.[28]

NOTES

1 The debate is analysed in the third chapter of John Christian Laursen, *The Politics of Skepticism in the Ancients, Montaigne, Hume and Kant* (Leiden: Brill, 1992).

2 Cf. Myles Burnyeat, "Can the Sceptic Live His Scepticism?" in *Doubt and Dogmatism: Studies in Hellenistic Epistemology*, ed. Malcolm Schofield, Myles Burnyeat, and Jonathan Barnes (Oxford: Clarendon Press, 1980).

3 Cf. Rodrigo Brandão, "Voltaire et le scepticisme," *Philosophique*, 35 (2008): 261–74.

4 "Que s'ensuivra-t-il de là? Nous Conduirons-nous autrement dans notre vie? Aurons-nous des idées différentes sur rien? Il faudra seulement changer un mot dans ses discours. Lorsque, par exemple, ont aura donné quelque bataille, il faudra dire que dix mille hommes ont paru être tués, qu'un tel officier semble avoir la jambe cassée, et qu'un chirurgien paraîtra la lui couper. De même, quand nous aurons faim, nous demanderons l'apparence d'un morceau de pain pour faire semblant de digérer." (What would follow from this? Would we behave in a different manner in our lives? Would we have different ideas about anything? It would be enough to change a word in their speeches. When, for example, during the war, it would be necessary to say that ten thousand men seem to have been killed, that an officer seems to have a broken leg, and that a surgeon appears to have cut it. Similarly, when one is hungry, one should demand the appearance of a loaf pretending to digest it.) *Traité de métaphysique*, ch. IV, in *The Complete Works of Voltaire* (Oxford: Voltaire Foundation, 1989), 14:446. This has some similarity with Locke's attack on the extreme form of skepticism that consists of denial of the certainty of existence of the self: "For man knows that he himself exists. I think it is beyond question, that man has a clear idea of his own being; he knows certainly he exists, and that he is something. He that can doubt whether he be anything or no, I speak not to; no more than I would argue with pure nothing, or endeavour to convince nonentity that it were something. If any one pretends to be so sceptical as to deny his own existence, (for really to doubt of it is manifestly impossible,) let him for me enjoy his beloved happiness of being nothing, until hunger or some other pain convince him of the contrary." John Locke, *An Essay on Human Understanding*, Book IV, ch. X, #2.

5 *Traité de Métaphysique*, ch. IV, 446.

6 *Traité de métaphysique*, ch. IV, 446–7 See also Locke, *An Essay on Human Understanding*, II, ch. 4.

7 See, for example: *Éléments de la philosophie de Newton*: "Le dessein, ou plutôt les desseins variés à l'infini qui éclatent dans les plus vastes et les plus petites

parties de l'univers, font une démonstration, qui à force d'être sensible, en est presque méprisée par quelques philosophes (…)." (The design, or better the infinitely varied designs which burst into the most vast and the smallest parts of the universe are a demonstration that, since it comes from the senses, is almost despised by some philosophers […].) *The Complete Works of Voltaire* (Oxford: Voltaire Foundation, 1992), 15:197.

8 "Plus j'ai vu des hommes différents par le climat, les mœurs, le langage, les lois, le culte, et par la mesure de leur intelligence, et plus j'ai remarqué qu'ils ont tous le même fond de morale; ils ont tous une notion grossière du juste et de l'injuste, sans savoir un mot de théologie; ils ont tous acquis cette même notion dans l'âge où la raison se déploie, comme ils ont tous acquis naturellement l'art de soulever des fardeaux avec des bâtons, et de passer un ruisseau sur un morceau de bois, sans avoir appris les mathématiques." (The more I saw men differing because of their climate, their manners, language, laws, religion, and their intelligence, the more I noticed they have the very same moral background; they all have a rough notion of just and unjust, without knowing one word of theology ; they all acquired that notion at the age reason develops itself, as they all naturally acquired the art of lifting burdens with sticks [...] without have learned mathematics.) *Philosophe ignorant.* Chapt. XXXI. See chapt. XXX –XXXVI and the article "Morale" of the *Dictionnaire philosophique.*

9 "La morale uniforme en tout temps, en tout lieu, /A des siècles sans fin parle au nom de ce Dieu. / C'est la loi de Trajan, de Socrate, et la vôtre. / De ce culte éternel la nature est l'apôtre./

Le bon sens la reçoit; et les remords vengeurs,/ Nés de la conscience, en sont les défenseurs; / Leur redoutable voix partout se fait entendre." (Morals are uniform in every time, in every place, / For centuries it talks in God's name / That's Trajans law, Socrates's, and yours / Of this eternal cult nature is the apostle. / Common sense receives it; and the vindictive remorses / Born from conscience, defend it; / Its formidable voice is heard everywhere.) *Poème sur la loi naturelle.* Première partie. On the criticism of Locke's rejection of innate moral principles see *Philosophe ignorant,* doubts XXXIV–XXXVI.

10 A good example of the context dependence of Voltaire's practical considerations is the case of lying. Despite the fact that Voltaire affirms that lies cannot be accepted in any society since oaths and promises depend on people being truthful, and the generalized use of lies would lead to the ruin of society, Voltaire claims that lies can be useful in particular cases, and the example he gives is the same as the one used by Kant to draw the opposite conclusion. See S. Charles. "D'un prétendu droit de plagier par humanité: Voltaire inspirateur de Constant," *Revue Voltaire* 9 (2009): 265–9.

11 For Voltaire and theodicy, see Richard A. Brooks, *Voltaire and Leibniz* (Geneva: Droz, 1964); William H. Barber, *Leibniz in France, from Arnauld to Voltaire* (Oxford: Clarendon Press, 1955); and Rodrigo Brandão, *A ordem do mundo e o homem:estudos sobre metafísica e moral em Voltaire*, http://filosofia.fflch.usp.br/sites/filosofia.fflch.usp.br/files/posgraduacao/defesas/2009_docs/2009.doc.Rodrigo_Brandao.pdf.

12 For the problem of evil in Voltaire's writings, see the first chapter of B. Baczko, *Job, Mon ami: promesses du bonheur et fatalité du mal* (Paris: Gallimard, 1997), and the article by Jean Goldzink, "La Métaphysique du mal," *Revue Europe* 72 (1994): 63–78.

13 *Voltaire's Correspondance*, ed. Theodore Besterman, vols. 6 and 7 (Geneva: Institut et Musée Voltaire, 1954).

14 See "Chaîne ou génération des événements," *Dictionnaire philosophique.*

15 For the case of Voltaire's dialogues, see S. Pujol, "Voltaire docteur ou douter," *Revue Europe* (May, 1994): 89–101, and "Misère du dialogue ou misère de la philosophie? L'impossible mot de la fin," *Revue Voltaire* 5 (2005).

16 "C'est précisément parce que je ne sais rien de tout ce que vous m'alléguez que j'ignore absolument si j'ai une âme, quand je ne consulte que ma faible raison. Je vois bien que l'air est agité, mais je ne vois point d'être réel dans l'air qu'on appelle cours du vent. Une rose végète, mais il n'y a point un petit individu secret dans la rose qui soit la végétation: cela serait aussi absurde en philosophie que de dire que l'odeur est dans la rose. (...) Quelques sages s'aperçurent que tous ces êtres imaginaires ne sont que des mots inventés pour soulager notre entendement; que la vie de l'animal n'est autre chose que l'animal vivant; que ses idées sont l'animal pensant, que la végétation d'une plante n'est rien que la plante végétante; que le mouvement d'une boule n'est que la boule changeant de place; qu'en un mot tout être métaphysique n'est qu'une de nos conceptions. Il a fallu deux mille ans pour que ces sages eussent raison." (It is precisely because I do not know anything about what you claim that I absolutely do not know if I have a soul, when I consult my feeble reason. I clearly see that the air is agitated, but I do not see a real being in the air that we call wind direction. A rose vegetates, but there is not a small individual hidden in the rose which would be vegetation: it would be as absurd in philosophy as saying that odor is in the rose [...] Some sages noticed that all those imaginary beings are nothing more than words invented to relieve our understanding; that the life of an animal is nothing else than the animal living; that its ideas are the animal thinking; that the vegetation of a plant is nothing more than the plant vegetating; that the movement of a ball is nothing more than the ball changing its place; in one word, that every metaphysical being is nothing more than one of our conceptions.) *L'A,B,C*, second dialogue.

17 "Quelle sera donc l'opinion que j'embrasserai ? Celle où j'aurai, de compte fait, moins d'absurdités à dévorer. Or je trouve beaucoup plus de contradictions, de difficultés, d'embarras, dans le système de l'existence nécessaire de la matière ; je me range donc à l'opinion de l'existence de l'Être suprême, comme la plus vraisemblable et la plus probable. Je ne crois pas qu'il y ait de démonstration, proprement dite, de l'existence de cet Être indépendant de la matière. Je me souviens que je ne laissais pas, en Angleterre, d'embarrasser un peu le fameux docteur Clarke, quand je lui disais: 'On ne peut appeler démonstration un enchaînement d'idées qui laisse toujours des difficultés. Dire que le carré construit sur le grand côté d'un triangle est égal au carré des deux [autres] côtés, c'est une démonstration qui, toute compliquée qu'elle est, ne laisse aucune difficulté ; mais l'existence d'un Être créateur laisse encore des difficultés insurmontables à l'esprit humain. Donc cette vérité ne peut être mise au rang des démonstrations proprement dites. Je la crois, cette vérité ; mais je la crois comme ce qui est le plus vraisemblable ; c'est une lumière qui me frappe à travers mille ténèbres'." (What is then the opinion I embrace? The one, after all, in which I would have fewer absurdities to face. Now I find much more contradiction, difficulties, obstacles in the system of the necessary existence of matter; I take the opinion then of the existence of the supreme Being, as the most verisimilar and the most probable. I do not believe that there is a demonstration, properly speaking, of the existence of this Being independent of matter. I remember when in England that I embarrassed a little the famous Doctor Clarke, when I told him that "We cannot call demonstration a chain of ideas that always leave some difficulties. Say that the square on the bigger side of a triangle is equal to the square of the two other sides, that is a demonstration, which being complicated as it is, does not leave any difficulty, but the existence of a Being who is the creator leaves insurmountable difficulties to the human mind. Thus that truth cannot be ranked as a proper demonstration. I believe in it, in that truth; but I believe in it as the most verisimilar; that is a beam of light which reaches me in total darkness.")

18 For an introduction to these almost unkown texts of Voltaire, see Gerhardt Stenger's introduction to Voltaire, *Lettres philosophiques et Derniers écrits sur Dieu* (Paris: GF, 2006).

19 That negative aspect is presented by Giorgio Tonelli, "The 'Weakness' of Reason in the age of Enlightenment," in *Scepticism in the* Enlightenment, ed. G. Tonelli, R. Popkin, and E. de Olaso (Dordrecht: Kluwer, 1997), 35–50.

20 Cf. "Préjugés." In *Dictionnaire philosophique.*

21 An important selection of Voltaire's political writings is also found in *Voltaire's Political Writings*, ed. David Williams (Cambridge: Cambridge University Press, 1994).
22 Cf. P. Gay, *Voltaire's Politics: The Poet as Realist* (Princeton, NJ: Princeton University Press, 1959), VIII.
23 Cf. R. Pomeau, *La politique de Voltaire* (Paris: Armand Colin, 1963), 8.
24 Ibid. 9
25 "Gouvernement," in *Questions sur l'Encyclopèdie, OCV* vol. 42[a] (Oxford: Voltaire Foundation, 2011), 117.
26 P. Lepape, *Voltaire le conquérant* (Paris: Seuil, 1997).
27 Here are some elements of the influence of Academic skepticism (the importance of the notions of probability, verisimilitude, and persuasion), but we can also trace this attitude back to his investigations in the domain of history and the epistemology of historical and juridical testimony. Evidence for that is the fact that most of the discussion about those notions appears in his historical texts where he attacks theology and biblical history.
28 Cf. Éliane Martin-Haag, "Diderot et Voltaire lecteurs de Montaigne: du jugement suspendu à la raison libre," *Revue de métaphysique et de morale* 3 (1997): 365–85.

chapter twelve

From General Skepticism to Complete Dogmatism: Jacques-Pierre Brissot de Warville

SÉBASTIEN CHARLES

At first blush, the relationship between skepticism and politics is far from obvious. Politics is often assumed to be a sphere in which decisions flowing from well-established principles are applied; and this seems to be in contradiction to the skeptical practices of *isosthenia* and the suspension of judgment. Skeptics for their part appear to grant little attention either to political theory – attacking it, like morality, on the basis of the argument from the variety of human laws and customs, which appears to make it impossible to guarantee the universalization of common public rules – or to political practice, which is partly dependent on lively passions such as ambition and thus seems hardly to be favoured by the *ataraxia* aimed at by the skeptical approach.

It is based on this general observation that the case of Brissot de Warville takes on a paradigmatic overtone, for in Brissot we have a man who professed radical skepticism and at the same time invested himself fully in political action during the revolutionary period as though, from his perspective, no real contradiction existed between these two approaches, both of which he wished to fully own. To try to understand this choice of simultaneous allegiance to the spirit of skepticism and the values of revolutionary France, it is important, I believe, first to call to mind the conception of skepticism peculiar to Brissot, which he hoped to see triumph during the Enlightenment. Next, we shall examine his political positions, which account for the privileged role he was led to play within the revolutionary movement; and finally, on this basis, we shall see what Brissot's case can in fact teach us about the very possibility of political skepticism or skeptical politics.

1. Brissot the Skeptic

We have Richard Popkin to thank for having on numerous occasions emphasized Brissot's significance for the history of ideas and more specifically for the history of skepticism in the early modern period.[1] Brissot's significance derives from the fact that he was one of the rare eighteenth-century authors to present himself (in his early writings) under the mantle of Sextus Empiricus, borrowing from Sextus the idea of a systematic critique of the sciences and scholarship and applying it to modern science and scholarship in order to demonstrate, in a single move, both their vacuousness and their uncertainty. In so doing he went against the tenor of a century that congratulated itself on the continuous progress of knowledge and the dissemination of the Enlightenment spirit. Thus many of Brissot's reflections take the form of a critical review of the knowledge of his time; and his ambition appears to have been to provide his readers with a skeptical encyclopedia that would compete with Diderot's and d'Alembert's *Encyclopédie.*

The first outlines of this monumental undertaking to undermine the scientific optimism of the Enlightenment are found in a manuscript stored in the Brissot boxes in the French National Archives. The manuscript's title has the merit of explicitness: *Plan du scepticisme universel appliqué à toutes les sciences* (Plan for applying universal skepticism to all the sciences).[2] This manuscript constitutes a general sketch of a vast project to critique modern science and scholarship, a project whose traces are found in several other boxes dedicated to specific fields of knowledge such as history. The project was intended to give rise to several volumes and was conceived by the young Brissot as a collective enterprise in which he would have liked to have the collaboration of such prestigious figures as d'Alembert. Indeed he contacted d'Alembert to this end; but clearly d'Alembert could not accept such an implicit critique of the project he himself had conducted with Diderot. Hence d'Alembert's flat refusal to Brissot, accompanied by a reproach for the latter's radicalism. For d'Alembert, a mitigated skepticism or reasonable Pyrrhonism is sufficient, in that they don't challenge the totality of knowledge or the possibility for continual progress in science and scholarship.[3]

It is undeniable that d'Alembert grasped perfectly the purpose of the project Brissot had put before him, which aimed to extend the skeptical critique to all the fields of science and scholarship and thereby strike down the idea of the possible superiority of the Moderns over the

Ancients, as is evident in this somewhat orotund opening passage in the manuscript:

> The fact is, in this century ornamented with the prodigal label of "philosophical," we believe that man has perfected all the sciences, scaled every step on their ladders; we believe that error has disappeared, that truth is no longer veiled, we believe we are in the middle of the light and yet we are still in darkness. We may not be making the errors of our forefathers, but we have traded them for new errors. Tossing us back and forth with their ebb and flow, they die out along with us; and the centuries to come will see the birth of more of them. They chase after each other; they reappear one after the other; and in the darkened circuit that they travel round, man is ever their toy. They rock him from infancy until white-haired old age.[4]

The radicalism of Brissot's project resides above all in his rejection of certainty in the sphere of science and scholarship. He argued that every discovery gives rise to new difficulties and increases the portion of the unknown, indeed the unknowable, as though the development of knowledge entailed a proportionate advance in ignorance, with each new stage in the acquisition of knowledge in no way guaranteeing true progress towards the truth, but assuring instead the increased complexity and obscurity of the world and an ongoing breakdown of scientific and scholarly disciplines. One proof of this is that the divisions specific to the new fields of science and scholarship, which were to have served as the organizing principle for Brissot's skeptical project (for Brissot's intention was to deal with all these fields), appeared to have undergone a perceptible conceptual inflation since Sextus's time. In particular, everything related to the fields of law and the natural sciences had in fact not stopped developing and becoming more complex over the course of the centuries.

Dividing his topic into three broad areas organized around three types of "science," namely, theology, the human sciences, and the natural sciences, Brissot generally adopts as his method of demonstrating the vacuousness of these purported sciences the destruction of their foundations, based on a review of the diversity of philosophical opinions, ancient and modern, on the issue in question. In the end he arrives at the adoption of a skeptical posture, which emerges as the most moderate position on all these subject matters. To illustrate the skeptical process employed by Brissot, relying above all on the classic skeptical argument from *diaphonia*,

I will cite just one passage about the nature of the divine and the impossibility of giving it a univocal definition:

> It is by examining all these authors, by examining their systems, the various attributes with which they have ornamented their respective divinities, the peculiar ideas that each party has formed of its own divinity: it is by reviewing their contradictions and their debates that it will be seen that, in the midst of this clash of opinions, doubt is the only position that the wise person should embrace. Everything comes together to make of doubt a law: the diversity of systems and ideas of all peoples about the divinity; the impossibility of ever managing to lift the veil that hides the first cause from our eyes; the enormous mass of contradictions into which the apologists for a divinity have fallen; the discordance between its negative and theological attributes; and a thousand other reasons that we will itemize.[5]

From theology to metaphysics and the natural sciences: the same method is used and reused, as though the clash between philosophical factions on every issue represented on its own a proof of the falsity of dogmatism. It would be tedious to trace each and every development. True, Brissot does sometimes set aside *diaphonia* in favour of other skeptical tropes. For example, he brings up the delicate question of how to determine the criterion for truth and shows how sensation and reason are untrustworthy judges since these instruments, purportedly providing guarantees of certainty, are in fact imperfect or limited.[6] But the fact remains that his preference often lies with confrontation between philosophical arguments, intended to give rise in the reader to doubts about the nature of knowledge such that these doubts may then lead to the suspension of assent to purported scientific truths.

Of interest in this jumble of contradictory facts are the reflections Brissot developed about what he calls moral man and social or political man, reflections that deal with the fields of moral philosophy and politics that lie at the heart of his subsequent commitment to human and civil rights. What, then, of moral philosophy, which will later justify many of Brissot's battles in favour of the weak, the enslaved, and oppressed peoples? Can it be conceived as universal, as based on sure and unshakeable principles? To judge by the manuscript text, nothing could be further from the truth. The text first ferociously seeks to demonstrate the eminently variable nature of moral philosophy, based on a catalogue of discordant historical facts; and then it conducts a critique of the purported principles that are supposed to base moral philosophy in reason.

It is therefore no surprise that, in the history of moral philosophy that Brissot projected, he set himself the task of managing to demonstrate these things. He dwells on the insurmountable variability of human customs, with an emphasis on the rise and decay of all the major moral systems that humanity has known; the influence of tradition rather than reason in the establishment of specific rules that claim to be general; and the divisions among philosophers on this precise point. While Helvétius comes through relatively unscathed, it is not because of the truth of his system based on personal interest, but rather because of the sequencing and the accuracy of his ideas on the issue.

As for the question of the bases for moral philosophy, it is approached in exactly the same way: Brissot opposes each philosopher's pronouncements on the essence of the good and the great moral principles, and on the possibility that human beings can freely follow such principles, to other philosophers' pronouncements. He proposes that, faced with this set of contradictory hypotheses, the reader suspend judgment and not recognize any moral law as intrinsically just, that is, as founded on reason. This leads Brissot to a critique of the customs of his own time, supposedly rational but in reality the product of tradition, and in particular to a critique of religious customs. It then leads him to raise questions, in terms very close to those ascribed by Sextus to Aenesidemus, about the condemnation of suicide, incest, conjugal infidelity, and homosexuality: he shows that this kind of interdiction is above all social and not natural, and that the Pyrrhonian has no basis for reproaching such practices, holding no particular dogma that makes it possible to assign the proper value to human actions:

> Nothing is good or bad in the eyes of the Pyrrhonian, *who has no scales with which to assess the value of human actions*. For the Pyrrhonian, all human actions have, like Janus in the fable, two faces; all can appear both criminal and virtuous, heroic or cowardly, beautiful or ridiculous, according to the perspective from which they are viewed … Given that all people are organized, situated, driven in different ways, they must all judge differently. Every nation has its own measure; indeed, so does every individual. Thus there is nothing surprising in the fact that customs do not resemble each other, given that there is so much dissonance within moral philosophy.[7]

Politics – which, ten years down the road, would seal Brissot's fate – politics, a discipline that deals not with human obligations, as moral philosophy does, but rather with rights, is also subject to this warning. In order to make a science of it, it would have been necessary to define what constitutes natural law. But Brissot forbids himself to conceive of natural law as a natural equality between individuals and once again opposes to each other the philosophical definitions formulated on the question, concluding with the uncertainty of the science of politics. He does – just barely – acknowledge need as a possible basis of real natural right and mentions the work he is conducting on this question; but he does so only to indicate right away that a system based on need would actually just constitute one more hypothesis destined to further increase the uncertainty of the political sphere. If the definition of natural law is hypothetical, it may be suspected that the same will be true of all other forms of law analysed by Brissot (the law of nations, social law, civil law, Roman law, canon law, feudal law), an analysis in which theories clash over origins, essence, value, and so on, producing real uncertainty and truly making of this manuscript by Brissot a handbook for radical skepticism.

2. Brissot the Politician

Based on a reading of this manuscript, it is hard to understand what motivated the revolutionary Brissot of some ten years later, the more so as some of his works that appeared after the presumed time of writing of the manuscript (around 1778–80) do not appear to clash with the skeptical frame of mind of the young Brissot. A work of Brissot's published at Neuchâtel in 1782, *De la vérité ou Méditations sur les moyens de parvenir à la vérité dans toutes les connaissances humaines* (On truth, or meditations on the means for arriving at truth in All spheres of human knowledge), reverts to the general idea presented in the manuscript and once again promises a series of volumes to come. Popkin sees in this work confirmation of a radical Pyrrhonism that constitutes "the most extended presentation of French Enlightenment skepticism"[8] and argues that we thus have Brissot to thank for having "carried skepticism beyond the usual moderate view of the preceding philosophers and scientists of the Enlightenment."[9]

However, what Popkin is advancing in these passages in fact relates only to the unpublished manuscript on universal skepticism. The actual project of the 1782 treatise on truth is no longer to demonstrate the vanity of the scientific enterprise, but rather to "seek *what there is that is certain in human knowledge.*"[10] True, at first sight, this project appears identical to the previous one, because it is a question of purging science and scholarship of the innumerable errors that continue to characterize them; but the end purpose is different, for Brissot acknowledges that this minutely careful work will allow him ultimately to cleanse the gold of the dross that surrounds it and thus arrive at a handful of indubitable truths. Above all, Brissot will henceforth acknowledge that there is a sure method in science and scholarship, that of *analysis* (which he borrows from Condillac, whom he had undoubtedly read in the meantime, since Condillac's name appears nowhere in the unpublished manuscript), and a new goal for scientists and scholars: *the good of humanity*. Hence a new definition of the philosopher, whose goal is not solely to arrive at the truth or be virtuous, but also to be *useful* to contemporaries, which amounts to making them happy.

Here, then, we see moral philosophy and politics rehabilitated and the project of universal skepticism decisively abandoned on account of its radicalism. Brissot now embraces in his turn the "reasonable skepticism" of his century (adopting that very expression), which consists at the theoretical level of developing a pragmatic concept of science and at the moral level of giving an ethical purpose, namely, human happiness, to the philosophical enterprise.[11] Moreover, Brissot expresses his hopes of establishing an organ intended to disseminate scientists' and scholars' observations in order to increase and perfect human knowledge, a project he followed up on in 1783, when he established in London both a "Lyceum" whose mission was to bring together scholars and scientists and a journal designed to publish their discoveries.[12]

Of course, obstacles lie in the path of the search for the truth and always will: the fallibility of the senses; confused and obscure ideas proper to certain fields such as metaphysics; the difficulty of grasping all the relationships that come together to produce a fact; the limits of the human mind; the misuse of words and especially abstract terms; the systematizing spirit; false erudition; passions and prejudices. All these factors lead us to recognition of the highly limited nature of the truths we can arrive at, but they do not for all that invalidate this enterprise of making us wise and happy.

From this perspective, philosophical enquiry should no longer seek to doubt for doubt's sake, but should aim rather to think things through in order to be useful to others and to oneself; and for this reason skepticism is to be condemned, since it turns philosophy away from consideration of the public good.[13] Gone now are the manuscript's skeptical reflections on moral philosophy and politics, which could provide no sure guide to action. Instead, Brissot turns moral philosophy and politics into the two fields of study worthy of commanding the attention of the Enlightenment philosopher, for only they lead human beings to happiness. Other disciplines are subject to moral philosophy and politics, because they procure the good of humanity solely through the mediation of latter.[14] This is the task that Brissot henceforth wishes to tackle, and from that perspective we can understand how his original radical skepticism came to evolve. Not that skepticism is now wholly hollowed out – after all, it remains useful to the extent that it contributes to a modest attitude that disavows the claims made by scientific dogmatists. Rather, it is useless in the spheres of moral philosophy and politics, fields in which uncertainty has no place.[15]

Nevertheless, two questions remain unresolved: What are the principles that could guide this science of human happiness that it is incumbent on a philosopher to acquire? And, assuming it is possible to determine the tenor of those principles, can and should the philosopher abandon reflection in order to commit to practical action? With respect to the first question, the manuscript had already left the door open to a possible answer by designating need as a basis for natural law. And indeed, with his *Recherches philosophiques sur le droit de propriété considéré dans la nature* (Philosophical research on property law as viewed in the state of nature), dating to 1780, Brissot takes up the idea once again and treats need as a source of natural legislation specific to living creatures, which by their nature have needs to satisfy, such as those of obtaining nourishment or reproducing. But since, as Hobbes had already observed, human needs vary in both quality and quantity, the state of nature can only be a state of constant war. This state allows, despite everything, for some degree of equality,[16] since the needs to be satisfied are few and can be met comparatively easily. True inequality arises within civil society when social human beings, in direct inverse to natural human beings, extend their needs indefinitely and are no longer content to satisfy the needs that nature implanted in them, going so far as to guarantee under law a right to property that nature never provided for. Thus the sole true title to property is need, and all other titles are fraudulent. All the social conventions that legitimize civil property thus appear subject to condemnation in Brissot's eyes. It is indeed civil property, disconnected from needs, that is the real basis for inequality and justice, since it takes away from some the possibility of satisfying their needs and confers on others riches that bear no relation to their real needs. Anticipating Proudhon, Brissot clearly conveys the idea that property is theft and that another theft is therefore legitimate as a way of redressing the initial injustice that authorized the legal recognition of the rich person's right to property.[17] He even goes so far as to conclude that nothing legitimizes the social inequality produced by the property of some to the detriment of others, thereby justifying a critique of inequality that on occasion flirts with hatred of the bourgeoisie:[18]

> If man, in society itself, continues to preserve the ineradicable privilege of property that nature granted him, then nothing can take it away from him, nothing can prevent him from exercising it. If the other members of society concentrate among themselves alone the property of the whole land base; if, with this spoliation, those who are deprived of it, being forced to resort to labour, cannot by that means procure for themselves their full subsistence, then they are within their rights to demand of the other proprietors what they require to fill those needs. They have a right to the riches of those other proprietors. They are within their rights to dispose of it according to their needs. Any force opposed to this constitutes violence. It is not the wretched starving man who deserves punishment, it is the rich man who is so barbarous as to rebuff his fellow's need who is worthy of torture. This rich man is the sole thief; he alone should be hung from those infamous gibbets that seem to have been raised up only to punish man, born in misery, for having needs; only to force him to stifle the voice of nature, the cry of liberty; only to constrain him to plunge into a hard slavery in order to avoid an ignominious death.[19]

Thus, in the name of the persistence of the state of nature within the social state, Brissot legitimizes theft by individuals driven by need, invoking the superior right of natural property over the "right" of civil property. Given this, he envisages the possible abuses of this acknowledgment of unpunished theft and, at the end, reintroduces a defence of private property. This he does, not in the name of private property's basis in natural property, which is illusory, but rather in the name of the preservation of the social order, thus advocating more a reform of penal laws that would punish less harshly those who steal because of need for food, as well as a better redistribution of wealth, than a truly revolutionary enterprise, which would challenge the whole social order.[20]

If it is the fact of responding to natural needs that serves as the theoretical basis for the philosopher's moral and political considerations, it remains to be seen whether the philosopher can and must be content to remain strictly at the level of reflection. In answer to this second concern, which is equivalent to the question of whether the philosopher should join theory to practice, the boxes in the French National Archives provide valuable information. In particular, there is a manuscript entitled

"Un politique philosophe doit-il se mêler de gouvernement?" (Should a philosopher-politician meddle in government?), a text that can with certainty be dated later than 1781, because it contains an allusion to Necker's first dismissal. In it, Brissot reviews his general principle about philosophical activity, which is to work for the happiness of others before one's own and thus to prefer public tranquillity over tranquillity of the soul, at least if circumstances permit. This last nuance is not insignificant: it allows Brissot to conclude that the philosopher can only truly act in a republican regime and that in a despotic regime, in which it is not possible to contribute to public happiness, it is better to turn away from all political activity. In such a case, rather than act, one must be content to influence public opinion through one's writings, aiming to enlighten and instruct public opinion to the extent that this is not prejudicial to the philosopher's safety. This indeed is what Brissot contented himself with doing during the pre-revolutionary period, taking up the pen against slavery and colonialism, practices that could not be justified in a supposedly enlightened century and that must come to an end. They must end, he thinks, not following a radical regime change but rather following an imperceptible process of reform that would lead to an improvement in the circumstances of the weakest.

I adduce as proof of this, for example, the way Brissot positions himself on the subject of British colonial policy in India, where for him it is more a question of denouncing the policy and calling for a more just treatment of Indians than of promoting a revolution, which would lead to nothing more than a bloodbath. For, as Brissot notes, "It is not for an author who works towards human happiness to hasten the onset of this period [of revolution], which will ever be a sad one, even when human freedom is the prize it yields."[21] A similar approach can be seen in connection with the abolition of slavery: this, he argues, must arise as the consequence of a reform that comes about through the transformation of public opinion. It will follow criticisms formulated by philosophers who are friends of humankind, who must bring their contemporaries to an understanding of the inhumanity of such treatment. For example, the Marquis de Chastellux was somewhat accommodating of slavery, which he had seen in operation in the United States and whose existence and persistence he justified in the name of a natural difference between blacks and whites that accounted for the softness of the former in contrast to the activism of the latter. Brissot argues in response that this difference is no more than the product of circumstances and that Chastellux is confusing cause with effect. The purported softness of the slaves is an effect of their conditions and not the cause of their passivity; and their masters, if they had been similarly circumstanced for generations, would prove to be just as passive. In short, "We should not ascribe to nature what is the product of society."[22] Given this perspective, it is easy to understand Brissot's subsequent battles in favour of abolition, in particular through the Société des Amis des Noirs (Society of friends of black people), of which he was a founding member, and more generally in favour of everything that struck him as constituting an exception to natural equality or to the social contract that forms the bond between the governing and the governed.[23]

Thus Brissot took up his pen to identify all forms of inequality, and he denounced them in accordance with the idea that it is up to the philosopher to protect the rights of the oppressed, to look out for collective happiness, and to mould public opinion and lead it to influence the government in power in order to attain its ends. No doubt he would have remained satisfied with this role of guide for consciences were it not for two significant events, one personal and one public, that shook his conception of the public role of the philosopher. The first of these events was his two months of imprisonment, which contributed to convincing him of the injustice of the existing system and the need to overthrow it rather than hope for gradual reform.[24] The second was the outbreak of the American Revolution, which made concrete the republican ideal that he secretly aspired to and partly accounts for his emigration to America. From then on, the time had come for the philosopher who was a friend to humanity to abandon theory in favour of practice. This undoubtedly explains his immediate return to France upon the announcement of the convening of the Estates General, even though he had apparently settled for good in the United States, a country that satisfied his wish for individual liberty and the public use of reason and of which he drew a somewhat utopian portrait.[25]

It is an understatement to say of Brissot's conduct during the revolutionary period that it was hardly marked by that spirit of moderation that had characterized his youthful attachment to skepticism. On this score, Leonore Loft is quite right to recall the comment made by Brissot's friend Dumont. As quoted by Loft, he wrote of Brissot that "He was one of those who really believed that everything could be sanctified by what is called the will of the people, and he did a lot of harm because of his enthusiasm for liberty, as so many others have done as a result of religious enthusiasm."[26] The *Patriote français*, the journal Brissot edited during the revolutionary period, had, in fact, a radical character and was committed to bringing a republican system into being as soon as possible.[27] As well, Brissot's actions as head of the Girondins hardly stood out for moderation, for he almost always preferred confrontation through war to negotiation through diplomacy.[28]

What are we to conclude about this transition from a radical skepticism to a dogmatism that was just as radical? Should we, with Popkin, see in it a form of "optimistic skepticism," a term Popkin uses in connection with both Brissot and Condorcet?[29] To do so would be to endorse a paradoxical term, because we must choose between two things: either Brissot's project was authentically skeptical, in which case it is hard to see why it would not be so in the political arena; or Brissot positioned himself favourably towards true social progress, in which case we must conclude he was not a universal skeptic. To argue, as Popkin does,[30] that the only reason Brissot did not carry through his project of universal skepticism is his tragic execution in 1793 is to pass over in silence Brissot's progressive adoption of a reasonable Pyrrhonism peculiar to his century, a stance that consisted of differentiating the spheres in which doubt should and should not be applied and of protecting politics and moral philosophy from Pyrrhonism. That stance unequivocally challenged his youthful project.

For my part, I think the interest of Brissot's case resides elsewhere than in the adoption of a purported "optimistic skepticism" and that we should use his case, rather, to try to deal with three difficulties specific to the link we are seeking to draw between skepticism and politics. First, his case shows that the hypothesis according to which the skeptical philosopher is by definition conservative in politics is simply false.[31] Next, it testifies to the significance of the socio-historical and political conditions in which the skeptic is immersed: these conditions sometimes constrain him or her to take sides, with all the risks that entails, especially during a revolutionary period when laws and customs are no longer effective and can no longer guide individual action. Finally, it makes it possible to picture the transformation of the role of the philosopher at the end of the century of the Enlightenment, which prefigures that of the role of the "intellectuel engagé" and renders the skeptical posture, if not impossible, at least extremely rare and dependent upon a different context within which it might assume a degree of legitimacy. Of this transformation, Brissot was himself conscious, emphasizing in the autobiographical sketch that he wrote a year before his death under the pseudonym Phédor that he "was formed to be a philosopher rather than a politician: politics was only a secondary subject of study for him. He wanted to liberate philosophy from the yoke of despotism; he sought the means to do so; he thought he had found those means in politics and he became a politician. Let liberty become strong and Phédor will revert to what he should have been, a philosopher."[32] But wishing to liberate the philosopher from the yoke of despotism, desiring the good of one's fellows, being an activist for equality and liberty: all this is to acknowledge value in things that, for a skeptic in antiquity, held none. Thus Brissot appears to have understood that the reactivation of skepticism in the eighteenth century presumed its readjustment – as though the only skepticism is one that is always begun anew; and that the skepticism of the Enlightenment authorized a different enquiry into moral philosophy and politics in the name of the new imperative of public utility, which the philosopher must henceforward adopt, thereby breaking with the Hellenistic ideal of the philosopher who is indifferent to the values shared in the public space.

NOTES

1 Richard Popkin devoted two articles to Brissot; I refer to them later in this paper. Besides these, though, he first made known his discovery of Brissot in 1992 in an article entitled "New Views on the Role of Scepticism in the Enlightenment," *Modern Language Quarterly 53* (1992): 279–97, and he devoted a paragraph to Brissot in his entry "The French Enlightenment" in *The Columbia History of Western Philosophy* (New York: Columbia University Press, 1999), 468.

2 Brissot, *De la vérité, ou Méditations sur les moyens de parvenir à la vérité dans toutes les connaissances humaines* (Neuchâtel: Imprimerie de la Société typographique, 1782), 361. We can be confident this is the title Brissot finally settled on, because the title *Plan raisonné du système de pyrrhonisme général* (Reasoned plan for a system of general pyrrhonism), which actually appears on the manuscript, has been struck out there. It was Popkin who first drew attention to the existence of this manuscript, although his knowledge of it was superficial. For example, he writes of a manuscript about ninety pages long, whereas even a brief examination reveals that, although the extant manuscript ends at page 86, it has been significantly altered (it is lacking a good quarter of its leaves). I had to work through several boxes in the archive to recover most of the missing passages and reconstruct the text almost in full. A more analytic and detailed description of this manuscript will be found in my article "From Universal Pyrrhonism to Revolutionary Scepticism: Jacques-Pierre Brissot de Warville," in *Scepticism*

in the Eighteenth Century: Enlightenment, Lumières, Aufklärung, ed. S. Charles and P. Junqueira Smith (Dordrecht: Springer, 2013), 231–44. James Burns recently provided an interesting synthesis of this manuscript ("Jacques-Pierre Brissot: From Scepticism to Conviction," *History of European Ideas* 38 (2012), 508–26), but without seeking the political and moral implications of Brissot's thought. If Burns's conclusion is close to mine on Brissot's skepticism, the arguments he uses to make the case for a conversion from Pyrrhonism to dogmatism are different.

3 Jacques-Pierre Brissot de Warville, *Mémoires (1754–1793)* (Paris: Alphonse Picard & Fils, 1910), vol. I, 121. On d'Alembert's skepticism, see Giorgio Tonelli, "The Philosophy of d'Alembert: A Sceptic beyond Scepticism," *Kant-Studien* 67 (1976): 353–71; and Véronique Le Ru, "Le scepticisme dans l'*Encyclopédie* de Diderot et d'Alembert," *Revue de métaphysique et de morale* 65 (2010): 75–92.

4 Brissot, *Plan raisonné du système de pyrrhonisme général* (Paris: Archives Nationales), pressmark 446 AP 21; (hereafter, *Plan raisonné*), leaf 1, recto.

5 Brissot, *Plan raisonné*, l. 6v–7r.

6 Brissot, *Plan raisonné*, l. 14r–14v: "If uncertainty prevails in the account given by our senses; if our senses alter, if they distort images of objects, what becomes of reason, this sublime gift that we claim to have been given by Heaven to enlighten us? Can a natural scientist be certain of his experiments and results if his lens is false and his instruments unreliable? Under what light will our doubts then be dispelled? Are we to turn to our senses? Their accounts are inaccurate. To reason? But reason only inquires and works things out based on those very accounts; but no reason can be established inside another reason, and, as Montaigne observes, we are faced with an infinite regress. Let modern philosophers then give up their belief in infallible reason! As the famous skeptic we have just cited writes, reason is a two-handled pot that can be wielded from both right and left. A thousand causes exist to give rise to error in us. We are forced to judge based on appearances that give differing accounts of objects. The passive faculty that receives sensations is modified in different ways in all beings, words have no fixed meanings, etc.; and for the thousand causes of our being misled, we have not a single cause for being led to obvious truth."

7 Brissot, *Plan raisonné*, l. 28r. Emphasis added.

8 "Scepticism and Optimism in the Late 18th Century," in *Aufklarüng und Skepsis. Studien zur Philosophie und Geistesgeschichte der 17. und 18. Jahrunderts*, ed. Lothar Kreimendahl (Stuttgart: Fromman Verlag, 1995), 176.

9 "Brissot and Condorcet: Skeptical Philosophers," in *The Skeptical Tradition around 1800*, ed. J. van der Zande and R. H. Popkin (Dordrecht: Kluwer, 1998), 31.

10 Brissot, *De la vérité*, 1. Emphasis added.

11 On the expressions "reasonable skepticism" and "mitigated Pyrrhonism" and their meaning, see my "What Is Enlightenment Scepticism? A Critical Rereading of Richard Popkin," in *Scepticism in the Eighteenth Century*, ed. S. Charles and P. Junqueira Smith, 1–15, and "Escepticismo Illustrado: entre pirronismo razonable y escepticismo radical," in *Dudas filosóficas. Ensayos sobre escepticismo antiguo, moderno y contemporáneo*, ed. Armando Cintora and Jorge Ornelas (Barcelona: Editorial Gedisa, 2014), 177–202.

12 On this score, see the mission Brissot describes for his *Licée*, or Lyceum, in the first number of the *Journal ou Licée de Londres, ou Tableau de l'état présent des sciences et des arts en Angleterre*, January 1784, I, 1, 5.

13 This is the basis on which Brissot distinguishes the ultimate aim of his own undertaking from Bayle's: "Exactly one hundred years ago, Bayle began his *Nouvelles de la République des Lettres* in Holland. Although he has often been put forward as a model, although I myself revere him, I will nevertheless refrain from imitating him in every respect. Of the two components of true philosophy, that is, the art of seeking out, of discovering, truth and the still more difficult art of only speaking useful truths, Bayle was in possession of one but not the other. He did not have that philosophical spirit that bends all knowledge towards the public good. Often he was no more than an adept dialectician, a skeptic difficult to shake. Bayle did a great deal for school philosophy, but he did little for the philosophy of the human being. He knew much, but did he always know well?" *Journal ou Licée de Londres*, January 1784, I, 1, p. 5.

14 This is the message conveyed by Brissot in the *Journal* issue for May 1784, 334–5: "Philosophers, who are accustomed to working out the first principles of things, must abandon the tortuous windings of metaphysics and the delicate manipulations of experimentations and consider that the existence and the evidence of the other sciences depend on the government's security and structures. They must become penetrated with the desire to provide the principles of government, to square with each other government's numerous and muddled arrangements, to find the remedies that must necessarily accompany the products of human industry. In our day, the greatest and best of men in every country except China are no more than passengers on a vessel in the hands of ignorant mariners. Our wise men apply themselves to all the sciences except that on which their happiness depends. Does the vessel come to grief? Then philosophers are plunged into the abyss along with their companions in misfortune. Of all the sciences worthy of human effort and attention, the most essential is without any doubt that related to the machine on board which humans are

making the voyage of life. All other interests, all other goals, can only take second place."

15 A passage in the *Journal* issue for February 1784 is explicit on this score: "For the sharply defined decisions whose dogmatism fills all the books, we must substitute modest doubt; that doubt that, even if it does not always lead to truth, at least draws us away from the well-worn path of prejudice and error. It is said that this state of suspension is cruel, that it throws the soul into numbness, into despair; that it thereby slows the progress of science. I don't believe it. No doubt there are categories of knowledge with respect to which doubt would be cruel, dangerous, would become a poison. Moral philosophy and politics are examples. Disorder would soon infiltrate a state whose leader allowed the reins to float at random, unsure of which road should be followed. No doubt a man who doubted whether he should be virtuous would be a proper object of fear to his fellows. Whatever faction we embrace, virtue is necessary. But is it equally necessary to believe, with Mr Lavoisier, that phlogiston is no more than a fancy and, with Mr Le Sage, that the sun's fire is an acid? No, no, these opinions have no bearing on either our own happiness or that of the state; we may, we must doubt them if we wish to arrive at the truth" (98).

16 In "The Roots of Brissot's Ideology," *Eighteenth-Century Life* 13 (1989), 21–31, Leonore Loft proposes an interesting connection between natural and religious equality: "Brissot explains that, originally, there were no distinctions between men, no hierarchy. He makes a parallel point about the primitive Church as established by Christ. There was originally one leader of the Christian Church, one founder, and when He died, no other was elected ... By implication, the system of political privilege, the political hierarchy, is not divinely decreed, it is man-made. If individuals have agreed to submit to a ruler it is with the stipulation that their happiness be ensured and, if it is not, the contract is nullified. In fact, those who attempt to hold power over others without mutual consent are rebels against society. The teachings of Paul, which instruct us to submit to a tyrant's rule, are unnatural. In this area Brissot makes quite clear that, when he is discussing early Church politics, he is discussing contemporary issues of power and politics" (28).

17 Cf. Paul Goupil, *La propriété selon Brissot de Warville* (Paris: A. Pedone, 1904), 79: "Thus, in sum, civil property constitutes a usurpation that nothing can legitimize; it consists purely of a state of affairs with no roots in natural principles, one against which human beings can subsequently rise up, one which they can always refuse to recognize when it makes the normal exercise of their faculties impossible."

18 Cf. Leigh Whaley, *Radicals: Politics and Republicanism in the French Revolution* (Phoenix: Sutton Publishing 2000), 14: "Brissot's essays tended to be politically radical, containing seeds of the future revolutionary in them, especially the *Théorie des lois criminelles.* It went beyond a critique of the penal system to an attack against tyrannical governments, the abuses by those responsible for the levying and collecting of taxes, the *fermiers-généraux,* and the faulty social system which was responsible for crime. Like Pétion and Billaud, Brissot was fiercely anti-clerical, denouncing the idleness of celibates, particularly the regular clergy, whom he regarded as parasites. Unlike Billaud, who was writing a few years later and who tended to be radical only when attacking religion, Brissot found fault with both the existing political system and the religious system. However, Brissot, unlike Pétion, never proposed concrete solutions to the old regime's problems."

19 Brissot, *Recherches philosophiques sur le droit de propriété considéré dans la nature, pour servir de premier chapitre à la* Théorie des lois *de M. Linguet, par un jeune philosophe* (1780), 109.

20 Brissot, *Recherches philosophiques,* 111–12: "Assuming that it is a crime to steal in order not to die of hunger, at least don't punish it as severely. There are so many gentler punishments with which the guilty person can even become useful to society; so why not use them? You would preserve a citizen for the state and you would not outrage nature. Legislators, you who hold in your hands the destiny of nations, do not limit yourselves to punishing the wrongdoing; dig it out by the roots; through the just distribution of the riches of the state, make unhappy beggary disappear, and there will be no more theft. It is only under bad governments that it is necessary to cause penal sentences to multiply."

21 Brissot, *Tableau de la situation actuelle des Anglais dans les Indes orientales et de l'état de l'Inde en général* (London: E. Cox, 1784), vol. I, 10–11. On Brissot's critique of British policy, see also the January 1784 issue of the *Journal,* 23.

22 Marie-Thérèse Isaac, "Le problème du 'Nègre-esclave': le témoignage du marquis de Chastellux et la polémique de 1786," *Revue de l'Université d'Ottawa* 56 (1986): 91.

23 See, for example, his political handling of the Transylvanian uprising of 1784 as discussed by Leonore Loft, "The Transylvanian Peasant Uprising of 1784, Brissot and the Right to Revolt: A Research Note," *French Historical Studies* 17 (1991), 209–18.

24 This is also the view of Robert Darnton in "The Grub Street Style of Revolution: J.-P. Brissot, Police Spy," *Journal of Modern History* 40 (1968): 309: "Those two months in the Bastille must have made him into a revolutionary." Cf. also "The Brissot Dossier," *French Historical Studies* 17 (1991): 199.

25 For Brissot's portrait of America, see Nicole Aronson, "Chastellux et Brissot: deux images de l'Amérique au dix-huitième siècle," *French Review* 49 (1976): 960–71.

26 Leonore Loft, *Passion, Politics and Philosophie: Rediscovering J.-P. Brissot* (Westport: Greenwood Press, 2002), 18.

27 Cf. Leigh Whaley, "A Radical Journalist of the French Revolution: Jacques-Pierre Brissot and the *Patriote français*, 1789–1791," *Nottingham French Studies* 31 (1992): 1–11.

28 If we are to believe a late-eighteenth-century manuscript presented by Marc Bouloiseau in *Annales historiques de la Révolution française* 57 (1985): 290–4, Brissot actually encouraged war rather than peace in order to get rid of two million surplus French people who were potentially hostile to the interests of the Revolution, arguing that, "just as with a delirious sick person who needs to be bled, it was necessary to *draw blood* from the body politic" (293, emphasis added).

29 Popkin, "Scepticism and Optimism in the Late 18th Century."

30 Popkin, "Scepticism and Optimism in the Late 18th Century," 176: "At the very end of his treatise, Brissot said that he hoped to discover in each science the very few truths that there are. He thought it would take him several years to do so. Then, in a footnote at the end, he said that if his work on legislation and politics permit, in two or three years he could present a 'tableau' of these truths along with a universal scepticism applied to all the sciences, and this would constitute a reasonable scepticism. Unfortunately Brissot was executed before he could complete his work because he was the leader of the Girondists."

31 On this point, my view is in line with tone of the conclusions reached by J.C. Laursen, "Skepticism, Unconvincing Anti-Skepticism, and Politics," in *Scepticisme et modernité*, ed. M.A. Bernier and S. Charles (Saint-Étienne: Presses de l'Université Saint-Étienne, 2005), 167–88.

32 Brissot, "Portrait de Phédor," in *Mémoires (1754–1793)* (Paris: Picard & Fils, 1910), vol. I, 15.

This article on modern skepticism has received an ordinary grant from SSHRC. A French version will be published in *Tangence* 106 (2014).

chapter thirteen

Carl Friedrich Stäudlin's Diagnosis of the Political Effects of Skepticism in Late Eighteenth-Century Germany

JOHN CHRISTIAN LAURSEN

Carl Friedrich Stäudlin (1761–1826) wrote the first substantial stand-alone history of philosophical skepticism that did not just weave skepticism into the history of philosophy as a whole, but that established its own canon of great figures and works and treated it as a subject worthy of study on its own.[1] I am going to draw attention to three aspects of his work. The first is his understanding of skepticism, the second his understanding of Kant, and the third his understanding of the political implications and effects of skepticism, both philosophical and non-philosophical. It will emerge that he liked some kinds of skepticism and disliked others; he liked Kant and Kantianism, but worried it could lead to the wrong kind of skepticism; and he worried about the political implications of the wrong kind of skepticism. He can be characterized as a skeptical, Christian Kantian; a Kantian, skeptical Christian; and a Christian and Kantian skeptic. Just what this means will be unpacked here.

Skepticism and Kantianism

The first sentence of the preface to Stäudlin's *History and Spirit of Skepticism Particularly in Regard to Morals and Religion* of 1794 is "Skepticism begins to be an illness of the age, and – a rare appearance in history – to spread among more classes and to express its influence at large."[2] Thus we start from the premise that something called skepticism is an illness, not a cure, and that it seems to influence human life in a wider sense than the purely philosophical. Staudlin's response to skepticism, I will suggest, places him in the eighteenth-century tradition of those who tried to tame skepticism for contemporary purposes, including Jean Henri Samuel

Formey, Louis de Beausobre, Jean-Bernard Mérian, and Louis-Frédéric Ancillon.[3] They developed an understanding of skepticism that both respected its philosophical acuity and kept it safe for Christianity and the eighteenth-century state. This school of thought sought to domesticate skepticism, to render it harmless in morals and politics.

Right after we learn that skepticism is an illness, we learn that it is related importantly to Kantianism. Stäudlin observes that "the latest revolution in philosophy" – by which he means Kantianism – has been "caused by it and has made it again the object of a deep philosophical investigation" (1.iii). But Kant does not refute skepticism: "If that revolution meant to overthrow it, by a new discovery shall no hair of its head be hurt, or indeed it shall have been strengthened" (1.iii). And towards the end of the 150-page "Philosophical dissertations" that introduce the history, Stäudlin observes that "Humean skepticism gave us Kantian dogmatism, which is the dogmatism most informative, prudent, and fitting for human tranquility and virtue that exists. One must however only return to the exaggerated presumption and claims of proud dogmatism in order to find that the critical philosophy sometimes leads to skepticism" (1.137). Stäudlin seems to be saying that rather than refuting skepticism, Kant's philosophy can be taken to support it, but this seems to be a paradox because Kantianism is then implicated in an illness of the age. We shall proceed to examine the mutual relations among skepticism, Kant, and politics in Stäudlin's account.

One problem, according to Stäudlin, was that very few people know what skepticism is, and that means that the word is used in widely varying and contradictory ways (1.iii–iv). So he decided to write the history of it. The idea of such a history was not new to him:

> Already in my university days various circumstances and contingencies led me to it. The first philosophical works that I read were written in the spirit of the Leibniz-Wolff philosophy. They pleased my youthful imagination, but they never completely convinced me. The writings of Sextus and Hume fell into my hands by chance and put me for a long time into a highly painful condition in that they made me aware of teachings that were very intertwined with my tranquility and ethics. In this predicament my unshakeable belief in virtue, for which I had to thank my education for the most part, was my anchor ... My interest in skeptical writings remained and was not a little nourished by the uncommon degree of sharpness and the giant mass of knowledge which are combined in many of these writings." (1.v)

Here we get back to Kant, because Stäudlin claimed to find a sort of answer to skepticism in Kant's writings: "they resolved many of my doubts and cleared up much that previously I had thought obscure" (1.v). On this account, Sextus and Hume had provoked Stäudlin's doubts, and Kant had answered them. Stäudlin ends his preface by observing that his publisher had supplied an illustration for the frontispiece that showed Hume facing Kant. Coyly, the last sentence of the preface reads that "The reader will divine the meaning of the juxtaposition of Hume and Kant" (1.x). Some people have read the facing figures as Kant refuting Hume. I am going to suggest here that in fact, in Stäudlin's interpretation, Hume and Kant agreed on skepticism in several respects, and that the latter did not refute the former. This brings out an apparent contradiction in Stäudlin's attitude towards Kant: the great philosopher is both an antidote to skepticism and a skeptic himself.

Kant and Stäudlin as Skeptics

Stäudlin was honest enough to admit that Kant's philosophy could lead to skepticism. He reported that Kant's work was read as "masked unbelief," and that an English journal had charged that it "leads to skepticism" (2.286).[4] Since God, freedom, and immortality are "not objects of knowledge and science," but only of "necessary thought and belief" (2.283), even "a convinced friend of this philosophy" had to admit that "it stood on the basis of Pyrrhonism, or even more on the basis of the Pyrrhonist method, in that it made everything without distinction doubtful, mathematics and natural science not excepted," he wrote (2.287). In a later work, billed as a third volume of his history of skepticism, Stäudlin observed that "In particular may I maintain that without the study of Sextus, Leibniz, and Locke it would be difficult to get to the bottom of the critical philosophy."[5] Many articles and books have been written about the influence of Leibniz, Locke, and other early modern philosophers on Kant's philosophy,[6] and one recent author has written of the influence of three early modern skeptics on Kant,[7] but it is rare to see him placed in the tradition of Sextus Empiricus.[8]

Not only could Kant be interpreted as a skeptic, but skeptics could also undermine the credibility of his enterprise. Stäudlin reported on the efforts of "Aenesidemus" Schulze and Ernst Platner to apply a "measured skepticism" (2.287) to Kant's philosophy. Schulze observed that Kant's claim that we cannot know anything about noumena must mean that we cannot know that the phenomena do not accurately represent them; and the fact that we do think in a certain set of categories does not prove that we could not think in others (2.289). In effect, Kant accepts Hume's skepticism rather than refuting it (2.288). And Platner mobilized skeptical strategies against Kant so well that Stäudlin observed that he "characterized the skeptical way of thinking better than any of his predecessors" (2.292).

Some have argued that even if Kant was a sort of skeptic in some respects, he was a dogmatist in politics. As Klaus Hartmann put it, "are republican institutions themselves in doubt? I do not think so. In Kant's philosophy of right one sees very clearly that he is adamant on the type of institutions we ought to have. And we seem to know that we ought to have them."[9] This much is true. But it is also true that in Kant's analysis republicanism is a noumenal aspect of our politics, and therefore we cannot know if we actually have it. To put it another way, something dressed up as republican politics might not actually be republican politics, but rather a mask for manipulative elites. I think we have enough experience of that to understand Kant's point that we might not ever know if we have the real thing, the thing in itself.

Stäudlin did not particularly like it that Kant could be challenged by skeptics, and even reduced to being one. "It is to be wished for," he wrote, "that the great father himself would vindicate himself" against Schulze and Platner (2.292). But since he had not, Kant could still be interpreted as a skeptic, if *malgré lui.*

It is worth observing that Stäudlin sent his book to Kant, who answered in a letter of December 1794 with some praise: the book is "a consummate work, as useful as it is careful and penetrating."[10] One wonders if he read the doubts about Kant's success at refuting the skeptics at the end of the book. If he did read them, and did not disagree, that would imply that Kant accepted the charges. And if Stäudlin was a loyal Kantian, which he thought he was, that must mean he was a skeptic, too. We shall also see other reasons below for understanding Stäudlin as a skeptic.

If it emerges that Stäudlin is himself a kind of skeptic even though he claims to refute some kinds of skepticism, this can be taken in at least three different ways. One is to read his claims to refute it as defensive writing, in which one claims to abhor what one actually respects, in order to gain a hearing for one's side, disarm criticism, and prevent persecution (a Straussian interpretation). There does not seem to be much evidence for this interpretation. The second is that Stäudlin did not quite face up to his own skepticism but that working through the texts he had developed sympathy for the skeptics, and that he had become a skeptic in spite of himself. The ambivalence that often emerges in his account suggests some truth to this one. And the third is that Stäudlin played a distinguishing and balancing game, distinguishing just the right kind of skepticism that would be harmless to morality, church, and state. I think this is the most obvious one. Whether it can be done well or not, Stäudlin wanted to have his cake and eat it, too: to be a Christian and a Kantian and at the same time admit a great deal of respect for some kinds of skepticism.

The Kinds of Skepticism

In his preface, Stäudlin remarked that "it would be wholly against my intentions if this work itself were to contribute to the promotion of skepticism" (1.ix). Rather, he has worked on the assumption that "it is often a better means to master an enemy that one gets to know him in his full strength" (1.ix–x). These (and other) remarks could certainly be taken to mean that Stäudlin was an anti-skeptic *simpliciter*, and that the book was written as an antidote to it.[11] But things are not so simple.

The key is Stäudlin's introductory "Philosophical Dissertations," the full title of which continues: "on the Spirit, Kinds, Sources, Effects, and History of Skepticism," and in which he distinguishes several sorts of skepticism. There is a "skepticism which arises purely out of shallowness and ignorance" (1.92). It often results in a "strange mixture of skepticism with superstition and dogmatism," and is the product of "ambition and love of paradox and novelty" (1.93). This "ambitious skepticism arises out of immoral [or non-moral: *unmoralisches*] sources and directs its followers in morals in ways that are often very harmful to them" (1.94). It becomes "fanatical and dogmatic," and can lead to "the spread of great moral and political revolutions" (1.95). At this point Stäudlin backtracks a bit: "I am far from saying that the ground of skepticism is always to be found in immorality, in willful obstinacy and closing of the eyes against the light of truth, and that all skeptics are careless, liars, and enemies of the human race," but one would not say this if one did not suspect that many skeptics do fit these categories (1.96). This "skepticism, grounded in the lust for evil," is an "immoral skepticism" (1.97). It is associated with "luxus" and flabbiness, affects all classes, and is especially disturbing if it reaches into the ranks of the powerful, where it becomes "highly dangerous to the welfare of society" (1.98).

The young are also susceptible to this wrong sort of skepticism. "One sees with astonishment in our times how unknowledgeable boys reject with contemptuous tones the truths which men of service and philosophical spirit hold holy as the hard-won result of long investigations and experience" (1.100). One suspects that this reflects personal experience in the classroom. As a result, "our age is an age of revolutions in the moral and political world and of secret political orders. Both work together for the spread of skepticism [*Zweifelsucht*]" (1.100). They "undermine not only the ruling forms of government and national religions, but also the ruling ways of thinking, education, and morals" (1.100).

There is yet another form of skepticism: "sad skepticism [*traurige Skepticismus*]," which is the result of "hypochondria, oppression and unlucky destiny in youth, and unregulated but strong and fast-changing feelings" (1.100). Here Stäudlin quotes a long letter from a youth who is the "victim of a despairing skepticism" (1.101). The young man writes that Pyrrhonism of the feelings is much worse than Pyrrhonism of the understanding, which may mean something to the effect that he cannot trust his feelings (1.103). In any case, he ends up in apathy and indifference (1.103). In another anecdote about a classmate's skepticism, Stäudlin writes of his psychological despair with pathos, observing that "he is no more" with the implication that he has killed himself (1.64). He also quotes and comments on many pages from Rousseau's Savoyard Vicar for an understanding of the psychology of skepticism (1.40–61). All of this may be best understood as personal psychology, with little relevance to politics. However, other sources of skepticism feed into political skepticism.

Skepticism can be caused by the study of the history of philosophy, Stäudlin notes, with so many contradicting schools (1.104). Political skepticism can be caused by the many contending forms of government. The travel writings of recent centuries have cast doubt on European morals, religion, and politics – and here Stäudlin mentions the influence of La Mothe Le Vayer in this field (1.106).

But in addition to immoral skepticism there are forms and degrees of skepticism to which Stäudlin is sympathetic. It has possible good uses against excessive dogmatism in science. "When the sciences have become too cocky, overrefined ... skepticism often grows up like a poisonous plant. But that can be good for the sciences. When pedantic dogmatism sleeps quietly on its arrogant contentions, skepticism can wake them up – when the sciences stand still, when one has taken in them for perfected what has only been begun, when one builds in them without having laid a foundation, when the spirit of investigation rests, then skepticism can bring out new activity for the spread of the sciences" (1.134). We have a "drive for dogmatism which is rooted in our nature" (1.135). It cannot be eliminated, Staudlin writes, but it can be moderated, and "for this moderation skepticism is an excellent means. It can moderate the pedantic pride, contemptuous disparaging, insulting rejection, and constant know-it-allness which the consciousness of greater mental powers and knowledge so easily lead to" (1.135).

And maybe most important, there is "philosophical skepticism," which is "very rare" (1.92). Already in the preface he had written that the topic of his book was skepticism "as an art of thinking that can be more or less philosophical" (1.vii). Much of what he describes as skepticism in the introductory dissertations and refutes is less philosophical, and rather immoral and shallow. But much of what he describes as skepticism in the main text of the book is more philosophical, and Stäudlin often approves of it. As he put it in one of the later, "third" volume articles, "I honor philosophical skepticism as much as I scorn the shallow and immoral kind."[12] One late eighteenth-century historian of philosophy called Stäudlin's book "a cure for skepticism," but it is not at all obvious that it is.[13] A late twentieth-century scholar has observed that Stäudlin prefigured Hegel's later distinction between ancient and modern skepticism, emphasis on the principle of *isosthenia* or equal arguments on both sides of every issue, and recognition of the merits of the right sort of skepticism.[14]

The Political Implications

Stäudlin was a self-professed Christian and a professor of theology at Göttingen for more than three decades, as well as author of numerous books on Christian theology and ethics. At many places in his writings he is concerned that skepticism undermines Christian belief. But there was a long tradition of Christian skepticism, sometimes described as fideism. At one point Stäudlin observes that complete skepticism will not even justify fideism (1.128). It dissolves not only knowledge but also belief (1.129). But moderate skepticism is another story. "One can earnestly doubt a lot, a great deal, of what the others believe and yet consistently believe with one's whole soul in a revelation like the Christian one. A man can consider the whole of metaphysics as a sea of uncertainty and even doubt the certainty of mathematics and the possibility of all objective knowledge. But if he can accept subjective certainty, which almost all skeptics do, then he can believe in a revelation like the Christian" (1.130–1). This sounds autobiographical, and may be Stäudlin's *modus vivendi* as a Christian with skepticism.

By contrast, the skeptical dissolution of Christianity by complete skepticism would be a bad thing, and Stäudlin usually associates the threat of skepticism to Christianity with the threat to morals and the state. In the "Philosophical Dissertations," he points out that by themselves the philosophical skeptics are not a direct threat to the state. As he notes, the Pyrrhonians reported that they acted in accordance with appearances and with "the customs in their country and inherited laws, morals, and religion" (1.108). But this is not especially reliable, Stäudlin thinks. Since "complete skepticism ... destroys all morality," "the skeptics act according to the laws and customs of their fatherland as long as they have to" (1.113). It is only external obedience to the laws that they exhibit, so if deeper commitment is required they will not have it, and in times of weak enforcement they will not have any incentive to obey. And further, if these laws and customs are morally bad, they will obey them without asking questions or appealing to higher standards simply because it is more comfortable (1.113–14). The ancient skeptics were not declared enemies of virtue, but they veiled it in fog (1.115).

Stäudlin quotes Bayle's argument that skepticism is bad for religion but not bad for the state (1.118), but he disagrees:

> I do not believe that skepticism is so innocuous concerning civil life, and so dangerous concerning religion, as Bayle maintains. I agree that the skeptics do not deny that that they must live according to the customs of their fatherland and in this and that case according to the moral laws, and they themselves can be good citizens – and that none of them, which one might have feared at first glance, had come down to us in history under the name of bad citizen. We are asked to believe that this means that even when skepticism has been spread wider among more classes of men there is nothing to fear for the tranquility, the security, and the welfare of the state. But this is false. The philosophical skepticism of the sharper minds will in its wider spread among the many turn into shallow, immoral skepticism, and can thus cause the greatest devastation in civil life. (1.121)

Ideas matter: "One would not believe, if history did not show us, that the lonely, withdrawn scholar who writes down his speculations in his room, and who seems to play an inert, unimportant role in the machine of state, often makes ready, without it being suspected, the most important revolutions" (1.121–2). This is because "metaphysics is not so far from common sense and the ideas on which people act as one is accustomed to think. Each man has a certain metaphysics ... put together out of the ideas of his education as a youth, the teachings of priests, and the basic principles of his particular inner needs" (1.122). If this is corrupted by public skepticism, "the seed of an unforeseeable moral decline, the destruction of common spirit, and the ruin of civil peace will grow up" (1.123). "Such a spirit of shallow skepticism, always mixed with much dogmatism, began to spread among the people with the entry of Christianity into the Roman world – and in France one heard long before the Revolution in all classes of men of religion spoken of as something about which nothing could be decided with certainty. There the Lucians mocked and the Ciceros doubted – here the Encyclopedists and Voltaire wrote" (1.123). This leads only to barbarity and brutality (1.124). Stäudlin is clearly worried about the effects of ideas both in the buildup to the French Revolution and after it.

At the end of the book, Stäudlin returned to these themes:

> Philosophical skepticism, not just pretended, not just imitative, not derived from an impure principle, has and can only have very few followers, but wherever it is taught and honored in writings and teaching it will little by little beget among the many the shallow skepticism that kills the spirit of investigation and promotes immorality. Philosophy will perhaps die out and the communal spirit among men and the common benefit of the educated class would uncommonly suffer if everyone was limited to describing the appearances of human feelings, and indeed in every subject could say only subjective things and no philosopher could say anything objective anymore. (2.293–4)

Note the particular concern with the educated classes.

Stäudlin goes on to observe that "We want to think of ourselves as not an isolated creature that lives in its own idea-world, but believe that we all have a claim to a certain sum of common truths" (2.294). As it is,

> there reigns in our times in almost all of the cultivated lands a very shallow and dangerous skepticism with respect to the most important objects that one still attributes value to if he is more informed and more tolerant than the way of thinking of believers and unbelievers is. This skepticism deserves however for most the name of a lazy and indifferent indecisiveness and for many the name of a wild, fanatical search for doubt. The main sources lie in that the drive for the sensual has uncommonly risen and the figure of a system is upheld such that interest in pure intellectual truth is uncommonly diminished. (2.295)

Clearly the emphasis is on the social effects here, and not on the philosophical merits.

Stäudlin's conclusion is kind of sad: this calamity has played itself out "in all the most famous capitals of Europe" (2.296). "But the writers of the cultivated states of Europe all agree [and here Stäudlin cites Raynal, Rigoley de Juvigny, Mercier, Vernet, and Wendeborn] that many new so-called philosophical productions are not the children of such a raw and unphilosophical skepticism" (2.296), with the implication that they might be the product of a more philosophical skepticism. Stäudlin must feel like a lone Cassandra, crying in the dark. "A variety of noteworthy events of our day can be seen as the results of a philosophy that makes everything unsteady and builds nothing, that leaves men in a lazy and careless indecisiveness about the most important things and changes them into just a sensuous and selfish being that is determined by time, chance, and circumstances and is driven here and there on the sea of this life without a rudder or compass, without a sure rule for his behavior and belief and without a determined goal for his hopes" (2.296). This last may echo some of the metaphors of Edmund Burke, who similarly decried the loosening hold of tradition on his contemporaries.

The beginning and the end of the book have Stäudlin articulating a common eighteenth-century educated elite's fear of the lower classes.[15] But throughout it is implied that there is still the other, more philosophical sort of skepticism. Stäudlin somewhat grudgingly, but also admiringly, admits that it may be a better philosophy, but he insists it is only for the few. He seems to be engaged in a balancing act: showing the merits of philosophical skepticism, but constantly aware that it can be harnessed by an unphilosophical way of thinking that has detrimental moral, religious, and political effects.

This worry is repeated in the "third" volume, especially in the third part, which brings out some of the positives for society and government of the critical philosophy. Stäudlin writes that the critical philosophy does not rule out revelation, and that he agrees with Kant that the "ordering of the state and the needs of the great masses" probably require the latter.[16] He stresses the Kantian "public" in emphasis on the importance of a public religion for order and tranquillity (5.347–8). He points out that metaphysics is important because every man has a metaphysics that helps him organize his life and follow the laws and his duties (5.358–9). He refers again to the dangerous spirit of the times (5.362). He admits that Kantianism has no sensitivity to "religious feelings, hopes, expectations, and desires," and some have carried it as far as "horrible philosophical intolerance, terrorism, and pride" (5.370). But he continues to defend Kant: the charges that he is a masked atheist are "ignoble and untrue"

(5.364), and claims that Kantianism will lead to "political and revolutionary ends" are both worthy of punishment and show little knowledge of human nature (5.372). As we can see, Stäudlin is fighting a two-front war, defending Kant and the critical philosophy, but making sure it does not go too far.

I am inclined to conclude that there are two very interesting things that we can find in Stäudlin, and one not so interesting thing. The interesting ones are his evaluation of Kant as a skeptic and Kantianism as a philosophy that could lead towards skepticism, and his recognition and respect for the philosophical acuity of much of the tradition of skepticism. The less interesting thing is his evaluation of the political effects of skepticism. It is almost too much of a cliché to understand skepticism as leading to the poisoning of minds in politics and the production of revolutionaries. To Stäudlin's credit, he does not worry one-sidely about the effects of skepticism on the minds of the lower orders, but sees a danger to the higher orders as well. But the idea that scepticism could have had some beneficial effects in politics such as leading to tolerance, moderation, and less fanaticism does not seem to have occurred to him.

NOTES

1 See J.C. Laursen, "Stäudlin, Carl Friedrich (1761–1826)," in *The Dictionary of Eighteenth-Century German Philosophers*, ed. Heiner Klemme and Manfred Kueh (London: Continuum, 2010), 1122–5. Remarks on Stäudlin's place in the historiography of skepticism can be found in Richard Popkin, "Some Thoughts About Stäudlin's 'History and Spirit of Skepticism'," in *The Skeptical Tradition Around 1800: Skepticism in Philosophy, Science, and Society*, ed. J. Van der Zande and R. Popkin (Dordrecht: Kluwer, 1998), 339–242; and Constance Blackwell, "Skepticism as a Sect, Skepticism as a Philosophical Stance," in Van der Zande and Popkin, *The Skeptical Tradition Around 1800*, 343–63.

2 Carl Fridrich [*sic*] Stäudlin, *Geschichte und Geist des Skepticismus vorzüglich in Rücksicht auf Moral und Religion* (Leipzig: Siegfried Lebrecht Crusius, 1794), vol. 1, iii. Hereafter cited in parentheses in the text by volume number and page. Some passages have been translated into English in R. Popkin and J.R. Maia Neto, eds., *Skepticism: An Anthology* (Amherst: Prometheus, 2007), 275–80.

3 See J.C. Laursen, "Tame Skeptics at the Prussian Academy," *Libertinage et philosophie* 12 (2010): 221–30.

4 See J.C. Laursen, "Kant in the History of Skepticism" in *John Locke und Immanuel Kant: Historisches Rezeption und gegenwärtiges Relevanz*, ed. Martyn

P. Thompson (Berlin: Duncker und Humblot, 1991), 254–68, and "Skepticism and the History of Moral Philosophy," in Popkin and Van der Zande, eds., *The Skeptical Tradition Around 1800*, 375ff.

5 C.F. Stäudlin, "C. F. Stäudlin über den Werth der kritischen Philosophie vornehmlich in moralischer und religiöser Hinsicht, den Gebrauch und Misbrauch derselben in den theologischen Wissenschaften, und den Geist und die Geschichte des Skepticismus," in *Beiträge zur Philosophie und Geschichte der Religion und Sittenlehre überhaupt und der verschiedenen Glaubensarten und Kirchen insbesondere* (Lubeck: Johann Friedrich Bohn, 1798), vol. 4, 169. This was one of three articles under the same title and in the same journal that were intended as a follow-up on the book: (vol. 3, 1797, 273–367; vol. 4, 1798, 83–189; vol. 5, 1799, 312–78). On the intention that it be the equivalent of a third volume, see vol. 3, 1797, 278; but at the end of the third installment he admitted that he had not arrived at what he had to say about skepticism (vol. 5, 1798, 378).

6 E.g., Thompson, ed., *John Locke und Immanuel Kant*; Ian Hunter, "Kant's Political Thought in the Prussian Enlightenment," in *Kant's Political Theory*, ed. Elisabeth Ellis (University Park, PA: Penn State University Press, 2012), 170–207.

7 Plínio J. Smith, "Kant's Criticism and the Legacy of Modern Scepticism," in *Scepticism in the Eighteenth Century: Enlightenment, Lumières, Aufklärung*, ed. Sébastien Charles and Plínio J. Smith (Dordrecht: Springer, 2013), 247–63.

8 But see Michael Forster, *Kant and Skepticism* (Princeton, NJ: Princeton University Press, 2008) for an in-depth analysis of Kant's use of Sextus's tropes.

9 Klaus Hartmann, "Response to Laursen and Minogue," in Thompson, *John Locke und Immanuel Kant*, 284.

10 I. Kant, *Kants gesammelte Schriften* (Berlin: Prussian Academy, 1900–), vol. 11, 532.

11 Ulrich J. Schneider, "Commentary: Stäudlin and the Historiography of Philosophy," in Van der Zande and Popkin, *The Skeptical Tradition Around 1800*, 379, seems to take these assertions at face value.

12 Stäudlin, "C.F. Stäudlin über den Werth," vol. 4, 179–80.

13 J.G. Bühle, quoted in Blackwell, "Skepticism as a Sect, Skepticism as a Philosophical Stance," in Van der Zande and Popkin, *The Skeptical Tradition Around 1800*, 360.

14 Klaus Vieweg, *Philosophie des Remis: Der junge Hegel und das 'Gespenst des Skepticismus'* (Jena: Fink, 1999), 69.

15 See Don Herzog, *Poisoning the Minds of the Lower Orders* (Princeton, NJ: Princeton University Press, 1998).

16 Stäudlin, "C.F. Stäudlin über den Werth," vol. 5, 342. References are to this edition and are hereafter cited parenthetically in the text by volume number and page.

Contributors

Rodrigo Brandão is Professor of Philosophy at the Federal University of Paraná, Brazil.

Daniel R. Brunstetter is Associate Professor of Political Science at the University of California, Irvine.

Sébastien Charles is Dean for Research and Creation at the University of Quebec at Trois-Rivières.

Jean-Charles Darmon is University Professor at the University of Versailles, St-Quentin-en-Yvelines, member of the Institut Universitaire de France, and Director of the Centre de recherche sur les relations entre littérature, philosophie et morale in Paris.

Pierre Force is Professor of French at Columbia University, New York.

Sylvia Giocanti is Associate Professor of Philosophy at Toulouse-Le Mirail University, Toulouse, France.

John Christian Laursen is Professor of Political Science at the University of California, Riverside.

Whitney Mannies teaches political theory at the University of California, Riverside.

Gianni Paganini is Professor of the History of Philosophy at the University of Piedmont, Vercelli, and a Member of the Research Center of the Accademia Nazionale dei Lincei, Rome.

Rui Bertrand Romão is Professor of Philosophy at the University of Oporto.

Andrew Sabl is Visiting Professor of Political Science at Yale University.

Emidio Spinelli is Professor of Philosophy at the University of Rome, "La Sapienza."

María José Villaverde is Professor of Political Science at the Complutense University of Madrid.

Index

www.ingramcontent.com/pod-product-compliance
Lightning Source LLC
LaVergne TN
LVHW090152080826
844660LV00013B/782/J

* 9 7 8 1 4 4 2 6 4 9 2 1 7 *